THE DEATH OF SECULAR MESSIANISM

THEOPOLITICAL VISIONS

SERIES EDITORS:

Thomas Heilke
D. Stephen Long
and C. C. Pecknold

Theopolitical Visions seeks to open up new vistas on public life, hosting fresh conversations between theology and political theory. This series assembles writers who wish to revive theopolitical imagination for the sake of our common good.

    Theopolitical Visions hopes to re-source modern imaginations with those ancient traditions in which political theorists were often also theologians. Whether it was Jeremiah's prophetic vision of exiles "seeking the peace of the city," Plato's illuminations on piety and the civic virtues in the Republic, St. Paul's call to "a common life worthy of the Gospel," St. Augustine's beatific vision of the City of God, or the gothic heights of medieval political theology, much of Western thought has found it necessary to think theologically about politics, and to think politically about theology. This series is founded in the hope that the renewal of such mutual illumination might make a genuine contribution to the peace of our cities.

RECENT VOLUMES:

The Fullness of Time in a Flat World
by Scott Waalkes

Christ, History and Apocalyptic
by Nathan R. Kerr

Redeeming the Broken Body
by Gabriel A. Santos

Paul, Philosophy, and the Theopolitical Vision by Douglas Harink

FORTHCOMING VOLUMES:

The End of Evangelicalism?
by David Fitch

The Politics of Practical Reason
by Mark Ryan

The Death of Secular
MESSIANISM

Religion

and Politics

in an Age

of Civilizational

Crisis

ANTHONY E. MANSUETO

CASCADE *Books* • Eugene, Oregon

THE DEATH OF SECULAR MESSIANISM
Religion and Politics in an Age of Civilizational Crisis

Theopolitical Visions 8

Copyright © 2010 Anthony E. Mansueto. All rights reserved. Except for brief quotations in critical publications or reviews, no part of this book may be reproduced in any manner without prior written permission from the publisher. Write: Permissions, Wipf and Stock Publishers, 199 W. 8th Ave., Suite 3, Eugene, OR 97401.

Cascade Books
An Imprint of Wipf and Stock Publishers
199 W. 8th Ave., Suite 3
Eugene, OR 97401

www.wipfandstock.com

ISBN 13: 978-1-60608-650-6

Cataloging-in-Publication data:

Mansueto, Anthony E.

The death of secular messianism : religion and politics in an age of civilizational crisis / Anthony E. Mansueto.

viii + 312 p. ; 23 cm. —Includes bibliographical references.

Theopolitical Visions 8

ISBN 13: 978-1-60608-650-6

1. Secularism. 2. Religion and politics. 3. History—Philosophy. 4. Theology of religions (Christian theology). 5. Metaphysics I. Title. II. Series.

BL2747.8 .M35 2010

Manufactured in the U.S.A.

This book is dedicated to my students at the University of New Mexico-Gallup, in dialogue with whom this work was born, to my grandfather, Salvatore, who connected me with a past in which humanity still believed in a future in which human beings would live lives of self-cultivation and ripening being, and to my daughter, Maria Coeli Tien Bo Xiao, who will live that future.

Contents

Introduction 1

CHAPTER 1   Theoretical Foundations 17

CHAPTER 2   The Human Civilizational Project 102

CHAPTER 3   An Imperfect Union 159

CHAPTER 4   An Era of Civilizational Crisis 201

CHAPTER 5   Between Cathedrals and Starships 258

Bibliography 301

INTRODUCTION

Statement of the Problem

Secular messianism is dead.

This, by itself, is hardly news. The *postmodern* condition, which understands itself as a skepticism regarding totalizing metanarratives in general (Lyotard 1974), is better understood as a skepticism regarding the grand metanarratives that have defined modernity as a great arc of progress that would carry humanity from the realm of necessity into the realm of freedom. What is much less well understood is that these metanarratives are *constitutive* of modern civilization itself. Not only the projects of transhumanist utopians and revolutionary sects, but also the ordinary work of creating and sustaining modernity—both capitalist and socialist—has depended on the usually unspoken hope that innerworldly civilizational progress would deliver to humanity the Good that human beings have sought by means of various spiritual disciplines since the evolution of sapience itself: the Good we have historically called Being or God or Brahmin or Tian.

Modernity has, historically, sought this end by two distinct means. What we will call positivistic modernity has sought to transcend finitude by means of scientific and technological progress. Humanistic modernity, has, on the other hand, sought to overcome contingency by creating a collective Subject—the democratic state or the communist party—which would allow humanity to shape its own destiny and that of the universe as a whole. It is in the name of these hopes that revolutions have been fought and millions of lives expended in the struggle for industrialization and capitalist development or socialist construction. And it is in the name of these hopes that billions still spend their lives toiling in factories and offices and stores—except that the hopes are dead and we are living an ideal in which we no longer believe.

What this means is that modern civilization, while *secular*, in the proper and literal sense of being *worldly*, is also no less *religious* than its predecessors, no less an attempt to realize humanity's transcendental vocation, our ontological hunger for Being. It is just that modernity kept its religion secret—usually even from itself. Partly this is because of the enduring strength of premodern religions, with which modernists were forced to reach public accommodations. But partly it is because the secret religions of the modern world, when their claims are made explicit, lack credibility and (because their claims are empirically testable) tend to be destabilizing rather than legitimating. We *know* that industrial technology, far from allowing us to transcend finitude, has turned us into batteries and now threatens the viability of our ecosystem. We *know* that even the most fully developed democracy cannot be "the actuality of the ethical Idea" (Hegel 1870/1990: 258) or communism "the definitive resolution of the conflict between existence and essence" (Marx 1844/1978).

We know this and we have known it for a long time, but our politics has, until very recently, been dominated by the struggle between capitalism and socialism, which are best understood as competing strategies for realizing the modern ideal (even if they often appealed to the people on some other basis, drawing on an alliance with premodern religious ideologies for legitimation). Since 1989, on the other hand, political discourse has increasingly thematized the problem of modernity as such, so that both explicit defenses and fundamental critiques of modernity, as well as positions in between, have entered the public arena in a new way. This suggests that we have reached a crossroads, a moment in which not merely the structure of our society but the very ideals that define our civilization are being called into question.

State of the Question

This deeper crisis is, however, still largely invisible to most current geopolitical analysis, which turns on the single question of *globalization*. According to this view the defining feature of the period since 1989 has been the formation of a single unified global market, with increasingly unfettered flows of capital across national borders. Analysts differ primarily in terms of what they think this means. There are, broadly speaking, four different responses to the phenomenon of globalization. *Neoliberalism* (Hayek 1988; Reich 1992) celebrates globalization and sees in it the realization of the modern ideal, the creation of a single, global civilization in which the ideological struggles of the past hundred and fifty years have finally come to an end, and capitalism, democracy, and secularism are finally victorious (Fukuyama 1989). Many on the modernist left (Hardt and Negri 2001, 2004; Arrighi 1994, 2007) agree that globalization represents real progress, but believe that, far from representing the "end of history," it has, at long last, finally created the conditions that Marx specified for socialist emancipation. The long history of Leninism was simply a detour caused by revolutionary impatience and the melding of authentically socialist aspirations with nationalism and resistance to capitalist modernization. Both trends regard the resurgent religious fundamentalisms of the past thirty years as atavistic reactions to modernity, a reassertion of fundamentally *premodern* social forms.

Against this celebration of globalization stands the neoconservative *Clash of Civilizations* thesis advanced by Samuel Huntington (Huntington 1993) but also embraced by Islamic fundamentalists such as *Hizbut-al-Tahrir* (Hizbut al-Tahrir n.d.). According to this view, the collapse of the Soviet Union has led not to a global victory for capitalism, democracy, and secularism, but rather to a renewed conflict between civilizations constituted by fundamentally incompatible ideals. What we will call the populist perspective, finally, reads the current situation as defined by a conflict between the global "North" and the global "South" that is as much cultural as economic and political and that understands socialism, which it often embraces in one form or another, as resistance to globalization and capitalist modernization.

I would like to suggest that all of these approaches are fundamentally inadequate. On the one hand, both neoliberal and socialist globalism take for granted the modern project and the inevitability of modernism's victory. They are thus unable to recognize neither the *structural* obstacles to the realization of the modern project nor the normative questions that people from many different civilizational traditions are raising about modernity itself. On the first count we should note the building ecological crisis, a product of the industrial technology on which modernity depends, the economic contradictions of both capitalism and socialism, a decline in authentic democratic participation, and a disintegration of the social fabric coupled with growing nihilism and despair.

This does not, however, mean that what we are facing is a "clash of civilizations" in the sense understood by Samuel Huntington—much less his looser interpreters in the neoconservative camp. First, the whole idea of a "Western Civilization" stretching from Ancient Israel and Ancient Greece up through the present is highly problematic. We need to think, rather, of at least two very different traditions that have been woven together, transformed, and disengaged from each other repeatedly over the course of the past five thousand years. Israel's encounter with God in the struggle for justice found very different expressions in Judaism, Christianity, and Islam. The classical humanistic ideal of life as a free human being and engaged citizen, who enters the public arena with rationally derived convictions regarding fundamental questions of meaning and value and struggles for those ideals in an open contest with similarly rational peers, *constituted* Hellenistic-Roman civilization, joined with Judaism, Christianity, and Islam to create a complex, internally differentiated civilizational complex during the Middle Ages, and then was forcibly disengaged from these traditions as the result of the Asharite and Augustinian reactions to constitute *one* strain of modernity. During the Middle Ages Christendom, *Dar-al-Islam*, and their Jewish minority subcultures were unified by a common Aristotelian philosophical language in which disputed questions of meaning and value were hashed out. Modernity, in both its humanistic and positivistic expressions, is the product of a rupture with that Aristotelian problematic.

There are, in other words, many Wests, ancient and modern, which have often been and continue to be in conflict with each other.

Finally, the clash of civilizations thesis fails to even describe correctly, much less really explain, the main lines of global conflict in the present period. The Jews and Christians who are most committed to sustained conflict with *Dar-al-Islam* are not, for example, secularized liberal interpreters of their tradition, but political-theological conservatives who actually *agree* with the fundamentalist Muslims with whom they are at war on a broad range of cultural questions, from the proper approach to the interpretation of the sacred Scriptures (literal inerrancy) through the nature of God (absolutely transcendent and sovereign) to church/state relations and the role of women in society. At even a rudimentary level of abstraction, in other words, this supposed *clash of civilizations* turns into a cultural convergence among groups that are, nonetheless, really and truly in conflict with each other on the geopolitical stage. East Asia, meanwhile, has embraced capitalism in a way that is hardly coherent with a traditional Confucian worldview and must be read either as representing a rupture towards modernity or a mobilization of other elements in their cultural heritage—a longstanding mercantile tradition and a statist authoritarianism associated more closely with Buddhism and Legalism respectively than with anything even remotely resembling a Confucian *ru xue.*

Nor is it really possible to analyze the current situation adequately in terms of a conflict between the global North and the global South. Where do China and India, the two largest and most powerful countries in the old "Third World," stand in this scheme? Can they meaningfully be assimilated to a global South that also includes Africa, much of which is in an advanced state of disintegration? And even within Latin America, where this analysis has the most support, there are sharp differences both in patterns of development and political line and strategy between the Southern Cone, Brazil, and populist regimes like Venezuela, Ecuador, Paraguay, and Bolivia.

Clearly something is lacking in all four geopolitical analyses. Specifically, all consider structural and ideological factors in isolation from each other, and regard civilizational ideals—when they are considered at all—as irrationally held and not subject to rational adjudication. For neoliberal and socialist globalism the issue is the global marketplace and its adequacy as a resource allocator. For neoconservatives and populists, the issue is one of cultural conflicts, even if those conflicts also involve a struggle over the resources necessary to advance their conflicting ideals.

This focus on structural factors reflects the roots of each of the geopolitical analyses we have identified in modern and postmodern social theory. Indeed, each reflects, to a greater or lesser extent, a well-defined trend in social theory and the debate between them is thus also a debate between the various trends of modern social theory. Here we can identify four "poles" between which the positions of most participants in the contemporary debate can be ultimately located. Neoliberal globalism is rooted in neoclassical economics and especially in theories of spontaneous self-organization such as that advanced by F. A. Hayek (Hayek 1988), which we will call *infokatallaxis*. According to this view human societies evolve as individuals seek to realize their self-interests under conditions of scarcity. In the process they develop various practices, some of which (like the marketplace) work and others of which do not. Selection operates across these practices, gradually creating the optimum social structure humanity has now achieved.

Socialist globalism, similarly, is rooted in a more or less orthodox historical materialism. According to this view the history is driven by technological progress, what Marx called "the development of the productive forces." When economic structures begin to hold back this development, revolutionary movements emerge that transform them. In the process, human beings, once merely the object of human history, become its subjects. And with the triumph of modern technologies that master the secrets of nature, they become the subjects of cosmic history as well.

The neoconservative clash of civilizations thesis is rooted in Weberian interpretive sociology. For Weber, human civilizations are constituted by meaning complexes that serve to orient action and legitimate authority. History unfolds as these various meaning complexes come into conflict with each other both within and between civilizations. While it is possible to read Weber as an evolutionary liberal for whom all societies ultimately tend towards capitalist modernity, it is more accurate to see him (like later neoconservatives) as a defender of Western liberal ideals in the context of what he once called a "war among the gods" (Weber 1918/1919).

Populist antiglobalism has the most obscure social-theoretical lineage. This is because, long allied with the Soviet Union and shaped by 150 years during which dialectical and historical materialism was the dominant ideology of the socialist movement, it tended to articulate itself in the language of dialectical and historical materialism, even when its real roots were elsewhere. Marx's political economy was, to be sure, among the influences that shaped the dependency/world systems theory (Amin 1978, 1979/1980, 1981/1982, 1988/1989; Frank 1967, 1975, 1998; Wallerstein 1974, 1980, 1989) that informed populist economic analysis. But the operative theory of social change that has informed this trend owes more to Durkheim (Durkheim 1911) or to indigenous thinkers such as Vasconcellos (Rommanell 1969) or Sandino (Hodges 1986) than to Marx. Specifically, it locates the principal catalyst for social transformation in the collective effervescence of the masses that generates or brings them into contact with a higher and deeper truth, often articulated in the language of national and/or religious traditions. In practice, until the collapse of the Soviet Union, populist ideologies of this sort served as "linking ideologies" (Lancaster 1988) that mobilized resistance to capitalist modernization in service to a thoroughly modern dialectical materialist socialism, a strategy made explicit by Gramsci (Gramsci 1949c). More recently however, this trend has been retheorized by thinkers who understand socialism not as a variant of the modern project but rather as a form of resistance to modernity and specifically to what John Milbank calls "the enclosure of the sacred" (Milbank 2006a).

But social theories are, also, at least implicitly, political theologies. Neoliberal globalism is one manifestation of "the secret religion of high modernity," what we have called *positivistic modernism*, which seeks divinization, understood as transcending *finitude*, by means of scientific and technological progress. Socialist globalism is another manifestation of this same religion, *humanistic modernism*, which seeks to transcend *contingency* by elevating humanity, through the medium of the proletariat and its party, to the status of unique subject-object of human history and then, by unleashing the development of the productive forces, to achieve comparable control over the larger cosmic evolutionary process of which human history is a part.[1] Interpretive sociology, on the other hand, is essentially the sociological form of Nietzschean theomachy, in which various forces vie with each other for power and legitimation in an endless struggle that no one ever wins. As such it falls clearly at one end of what we will call the postmodern spectrum. At the other end of this spectrum lie Radical Orthodoxy (Milbank 1991, 1999, 2006a, 2006b) and other religious postmodernisms that explicitly reject both the modern aspiration for technopolitical self-divinization and the postmodern theomachy in favor of an ontology of peace and respect for the Other.

Of these various alternatives, only neoliberalism and the Radical Orthodox ontology of peace are represented *directly* in the contemporary debate. Other participants fall somewhere between the poles we have defined. Thus most of contemporary socialist globalism (Hardt

---

1. There are, to be sure, positivistic socialists—e.g., much of the Soviet tradition—and humanistic liberals, and we will note these variations in the course of our argument. But for the most part, we will argue, embracing the positivistic variant of the modern ideal tends to pull one towards capitalism, because of its long term superiority as an engine for pure, quantitative growth, while humanism tends to pull one towards socialism which alone offers a real hope of transcending contingency and thus rising to the status of Necessary Being.

and Negri 2001, 2004; Badiou, 1988, 2006) explicitly rejects both Leninist theory and strategy and its associated political theology that seeks divinization by becoming the unique subject-object of human history, a point around which Badiou in particular has been very explicit (Badiou 2005). But as we will see there is still a strategy for divinization at work here, located somewhere between that of classical dialectical materialism, neoconservative theomachy, and postmodern ontologies of peace and respect for the Other. Neoconservative theomachy is rarely articulated explicitly, but joined to the defense of a specific civilizational tradition, either "the West" (Huntington 1993) or *Dar-al-Islam* (*Hizbut-al-Tahrir* n.d.), pulling it towards either neoliberalism or religious postmodernism. And between Radical Orthodoxy and neoconservative theomachy lie a whole spectrum of postmodernisms: "weak theologies" (Caputo 2006), Derridian "acts of religion" (Derrida 2001), and what remains of the earlier deconstructionist postmodernism (Derrida 1967/1978).

Thesis, Method, and Outline

It is the aim of this book to advance a fundamentally new understanding of the current situation, grounded in a new social theory and political theology. Specifically, I will argue that the present period marks the early stages of what I will call a period of *civilizational crisis* in which both the positivistic and the humanistic variants of the modern ideal are increasingly being called into question, but in which no new ideal has, as yet, emerged to replace it. This crisis is partly the result of the inability of modern social structures, capitalist or socialist, to realize the modern ideal but stems ultimately from the inherently unworkable character of the modern ideal as such. The result is, on the one hand, a rising tide of nihilism and despair, of which deconstructionist postmodernism represents the high, self-conscious form and, on the other hand, a reversion to what I hope to show are *early modern* ideologies centered on submission to a divine sovereign, and to Christian and Islamic fundamentalism in particular.

Woven into this *crisis of modernity* is a still deeper *crisis of classical humanism*, the aims of which, while far more modest than those of modern humanism, also remain unrealized and are under increasing threat. In this case the problem is not that the ideal is unworthy or unworkable, but rather that we are still very far from creating for it an adequate material base.

This thesis depends, in turn, on a substantial departure from modern social theory, which I call *dialectical sociology*. I retain much from modern social theory. From historical materialism I retain the conviction that human societies grow up on a definite material basis, and that they develop certain structures (technological, economic, political, and ideological or cultural) that initially permit growth and development but that may, eventually, also become obstacles to development, leading either to revolutionary transformation or civilizational collapse. From functionalism I retain a focus on the role of social structures in shaping forms of knowledge and especially approaches to fundamental questions of meaning and value, as well as the critical importance of moments of collective effervescence in catalyzing social transformation. And from interpretive sociology I retain a focus on history as a contest among ideals that both order action and legitimate authority. Unlike the whole tradition of modern social theory, however, I argue that human societies are teleologically ordered to a transcendental end—Being. In this understanding, particular civilizational ideals, shaped by social structures and instruments of legitimation though they may be, are nonetheless real approaches to Being. In other words, I join the insights of modern social theory to an epistemological and metaphysical realism. Social structures are simply ways of realizing a civilizational ideal under definite material conditions. *Crises of regime* occur when one set of policies no longer works and must be replaced by another that, however, does not call the social structure itself into question. *Structural crises* take place when existing structures no longer serve the dominant civilizational ideal and must be replaced. A *civilizational crisis* is much deeper and occurs when a civilization's ideal itself becomes unworkable and must be abandoned. But these crises and the ensuing social struggles are not an open theomachy, but rather a difficult, often contradictory, groping towards a real common end, which is Being.

This implies a political theology that is oriented not towards innerworldly divinization, whether technological or political, but rather towards a holistic growing and deepening of participation in the creative power of Being as such. This can be seen as a return to a revitalized Catholic, and specifically Thomistic, political theology, which recognizes the religious significance of the struggle for human development, civilizational progress, and social justice, but does not seek from these a divinization they cannot deliver. Divinization, rather, comes as we respond to grace in the form *both* of the attractive power of God *and* the limits imposed by our finite and contingent condition, which stretch us beyond the merely human, challenging us to love God and neighbor for their own sake and not merely as means to our own development, and thus to love them with God's own love, something that results in a connatural knowledge of God and a kind of accidental[2] (but never essential) deification. But the point can also be made in the language of humanity's other great spiritual traditions—Islam, Hinduism, and the Buddhist/Taoist/Confucian synthesis of Chinese civilization. The result will be a world *Convivencia* theology that re-engages the spiritual traditions and the great Silk Road tradition, and brings them into dialogue with each other.

Such a political theology can support the aims of classical, if not of modern, humanism, but it sets them in a larger context. Specifically, it sets them in the context of the larger Axial Age project of religious problematization, rationalization, and democratization. This project, which goes back to the period between 800 and 200 BCE treats spiritual questions as *questions*, which can be rationally explored and around which real deliberation and persuasion is possible, if never definitive. It aims to expand the sphere of deliberation to include the whole people. But unlike some formulations of this ideal, such as Hannah Arendt's *The Human Condition* (Arendt 1958), it does not regard this deliberation as an end in itself, but rather as a means of advancing our understanding of questions that are critical to both human civilizational progress and spiritual development.

This approach allows us to understand the distinctiveness of the modern ideal in a way which was not previously possible, showing that it is both a *religious* ideal in the sense of bearing on fundamental questions of meaning and value, and indeed *a strategy for divinization*, and yet very different both in its understanding of the divine and in its strategy for realizing the divine from earlier civilizations—and

---

2. The term "accidental" is used here in its technical philosophical sense: as a quality inhering in something the fundamental nature of which is defined by another substantial form or essence. A simple example would be a star (the substantial form) that is blue (the accident).

specifically the civilization of ancient and medieval Europe with which postmodernism attempts to link it. I will show that the modern ideal emerged out of a series of conquests undertaken by Europeans (and to a lesser extent the Turks and Mongols) during the later Middle Ages, which led to the formation of sovereign nation-states and eventually to industrialization and capitalist development. These changes in social structure led in turn to a new understanding of the divine as *infinite power*, an understanding shared by both early modern ideologies of authority and submission (Protestant Christianity and Asharite Islam) and by high modern ideologies that seek divinization by means of scientific and technological progress—what I call the positivist variant of the modern ideal. The humanistic variant of the modern ideal emerged in reaction to this. Marginalized Radical Aristotelians and other humanistic intellectuals translated their ideal of intellectual identification with the Agent Intellect into innerworldly historical terms. This meant aspiring to organize and direct the cosmohistorical evolutionary process through the medium of the revolutionary party with the support of the working classes.

I will also show why these ideals are not workable. It is not so much that humanity cannot transcend the limits of finitude by means of scientific and technological progress (this seems unlikely, but the jury is still out) but rather that the end we seek is not what Hegel called the "bad infinity" of endless existence and unlimited power but rather Being as such, a creativity and generativity that requires progress of an entirely different order. The humanistic modern ideal, on the other hand, is internally contradictory. A revolutionary politics that elevates humanity to the position of "unique subject-object" of the historical process is incompatible with the rational autonomy such subjectivity requires for all but one individual. Thus the designation of the great revolutionary movements of the modern era by proper names that Badiou (Bosteels 2005) points out.

We increase our participation in Being by cultivating increasingly complex capacities, individual and collective, though without ever crossing the fundamental ontological frontier between contingency and necessity. Divinity is always and only a horizon—but it is our horizon, and it defines us.

The fundamental flaws in the metaphysical foundations of the modern project are reflected in the developing crisis of modern civilization. Indeed, far from progress towards a technological utopia, we face a building ecological crisis, technological and economic stagnation,[3] a decline in authentic democratic participation, and—as we noted above—an abandonment of autonomous rationality in favor of either religious fundamentalism or irrationalist nihilism. And this is not simply a result of a failure to be sufficiently capitalist or sufficiently socialist—to submit ourselves with sufficient rigor or to transcend more fully the discipline of the marketplace—as neoliberal and socialist theorists would have us believe. The failure is, rather, at the level of the modern civilizational ideal of innerworldly divinization.

To the extent that classical humanism remains alive, it faces a rather different problem. This ideal emerged, in the first place, out of the class struggles of sixth-century Athens, as hitherto marginalized peasants, taking advantage of new specialized agricultural technologies (wine and oil production), which gave them a privileged place in the global economy, claimed for themselves a place in the *polis* and thus in its cult. As these technologies spread, the Hellenistic and later Roman civilizations that embraced classical humanism turned to chattel slavery and empire building to support their free citizen populations—structures that ultimately strangled the very ideals they were intended to support. Classical humanism was reborn in the communes of medieval and early modern Europe as that region carved out for itself a high-wage, high-technology niche in the global economy and once again became bound up with chattel slavery and empire building as the artisan class was broken and petty commodity production gave way to capitalism. Never really compatible with industrialism (capitalist or socialist) and surviving on the margins even in high-wage economies, classical humanism is threatened today with extinction as high-wage economies are overwhelmed by the emergence of India and China, and the global

---

3. Our claim of technological and economic stagnation may seem surprising, given all of the talk about the emergence of a knowledge economy, not all of it wrong. As Eric Lerner (Lerner 1990) points out, however, current technological advances are based on basic science (relativity and especially quantum mechanics) that is nearly a century old. And much of the technology that quite literally drives our civilization (e.g., the internal combustion engine) is even older than that. In the technological utopia of high modernism, we would long ago have transcended the use of polluting and nonrenewable fossil fuels, and would have made advances in basic science of the same import as those of the beginning of the twentieth century, something that simply hasn't happened.

market demands the total mobilization of human creativity and energy in the production process.

It is not yet clear how this crisis will unfold. Indeed, I will argue, we may be able to shape its progress, opting for a transition by means of reform or revolution rather than a transition through decadence or a civilizational collapse. In any case, the next steps in the human civilizational project will be inspired by a re-engagement with a much older and deeper stream of civilizational progress, one rooted in what Karl Jaspers (Jaspers 1953) called the Axial Age, the period of religious problematization, rationalization, and democratization between 800 and 200 BCE during which humanity began to cultivate the capacity to make rational decisions regarding fundamental questions of meaning and value and ordinary people began to claim their place in that great conversation.

Our vision for the future is centered on the resumption and radicalization of this archaeorevolutionary process. We seek a technological regime that perfects rather than dominates nature, an economic structure that is open to innovation and entrepreneurship but that restores control over the means of production and the production process to the direct producers and that orders allocation of surplus to the common good, a democracy that is rooted in humanity's shared capacity for reason and that extends to deliberation not only around means, but also around ends, and a new spirituality of meaning and self-cultivation that respects the possibility that human beings follow different paths, and may even seek different ends, without banishing the language of meaning and hope from the public square.

My method in this undertaking reflects my theory, which joins dialectical sociology, and especially the tradition of ideological criticism, to a metaphysically realistic dialectics. We will analyze the social basis and political valence of various ideological trends and tendencies and draw out their internal contradictions, both political and spiritual, and in so doing articulate a constructive alternative. A focus on trends and tendencies, as opposed to an in-depth engagement with specific thinkers understood in their own terms, is essential to the project. This is because our thesis depends on a claim that something is going on in modern and postmodern geopolitical analysis and social theory that its proponents do not generally acknowledge. Specifically, these geopolitical analyses and social theories are also political theologies, and the struggles they articulate are metaphysical as well as political.

Because of the scope of this argument—and since neither I (nor any one else, to my knowledge)—possesses specialist knowledge of each and every epoch of human history, I have had to rely extensively on the work of other scholars who have devoted their lives to the understanding of particular epochs.[4] Sources important for the analysis of particular historical periods but not for the overall argument of the book are indicated in the relevant chapters and in the bibliography. A few works, however, stand out because they have shaped my overall thesis, because they argue theses so diametrically opposed to my own that my entire work is shaped in some significant degree by argument with them, or because they have contributed key conclusions that are essential to my overall argument. The most important work in the first category is Karl Jaspers's *The Origin and Goal of History* (Jaspers 1953), which articulated the Axial Age thesis that is so fundamental to my larger argument. Works that offer competing approaches to common questions, and that have shaped my argument through debate, include Eric Voeglin's *Order and History* (Voeglin 1956, 1957, 1974), Samir Amin's *Class and Nation, Historically and in the Current Crisis* (Amin 1979/1980), Francis Fukuyama's "The End of History" (Fukuyama 1989), Samuel Huntington's *The Clash of Civilizations* (Huntington 1993), Charles Taylor's *A Secular Age* (Taylor 2007), and John Milbank's "Geopolitical Theology" (Milbank 2006a). Works that have shaped my understanding of particular periods in history include Geoffrey de Ste. Croix's *The Class Struggle in the Ancient Greek World* (de Ste. Croix 1980), Perry Anderson's *Passages from Antiquity to Feudalism* and *Lineages of the Absolutist State* (Anderson 1974a, b), Barrington Moore's *Social Origins of Dictatorship and Democracy* (Moore 1966), Theda Skocpol's *States and Social Revolutions* (Skocpol 1979), Andre Gunder Frank's *ReOrient* (Frank 1998), and other works from the world-systems trend. I often disagree with these authors and make it clear where I do so and why, but am substantially dependent on their mastery of the primary sources and their pioneering work in the development of *longue durée* and comparative historical analyses.

---

4. See Andre Gunder Frank's excellent defense of the use of secondary analysis in the introduction to *ReOrient* for an extended treatment of this problem (Frank 1998).

Our argument will begin with a statement, in chapter 1, of the theoretical apparatus necessary to our analysis of the current situation. We will address in greater depth than we have in this introduction the link between geopolitical analysis, social theory, and political theology, show why we believe the principal existing approaches to be inadequate, and explain our alternative. From there we will proceed inductively. Chapter 2 will argue that the process of religious rationalization and democratization that began with the Axial Age pointed not to modernity but to the spirituality of meaning and self-cultivation that was emerging towards the end of the Silk Road Era, and that this process was interrupted by the series of conquests that gave birth to modern civilization. We will show where modernity came from and how it has unfolded.

Because this is a book that intends first and foremost to address the current situation, and because the United States not only plays a dominating role in the present period but also had a rather unique experience of modernity that creates both special problems and distinct opportunities, we need also to address the special case of the United States. This will be the topic of chapter 3.

Only after these preliminary tasks are completed will it be possible to argue convincingly for our first thesis, that the present period represents the early stages in a civilizational crisis. Chapter 4 will locate the roots of the crisis in modernity's option for a univocal metaphysics and outline its dimensions: ecological, technological, economic, political, and cultural. It will also show how it bears on more immediate developments, such as globalization and the conflict between those who have found ways to benefit from it and those who have not. This will allow us to elaborate a detailed strategic analysis and make an assessment regarding the relative likelihood of various scenarios: civilizational progress through reform or revolution, a transition through decadence, or civilizational collapse.

From here it will be possible to map out a vision and a strategy for the future. Chapter 5 will show how it is possible to rationally ground a new civilizational ideal rooted in the archaeorevolutionary process reaching back to the Axial Age, and will answer objections from neoliberal, neoconservative, socialist, and populist critics. It will then try to show what the next steps in the human civilizational project might look like. Specifically it will argue for the development of new technologies that tap into the immanent drive towards growth that characterizes all forms of matter, physical, biological, and social. We will show how it is possible to transcend the limits of both market and state allocation of resources in a way that allows for diversity and innovation and ensures that surplus is used in a way which promotes human development. We will argue for creation of a new type of public arena *constituted* by debate around fundamental questions of meaning and value. Only such a public arena can realize the full promise of the first democratic revolution—that of the Axial Age—and only such a democratic arena can overcome the limitations of both secularism and confessionalism. Finally, we will argue for a spirituality of meaning and self-cultivation and for the central importance of reconstituted powerful and credible sapiential authorities—teachers of wisdom who can guide humanity in its search for wisdom and its process of development without constituting themselves as a new exploiting class. Chapter 5 will also discuss strategies for change, joining a rigorous and sober analysis of the strategic situation in the present period with an argument that, the apparent strength of modernity—and its dominant capitalist form in particular—notwithstanding, change is inevitable. Specifically, we will show how to work for a transition through reform or revolution while preparing for a more likely "transition through decadence" in which the old order declines because it is incapable of addressing an impending ecological crisis and internal economic contradictions, while a new civilization grows up in its crevices and on its margins. We will show what, in either case, we need to do to build the new order as the old one declines.

CHAPTER 1

Theoretical Foundations

In the introduction we noted briefly the inadequacies of most contemporary geopolitical analysis and traced this inadequacy to its roots in modern social theory and a modern civilizational ideal centered in divinization by means of innerworldly civilizational progress, whether scientific and technological or philosophical and political. In this chapter we will explore in greater depth the relationship between geopolitical analysis, social theory, and political theology. We will then go on to amplify our critique of the principal contemporary geopolitical analyses, showing in more detail why we believe them to be inadequate. We will extend this critique to the principal forms of modern social theory. We will also show in general terms why the modern ideal to which most modern social theory is committed is inadequate. Finally, we will outline the alternative geopolitical analysis, social theory, and political theology that will be developed throughout the subsequent chapters of this book.

Geopolitical Analysis, Social Theory, and Political Theology

It is one of the aims of this work to bring together three disciplines that have not generally been associated with each other, at least in the modern era: geopolitical analysis, social theory, and political theology. We would do well, therefore, to begin, by addressing formally the way in which these disciplines are related to each other.

Geopolitical Analysis

Geopolitical analysis is, first and foremost, analysis that attempts to specify the balance of forces on a global scale in any given *conjuncture* or *period*. The analysis may be primarily economic, political, or cultural or may address in an integrated way all three forms of practice, but it focuses on surface features and on a (relatively) short-term perspective. Let us examine in greater detail what this means.

By a conjuncture (Althusser 1965/1977, 1968/1970, 1966–1969/1971) we mean a political moment defined by a precise combination of forces. These forces may be the discovery or depletion of natural resources, new technological developments or technological impasses, flows or blockages in the flow of labor or capital, strikes, elections, or other political actions, military maneuvers either traditional or nontraditional (e. g. guerilla raids or terrorist acts), or cultural events such as an influential movie or television series, the publication of a major novel or philosophical work, a scientific discovery, or a major new initiative by a religious leader or organization. A conjuncture is, in other words, the immediate context of the acts of others in which we ourselves (whether we are individuals or major geopolitical actors) must in turn decide how to act. It is the field on which tactical analysis takes place and tactical decisions are made.

A period, on the other hand, is defined by a relatively stable alignment of economic, political, and cultural forces. At the economic level, this is generally what Michel Aglietta (Aglietta 1976) called a *regime of accumulation*, a specific, long term strategy for economic development within the context of a given economic structure, usually one that addresses more or less successfully over a period of decades the contradictions of that economic structure. Examples from the capitalist context would include the consumer durable demand led regime (what Aglietta calls "Fordism") of the postwar period and the neoliberal regime that has prevailed since the late 1970s (Davis 1986). Examples from a socialist context would include Lenin's New Economic Policy and Stalin's subsequent regime of primitive socialist accumulation (Bettelheim 1976). At the political level periods are defined by the global alignment of and struggle between great powers. For example, consider the struggle between the U.S. and Germany to succeed England as the global hegemony between 1914 and 1945 and the subsequent struggle between the U.S. and the Soviet Union between 1945 and 1989. These great powers, we should note, need not be nation states. More often they have been multiethnic empires. And it is important to watch for the emergence of new types of great power that might be invisible to more traditional forms of geopolitical analysis. At the cultural level periods are defined by broad trends: the counterculture of the sixties, the resurgent Evangelical Christianity and Islamic Fundamentalism today, as we will argue later, coming to a close.

At both the level of the conjuncture and the level of the period there are always many different ways to define the alignment of forces. Is the present conjuncture best defined by the 9/11 or by the rise of China and India? The period of Fordism and the period of the Cold War do not correspond exactly to each other and neither corresponds exactly to "the sixties." The most effective geopolitical analysis will be one that is able to account, under a single principle, for as many different forces (economic, political, and cultural) as possible, and to actually *explain* the disjuncture between apparent economic, political, and cultural conjunctures and periods.

Social Theory

Even if we pretend to be "pragmatic" in our geopolitical analysis, conscientiously looking for the most powerful and economic explanation, our choices will always be theory laden. This is because the only way to bring together under a single principle the diverse array of actions and forces that define a conjuncture or a period is with respect to a specific understanding of how human societies work, in other words, a social theory.

These theories come in several different types. Liberal theory does not, strictly speaking, recognize "society" as a formal object (Hayek 1988). Rather, it refers to the "extended order of human cooperation," or simply to the patterns that can be observed in the actions of human individuals, who are understood to seek their self interest under conditions of scarcity.

Historical materialism, on the other hand, while not denying the reality of the human individual, takes as its formal object *structures*, technological, economic, political, and culture. The most important of these are the *forces of production*, the *relations of production*, and the political and cultural *superstructure*. It proceeds by analyzing contradictions between the forces and relations of production that are understood to lead to either revolutionary transformation or civilizational collapse.

Functionalist theories in the Durkheimian tradition claim to take society itself as their formal object (Durkheim 1911/1965), but in most cases this actually means reading cultural forms (art, science, philosophy, religion) as a "collective representation" of social structure, and moments of "collective effervescence" (times when people relate to each other with unusual intensity, and outside of the usual structured patterns) as catalysts for structural transformation. This opens up significant room for synthesis between functionalist and historical materialist approaches, an option that has rarely been acknowledged but that is reflected in much socialist theory from both Europe and the Third World in the twentieth century (the populist synthesis mentioned earlier).

Interpretive sociology (Weber 1920/1968), finally, returns to the individual and the well defined organization as its object of analysis, but this object is conceived formally as a carrier or meanings and a participant in struggles over power and legitimation. There is also significant room for synthesis between the functionalist and interpretive approaches an option reflected most obviously in the work of Talcott Parsons (Parsons 1964).

It should already be apparent how social theoretical decisions will drive geopolitical analysis. Neoliberal analysis will always focus on the actions of specific individuals or well-defined organizations (corporations, parties, states, etc.) and will treat those actions as attempts to adapt to an environment of scarcity. It will also expect conjunctural and periodic contradictions to resolve themselves by means of the selection of the effective adaptation available. Historical materialism, on the other hand, will treat specific actors (individuals, organizations) as representing social classes or class fractions. Classes and class fractions, in turn, will be treated as products of the underlying relations of production, and the contradictions between them as expressions of deeper contradictions between the forces and relations of productions, contradictions that are resolved ultimately only by changes in the relations of production. Functionalism might seem poorly adapted to geopolitical analysis, especially at the level of the conjuncture, given its emphasis on the dominance of structure over action, but the concept of collective effervescence can contribute powerfully to explaining otherwise unexpected changes in the balance of forces. And in synthesis with historical materialist or interpretive theories it can contribute powerfully to understanding the role of cultural forces generally and religion in particular in shaping a conjuncture or period.

Political Theology

Modern social theory pretended to be scientific, in the sense of explaining rather than evaluating social patterns, and even postmodern theories that resist the term "science" generally claim to be value neutral. But these claims are specious. Each of the theories has embedded in it a definite orientation towards an *end*. For neoliberal theories this is the interest of the human individuals who are its formal objects, an interest first and foremost in survival, and ultimately in whatever else they choose. And the realization of these interests comes through control over the physical and social environment. Effective adaptations, in other words, are those that remove material constraints. Extended logically, in a way that is implicit in most liberal theory but that has been made explicit only by a few thinkers in this tradition, such as Frank Tipler (Tipler 1994), this trajectory points beyond finitude towards a kind of scientific and technological divinization.

For historical materialism, on the other hand, the goal is not simply to realize individual interests but rather to make conscious and rational an historical process that has hitherto proceeded unconsciously and often irrationally. By understanding the way in which human societies develop, the proletariat can, through the medium of its political party, become the subject as well as the object of history, transcending not so much finitude as contingency. And by reorganizing society so as to unleash the development of the productive forces, it becomes the master of cosmic history as well: a different sort of divinization, but divinization nonetheless.

Functionalism and interpretive sociology are, as we will see, postmodern theories and reject, at least implicitly, the modern ideal. But this does not mean that they are not the carriers of definite values. Durkheim's critique of modernity (Durkheim 1897/1951) focuses on the tendency toward anomie and egoism and thus a loss of meaning and solidarity, which are thus marked as values. Weber, on the other hand, vacillates between mourning the loss of meaning entailed by the triumph of instrumental reason in the modern world (Weber 1921/1958)—what he called the iron cage of capitalism—and prophesying a continued "war among the gods," that is, a continuing struggle between meaning complexes and those who carry them (Weber 1918/2004).

What this means is that, whether they like it or not, social theories are also political theologies and the geopolitical analyses they motivate are geopolitical theologies (Milbank 2006a). By a political theology we mean a theory that engages the ends (transcendental or otherwise, because it is possible to have an atheistic political theology) to which social structures are ordered *and* the way in which these ends themselves order human societies. When we move to the political theological level, in other words, we treat transcendental principles and values (or the lack of them) as factors apart from which the working of human societies, both over the *longue durée* and in any given period and conjuncture, cannot be properly and fully understood.

What this will immediately accomplish will be to bring to light the theological aims of both the positivistic and the humanistic variants of the modern ideal, apart from which they are incoherent, and the religious interest, if not necessarily theistic conviction, which is embedded in postmodern theories such as functionalism and interpretive sociology. But it will also allow us to understand the current situation in a way that modern and postmodern social theory cannot. Having specified the modern ideal, its unworkability and internal contradictions, and thus the profound discontent of the present period, immediately become apparent. It allows us, in other words, to see the gathering storms of a civilizational crisis that has remained invisible to most contemporary geopolitical analysis and the modern and postmodern social theory in which it is rooted.

But before we can do this we need to identify in more detail the shortcomings of the modern and postmodern approaches.

Critique of the Principal Alternatives

Geopolitical Analysis

The forgoing discussion has, in fact, given us some very specific formal criteria by which to evaluate the principal geopolitical analyses that dominate the current debate. Specifically, we will look at how well—both how *powerfully* and how *economically*—each analysis explains the combination of forces at work in the present conjuncture and period.

The End of History

As we noted above, the much-vaunted "end of history" thesis claims that, with the collapse of the Soviet bloc the great ideological struggles that have dominated the past hundred and fifty years (or from a broader perspective, the whole of human history) have come to a more or less definitive end and that capitalism, democracy, and secularism have won a definitive global victory. Any struggles that remain are mere mopping up operations; real politics is over and has been replaced by a largely technocratic public policy focused on how best to implement and manage a system that is now universally accepted.

Some have read recent statements by Fukuyama (Fukuyama 2006) as at least a partial retraction of his original 1989 thesis, and thus question whether or not the "end of history" thesis still plays a significant role in the current debate. I would suggest, first of all, that, as the following selection indicates, he has not altered but rather only nuanced his basic claims regarding the triumph of capitalist modernity.

> Many people have also interpreted my book "The End of History and the Last Man" (1992) as a neoconservative tract, one that argued in favor of the view that there is a universal hunger for liberty in all people that will inevitably lead them to liberal democracy, and that we are living in the midst of an accelerating, transnational movement in favor of that liberal democracy. This is a misreading of the argument. "The End of History" is in the end an argument about modernization. What is initially universal is not the desire for liberal democracy but rather the desire to live in a modern—that is, technologically advanced and prosperous—society, which, if satisfied, tends to drive demands for political participation. Liberal democracy

is one of the byproducts of this modernization process, something that becomes a universal aspiration only in the course of historical time.

"The End of History," in other words, presented a kind of Marxist argument for the existence of a long-term process of social evolution, but one that terminates in liberal democracy rather than communism. In the formulation of the scholar Ken Jowitt, the neoconservative position articulated by people like Kristol and Kagan was, by contrast, Leninist; they believed that history can be pushed along with the right application of power and will. Leninism was a tragedy in its Bolshevik version, and it has returned as farce when practiced by the United States. Neoconservatism, as both a political symbol and a body of thought, has evolved into something I can no longer support.

Second, regardless of the details of Fukuyama's position, the "end of history" thesis continues to shape much U.S. domestic and foreign policy. In the terms used in this work, neoliberal "end of history" theorists—most Democrats and more moderate Republicans—resist neoconservative attempts to advance capitalist modernity by force because they believe that such force is unnecessary given the long range tendency of human history.

The appeal of this analysis, and its apparent power, come from the fact that the basic framework of capitalism and, to a very large extent, the opening of markets to global capital flows, the "loosening" of labor markets by the restriction of social protections for workers, and a general scaling back of the social wage and social "entitlements" are accepted across a broad political spectrum from the far right through not only social democracy but many "reformed" communists. The analysis is made all the more attractive by the fact that the latter defend their concessions to liberalism with the claim that "there is no alternative." They do so not because they have been persuaded that they were wrong in the great ideological struggles of the last hundred and fifty years, but because "reality" has won out over ideology as such. And especially for those who read history from the standpoint of modern social theory (liberal or socialist) and share the modern ideal of transcending finitude by means of scientific and technological progress, this looks like a very strong argument.

This strength is, however, only apparent. There are vitally important facts that it cannot accommodate. First and foremost, as we will demonstrate later in this work, the apparent victory of capitalist modernity comes on the eve of an ecological and demographic crisis that calls the whole modern project radically into question. We will spell out the details of this impending crisis later. For now it is enough to note that such a crisis simply does not fit within the neoliberal narrative, or at least requires a technological fix that capitalism has thus far shown no signs of generating.

Second, there is very little evidence that the acceptance of capitalist modernity has brought a global victory for liberal democracy in its train. Societies throughout Asia, from the Arabian Peninsula to China, have embraced significant elements of capitalist modernization while decisively rejecting what the West understands by liberal democracy. This is a point on which Fukuyama has nuanced his position, but such nuancing significantly changes what is being claimed. A history that ends in an authoritarian/technocratic capitalism is going to be far less attractive—and invite far more resistance—than one that ends in a democratic capitalism.

Finally, the "end of history" thesis simply cannot accommodate the persistence of religion in the modern world. At issue here are not simply the ethnoreligious conflicts of the past two decades that motivate the competing "clash of civilizations" thesis, but also the persistence of religious belief, practice, and seeking in societies that, by any reasonable measure, have accepted capitalist modernity as an economic model. The United States, by any measure, one of the principal homelands of capitalist modernity, continues to be characterized by a richly diverse and vibrant religious practice that extends from dispensational premillennialism through various immigrant religions up to the New Age. China, while clearly modernizing, is also experiencing a religious revival. And many other states in Asia (Saudi Arabia, for example, and on a somewhat different model the Gulf States) have tried to synthesize economic and technological modernization with hereditary monarchy and a conservative Wahabi Islam.

The Clash of Civilizations

Like the "end of history" thesis to which it is largely a reaction, the "clash of civilizations thesis derives its appeal from the fact that it highlights one of the obvious—and for many social scientists unexpected—

characteristics of the current situation: the persistence, and indeed the intensification, of ethnoreligious conflicts just as the great ideological war of the past hundred and fifty years seemed finally to be dying down. The thesis also has the merit of seeming more honest in recognizing the extent to which liberal ideals generally continue to be contested. This is true globally: consider the persistence of authoritarian regimes and of conservative religiosity throughout Asia.[1] But is also true within the West. Consider the persistence of Christian fundamentalism in the U.S. and of neofascist tendencies in Europe.

This said, the "clash of civilizations" thesis simply ignores too many facts to be credible. First, as we noted above, the whole idea of a "Western Civilization" stretching from Ancient Israel and Ancient Greece up through the present is highly problematic. This is really a question for the comparative historical sociology against which fundamental social theory tests itself, and we will examine the question in greater detail in the next chapter. To put the matter briefly, however, as we noted in the introduction, there are *many* Wests, deriving from both the Jewish and the Hellenic experience, which have flowed together—and been in as much conflict with each other as with other civilizational traditions—over the course of the past five thousand years.

Second, as we also noted in the introduction, the "clash of civilizations" thesis fails to even describe correctly, much less really explain, the main lines of global conflict in the present period. The Jews and Christians who are most committed to sustained conflict with *Dar-al-Islam* are not, for example, secularized liberal interpreters of their tradition, but fundamentalists who actually *agree* with the fundamentalist Muslims with whom they are at war on a broad range of cultural questions, from the proper approach to the interpretation of the sacred Scriptures (literal inerrancy) through the nature of God (absolutely transcendent and sovereign) to church/state relations and the role of

---

[1]. I recently interviewed for a position at a university in the Persian Gulf region where the (mostly American expatriate) search committee made it clear to me that students in the Gulf do not attend the university in order to develop an autonomous approach to fundamental questions of meaning and value, and that while they are quite curious about *other* philosophical and religious traditions, the application of historical critical methods to the study of Islam or *any* engagement with normative philosophical or religious questions which might challenge the dominant Wahabi tradition, however, respectfully, would not be welcome. One does not have to be a neoconservative or a Weberian to recognize a civilizational conflict here.

women in society. At even a rudimentary level of abstraction, in other words, this supposed *clash of civilizations* turns into a cultural convergence among groups who are, nonetheless, really and truly in conflict with each other on the geopolitical stage. East Asia, meanwhile, has embraced capitalism in a way that is hardly coherent with a traditional Confucian worldview and must be read either as representing a rupture towards modernity or a mobilization of other elements in their cultural heritage—a longstanding mercantile tradition and a statist authoritarianism associated more closely with Buddhism and Legalism respectively than with anything even remotely resembling a Confucian *ru xue*.

This latter point suggests that if neoliberalism ignores the persistence of the sacred even in otherwise modernizing contexts, neoconservatism ignores modernization and pretends that China, India, and *Dar-al-Islam* are still the ancient spiritual civilizations they once were, rather than complex social formations in which ancient spiritual traditions certainly survive, but only in complex and contradictory combination with modern capitalist and socialist structures and ideals.

Neosocialism

We noted above that, the collapse of the Soviet Union notwithstanding, modernist socialism still has forceful advocates. At the level of geopolitical analysis, this trend is defined by the claim that the apparent victory of capitalist modernity, and especially the creation of a global market in capital, is only now creating the conditions that Marx specified for the emergence of an authentic socialist movement. The socialisms of the past hundred and fifty years were something else: an effort on the part of the organized working class to ameliorate its conditions under capitalism (what is usually called social democracy) or an effort to force a socialism for which the conditions had not yet emerged, often by tapping into populist or nationalistic sentiments (Leninism) (Hardt and Negri 2001, 2004; Arrighi 1994). A version of this theory that is more "orthodox" in focusing more on technological development than global integration and in conserving the leading role of the Communist Party defines the political line of at least one tendency in the Communist Party of China (Zhao 1987).

This theory's main attraction is the fact that it is probably *right* both in arguing that it is only now that the planet has become sufficiently capitalist to generate the contradictions that Marx described, at least on a global scale, and in pointing out that the socialisms of the past hundred and fifty years were about something other than a transition to *Marx's* communism. But this does not mean that Marx was right. We need an analysis that can explain the rise and fall of the *actually existing socialism*, not one that simply dismisses it as the wrong or an inauthentic socialism. And before we believe that we are an the eve of a "true socialist" revival, we would need to see not only the operation on a global scale of the capitalist contradictions that Marx identified (and we will show that these *are* emerging) but also evidence of a global, internationalist, *proletarian* movement aiming at *communism* in Marx's sense: the construction of a classless and stateless social order of rationally autonomous social individuals. The many and diverse social upheavals of the present period notwithstanding (including the World Social Forum and the socialist resurgence in Latin America) *there is no evidence of such a movement*.

Populism

One of the reasons why modernist, alterglobalist neosocialism lacks credibility is the fact that much of the contemporary socialist movement, while certainly distancing itself from the Leninist heritage, has also distanced itself from modernism and made explicit what was always implicit in previous socialist movements: that much socialism is about *resistance to*—rather than *transcendence of—capitalist modernization*.

As we noted in our introduction, this trend is complex and amorphous and has rarely had "its own" social theory, at least until very recently.[2] But it has had and continues to have a distinctive geopolitical analysis. Specifically, it reads global dynamics in terms of a North/South conflict that has not only economic and political but also cultural

---

2. There have been some brief exceptions to this. The Russian *Narodniki* argued that capitalism is impossible apart from imperialism because the dispossession of the peasantry drives demand down so low that it is impossible to sustain growth (Radkey 1958, 1962; Lewin 1968). It would also be possible to regard a thinker like Vasconcellos (Romannell 1969) as articulating an independent theory for the Mexican Revolution.

dimensions. For most of the twentieth century this was articulated in terms of the Leninist theory of imperialism and national liberation. As capitalism develops and technology advances, the rate of profit falls. Advanced capitalist countries respond by exporting capital to less developed countries precisely because they are less developed, and their low technology, low wage economies offer the prospect of higher profits. They make alliances with local landed elites that hold back or at least distort development, focusing it on the export sector. Because the national bourgeoisie is so small and weak, national liberation and democracy are possible only under the leadership of the working class and the Communist Party (Lenin 1916/1971). Later, dependency/world system variants of this theory traced imperialism all the way back to the beginning of the capitalist era and argued that it was the *source* of the primitive accumulation of capital that made capitalist modernization possible in the first place. Capitalism is intrinsically imperialist, and anti-imperialist struggles intrinsically anticapitalist (Frank 1974).

The collapse of the Soviet Union has "liberated" the planet's peasant masses and their organic intellectuals from the hegemony of their Leninist sponsors, and they are gradually finding their voice. We will look at what this has meant at the level of social theory and political theology later in this chapter, but it is worth noting here a very distinctive analysis with profound implications for the way we understand the current situation: John Milbank's claim that the current resurgence of religion (and indeed the whole history of socialism) represents forms of resistance to what he calls the "enclosure of the sacred." Specifically,

> as Karl Polanyi long ago acknowledged in *The Great Transformation*, what capitalism initially accumulates or 'encloses' is not simply that which serves people's 'real' needs. Beyond the most basic level of subsistence the latter is indefinable. What capitalism really encloses . . . is 'the sacred', taken in the very broadest sense. That is to say, it seizes both land and people who previously have been considered to occupy positions, arrangements and roles of social, political, cosmic and religious as well as merely 'economic' significance. . . .
>
> Refusal now is likewise is [sic] liable to take on a more absolute and global political form: as David Harvey notes, contemporary struggles are less over relative wage and working conditions as over attempts to resist further enclosures of whole ways of life. Hence they tend to occur in areas still 'on

> the margins' of the globalizing process (South America and India: resistance to crop-patenting, ending of Coca production, dam projects etc) but can nonetheless enlist to some degree the solidarity of concerned consumers in the richer parts of the world—thus globalization also permits the possibility of world-networks linking worker with consumer co-operatives . . .
>
> . . . . today the only persisting struggles against capital are in some measure struggles to protect sacrality and often include specifically religious dimensions (Milbank 2006a, 20, 47–48).

The great attraction of this analysis is the fact that it speaks to the interests of and tries to give voice to the aspirations of the vast majority of the people of the planet, most of whom are not members of the industrial proletariat, much less "knowledge workers" benefiting from the global information economy or humanistic or clerical intellectuals trying to defend *their* civilizational tradition in a global theomachy, but rather poor peasants or semiproletarian and often unemployed or underemployed urban slum dwellers.

This said, it is simply not possible to define rigorously a global "South" that includes India and China as well as Africa and Latin America. The differences in ecological endowment and economic trajectory are too great. And there *is* a growing urban proletariat in places like India and China that sees itself as having benefited from globalization and capitalist development, even if it does not want to *stop* there. Furthermore, it is not really possible to treat the whole "resurgence of religion" as a unitary phenomenon. Islamic, Christian, and other fundamentalisms, we will argue, represent an attempt on backward sectors of capital to use early modern ideologies to resist globalization while keeping the people passive. Other popular religious movements (the popular church in Latin America, but also important trends in India and China) could be described quite well as movements of resistance to capitalist modernization. But still others (the New Age) seem to thrive in the knowledge economies of the global metropoles. Similarly, not all socialisms can be described as forms of resistance the enclosure of the sacred: witness the alterglobalists we noted above.

All of the principal analyses, in other words, are far too monolithic. They reduce the current situation to one or two of its most dramatic features and ignore not only subtle details but entire dimensions of contemporary social reality, to which their adversaries quite rightly try to draw attention. We need a new analysis that can accommodate the fully complexity of the current situation. But before we begin to develop that analysis we need to look more closely at the roots of contemporary geopolitical myopia in the traditions of modern social theory.

Social Theory

We have already noted in the introduction that in order to carry out the sort of analysis we propose, we will need a new kind of social theory, one that takes seriously *both* the material basis on which human civilizations develop *and* humanity's ordering to transcendental ends as well as the structural factors that have concerned modern social theory. Our aim in the present section is, first of all, to explain in greater depth why modern and postmodern social theory is inadequate. The basic outline of our argument is straightforward. The current situation can be understood properly only in the context of the crisis of the modern ideal, including both its positivistic and humanistic variants. High modern social theory,[3] even when it mounts a critique of certain aspects of modernity, actually *presupposes* and *serves* the modern ideal, and thus cannot adequately thematize the problem of modernity. This is because high modern social theory, whether liberal or socialist, is fundamentally an attempt to understand how society works in order to bring it under rational, human control. As a result of this aim, it theorizes only those aspects of human society that are potentially subject to such control. This includes technology, economics, politics, and culture. The material base *as material*, as an ecological context that *constrains* potential patterns of development, is generally outside the scope of modern social theory. And it is taken for granted that human civilizations aim at material progress, even if they do not know that this is what they are doing, and even if they do not do it as effectively as they might due to technological or cultural backwardness, or oppressive economic and political structures. The specificity of the modern ideal, which *is* focused on such progress, is thus obscured, and the current situation—an emerging civilizational crisis rooted in the unworkability of the modern ideal—becomes impossible to understand.

---

3. A category in which we include both classical and neoclassical political economy and the more technicist variants of historical materialism.

Postmodern theory, on the other hand,[4] recognizes the specificity of the modern project only to resist it in the name of the values of meaning and solidarity that remain inadequately grounded or treat it as one of a potentially infinite number of ideals all contending with each other in an endless clash of civilizations.

We will begin with a critique of the two principal variants of high modern theory: those that attempt to apply directly to human society the concepts developed by mathematical physics and its derivatives, such as Social Darwinism, sociobiology, and the information-theoretical neoliberalism of F. A. Hayek, and the technicist variant of historical materialism. We will then go on to assess the contributions and limitations of theory in the postmodern spectrum, from Radical Orthodoxy at one end, through populism and functionalism, up to deconstructionism and interpretive sociology at the other. Once we have shown why both modern and postmodern social theory are inadequate, we will be in a position to explain just what sort of theory is required, and to outline and argue briefly for that theory in anticipation of the more developed argument we will make in the next two chapters.

Positivism

At the heart of modernity is the hope that science, by telling us how the world works, will allow us to bring the world under our control. And the architectonic discipline of modern science is mathematical physics that attempts to formalize physical systems mathematically. It should come as no surprise that modern social theory should begin with an attempt to do the same for social systems.

Mathematical physics can be applied to the study of human society either directly or through the mediation of derivative disciplines such as evolutionary biology. The first approach has largely been confined to the discipline of economics: the development of formal models of the market system that allow economic actors to predict and control their economic environment. Global social theory, even of the most reductionist stripe, has tended to take the second approach, treating

---

4. And we will include in this category not only deconstructionist postmodernism in the narrower sense, but also social theories such as functionalism and interpretive sociology that emerged as people first began to question the modern project during the later part of the nineteenth century.

sociology as a branch of evolutionary theory. Ultimately, we will see, these two approaches converge in the information theoretical neoliberalism of thinkers such as F. A. Hayek, in which economics appears as a special case of a larger evolutionary theory.

What is actually taken from mathematical physics is really very simple: the idea that the universe is devoid of any underlying teleological ordering, and that complex organization, where it develops at all, does so by means of random variation and by a process of natural selection for structures that have thermodynamic stability, generally speaking because of their ability to import from the environment the energy necessary to sustain organization—which is, from this point of view, precisely what an economy is for.

There have historically been several attempts to develop a global social theory on this model. These attempts differ largely based on what they regard as the proper unit of selection. Thus early Social Darwinists (Spencer 1857) treated the individual or even the "race" as the unit of selection. This view was discredited, because it failed to take into account the fact that even if the poor (who are assumed to be less fit in this perspective) die younger than the rich, they nonetheless live long enough and produce enough offspring for their population to grow more rapidly than that of the rich, effectively evading the mechanism of selection.

It is more common in the present period to argue that it is the *gene* that is the actual unit of selection and that human beings are no more than machines for reproducing our genes. This is the claim of most sociobiology (Wright 1995). According to this view moral norms emerge because they help people to survive long enough to reproduce and pass on their genes, and they are regularly violated for the same reason. Thus Wright argues that women should feel lucky to be raped, because the children born of the rape will share their father's aggressive and powerful genetic heritage.

This approach has a number of problems, the most serious of which is it that it fails the text of Occam's Razor. It is true that it is possible, with some creativity, to mount *an* explanation of human behavior in terms of its utility in reproducing our genes. But there are many alternative explanations as well. Is sociobiology really the most economical approach? Only if we confuse economy of explanation with reductionism. The truth is that all we really know about genes is that they code for the production of proteins. While there is clearly an association of some kind between genes and more complex biological characteristics, such as eye color, we know very little about how genes are expressed, even in terms of basic morphology. Sociobiology assumes, in effect, a whole chain of causation, and thus fails to meet the test of Occam's Razor.

Of rather more importance is the neoliberal position, which treats *practices* rather than a gene or a biological individual or collectivity as the appropriate unit of selection. This approach derives ultimately from Adam Smith's defense of the free market (Smith 1776), of which it is simply a generalization. Arguing against tariffs, Smith reasoned that wealth was the product of labor, and that labor was set into motion by capital. The prosperity of a society thus depended in the long run on its capital supply. Individuals would, furthermore, naturally seek the most rational and productive employment of their capital. Any attempt to regulate investment by means of tariffs or other laws would merely distort the allocation of capital, resulting in lower productivity and less wealth.

Smith's theory conceded too much to labor to be really palatable to later capitalist theory. Neoliberals such as Hayek (Hayek 1988) remedy this by restating the theory in a way that makes no direct mention of labor whatsoever. Individuals seek to survive and realize their other interests under conditions of scarcity. They develop various practices in order to do so (technologies, economic and political structures, ideologies). Some work but others do not. Those that work become part of an ongoing social tradition. We know that markets are superior to centralized planning systems partly for the simple reason that they have proven themselves. Capitalism survived, socialism fell (or so the story goes). But this result also accords with the expectations of the theory. Markets allow practices to be tested without protection and subsidy and thus do a better job of selecting for those that actually have survival value. They are, furthermore, much better at accessing and processing information regarding the diverse interests and abilities of people in a complex society, something no individual mind or group of minds (such as a central planning commission) could ever even hope to accomplish.

This understanding of human society directly implies the end of history thesis advanced by Francis Fukuyama. In effect, over a period of time, human societies will figure out which practices work and which don't. According to most neoliberals this process has been completed, and capitalism, democracy, and a basically secular worldview centered on modern science and governed by an instrumental rationality have all demonstrated their superiority. Reactionary holdouts as well as alternative modern projects such as socialism were doomed from the beginning, and their remnants will now quickly disappear.

Hayek's specific critique of socialism and his defense of the marketplace have merit, and we will see later that this is, in part, why markets—especially markets in goods and services—are so difficult to transcend. But it becomes compelling only if we believe that there is no larger end or purpose to human life, a purpose that transcends the consumption interests of individuals, as they currently understand them. If, as we have argued elsewhere (Mansueto and Mansueto 2005), there *is* such a purpose, then the problems with Hayek's theory become obvious. First, even if we accept the view that the marketplace is an information processing system, it turns out to have real limits. It knows only what people want, and how badly, and what they can produce, and at what cost. It has no access to information regarding the impact of various activities on the integrity of the ecosystem and the social fabric or on the development of human capacities. Second, the model fails to theorize the actual conditions for production. Modernist to the core, liberal theory simply assumes that with an adequate supply of capital people can create whatever they wish, regardless of the material or social conditions. The absurdity of this position was nicely illustrated by the recent proposal by former Undersecretary of Defense and World Bank President Paul Wolfowitz to create a market in information regarding terrorism threats, as a substitute for real investment in understanding the complex dynamics of the current global situation.

This approach also misses the profound contradictions in the modern project. The defeat of the Soviet bloc did not resolve the contradictions of capitalism. On the contrary, as we will demonstrate later, the ecological crisis is becoming more serious with each passing year and the dynamics of neoliberalism point to both difficulties in capital formation and global underconsumption. The pressure to work and produce—often cited as a strength of markets—is rapidly undermining our social fabric. But most important, there is little evidence that capitalism is going to deliver on the full promise of the modern ideal—

to lift humanity out of finitude and towards a kind of technologically grounded divinity. This is why people, even though they continue to *live* the modern ideal, no longer believe in it but have turned increasingly to older spiritual traditions that have more credibility. Neoliberalism is at a loss to explain this turn.

Historical Materialism

The limitations of liberal theory were apparent from the beginning. The ink was not dry on Adam Smith's defense of the free market before the cities of England began to burst at the seams with displaced peasants seeking work—and often starving even when they found it. Just as the physical sciences in the nineteenth century began to generate results, such as the Second Law of Thermodynamics or the Poincaré Recurrence Theorem, which questioned the possibility of unlimited technological progress, so too did the social sciences begin producing results that questioned the possibility of unlimited social progress. At first these theories simply pointed out that progress would have its costs and that we ought not to assume that it would spontaneously resolve all social problems. This was the message of Thomas Malthus, who pointed out that while food production grows arithmetically, population grows geometrically, resulting in inevitable overpopulation—something that is only made worse by interventions to alleviate poverty, which increase the rate at which population grows even further, until it exceeds the carrying capacity of the land (Malthus 1798). At this point in history, however, the modernist ideal was far from exhausted, and creative thinkers began to look for ways to actually realize the promise of modernity, even if that meant breaking with key elements of modern social structure.

It is in this context that we must understand historical materialism. Most systematic statements of historical materialism, beginning with Marx's own sketch in the Preface to the *Contribution to the Critique of Political Economy* (Marx 1859/1966), and Engels' later systematization in *Socialism* (Engels 1880/1978), attempt to explain the development of human society in terms of the complex interaction of the "forces" and "relations" of production. Working under given material (ecological) conditions, human beings develop increasingly sophisticated technologies that amplify their productive capacity. These developing forces of production imply definite ways of organizing the production process and of centralizing and allocating resources for production—what Marx calls productive relations. And the forces and relations of production in turn imply various legal and political structures, and certain definite forms of social consciousness. At certain points in development the relations of production, the way of centralizing and allocating resources, become an obstacle to further technological development, setting in motion economic crises, class struggle, and revolution. If a civilization can successfully reorganize itself in such a way as to unleash renewed technological progress, it recovers and thrives; if not it collapses.

Now Marx is quite correct to point out that human beings, however else they might be distinguished from other animals, distinguish themselves through the act of production (Marx 1846/1978). While minerals seek Being by conserving their form, plants by nutrition, growth, and reproduction, and animals by sensation and locomotion, we humans are unique in actually bringing into being entirely new forms of organization. The question, however, is just what this act involves. Human beings are, before we are anything else, animals inhabiting definite ecological niches. It is one of the great limitations of historical materialism, and a mark of its modernist assumptions, that very little attention has been paid to the question of ecosystem, whether as a constraint on human development, as something that shapes it, or as something shaped by it. And yet it can hardly be a coincidence that the first urban civilizations developed in fertile river basins or that those who turned to warfare as a strategy for economic development generally inhabited arid steppes where agriculture was more difficult. It is true, to be sure, that the way in which ecosystem affects development changes over time. A more complex society like ours, which effectively inhabits the entire planet, is affected less by the particularities of local ecosystems than by global questions such as the supply of fossil fuels or the impact of human society on climate change. But these nonetheless remain vitally important questions—questions that may ultimately catalyze global crises and require revolutionary transformations far greater than any envisioned by Marx—and historical materialism ignores them at its peril.

At the same time, the act of production is, from the very beginning, an *intellectual* act. Whatever impact technology may have had on human intellectual development, and that impact is no doubt significant, it was made possible to begin with by human physiology—by our big brains and our opposable thumbs, as well as by the absence of fangs and claws or stomachs that can digest grass. Human beings survive by transforming our environment and by bringing into being entirely new forms of organization. The intellectual processes involved in production are, furthermore, never purely *technical*; they do not, in other words, involve simply methods of transforming a raw material. They also involve *science* or at least an *empirical lore*, which provides us with an understanding of how the raw material (which is often the whole ecosystem itself) is organized, and thus of its latent potential. Unless we know that plants grow from seeds and require soil, water, and light, agriculture will be impossible. But production also presupposes definite *aims*, and it is not enough to say that that aim is survival. On the one hand, we always aim for much, much more: we seek an unlimited and autonomous creative power. It is in this sense that I would insist that our aims are always transcendental. On the other hand, different civilizations and different technological regimes understand and pursue these ends very differently. The alchemical technologies of the Silk Road Era sought to tap into and catalyze potentials latent in matter; modern industrial technologies, on the other hand, break down existing organization in order to release energy and do work. These immediate technological aims are, furthermore, embodied in larger complexes of religious and metaphysical ideas in the context alone of which they make sense. Technologies that tap into and attempt to catalyze and further already existing dynamics of growth and development presuppose that such dynamics of growth and development are present—they presuppose, that is, a broadly teleological worldview. Modern industrial technology assumes that matter is inert and that order is something imposed on inert matter from the outside, whether by a sovereign God, as in the case of early modern theologies, or by humanity itself.

It is important to understand, furthermore, that this criticism cannot be answered by pointing to the significant achievements of Marxist cultural theory, whether in the historical materialist or critical theoretical traditions. The difficulty is not a neglect of culture; it is a failure to recognize the immanent teleological ordering of humanity and indeed of the universe as a whole, a failure to recognize as *real* the transcendental principles about which cultures speak.

Any revision of historical materialism that is going to be adequate to understanding the current situation will, on the one hand, have to take even more seriously than Marx did the role of really material (ecological) constraints on development, *and* the teleological ordering that is already implicit in the act of production itself, an act that is intellectual from the very beginning and presupposes a distinctly human way of seeking Being.

But before we attempt such a revision, let us see what the other trends in modern social theory can offer us.

Interpretive Sociology and Right Postmodernism

We are not accustomed to thinking of Weberian interpretive sociology as a postmodern theory. In one sense, after all, it is *the* theory of modernization *par excellence*. Weber's driving question was why industrial capitalism, bureaucratic organization, and the instrumental rationality that inspire them emerged when and where they did. Weber's approach to this problem, however, reflects a vantage point outside the modernist paradigm. He is, first of all, profoundly aware of the *specificity* of modern civilization, and does not regard modernity as the inevitable *telos* of either an adaptive evolutionary process or of the materialist dialectic. On the contrary, he reads it as the product of distinctive and rather surprising political-theological struggles that took place in a very specific time and place: the northwest fringes of Europe, hitherto a backwater by comparison with the civilizational heartlands of China, India, and *Dar-al-Islam*. Second, he is interested in the problem of modernization largely in order to better understand Germany's precarious position in the emerging European imperial hierarchy. And even if his *politics* (like those of many right postmodernists) remain those of a liberal-conservative, his approach to this problem reflects the Nietzschean and (later) Heideggerian conviction that history is not so much an evolutionary process that selects the most fit (races, individuals, practices) as it is an open-ended struggle between civilizations driven by competing ideals and by a common will to power.

The explanation that Weber offers for industrialization is a process of rationalization that reaches back to what Karl Jaspers later called the Axial Age—the period between roughly 800 and 200 BCE when magic and nature religion gradually began to give way to religions focused on either transforming the world or achieving salvation from it. Weber acknowledges that this process, while not universal, affected all of the great civilizational centers of Eurasia. Some paths of rationalization, however, were more promising than others. The "salvation religions" that emerged during this period can be classified as either mystical or ascetic, otherworldly or innerworldly. Mystical religions seek salvation through union with the sacred, ascetic religions by doing the will of God. Otherworldly religions are focused primarily on redemption *from* the world, innerworldly religions on the redemption *of* the world.

From here Weber's explanation of why it was Europe and not China or the Islamic world that industrialized falls out neatly (Weber 1921/1968). Asian religions tend to be mystical rather than ascetic, and are thus less world-transforming. Taoism is a classic example of innerworldly mysticism and Buddhism of otherworldly mysticism. The "West," for Weber and his followers is defined by ascetic religion, and specifically by the ethical monotheism that characterizes Judaism and its derivatives. Asceticism by itself, however, is not enough. Catholicism, for example, gives an otherworldly cast to the ascetic impulse. Ethical conduct finds its fulfillment in the beyond, in the beatific vision, and not in this world. Nor is even *innerworldly* asceticism sufficient to spark modernization. Judaism and Islam are both intensely focused on realizing God's will in the world, but neither sparked an industrial revolution or capitalist development—and this in spite of the high material and scientific level of the Islamic civilization in which both religions flourished throughout most of the middle ages. This, Weber argues, is because they fail to create the peculiar psychic tension that modernity requires. Either one fulfills the law, or one does not. It may be difficult to be a good Jew or Muslim, but one's spiritual status is at least transparent and under one's own control. The psychic tension essential to modernity, Weber argues, is the unique contribution of Protestantism generally, and Calvinism in particular. On the one hand, he claims, the Protestant doctrine of the Christian vocation valued all useful work, and not merely the contemplative activity of the monastic or the religious scholarship of the rabbi or Islamic jurist. On the other hand, the Calvinist doctrine of double predestination left believers constantly wondering about their spiritual state—about whether they were among the saved or among the damned. This was something that they could never know for sure, but there were signs. Those who were productive, fulfilling God's command to "fill the earth and subdue it," were more likely among the saved than those who were lazy and incompetent. Those who saved and invested, putting the fruits of their labor to good use, were more likely among the elect than those who consumed everything they produced in useless luxuries. While there is nothing one could do to alter one's state, believers naturally rationalized their behavior in order to make it compatible with the belief they were saved, and thus ended up working, saving, and investing with unprecedented intensity. Since any relaxation or lapse was not merely a fault to be confessed, but a sign that their earlier confidence had been misplaced, believers were careful never to let up, something that created the unique, frantic pace of activity that capitalism required (Weber 1920/1958).

Later Weberian scholars have used Weber's theory to analyze in depth why China, which was almost certainly the technologically and economically most advanced region on the planet up until 1800, fell so rapidly behind, and why Japan, which was merely a periphery of the Chinese trade system, was able to industrialize and contest Western dominance. Ho Ping-ti (Ho 1959), for example, argues that there were a number of features of Chinese culture that weighed against industrialization and capitalist development: a preference for safe investments such as trade monopolies and tax farming, a Confucian ethos that required the redistribution of wealth through kin networks and that favored investment in literary and philosophical activity rather than in science and technology, and that valued status (academic degrees and civil service ranks) more than wealth. Robert Bellah (Bellah 1957), similarly, has shown how, after the pacification of Japan undermined the traditional social function of the *samurai*, this group drew on their *bushido* ethic to transform themselves into industrial capitalists, the discipline of hard work, savings, and investment in this case legitimated as service to the Mikado or emperor.

It is easy to see why interpretive sociology might look not only irreducibly modernist, but a mere scholarly recasting of the story that the West tells about itself, giving a slight nod to other great civilizations and lauding the contributions of Weber's own Germanic people as opposed to the Greeks and Romans. If we look more deeply, however, at the underlying theoretical foundations of Weber's work, we can see that he breaks in important ways with high modernism and more nearly prefigures the stance of contemporary postmodern theory.

In order to demonstrate this, we need only read the opening theoretical sections of Weber's *Economy and Society*. The object of sociology, according to Weber, is social action. Social action is defined by the meanings that individuals give their actions. It is these meanings and the relationships between them that sociology attempts to elucidate and understand. The only real difference between sociology and a humanistically written history is the fact that sociologists look for typical meanings, for the universal or at least relatively general rather than the particular. Thus Weber's ideal types, which are all specifications of four general types of meaning orientation: affective (driven by feeling), traditional (determined by the fact that things have always been done that way), instrumental (means/ends) rationality, and substantive or value rationality.

These meaning orientations are important to Weber because they play a central role in legitimating power and in motivating economic action. It is not so much that people see the universe in a certain way and act accordingly—a rather simple-minded but not necessarily wrong-headed approach to understanding human society. It is that human beings are engaged in a constant struggle for power in which their basic meaning-orientations function first and foremost as weapons in what Weber once described as a kind of "war among the gods" (Weber 1918/1919). From this standpoint the process of rationalization sketched out through *Economy and Society* and *The Protestant Ethic* are not so much an inevitable evolutionary process, but the chronicle of an open-ended struggle between competing civilizational ideals.

However one reads Weber, there are a number of difficulties with his approach. First, at the most abstract level, we must note that Weber leaves the origin and development of the various meaning orientations or civilizational ideals largely unexplained. In this sense he merely replaces historical materialist reductionism with an historical idealist reductionism; neither is scientifically complete.

Second, Weber's account of the origins of modernity is deeply flawed. Even if we accept that the Protestant Ethic Thesis captures part of what makes European modernity unique, it is only a partial explanation. Where did the Protestant Ethic come from? Why did it emerge when and where it did? What catalyzed the radicalization of Augustinian Christianity in the late middle ages and catapulted it to dominance? Conversely, many of the obstacles to development that

Weberians such as Ho Ping-ti identify in China—state monopolies, tax-farming, office selling, etc—were also present in Europe. France, in some ways the homeland of high modernism, had to overcome all of these obstacles—and did (Skocpol 1979). And the pride of place that the Confucian school gave to philosophy and literature over science and technology does not seem to have prevented China from being *the* global leader technologically until the early modern era. What changed and why?

Third, while the Weberians are quite correct in pointing out that dependency/world systems theorists must explain why Europe was able to *win* the contest it began in the late middle ages, especially given the fact that it started from so far behind, it is simply impossible to explain the rise of Europe without taking into account the reality of the conquests and their implications for the primitive accumulation of capital, the formation of the modern state—and of these for the emergence of the civilizational ideal we call modernity.

These weaknesses all bear on the adequacy of interpretive sociology as a tool for understanding the current situation. If high modern social theory (liberal or socialist) attempted to reduce human civilization to simply a material adaptation to our physical and biological environment, right postmodernism reduces it to an attempt to realize ideals which, because they are utterly independent of material conditions, cannot be tested. They can only be contested. Civilizational conflict follows inevitably and interminably. And with globalization and the development of modern weapons, the prospects for humanity are not pleasant.

Fortunately, civilizational ideals are not independent of reality—either the underlying material basis on which they grow up or the transcendental ends that they pursue. And because of this they are neither irreducibly incompatible nor incommunicable. And while no civilization can claim to represent the "definitive solution to the riddle of history," and while every civilization has contributed *something* to our understanding of what it means to be human, some ideals turn out to be more compelling than others.

This said, we must note that interpretive sociology contributes something important to our understanding of human history. There *is* a struggle between competing civilizational ideals, even if this struggle takes place within a certain material and metaphysical context. It will be one of the aims of the theory we propose to capture this aspect of the historical process while situating it properly in the context of the material and spiritual factors that alone can explain it and endow it with meaning.

Functionalism

The position of functionalist sociology in the Durkheimian tradition with respect to the modern project is equally complex. This school traces its roots back, ultimately, to French traditionalism. Traditionalism was a reaction against the Enlightenment, and specifically against the Enlightenment ideal of rational autonomy. Thinkers like de Maistre and de Bonald, the principal theoreticians of reaction in the wake of the French revolution, focused attention on the role of religion generally, and ritual in particular, in constituting and maintaining the social order. They regarded the social order, including language and religion, as part of a primitive revelation that provided humanity with the tools it needed in order to think—and indeed survive (McCool 1977; Milbank 1990). The central social category for the traditionalists was that of violence and especially the ritualized violence of sacrifice which, they believed, *constituted* the social order. In this sense, they put forward not only a *critique* of the French Revolution, but also a kind of hidden *reading* of that revolution, which was nothing if not a reconstitution of the social order through violence.

Traditionalism runs like a secret thread through postmodern social theory. In its original "rightist" form, it represents, of course, simply another way of theorizing history as a kind of theomachy, and a fully developed sociology in this vein (which we do not have) would complement Weber's interpretive sociology, which is distinctively Protestant in its understanding of religion as "word" with a Catholic focus on religion as liturgy and sacrament. But there is also a left traditionalism—or perhaps many different left traditionalisms—and a "center" traditionalism. John Milbank (1990: 69) has, for example, recently called attention to the work of Pierre Simon Ballenche, who argued that the Axial Age represented a radical democratization of the religious arena as the popular classes struggled to gain full access to the cult and thus claim their full humanity. But any theory that regards the spontaneous dynamism of the people, especially as expressed in revolutionary upheavals, as somehow constitutive of social order, is ultimately a leftist inflection of the traditionalist emphasis on violence as constitutive of social order. Alexis de Tocqueville, finally, is an example of "centrist" traditionalism. De Tocqueville shared traditionalist concerns about the violence of the French revolution but responded not by rejecting democracy as such, but rather by looking for an alternative form of democracy, something he found in the complex, pluralistic civil society of the young United States.

This whole history has been obscured somewhat by the refraction of the original insights of the traditionalists through the lens of positivism. Auguste Comte and the other positivists turned traditionalism on its head, arguing that society was not a divine creation, but rather that God was a social creation, and that it is human society itself that is the real object of worship, something that Comte attempted to make explicit with his system of socialatry. It is in Comte, of course, that we see the most explicit form of modern secularism, with science actually replacing not only theology but also philosophy.

Durkheim took the ideas developed by this already contradictory tradition and developed them in new and far more subtle ways. A Jew and a man of the republican and socialist left he celebrated the victory of the Third Republic and began his career by attempting to define for the Republic a secular and modern approach to moral education. Increasing demographic pressure, he reasoned, gradually forced humanity to develop new technologies, something that lead ultimately to first the social division of labor between various trades and occupations and eventually to the technical division of labor within trades characteristic of modern industry. This, in turn, led to a change in the way human societies maintained their cohesion. Preindustrial societies, in which most people did the same thing, relied on a "mechanical solidarity" based on shared beliefs and values. But as peoples' lives diverged so too did their beliefs and values. Mechanical solidarity gave way to an "organic solidarity" based on material interdependence. This was, he argued, basically a positive development, since it permitted an unprecedented degree of ideological pluralism. In this sense, he clearly affirmed the Enlightenment ideal of rational autonomy. But he also noted the existence of serious contradictions in the economic system: what he called the "anomic" and "coercive" forms of the division of labor. The anomic form derives from insufficient economic regulation, and results in a loss of meaning. The forced form results from the existence of inequalities between contracting parties, and leads to exploitation (Durkheim 1893/1964). These contradictions were further reflected in rising suicide rates in the most advanced industrial countries (Durkheim 1897/1951), which he attributed to a deepening moral crisis. People seemed to find less and less meaning in their lives, and to feel less and less connected to each other and to society as a whole. While capitalism had increased the level of material interdependence, it was also undermining our ability to understand the social significance of our work and to feel like members of a cohesive social group.

In response to this situation Durkheim advanced a far-reaching proposal for the development of occupational groups or "corporations." This proposal amounts to a comprehensive attempt to adapt the tradition of the medieval guilds and journeymen's associations to the new and much more complex conditions of an industrial society. These corporations were not only to regulate wages, hours, and working conditions; they were eventually to collectively control the means of production, and connect them to the "directing and conscious centers of society." They were, further, like the guilds, to serve as the center of a rich social life, and the locus of new moral forces that would combat the egoism and anomie that was gradually eating away at the social order (Bellah 1973: xxxi).

Durkheim argued, furthermore, that the social basis for the implementation of his proposal lay in the popular religious traditions of the people themselves. His study of Australian religion had convinced him that religious symbols were "collective representations" of the structure of human society. Indeed, God *is* the community, in transcendent form, binding the individuals together into a social being that is greater than themselves, to which their ties are stronger than any tie of self-interest, and which has the moral authority, but also the compelling beauty, to command self-sacrifice. In ritual gatherings he found a "collective effervescence" that catalyzes the formation of a sense of unity and oneness that transcends the existing empirical forms of social order and that opens up the possibility for the emergence of radically new social forms that later on become embodied in new economic and political institutions.

> In such moments of collective ferment are born the great ideals upon which civilizations rest. These periods of creation or renewal occur when men for various reasons are led into a closer relationship with each other, when reunions and assemblies are most frequent, relationships better maintained and the exchange of ideas most active. Such was the great crisis of Christendom . . . in the twelfth and thirteenth centuries. Such were the Reformation and the Renaissance, the revolutionary epoch and the Socialist upheavals of the nineteenth century. At such moments this higher form of life is lived with such intensity and exclusiveness that it monopolizes all minds to the more or less complete exclusion of egoism and the commonplace. At such times the ideal tends to become one with the real, and men have the impression that the time is close when the ideal will in fact be realized and the Kingdom of God established on earth. (Durkheim in Bellah 1973: 1)

Durkheim hoped fervently for the renewal of such collective effervescence in his own time, and had little doubt concerning its probable source.

> Who does not feel . . . that in the depths of society an intense life is developing . . . We aspire to a higher justice which no existing formulas express . . . One may even go further and say with some precision in what region of society these new forces are forming: it is in the popular classes (Durkheim in Bellah 1973, xlvii).

What Durkheim has done, in effect, is to gradually and partly rescue left traditionalism from its positivistic (and modernist) captivity, while developing a more complex and subtle account of the dynamism that earlier traditionalists of the left and the right saw in sacrificial and revolutionary violence. Even if Durkheim's analysis of the internal contradictions of capitalism is rather undeveloped and schematic, his theory nonetheless captures better than Marx the actual dynamics of mass socialist movements. It is now well established that the principal social base of the socialist movements of the late-nineteenth and twentieth centuries was not the urban proletariat, but rather the peasantry, that these peasants were struggling not so much to transcend capitalist modernity as to resist it, and that they did so by drawing on popular communal institutions and religious traditions (Wolf 1969; Lancaster

1987). But even in the cities, socialism found its base in popular communal institutions and religious traditions. William Sewell (Sewell 1980) has argued at great length that French socialism emerged out of the struggle of the *compagnonages*, associations of journeyman artisans, against the penetration of market relations into French society, in the years following the revolution of 1789—long before "socialized" industrial forces of production had become important in the French economy, which retained an agricultural and artisanal character. Some of these guilds maintained traditional Catholic cults centered on patron saints while others were Masonic and neopagan, but nearly all were, in some sense, religious. And the development of urban working-class socialism showed similar patterns even in countries such as the United States where there was no formal guild structure (Mansueto 1985, 1995, 2002a). John Milbank's recent (Milbank 2006a) attempt to retheorize socialism as a movement of resistance to the enclosure of the sacred and in defense of a "general economy" that orders material production to higher and ultimately transcendental ends, falls clearly within the theoretical space created by Durkheim, even if Durkheim himself retains too much of the taint of modernism for Milbank's tastes.

This said, there remain serious difficulties with Durkheim's theory. The full theological implications of Durkheim's social metaphysics of participation are not drawn out. While he is able to recognize the progressive potential of popular religious beliefs and practices in a way other modern social theorists cannot, he remains reluctant to take seriously the metaphysical *objects* of these beliefs and treats them as simply an imaginative way of expressing devotion to human society and to the human civilizational project. He never formally considers the possibility that human civilization might be ordered to transcendental ends—and to this extent his thought remains within modernist/postmodernist horizons.

Because of this the whole dynamic of human development is left at once unexplained and unvalued. Why do human societies develop in a way that generates demographic pressure and why do we respond with technological innovations that eventually lead to the social and technical division of labor? Why do moments of collective effervescence occur when and where they do? It is, perhaps, because of these weaknesses that functionalism and left traditionalism have never been taken up as autonomous revolutionary theories by the populist tendencies they describe so well. Rather, functionalist and left traditionalist ideas have generally entered the political field in a combination with ideas drawn from the broader historical-materialist tradition: a populist or dependency/world systems analysis of the global economy and Gramscian analysis of cultural hegemony.

The first of these theories was originally articulated, as we noted above, by the Russian *Narodniki*, who argued that capitalism was impossible in Russia or other countries lacking a colonial empire because the dispossession of the peasantry would so drive down incomes that it would undercut the effective demand required to sustain a national market for manufactured goods. Ultimately this claim proved incorrect: a national market turns out not to be necessary for capitalism, which can develop equally well on the basis of an *external* market, whether for agricultural or industrial goods. But it did suggest two useful insights. First, it focused attention on the intimate connection between colonialism and the primitive accumulation of capital, something to which thinkers such as Andre Gunder Frank (Frank 1967) devoted considerable attention. Second, it suggested that even if capitalism was possible for colonies or neocolonies, *authentic human development* is not, for the simple reason that export-oriented capitalism orders the economy to the needs of the imperial metropoles rather than those of the people.

This, in turn, led to a claim, never fully articulated except by a few extremist groups, that the "Third World" countries of Asia, Africa, and Latin America—the situation of their people made increasingly impossible by global capital—were in a more or less permanent revolutionary situation. This revolutionary discontent might be articulated in the form of nationalistic or religious ideas, but it was objectively anticapitalist.

Here Antonio Gramsci's concept of cultural hegemony (Gramsci 1949c) provided a way to theorize the linking of these national and religious ideas to ultimately socialist aims. Gramsci argues that a stable ruling class must govern not by coercion or co-optation, but by linking the national, popular, and religious traditions of the people to its own class project. This is no different for the working class. Seen from this point of view movements like the theology of liberation become just such linking ideologies (Lancaster 1988), yoking the peasantry and the semi-proletarian urban masses of the Third World to the socialist project.

Maoism provides another way in which the populist project was linked to modern socialism. Indeed, Maoism can be seen as simply the culmination of a project begun by Lenin and Gramsci. The first gives us the vanguard party and a strategy centered on leveraging conjunctural crises to bring the party to power. The latter adds a strategy for tapping into deeply held beliefs and values and linking them to the party's project. Mao's early thought (Mao 1927/1972) remained largely within the limits of an application of Leninism to the social conditions of the Chinese revolution. But increasingly Mao began to dissociate political analysis from the larger context of social theory. Maoism began as a protocol for analysis of the current situation in terms of its constitutive contradictions, with little more than lip service to the core historical materialist categories of forces and relations of production, superstructure, etc. (Mao 1937a/1971, 1937b/1971, 19571/1971; Bosteels 2005). Mao himself used this sort of analysis to gain control of the party and bring it to power and, when the party became a constraint on his power, to attempt to liberate himself from it by means of the Cultural Revolution, which exploited the contradictions between the children of the revolutionary generation and their parents. For these young Red Guards, however, and for their admirers around the world, Maoism represented the possibility of a politics without or beyond the party, a development the significance of which we will consider shortly.[5]

What has happened, of course, is that that socialist project has largely collapsed, freeing the populist and left-traditionalist elements from the Third Worldist synthesis, but also depriving them of a complete social theory. Efforts such as John Milbank's "geopolitical theology" (Milbank 2006a) are, among other things, an attempt to remedy this situation, but are thus far tentative and incipient.

---

5. It should be noted that there were *also* Western Maoists for whom Maoism was, first and foremost, a technique for restoring the party which, under the leadership of the Soviet Union, had become so implacably reformist that it could no longer fulfill its *metaphysical* function of constituting the revolutionary intelligentsia as the subject of the historical process. That is why the New Communist Movement in the U.S., and similar movements elsewhere, are properly understood as party-building movements rather than as tendencies within the workers (or other popular) movements as such.

We will conserve much of the left-traditionalist and functionalist perspective. Specifically, we will conserve the link between social structure and collective representation and the role of collective effervescence in catalyzing social transformation. We will also draw significantly on de Tocqueville's analysis of mediating institutions. But we will set them all in a larger context that remedies their weakness as scientific theories.

Political Theology

It may, perhaps, seem odd that we have discussed *postmodern* social theory without even mentioning the principal varieties of *postmodernism*, especially the deconstructionist postmodernism associated with Derrida. This is, because, strictly speaking, *postmodernism* is not so much a social theory as it is a political-theological position. Indeed, each of the social-theoretical alternatives we have analyzed encodes a distinct, if often implicit and hidden, political theology.

Once again, we have four basic poles between which the principal political-theological alternatives of our time are arrayed:

1. information-theoretical neoliberalism,
2. dialectical materialism,
3. nihilistic theomachy, and
4. religious postmodernism, especially Radical Orthodoxy.

Let us consider each of these briefly in turn, noting prominent positions that stand in between.

Information-Theoretical Neoliberalism.

God building, it turns out, is alive and well. There is, in fact, a broad transhumanist trend that continues to argue that human beings are on the verge of a major breakthrough that will significantly push back the limits of finitude and lead us, if not to full divinity, then along a trajectory that points clearly in that direction. Many of these transhumanisms focus on technologies that may result in significantly lengthening of human life or augmentation of human capacities in the short-term. These do not address the difficult question of the generally pessimistic outlook for complex organization, life, and intelligence in most standard cosmologies, which point either towards the infinite expansion of the universe, until matter is too thinly dispersed for complex organization to develop, or else a big crunch that destroys all of the achievements of a single cosmic cycle.

The single exception to this is the work of Frank Tipler, who has advanced a highly developed, if also very controversial, argument for technological self-divinization that clearly shows what we mean when we talk about the "secret religion of high modernity." Tipler takes as his starting point a high-technology variant of Berkeley's subjective idealism. The universe is a vast information processing system. Matter is the "hardware" component of the system, the laws of nature the "software." Drawing on the information theory developed by Shannon and Weaver (1949), Tipler argues that the organization of a system is its negative entropy, or the quantity of information encoded within it. "Life" is simply information encoded in such a way that it is conserved by natural selection. A system is intelligent if it meets the "Turing test," that is, if a human operator interrogating it cannot distinguish its responses from those of a human being (Turing 1950). The mathematical physical reductionism of Tipler's model should be apparent

What is distinctive, about Tipler, however, is his technological triumphalism, which promises eternal life on a technological basis. Intelligent life continues forever, he argues, if

1. information processing continues indefinitely along at least one world-line γ all the way to the future c-boundary of the universe; that is, until the end of time.
2. the amount of information processed between now and this future c-boundary is infinite in the region of spacetime with which the worldline γ can communicate; that is the region inside the past light cone of γ.
3. the amount of information stored at any given time τ within this region diverges to infinity as τ approaches its future limit (this future limit of τ is finite in a closed universe, but infinite in an open one, if τ is measured in what physicists call "proper time"). (Tipler 1994, 132–33)

The first condition simply states that there must be one cosmic history in which information processing continues forever. The second condition states that it must be possible for the results of all information processing to be communicated to world-line γ. This means that the universe must be free of "event horizons," that is, regions with which an observer on world line γ cannot communicate. It also means that since an infinite amount of information is processed along this world line, an observer on this line will experience what amounts subjectively to eternal life. The third condition avoids the problem of an eternal return, i.e., an endless repetition of events as memory becomes saturated and new experience thus impossible.

Tipler then goes on to describe the physical conditions under which "eternal life" is possible. In accord with the currently divided state of physics, he presents separate "classical" or "global general relativistic" and "quantum mechanical" theories. I will examine his "classical" theory first. Information processing is constrained by the first and second laws of thermodynamics. Specifically, the storage and processing of information requires the expenditure of energy, the amount required being inversely proportional to the temperature.

> ... it is possible to process and store an infinite amount of information between now and the final state of the universe only if the time integral of P/T is infinite, where P is the power used in the computation and T is the temperature. (Tipler 1994, 135)

Eternal life thus becomes essentially a problem of finding an adequate energy source. Tipler proposes finding this source in the "gravitational shear" created as the universe collapses at different rates in different directions. This imposes a very specific set of constraints on the process of cosmic evolution. Only a very special type of universe, the so-called "Taub" universe, named after mathematician Abraham Taub, collapses in just precisely the way required. And even most Taub universes tend to "right" themselves, returning to more nearly spherical form. For information processing to continue forever, life must gain control of the entire universe, and force it to continue its Taub collapse in the same direction far longer than it would spontaneously (Tipler 1994: 137). Thus the requirement that intelligent life gain control of the universe as a whole, and control the rate and direction of its collapse, so as to create the enormous energies necessary to guarantee eternal life.

Meeting the second and third conditions outlined above requires, furthermore, that the universe be closed, because "open universes expand so fast in the far future that it becomes impossible for structures to form of sufficiently larger and larger size to store a diverging amount of information" (1994: 140). It also requires that "the future c-boundary of the universe consist of a single point . . . the Omega Point" (1994: 142). Finally, in order to meet information storage requirements, "the density of particles must diverge to infinity as the energy goes to infinity, but nevertheless this density of states must diverge no faster than the cube of the energy" (1994: 146). Tipler identifies, in addition to these requirements, which he calls "weakly testable," a variety of other predictions that can be used to test his theory, including the requirement that the mass of the top quark be 185 +/- 20 GeV and that the mass of the Higgs boson must be 220 +/- 20GeV (1994: 146). Fermilab recently measured the top quark at just a little bit below this mass.

In order to understand Tipler's Quantum Omega Point Theory, it is necessary to understand some of the internal contradictions of current quantum cosmology. In general relativity the spatial metric h and the nongravitational fields F are taken as given on the underlying three-dimensional manifold S. Cosmologists then attempt to find a four-dimensional manifold M with a Lorentz metric g (the gravitational field) and nongravitational fields F such that M contains S as a submanifold, g restricted to S is the metric h, and K is the extrinsic curvature of S, or, to put the matter differently, K says how quickly h is changing along the fourth, "temporal" dimension (1994: 162). In quantum cosmology, on the other hand, the universe is represented by a wave function $\Psi(h,F,S)$, which determines the values of h and F on S (1994: 174–75). One feature of the system, however, remains arbitrary: the selection of the fixed three-dimensional manifold S. Hartle and Hawking have proposed to eliminate this contingency by allowing the wave function to be a function of any three-dimensional manifold. According to this view, the domain of Ψ includes all possible values of h, F, and S (1994: 178). The Hartle-Hawking formulation, however, still requires h to be spacelike on all three-dimensional manifolds S. This restriction brings the formulation into conflict with classical general relativity, which does not distinguish so sharply between space and time.

Tipler points out, however, that the requirement that h be spacelike derives from a subjectivist interpretation of quantum mechanics, which interprets the wave function as a probability amplitude at a given time. This, obviously, requires times to be sharply distinguished from space. Tipler, however, favors a Many-Worlds interpretation of quantum mechanics, according to which all possible values of the wave function exist mathematically, and all those that permit the existence of observers exist physically. This removes the need to distinguish between space and time, and thus the requirement that h be always spacelike. Tipler proposes instead to allow the domain of the wave function to include all four-dimensional manifolds that permit a Lorentz metric g. All such manifolds permit what is known as a foliation. They can, that is, be represented as a "stack" of three-dimensional manifolds S(t), each representing the topology of a possible universe at a different moment of time. Each foliation will have a metric h, which need not be space like, as well as nongravitational fields, induced by the enveloping space-times (M,g). Any (h,F,S) that cannot be represented this way has $\Psi=0$; it does not exist. Similarly, there will be many spacetimes that permit the same (h,F,S). Some of these may have a future c-boundary that is a single point—the Omega Point (1994: 174–81). Thus the "Omega Point Boundary" condition on the universal wave function:

> The wave function of the universe is that wave function for which all phase paths terminate in a (future) Omega Point, with life continuing into the future forever along every phase path in which it evolves all the way to the Omega Point. (1994: 181)

Now, the Four-Manifold Non-Classification Theorem states that there does not exist any algorithm that can list or classify all compact four-dimensional topological or differentiable manifolds without boundary, nor is it possible to tell if any two given manifolds are the same or different (1994: 190). This means that it is impossible to derive the system as a whole from any one of its elements—a situation that, following William James, Tipler identifies with radical, ontological indeterminism (1994: 187). This means that the existence of life and intelligence, and the *decision* on the part of intelligent life to guide the universe towards Omega, is in fact logically and ontologically prior to the universal wave function itself (1994: 183): "The wave function is generated by the self-consistency requirement that the laws of physics and the decisions of the living agents acting in the universe force the universe to evolve into the Omega Point" (1994: 203). Indeed, in so far as the equations of both general relativity and quantum mechanics are reversible, there is no scientific reason to assume that causality runs only in one direction: from the past, through the present, into the future. It might just as well be seen as running from the future, through the present, into the past. From this point of view it is God, the Omega Point, which, existing necessarily, brings the entire universe into existence and draws it to himself.

> At the instant the Omega point is reached, life will have gained control of *all* matter and forces not only in a single universe, but in all universes whose existence is logically possible; life will have spread into *all* spatial regions in all universes that could logically exist, and will have stored an infinite amount of information, including *all* bits of knowledge that it is logically possible to know. And this is the end. (Barrow and Tipler 1986: 677)

The question arises, quite naturally, just how we are to reach Omega. The key link between actually existing carbon-based life, and this nonmolecular intelligent living system is a "race" of intelligent, self-reproducing, interstellar probes (the so-called von Neumann probes). Tipler proposes launching a series of such interstellar probes in the expectation that as they evolve they will grasp the conditions for the long term survival of intelligent life in the cosmos, and eventually reorganize the universe on a cosmic scale in order to bring into being the nonmolecular life form(s) that can survive into the final stages of cosmic evolution.

Such probes would, of course, be extremely expensive. It thus becomes necessary to identify an optimum path of economic development. Barrow and Tipler draw on Hayek's reasoning to argue that in a market system the technological and economic development necessary to support the construction of interstellar von Neumann probes will take place spontaneously (thus marking their theory as the political-theological correlate of Hayek's information-theoretical neoliberalism.) They argue that insofar as

> the economic system is wholly concerned with generating and transferring information ... the government should not interfere with the operation of the economic system ... if it is argued ... that the growth of scientific knowledge is maximized by information generation and flow being unimpeded by government intervention, does it not follow that the growth of economic services would be maximized if unimpeded by government intervention? (Barrow and Tipler 1986: 173)

Indeed, they argue that if the operation of the marketplace is left to run its course, the cost of energy and raw materials relative to wages will decline to the point that humanity will become capable not only of interstellar travel, but ultimately of reorganizing the structure of the cosmos on a macroscale—developments that are both critical for their meliorist physical eschatology.

> ... the price of raw materials and energy have, on the long term average, been decreasing exponentially over the past two centuries ... (Barrow and Tipler 1986: 172)

The sort of interstellar probes that Barrow and Tipler believe are necessary in order to secure the destiny of intelligent life in the cosmos would currently cost between $3x10^{10}$ and $2x10^{14}$, depending on their speed.

> These costs ... seem quite large to us, but there is evidence that they could not seem large to a member of a civilization greatly in advance of ours ... the cost relative to wages of raw materials, including fuel, has been dropping exponentially with a time constant of 50 years for the past 150 years. If we assume this trend continues for the next 400 years ... then to an inhabitant of our own civilization at this future date, the cost of a low velocity probe would be as difficult to raise as 10 million dollars today, and the cost of a high-velocity probe would be as difficult to raise as 70 billion dollars today. The former cost is easily within the ability of ... at least 100,000 Americans ... and the Space Telescope project budget exceeds $109 billion. If the cost trend continues for the next 800 years, then the cost of a $3x10^{10}$ probe would be as difficult to raise as $4000 today. An interstellar probe would appear to cost as much then as a home computer does now ... In such a society, *someone* would almost certainly build and launch a probe. (Barrow and Tipler 1986: 583)

Tipler's theological position is quite explicit. Despite his frequent references to Aristotle and Aquinas, and his effort to show the compatibility of his theory with most of the principal religious traditions, these implications tend very clearly towards Calvinist Christianity. This is because of the centrality of what he calls "agent determinism." Realization of the Omega Point is, in one sense, inevitable; it is required by the very existence of the universe itself. But it presupposes the subordination of the interests of individual carbon-based organisms to a larger cosmic plan that involves the displacement of carbon based by machine, and eventually by nonmolecular intelligence. And in so far as this transition is best carried out through the unimpeded operation of rationally inscrutable market forces, it requires the submission of individual carbon based organisms to cosmic imperatives that they cannot understand, and with which, at the very least, they cannot fully identify. Eternal life, furthermore, is not something the soul achieves, by becoming actually capable of infinite self-organizing activity, but rather something bestowed on it by the nearly omnipotent and omniscient beings near Omega, simply because it is in *their* self-interest. Tipler makes a game-theoretical argument (1994: 245–59) that these beings will resurrect us, and will bestow eternal life upon us, and that this will be a life of potentially infinite richness and joy—but ultimately the decision is theirs. We have here, in effect, an anthropic cosmological argument not only for neoliberal economics but for a peculiar, high-tech, Calvinism.

What are we to make of all this?

I have published detailed critiques of Tipler's *science* elsewhere (Mansueto 1995, 2002b, 2005). From the standpoint of this work his project is interesting precisely because it illustrates that behind the high modern drive towards scientific and technological progress is nothing less than demand for divinization. What Tipler proposes to build is, in effect, the God of univocal metaphysics: a being like us, but infinite in knowledge and power. This is quite different from *Esse* as such, which *is* in a qualitatively different way than we are, and which is defined not by sovereignty but rather by creativity.

This difference may, perhaps, be better illustrated at the imaginative level. The God of Judaism, Christianity, and Islam, the God understood by analogical metaphysics as *Esse* as such, appears to the prophet Elijah, for example, not in wind, earthquake, or fire, but rather in a gentle nurturing breeze (1 Kgs 19:11). Attempts to illustrate something like Tipler's strategy of technological god building, on the other hand, have yielded such images as that of the Borg Collective in the *Star Trek* universe, which assimilates cultures and annihilates all difference, *The Matrix,* or the Replicators in *Stargate SG-1*, who consume everything around them in order to replicate and eventually take over the universe—exactly the economy of salvation that Tipler proposes for us.

These imaginative comparisons make it clear where Tipler—and the whole high modern project—go wrong. The divinity humanity seeks is not that of endless existence and infinite power, which turns out to be more like a kind of hell, but rather that of eternal life and the creative power of Being as such, a possibility that is invisible to Tipler precisely because he allows science to displace wisdom in the hierarchy of the intellectual virtues and tries to achieve by scientific and technological progress what is possible only by means of spiritual discipline.

Dialectical Materialism

We have already suggested that the modern socialist movement is a complex phenomenon by means of which modernist intelligentsias leveraged the support of both displaced peasants and the emerging industrial proletariat to make a bid for class power (Konrad and Szelenyi 1967). And these modernist intelligentsias have, in fact, differed significantly among themselves. There have been tendencies within the communist movement that would have differed with Tipler only with regard to the economic structure most likely to produce the scientific and technological progress he desires (Bogdanov 1928; Rowley 1987). But such tendencies have historically been treated, and not without reason, as "bourgeois" deviations. The distinctively *dialectical* variant of the secret religion of high modernity is quite different. It derives from the humanistic tradition and its metaphysics is not univocal but analogical. It defines divinity, that is, not in terms of infinite power, but rather in terms of necessary being or, to use more modern language, subjectivity. To become God, for the modern dialectician, is to organize and direct the cosmohistorical evolutionary process. Technological process is certainly an element of this vision, but it is not central. Revolution here takes on directly metaphysical dimensions.

The most explicit example of this metaphysical aspiration comes in the early Marx and in the critical theorists who continued to develop his insights during that period. This variant of dialectical materialism has deep roots in the older dialectical tradition that reaches back to Socrates, Plato, and Aristotle, and more directly in the Radical Aristotelianism of the Silk Road Era. This latter tradition had as its ideal the achievement of a degree of philosophical wisdom that made the individual human intellect (known as the "potential intellect") identical with the Agent Intellect, the angelic intelligence that governs the sublunar world. This was, for thinkers like ibn Sina and Moshe ben Maimon the degree of wisdom achieved by the prophets. For Radical Aristotelians such as ibn Rusd and Levi ben Gerson it represented the only possible immortality.

In the Jewish and Islamic context in which it grew up, this ideal represented, if anything, a sober limitation of human aspirations for the divine. This sobriety is still apparent in the work of Spinoza, for whom any notion of *divinization* would have been absolutely foreign. As it filtered into Christendom, however, most likely through the channel of *converso* communities and through the mechanism of a kind of Radical Aristotelian counter-reaction to the Augustinian revival of the late Middle Ages, the idea gradually emerged that by achieving mastery of nature and history human beings achieved a kind of divinity. This was, undoubtedly, assisted by the Scientific Revolution, which undermined the Aristotelian distinction between the changeable world of the sublunar sphere and the divine realm of the planetary and sidereal heavens, so that understanding how the world works, and why it is the way it is, came to mean, increasingly, understanding *everything*, a kind of divine and absolute knowledge.

What set this tradition apart from the positivistic forms of high modernity was the insistence on understanding *why*. It is the inability of the understanding (*Verstand*) to answer this question that caused Kant to separate morality and religion from science and that led Hegel to posit a higher reason (*Vernunft*) that *could* explain as well as describe. And it is, of course, in Hegel that we find the clearest formulation of the claim that philosophical wisdom and political practice can, in fact *do*, lift humanity above contingency and to a kind of divinity.

Modern dialectics emerges out of this Hegelian moment. Specifically, it derives from Marx's recognition that the democratic revolutions alone were not enough to lift human beings out of contingency; it would be necessary to transcend capitalism as well. More specifically, Marx argues in such early works as the *Contribution to the Critique of Hegel's Philosophy of Right* (Marx 1843/1978) and the *Paris Manuscripts* (Marx 1844/1978) that the bourgeois state, far from realizing the Enlightenment ideal of rational autonomy, merely establishes a realm in which such autonomy may be exercised, while leaving the structure of civil society (the economic system) untouched. But at the heart of this system is the wage relation, which takes what ought to be the most fundamental expression of human nature, our labor or creative capacity, and transforms it into something oppressive, alienating human beings from nature, from each other, and from our "species being." Communism, which is the collective appropriation of the social surplus product, overcomes this alienation by restoring control over the product of labor to the laborers themselves, through the medium of the collectivity. This is why Marx calls communism

> . . . the definitive solution of the contradiction between man and nature and between man and man, the true solution of the contradiction between existence and essence, between objectification and self-realization, between freedom and necessity, between the individual and the species. Communism is the solution to the riddle of history and knows itself to be that solution. (Marx 1844/1978: 84)

The claims of Althusser (Althusser 1965/1977, 1968/1970) and his followers to the contrary, Marx probably never regarded this "humanistic" concern for transcending contingency as in contradiction with the focus in his later works with the development of the productive forces. Like ibn Rush and Levi ben Gerson (and like Hegel) Marx regarded *all* knowledge and *all* mastery as contributing to a human self-realization which, even though the religious language has dropped away, still amounts to a kind of divinization. Why, after all, couldn't socialism *both* unleash a level of technological progress that allowed human beings to transcend the limits of their finitude *and*, by making humanity, through the medium of the social collectivity, the master of its own destiny, also realize the Enlightenment ideal of rational autonomy?

The answer to this question became apparent only as socialism itself developed, both as a social movement and, in the twentieth century, as a form of social organization. The socialism of Marx's time was a movement of artisans and humanistic intellectuals who, while they embraced the democratic revolutions, vigorously resisted capitalist modernization and specifically proletarianization (Sewell 1980). The socialist movement of the later part of the nineteenth century was increasingly a movement of industrial workers and technicist intellectuals. This movement became deeply wedded to a gradualist electoral strategy. While there were thinkers, such as Eduard Bernstein, who theorized gradualism in moral terms, drawing especially on the Kantian tradition, most looked to Engels' *Dialectics of Nature* (Engels 1880/1940) and his *Socialism Utopian and Scientific* (Engels 1880/1978). Engels argues in the first work that quantitative changes throughout the material world gradually become qualitative. In the second work he theorizes the transition to socialism in precisely this way. Industrialization gradually increases the size of the proletariat, eventually giving them a majority and the ability to win elections. This tied the development of socialism to underlying technological processes and favored the technicist variant of the socialist project and a socialist variant of the godbuilding of the sort we analyzed in the previous section.

But there is a deeper problem with the modern dialectical strategy for divinization. Its metaphysical aspirations depend on the mediation of the *party*, which alone allows human beings to build the power necessary to master the historical process and thus to move from necessity to freedom and from objecthood to full and free subjectivity. Perhaps the best example of this trend is the thought of Georgi Lukacs, who argues that it is precisely through the medium of the Communist Party that the proletariat becomes the "unique subject object of human history" (Lukacs 1922/1971).

The difficulty is that the party is not and cannot be a true collective subject in which all participate equally or even meaningfully. Rather, it is an instrument by which a leader or a small group of leaders use a disciplined cadre of organizers to carry out *their* strategy and realize *their* vision. Indeed, all effective communist parties have been the instruments of the great leaders who built them or inherited and transformed them: Lenin, Stalin, Gramsci, Mao, Castro. This is why, as Badiou notes (Bosteels 2005), the principal political tendencies within the communist movement have been known by proper names: Leninism, Trotskyism, Stalinism, Maoism . . . Deification as "organizer and director of the historical process" is possible only for a single individual and then only in a limited and qualified way. Great leaders still die and history ultimately escapes them. Communism, it turns out, is a kind of modernist sacral monarchy.

We have already noted above that Leninism, Gramscianism, and especially Maoism progressively cut the communist project off from the underlying social forces that are supposed to give birth to it in favor of a more or less pure *techne* of conjunctural power politics. This does not strip the communist project of its metaphysical aims, but it does change them. The difference is marked in the distance between, say, the early Marx or Lukacs and the later Althusser or especially Alain Badiou.

Badiou argues that mathematics—and more specifically set theory—*is* ontology. This immediately generates severe constraints on what kind of metaphysics is possible. On the one hand, the Russell paradox and the axiom of foundation imply that a set can neither contain nor belong to itself. This means that there is no "set of all sets," whether we call that set Nature, History, or God, but only what Badiou calls "multiplicities." On the other hand, precisely because of this, sets are defined disjunctively and in relation to one another. This means that they are defined by something outside themselves and thus indiscernible by ontology. This void is the site of what Badiou calls the "event."

Badiou identifies four distinct types of events: art, science, politics, and love. In each case, the event involves naming the indiscernible and thus the term in terms of which all sets are defined. The event is, in effect, a kind of ontological revolution. The subject is constituted in and through this process, by the naming of and fidelity to the event (Badiou 1988/2006). Some thinkers have charged that Badiou arbitrarily excludes the religious from his typology of events (Dews 2004; Zupanic 2004). Might not God be defined here, *outside* ontology, as the "event of events" (Dews 2004)? But such complaints misunderstand Badiou, whose atheism is, ultimately, not of the intellect but rather of the will. The event defines—or rather redefines—the ontological structure of reality itself, constituting the subject as, in effect, divine. There is thus no room for being called by a pre-existing God.

It is only when we reach this point that the relationship between Badiou and his mentor Sartre becomes apparent. As for Sartre (Sartre 1943), Badiou understands human beings as constituted by the desire to be God, and as fully human only when they are engaged in metaphysical revolution.

Like most philosophical products of the New Left, however, Badiou's philosophy is not simply wrong; it is founded on a fundamental misunderstanding. We have already shown elsewhere (Mansueto 2002b) that attempts to demonstrate the existence of God within the context of a purely formal reason—the ontological argument—inevitably fail for the simple reason that they are based on bad mathematics. Thus the ontological argument—the claim that God exists because "that than which nothing greater can be thought" would not meet the terms of its definition if it *didn't* exist, is convertible with Zorn's Lemma, which claims that a partially ordered set with an upper bound must have a maximal element. This lemma, while intuitively obvious, cannot be proven. Badiou, similarly, sets up a set theoretical definition of and argument for the existence of God that he then knocks down. But this argument is based on a confusion between the numerical and the transcendental One. The numerical One—the One that can be defined set-theoretically—is simply a function of the ordering of sets by inclusion, and has none of the properties historically associated with the divine. The transcendental One, on the other hand, is One in the sense of being integral: it cannot be divided without ceasing to exist, and is thus convertible with Being. It cannot be defined set-theoretically. The "god" whose existence Badiou disproves, in other words, is not God at all, but merely a number.

By dissociating communist political strategy from its underlying social theory, Maoism generally, and Badiou in particular, shift it along the ideological spectrum in the direction of a nihilistic theomachy. Indeed, Badiou's option for an emancipatory politics is, in the end, *worse than arbitrary*. It is a function of the fact that he, and the humanistic intelligentsia to whom he appeals, stand outside the current bloc in power and outside the ontology that that bloc has defined. But if the motivation behind politics is the self-constitution of the subject through an act of ontological revolution, it is unclear why such a revolution might not be carried out, as it was for Heidegger, by and on behalf of a fascist movement. Third World Maoism was held back from this danger by its peasant base; Western Maoism is not. We are probably fortunate that so many humanistic intellectuals have been drawn to apolitical "events" such as art and love that do not lead to violence. In the end Badiou's theory is an ideology of pure terror, the nightmare nihilism against which Dostoevsky warned us in *The Possessed* in which alienated intellectuals cut off from any broader sense of meaning and any solidarity with the working classes, and without the discipline of the party, *individually* play God.

∽

It is worth pausing at this point to make explicit the claim that *all* high modernisms, and not simply their more extreme manifestations, should be regarded as secular messianisms. By *secular*, in this context, we mean very simply *innerworldly*. High modernism in all its forms seeks divinization in and through innerworldly civilizational progress. By *messianism* we mean the claim that some individual or organization is capable of carrying humanity as whole to this end, of *substituting*, in effect, for the long march of intellectual and moral and thus spiritual development. And of course both positivism and modern dialectics are messianic in this sense. In the case of positivistic modernity it is the scientist, the engineer, and the entrepreneur who play the messianic role; in the case of modern dialectics it is the dialectician, but above all the General Secretary whose knowledge of the "conditions, ultimate general results, and line of march" of the historical process elevates him above that process to a quasi-divine status. Indeed, it is *in and through* the General Secretary that the proletariat, and with it humanity, is redeemed.

Nihilistic Theomachy and Deconstruction

There are, as far as I am aware, no thinkers who actually advocate an explicitly nihilistic theomachy. But Nietzsche and Heidegger themselves both came close to this position, and it thus lurks in the background of contemporary postmodernisms. Let us look more closely at Heidegger's position, since it is the one more often embraced.

Heidegger's work is notoriously complex and obscure and has been buried in layer upon layer of commentary, so that it becomes difficult to say anything about him without risking exposure for some scholarly *faux pas*. This complex of defensive ramparts, however, in fact conceals a cluster of relatively simple claims. Heidegger's early critique of metaphysics, set forth in *Problems of Phenomenology* (Heidegger 1927) and *Being and Time* (1928) focuses on the failure of thinkers, beginning with Plato, to grasp the distinction between Being and beings, and instead attempts to theorize Being as the beingness of beings—it thinks Being in entitative terms. Where the pre-Socratics, according to Heidegger, were able to think the self-manifestation of Being, something he associates with the term *physis* or nature, Plato and Aristotle increasingly use the language of *morphe* (form) and *energeia* (actuality). Form, and especially the Good or the "form of forms," is, for Plato, what really *is* and that in terms of which this world of appearance must be explained and judged. Aristotle goes even further down this road, arguing that it is form that actualizes matter, bringing things into being. Rather than simply allowing Being to manifest itself, to present itself as a question, it is reduced to something other than Being, something that can be comprehended—and once comprehended, used to ground our own process of making, our own process of bringing into being. Indeed, as Heidegger points out, the very notion of *morphe* derives from the language of the craftsman: it is the look or appearance given to something by its producer. *Energeia* similarly, is rendered in German as *Wirklicheit*, from the root for work. Metaphysics thus grounds technology, and the larger technological mode of relating to the world.

Later Heidegger (Heidegger 1941) modified both his historical analysis and his philosophical position. Increasingly identifying ancient Greek and German romantic thought, he claimed to hear in Plato and Aristotle echoes of the earlier Greek *aletheia* or unconcealment of Being. Thus he located the crystallization of metaphysics in the "translation" of Greek thought into Latin, the language of road builders and empire makers, a crystallization that is completed in the Middle Ages when Being is identified with the supreme maker, the Christian Creator God. This process culminates, of course, in Thomas Aquinas, who is the supreme philosopher of the "ontotheologic," the universal causal-explanatory system in which Being is simply an instrument for explaining and ultimately manipulating entities. Modern metaphysical theories, such as those of Descartes and Hegel—or for that matter Marx—differ only in giving human rather than divine subjectivity or labor pride of place. Nietzsche's claim that the world is just the "will to power" is simply the culmination of this long metaphysical tradition, and offers just one more formulation of the first principle.

Being, for the later Heidegger, manifests itself in a people only through the voice of the few who help it to discover its "god," a sort of mythos under which Being is revealed.

> ... the essence of the people is its "voice." This voice does not, however, speak in a so-called immediate flood of the common, natural, undistorted and uneducated "person." The voice speaks seldom and only in the few, if it can be brought to sound ...
> (Heidegger >1934/1989: 319)

> A *Volk* is only a *Volk* if it receives its history through the discovery of its god, through the god, which through history compels it in a direction and so places it back in being. Only then does it avoid the danger of turning only on its own axis . . . (Heidegger >1934/1989: 398-99)

Heidegger sees humanity as a passive instrument of Being rather than an active creator of meaning. After the "turn" in his thought, however, Heidegger also becomes more interested in analyzing the historical process by which Being is unconcealed—or by which it "withdraws" leaving the world subject to *techne* and to the will to power—than he is in the existential analysis of *Dasein* (human being or literally "being-there") as an opening to Being. While the historical process is treated here simply as a product of Being's unconcealments and withdrawals, the effect is, nonetheless, to reinstate the Nietzschean focus on the nexus between power and meaning, while endowing this nexus with an ontological legitimation that makes the forcible irruption of meaning in history no longer the product of finite human organizing activity, but rather an epiphany of Being itself. It is this notion of the historical destiny of the people as an unconcealment of Being, by Being, which made Heidegger vulnerable to the appeal of Nazism, which appeared to him as the possible occasion of just such an unconcealement.

In what sense is this a theomachy? For Heidegger, in effect, one "unconcealement" of Being vies with another, without any underlying onto-logic that relates them as aspects or progressive revelations of a single truth. Through the medium of national myths or "gods" these unconcealements of Being constitute nations that are then locked in what can only be a mortal combat.

The deconstructionist postmodernism of Jacques Derrida (Derrida 1967/1978) can be seen as developing dialectically out of Heidegger's position. Derrida accepts Heidegger's critique of metaphysics but rejects his continued use of the language of "Being" and of gods, which, he suggests, reinstates the "violence" of metaphysics. What Derrida suggests is that violence is unavoidable: there is no escape. The best that we can do is to unmask the violence embedded in our own discourse and that of others in an effort to contain the damage. To this Heideggerian lineage Derrida joins that of a dialectics, and mores specifically that of a critical theory turned back on itself and shorn of any constructive ambition. Just as Marx extended the Hegelian dialectic to expose its internal contradictions and residual essentialism to reveal it as an apologia for an intelligentsia anxious to reach an accommodation with the rising Prussian state, so deconstructionist postmodernism exposes the residual essentialism in Marx and shows how it became an apologia for rising statist elites.

As a political theology this position differs from a nihilistic theomachy primarily in its decision to retire from the *agon* or struggle. By exposing *all* ontologies as bids for what amounts to divinity, deconstructionism claims to make room for a properly human life, freed from the totalitarian delusions of the past century. Postmodernists apply themselves to the task of "deconstruction," that is of unmasking claims to universality and showing them up for what they are: claims to power. More specifically, postmodernists argue for the conservation of "difference" and are thus at the forefront of struggles for multiculturalism, gender equality, etc.

This position is, however, characterized by profound internal contradictions. If values are purely and simply the product of human social action, and lack any ground in the structure of Being as such or the nature of the universe, then any claim to universal authority on the part of a particular moral vision (including a critical, emancipatory vision) must be regarded as a claim to power on the part of the social class, ethnic group, or gender group that developed the vision. If, however, there is no universal standard outside of the array of competing moral systems developed by different cultural traditions, then on what basis can we argue with moral authority that diversity, the preservation of difference, and "multiculturalism" are values? The matter is complicated by the fact that many, if not most, of the cultural traditions that postmodernists are anxious to defend against the totalitarian hegemony of "Western Civilization" in its Christian-conservative, market-liberal, or secular-socialist forms in fact differ very sharply with postmodernism regarding the fundamental question of the meaningfulness of the universe. More generally, we should point out that postmodernism gives us neither a positive vision of the Good nor any method of adjudicating the competing claims of rival individuals, social classes, ethnic groups, gender groups, etc. As such, we must say that it fails as a political theology.

Religious Postmodernism

It is interesting to note, in this regard, a recent turn among deconstructionist postmodernists back towards religion. This turn has, of course precedents in the work of Soren Kierkegaard (Kierkegaard 1848), and of Emmanuel Levinas. Levinas (Levinas 1965), for example, argued that Heidegger's continued use of the language of Being perpetuated the effacement of the Other in the interests of power and domination that had characterized the whole Greek philosophical tradition, which he refers to as "ontology" and advocates a new "metaphysics" rooted in confrontation with the radically Other, the victim, in which alone we can discover—but never conceptually possess—God. This line of reasoning has been taken up by *some* Latin American liberationists, explicitly by Miranda (Miranda 1972, 1973) and Dussel (Dussel 1998), and more loosely and eclectically by others, for whom the encounter with the poor and oppressed becomes the unique privileged hermeneutic key for reading the Scriptures—and reality in general.

In his early works Derrida argued that finding God in the face of the other was simply another act of violence, because it effaced the specificity of the particular person. More recently, however, he has turned back to a position not too different from that of Levinas (Derrida 2001), a move that has been extended in the work of John Caputo (Caputo 2006). Derrida begins by identifying sources or senses of the religious: belief or the fiduciary and the unscathed (Derrida 2001: 70). These two senses "reflect and presuppose each other" and lie behind the "instituted apparatus consisting of dogmas or articles of faith that is both determinate and inseparable from a given historical socius" (Derrida 2001: 93).

The religious, thus understood, has a complex and ambiguous relationship with high modernity, which Derrida glosses as "technoscience." On the one hand, it makes use of technoscience and merges with it, creating anew the "globolatinity," which has defined the West since at least the time of Constantine. As Carl Raschke explains,

> According to Derrida the "Latin" is the word for the West. The Latin is what overreaches with its sumptuous signatures of power and meaning; it is a perfection of the organizational, a vast economy of coding as well as a "reterritorialized" . . . sys-

> tem of administration necessary for the expansion of a planetary sociopolitical apparatus . . .
>
> As in Old Rome, the notion of "religion" functions as an aggregate signifier for the "re-binding" (*re-ligio*) together of previously profuse and dissociated particularities of faith and devotion with their own indigenous or "territorial" characteristics into a grand ideology of "unity in diversity." (Raschke 2005)

On the other hand, religion also reasserts the particular and the territorial against the global culture of technoscience.

> The fundamentalist war machine is quintessentially a *jihad* of de-territorialized faith-nomads exploding, like the Islamic armies after the death of Mohammed, across the vast and crumbling empire of technoscientific rationality. (Raschke 2005)

There is, however, a deeper layer to Derrida's analysis. He first suggests this layer when he insists that

> There is no opposition, fundamentally, between "social bond" and "social unraveling." A certain interruptive unraveling is the condition of the social bond, the very respiration of all community. (Derrida 2001: 99)

Derrida develops this insight—which has its roots in the French Traditionalist claim that violence is the foundation of the social bond—in his distinction between Law and Justice. Where Law, he argues, is deconstuctible, Justice is not. Indeed, Justice is *the undeconstructable* and the condition of any possible destruction.

> The operation that amounts to founding, inaugurating, justifying law, to making law, would consist of a *coup de force* of a performative and therefore interpretive violence that in itself is neither just nor unjust and that no earlier and previous founding law, no pre-existing foundation could, by definition, guarantee or contradict, or invalidate . . .
>
> Justice in itself, if such a thing exists, outside or beyond law, is not deconstructible . . . Deconstruction *is* justice . . . Deconstruction takes place in the interval that separates the undeconstructibility of justice from the deconstructibility of law. (Derrida 2001: 241–43)

Derrida goes on to distinguish (following Benjamin) two different types of founding violence. Mythological, or Greek violence, founds law and demands blood sacrifice; divine or Jewish violence accepts sacrifice, it "sacrifices life to save the living" (Derrida 2001: 288). Here we see echoes, perhaps unconscious, of de Maistre and de Bonald, as well as a conscious attempt to transcend them.

> Divine violence is the most just, the most historic, the most revolutionary, the most decidable or the most deciding. Yet, as such, it does not lend itself to any human determination. (Derrida 2001: 291)

The result of this analysis is to point Derrida towards the idea of "messianicity without messianism" (Derrida 2001: 56), a distant horizon of justice that leaves room for revolutionary violence as the condition of justice, in fact as *justifying*, without ever appealing to some higher principle in terms of which it might itself be justified. This is, in effect, a reinstitution of the old prophetic office—but without the "transcendental signifier"—God—in terms of which this office was traditional carried out.

Caputo takes this a step further and advances what he calls a "weak theology," which reinterprets and radicalizes the traditional Christian concept of the "weakness of God."

> On the classical account of strong theology, Jesus was just holding back his divine power in order to let his human nature suffer. He freely chose to check his power because the Father had a plan to redeem the world with his blood. . . . That is not the weakness of God that I am here defending. God, the event harbored by the name of God, is present at the crucifixion, as the power of the powerlessness of Jesus, in and as the protest against the injustice that rises up from the cross, in and as the words of forgiveness, not a deferred power that will be visited upon one's enemies at a later time. God is in attendance as the weak force of the call that cries out from Calvary and calls across the epochs, that cries out from every corpse created by every cruel and unjust power. The logos of the cross is a call to renounce violence, not to conceal and defer it and then, in a stunning act that takes the enemy by surprise, to lay them low with real power, which shows the enemy who really has the power. That

is just what Nietzsche was criticizing under the name of ressentiment. (Caputo 2006: 44)

This analysis in turn defines a significantly new attitude towards the current situation. There is, on the one hand, a radical extension of "globolatinity," as well as a diversification of its forms: the purely "secular" language of technoscience, the integrating ideologies of official inter-religious dialogues of the sort pursued by UNESCO or the United Nations Alliance of Civilizations, and any variants in between. At the same time, we are witnessing a global rebellion against this universal, cosmopolitan culture in all its forms, a rebellion led by resurgent religious fundamentalisms. Against both of these trends Derrida and the weak theologians raise the specter of a "weak force"—a messianicity without messianism, an ungrounded but revolutionary demand for justice.

There are numerous difficulties with this approach. Like all postmodernisms, it is ultimately idealistic, explaining history as if it was *only* a battle of ideas, without reference to the complex material factors that also shape historical struggles. This means that, while "globolatinity" is presumably a form of legitimation for the global market, fundamentalism is made to look more anticapitalist than it really is, or its attitude towards capitalism rendered irrelevant. All globolatinities are, furthermore, conflated with each other, without reference to the ideals they embody or the structural means by which they pursue them. Second, the ungroundedness of the demand for justice advanced by Derrida and the weak theologians it itself a reflex of their impotence. This is an ideology of proletarianized (if also rather privileged) humanistic intellectuals who have abandoned any serious effort to listen to, teach, speak with, or even speak for the people. The result is a kind of intellectual terrorism that *either* posits the suffering of the oppressed as itself the principal force for justice (this seems to be Caputo's position) *or* opens a space for real terror which, however unjustifiable it may be, is nonetheless "divine" justice, the founding moment of a new Law and a new epoch. If this sounds a bit like Heidegger's expectation of a new advent of Being, and if it inspires a similar fear, this is not accidental.

We find a further—and much more substantive—engagement with religion in the Radical Orthodoxy of John Milbank and his associates, whose tentative interventions in the field of social theory we have already noted above. Milbank began his work with a global critique of modern social theory, arguing that it is irreducibly secularist (Milbank 1991). In this early work, Milbank largely accepts the Heideggerian critique of metaphysics and argues, in effect, that the whole dialectical tradition is ultimately grounded in an ontology of violence in which will is pitted against will. This is illustrated for him not only in modern social theory, but also in the older dialectical ethics of Socrates, Plato, and Aristotle. Even Plato's ideal state, he claims, is an "armed camp," and Aristotle's whole concept of virtue is really just transformation of a fundamentally military ethic of heroism. Indeed, Aristotle counsels his students to be haughty to those beneath them in station and to make sure that others depend on them (Milbank 1991: 352).

Against this ontology of violence, Milbank proposes an ontology of peace, the carrier of which is the Christian church that, following Augustine, he calls the "Other City," founded on different loves. Milbank argues that when we recognize Being as difference, we learn a nonpossessive love that at once cancels and preserves the distance between persons. This is the creative love of God, who brings into Being creatures different from himself and authentically free, and who calls us to love each other in the same way. There is, Milbank argues, no way to ground this ontology dialectically; indeed, to try to do so is to yield to the very ontology of violence that seeks truth through struggle and contradiction.

Gradually, Milbank has pulled back from this position, and granted greater space for metaphysics. Even in *Theology and Social Theory* we find the seeds of an alternative critique of philosophical modernity, one that locates its point of origin not in Plato and Aristotle, or even in the Latin Middle Ages generally, but rather in John Duns Scotus, whose doctrine of the univocity of Being laid the groundwork for both the Reformation and secular modernity. What this doctrine does (and here I am clarifying and extending Milbank a bit) is to make the difference between God and human beings quantitative rather than qualitative. On the one hand, this approach grounds divine authority in power rather than love; on the other hand, it opens up the possibility, which defines humanity, that human beings, by building power (through, for example, scientific and technological progress), might be able to transcend finitude and achieve divinity.

In a recent paper (Milbank 2006b) Milbank further develops this thesis, dating the "ontotheological lapse" clearly to around 1300 and, following Benedict XVI, attributes this ontotheological lapse to the growing influence of Islam, which, together with Judaism, because of the primacy that they both give to the law over the image as disclosing the divine, he deems resistant to an analogical metaphysics of participation. Thomas Aquinas, along with Nicholas Cusanus and a few others, are deemed uniquely resistant to this lapse.

Milbank makes a number of critical errors of sociohistorical analysis. His claim that the traditional religions of Japan, China, and India lack the resources to mount an effective resistance to global capitalism is merely asserted, and his argument that Catholicism does (which I accept, albeit on somewhat different grounds) is more a suggestion of a strategy than a demonstration of effective resistance. But it is not only possible to define hypothetical strategies for Buddhist, Confucian, or Hindu resistance to capitalism; one can identify actually existing movements (cf. Sarkisyanz 1965), as one can in the case of Catholicism (Lancaster 1988).

Far more serious, however, are his errors with respect to Judaism and Islam. His claim that the univocal metaphysics that lies behind the modern project is a result of Islamic influence (Milbank 2006b), for example, is simply indefensible. This metaphysics developed rather, as we will see, in both *Dar-al-Islam* and Christendom, in response to the emergence of sovereign, absolutist state structures, itself the product of the Norman, Mongol, and Turkic conquests (and reactions to them), and not "Nestorian" and "semi-Arian" christologies.

But his mistake here is not merely historical; it is theological. What Milbank is missing here is the long tradition, reaching back to the prophets, and extending into Christianity as well as Judaism and Islam, which identifies *doing justice* and *knowing God*. Thus when the prophets speak of *da'ath 'elohim* (knowledge of God) they are not speaking of something theoretical, but rather an experiential and nonconceptual knowledge that we gain in actually realizing the divine will (cf. Hos 4:1–2, 6:3).

Doing justice, in other words, leads to a real participation in the life of God—a spirituality fully compatible with an analogical metaphysics of *Esse*, and very far from the "wooden legalism," which Milbank scorns.

Finally, Milbank's critique of Protestantism is flat and one-dimensional. Among other things, he fails to distinguish between the postmillennial reformism of most North American Protestants (liberal and evangelical) and the premillennial dispensationalism that emerged out of the disappointment of Protestant hopes after the Civil War. It is the latter theology alone that abandons social reform in favor of geopolitical support for a restored Israel (as a sign of the end times). And while there certainly *is* a relationship between Protestantism and capitalism, it is a complex one. There has been resistance to capitalism in both evangelical and liberal Protestant communities. While I am inclined to agree with Milbank that Protestant Christianity has more difficulty grounding such resistance than does Catholicism, it must be both acknowledged and explained.

Milbank's most serious error of analysis, however, concerns the modern project itself. He assimilates modernity far too completely to the Protestant project, and misses the modernist dynamic within socialism, which existed alongside the conservative element of resistance to enclosure of the sacred that he quite correctly points out. Protestantism represents *early* modernity, which was centered on the ideal of human vice-regency to a sovereign God; *high* modernity rejects this God altogether in favor of a project (rarely acknowledged explicitly) of divinization (understood here as transcending the bounds of finitude) by means of scientific and technological (or philosophical and political) progress. This, and not a heretical Christianity, is the true secret religion of high modernity.

This, in turn, leads Milbank to miss one of the most important features of the current situation. He quite correctly acknowledges that the current religious revival is not all of one piece. It is not all a "resistance to enclosure of the sacred," and includes much that he is reluctant to embrace. But because he does not theorize the break between early and high modernity, he cannot properly theorize the problem of fundamentalism, whether Christian or Islamic. These latter movements, I would like to suggest, represent a turning back to early modern dynamics by elements of the population "left behind" by globalization and disenchanted with the high modern ideal, but at the same time reluctant to break cleanly with capitalism, from which they benefit in important ways.

Unable to properly theorize the problem with fundamentalism, but rightly suspicious of identifying with it, Milbank opts for a Catholic restorationism that is all the more troubling because of his inability to see clearly the potential in other traditions.

What is the social basis of Milbank's error? As European social democracy has begun to erode under pressure from the global market, Europeans have become increasingly dissatisfied with the radical secularism of the postwar settlement—a tendency that is evident in the turn of even radical deconstructionists such as Derrida to a sort of religion. At the same time, Europe is deeply threatened—in a way the United States, for example, is not—by its growing internal diversity, and specifically by its growing Islamic population. Thus the need to redefine European identity. Milbank, like Wojtyla and Ratzinger (to whom he is much closer than he imagines), locates this identity in the Catholic tradition.

> ... the *real* peculiarity of Europe is *not* the triumph of reason, but rather the idea that one should proceed through reason towards a faith whose intellectual scope is even greater ... in this way it is "catholicity" not enlightenment that defines the west and catholicity not enlightenment that is incommunicable to other religious civilizations. (Milbank 2006a: 83–84)

Indeed, in many ways this statement sums up both the brilliance and the tragedy of Milbank's position. The first part of this statement contains a powerful insight, that Europe (and indeed the West, including Latin America) ignores at its peril: it reasserts the distinctly Catholic element in Europe's heritage. But the second part of the statement is simply false. There is *nothing* incommunicable about catholicity. There is, rather, a long tradition of dialogue between Catholicism and other traditions, both at the level of the "high tradition" (consider both the *Convivencia* in medieval *al-Andalus* and Matteo Ricci's creative engagement with the Confucian tradition) and at the popular level, in the countless syncretisms that have linked Catholicism to the popular traditions of every continent. Indeed, the idea that we can establish rationally the reasonableness of supra-rational knowledge and the idea of a metaphysics of participation are quite widespread, and find powerful echoes even in traditions like Buddhism that are nontheistic (e.g., in the focus on integrating dialectics with meditation and in the idea of the

Buddha-nature shared by all beings). The specifically Catholic claim that we can not only participate in the divine, but actually undergo a sort of divinization is, to be sure, unique. But that uniqueness in no way constrains dialogue with other civilizations or even the creation of a public arena constituted by authentic deliberation around such fundamental questions of meaning and value as the end to which we are ordered, as well as the means for achieving those ends—a polity that is authentically pluralistic and that transcends radically both secularism and confessionalism in a kind of extended *Convivencia*. This, and not a simple primacy of the ecclesial, is the true solution to the current crisis not only for Europe, but for humanity as a whole.

What has happened here is, of course, that postmodernism, which deconstructed Heidegger's philosophical fascism into a radically secular and militantly pluralistic ontology—and politics—of difference, has, due to the internal instability that we identified above, "returned" to an ontology of power and a politics of civilizational conflict, even if the civilization being defended is a Catholic Christian civilization, understood as a civilization of nonpossessive love.

If we are actually going to transcend the secularism of modern social theory, and not merely counterpose to it a set of ungrounded claims, we need to develop an alternative that *demonstrates* that human beings really are ordered to transcendental ends. Partly, of course, this is a task for metaphysics itself, and for philosophical anthropology, and as such it is beyond the scope of this book (cf. Mansueto and Mansueto 2005). What we can, however, do is to show that a social theory that takes into account this transcendental ordering has superior explanatory power both globally and in reference to the current situation. It is to this task that we now turn.

Spirituality and Civilization

A *Global* Convivencia *Theology*

It is not possible in this context to explain fully, much less argue for, the philosophical and political-theological perspective that lies behind this work. I have laid out the philosophical foundations briefly in *Spirituality and Dialectics* (Mansueto and Mansueto 2005) and more extensively in my *Knowing God* series (Mansueto 2002b, 2010) and am in the process of extending that argument into the properly theological realm. Here it is possible only to offer a few key guideposts and indications, sustained as much by the foregoing critique of the principal contemporary alternatives as by a positive argument.

Philosophical Foundations

The perspective that follows is grounded in a restored rational metaphysics and natural law ethics located broadly in the Aristotelian and Thomistic tradition, but enriched through dialogue with recent developments in the physical, biological, and social sciences and with humanity's principal wisdom traditions. Let me outline briefly how this restored dialectics approaches the principle philosophical problems.

Consider the problem of knowledge. Relativism and subjectivism of one sort or another have been almost *de rigueur* in bourgeois philosophical circles since the middle of the nineteenth century. Any claim that we know real objects has been treated as a sure sign of a lack of philosophical sophistication. But recent work in neuropsychology (Luria 1973; Sacks 1985; Damasio 1994) suggests that sensation does in fact produce an image in the brain that records data about the organization of the universe, rather than merely organizing sensations in a way that has little or no relationship to the objective determinations of the things that give rise to them. Cognitive development theory (Luria 1976) and the sociology of knowledge (Durkheim 1911/1965; Lukacs 1922/1971; Fromm 1941, 1947) have certainly demonstrated that the way in which we abstract the intelligible content of these images is radically dependent on participation in human society and indeed on the specific structure that shapes the way in which we live. But far from implying a radical relativism, this evidence in fact provides a new way in which to understand the medieval debates around the Agent Intellect and the Thomistic doctrine of connatural knowledge. The Agent Intellect in Aristotelian psychology (Aristotle *De Anima* III) is the faculty that illuminates the images we garner from experience and reveals their intelligible content. Due both to ambiguities in Aristotle's thinking on the matter, and contemporary socioreligious interests, the Middle Ages witnessed a vigorous debate between those (including most of the Arab commentators) who saw the Agent Intellect as a single unified intelligence illuminating all of humanity, and those who, like

Thomas, treated it as a faculty of the human person (von Steenberghen 1980). Connatural knowledge is knowledge we have preconceptually due to a similarity of nature with the object known (Aquinas *Summa Theologiae* II–II, Q45, a2). I argue, against both Thomas and the Averroists, that the "Agent Intellect" is both individual and collective—that it is in fact nothing other than human society. By living in the way social structures of varying degrees of complexity require us to, and thus in a very real sense "living" these social structures, we gain a kind of preconceptual connatural knowledge of these structures that then illuminates the images we garner from experience, revealing their intelligible content. This "social intellect" is of course internally differentiated across different social systems, and is internalized differently by each individual within each society, depending on social location, the specifics of family structure and socialization, etc. Together these ideas help us to transform the "hermeneutic circle" in which the theory of knowledge has been caught at least since Kant, and which the sociology of knowledge has only tightened, into a dialectical spiral that permits an authentic ascent to Truth.

Once the epistemological problems facing us have been resolved, it is then necessary to demonstrate that the universe is structured in such a way as to point to a principle infinite, necessary, and perfect in character. We have come to take for granted claims rooted in science that is over a century old that the universe is governed by chaos and contingency, and that meaning and value are at best temporary and fragile constructs of the human individual and human society—and at worst illusions that cover a weak-hearted inability to confront the darkness and the abyss.[6] And a universe that is itself little more than a

---

6. The most devastating "scientific" results from the standpoint of the friends of meaning have clearly been the Second Law of Thermodynamics and the theory of natural selection. The first theory, which holds that closed systems of particles tend towards disorder and dissipation of energy, seemed to point towards a future of gradual but inexorable cosmic degeneration through heat death and entropic disintegration; the second seemed to claim that what "progress" there is can be explained through random variation and natural selection based on survival value. Neither seemed to leave much room for either an intelligent and benevolent divine creator and architect or for secular doctrines of evolutionary progress of the kind proposed by dialectical materialism. But other results as well have tended to undermine traditional arguments for the existence of God and/or the ultimate meaningfulness of the universe, including relativistic cosmologies that seem to limit the magnitude of the universe in space and time, and thus close off the possibility of unending growth and development, and

"quantum fluctuation," and the behavior of which is governed by chaos and contingency, hardly requires for its explanation (indeed would seem to *exclude*) a principle infinite, perfect, necessary, and thus divine. Only such a principle, however, can ground meaning that is ultimate in character. All else is partial and contingent.

And yet this science is in crisis—and has been almost since its inception—because of a complex of internal contradictions. First of all, the claims of evolutionary theory seem to contradict those of equilibrium thermodynamics—the one pointing towards increasing and the other towards decreasing complexity. Both together, furthermore, with their emphasis on directional change over time (be it disintegration or evolution) contradict the time-reversible laws of both classical and quantum mechanics. Finally, mechanics (which, contradiction or no, forms the basis of the entire edifice of modern science) has shown itself unable to resolve contradictions between relativistic and quantum descriptions of the universe (Prigogine 1977, 1979, 1984, 1989; Lerner 1991; Mansueto 1998).

In the light of this crisis of the sciences, perhaps it is time to review the seventeenth-century verdict against Aristotelian physics and teleological explanation. Aristotle's physics was rejected for two reasons. First, it was unable to advance a unified theory of motion. How does one explain teleologically a decaying corpse or a thrown javelin? These processes do not seem in any sense ordered to the perfection of form. Thus the distinction between natural and violent motion. This in turn led to a distinction between the celestial realm, where all motion is natural, and the sublunar realm where both kinds of change occur. Second, Aristotelian science had considerable difficulty coming to terms with the growing evidence that even the heavens were not ordered in the perfect manner required by his theory (Murdoch and Sylla 1978; Grant 1978; Lindberg 1992).

There were two ways to resolve this problem. One would have been to generalize the concept of teleology in such a way as to accommodate the reality of violent motion, and to abandon the particular cosmological models developed by Aristotle in order to save the principle of teleological ordering. There were powerful reasons to take just pre-

---

quantum cosmologies that call into question the very idea of causality, and thus the possibility of arguing from the universe to God as first cause.

cisely this approach. Aristotle and his interpreters had, after all, already implicitly shown that the only complete explanation is a teleological explanation. This is because a complete explanation must terminate in a principle that (directly or indirectly) explains everything else while being self-explanatory. Such a principle must be necessary, infinite, and perfect (and thus divine), and it must cause exclusively by the attractive power of its own perfection (otherwise it would be in motion itself and would thus require some other explanatory principle, resulting in an infinite regress) (Aristotle *Metaphysics* 1071b–1076b; Aquinas *Summa Theologiae* I, Q2).

This was not, however, the road taken. Teleology was abandoned altogether, and (though this was never acknowledged, or perhaps, even really recognized) the possibility of a complete explanation along with it. Instead, an attempt was made to develop increasingly general mathematical formalisms that describe motion (now conceived exclusively as change in place). Thus the whole history of mathematical physics, beginning with the special theories of Galileo and Kepler, up through the "first unification" by Newton, and each of the successive generalizations and unifications: Hamiltonian dynamics, Maxwell's equations, relativity, quantum mechanics, and most recently quantum cosmology.

But is mechanistic mathematical physics any better able than its Aristotelian predecessor to offer a unified theory of motion? The contradictions cited above suggest rather pointedly that it is not. Perhaps it is time to consider the road not taken. And this is precisely the direction implicit in the work of a number of physicists and biologists who are (sometimes in spite of themselves) rediscovering the necessity of teleological explanation to a complete science, and gradually helping to reground a teleological cosmology. One need only mention the work of such diverse thinkers as David Bohm (Bohm 1980), Benjamin Gal-Or (Gal-Or 1986), Ilya Prigogine (Prigogine et al. 1977, 1979, 1984, 1989; Eric Lerner 1991), and Lynn Margulis (Margulis and Fester 1991). Recognition of the radical interconnectedness of all things, of the finetuning of key physical constants, which seem to be fixed in just such a way as to make possible the development of complex organization, life, and intelligence, and of the tendency of all matter to develop towards increasingly complex forms of organization: these are the marks of a resurgent teleological science that has not yet broken through the bonds of the hegemonic mathematical physics, but that will ultimately make such a break not only possible but necessary.

If we can establish cosmic teleology then we can also prove the existence of God. A system that evolves infinitely towards ever-higher degrees of organization must have a sufficient cause. And the only cause sufficient for such a universe is *Esse*, or Being as such. And the teleological character of the divine causality that we are proposing effectively answers the old historical materialist critique of religion. God is a lure the incredible Beauty of which attracts the potential latent in matter, not a cosmic tyrant who imposes order on something inert or who creates *ex nihilo* beings that are merely dependents. Knowledge of such a God awakens our powers; it does not dope them. And we can say with confidence to the postmodernists that such a God, which is the power behind the infinite diversity of a rich and growing universe, is never the Same, never effaces creative difference.

Finally, only after we have demonstrated the ultimate meaningfulness of the universe—only after we have shown it to be a system evolving necessarily, if often in a hesitant and contradictory manner, towards God—can we return to harvest the principle of value and the criterion of judgment that makes it possible to challenge the market order. This principle is, of course, nothing other than the drive of matter towards ever higher degrees of organization, a drive grounded in the attractive power of a God whose Beauty, Truth, and Goodness inspires in all things a dynamic of growth and development. Knowing this principle, we also know what we must do—and how resources must be allocated. We know that resources must be allocated first and foremost to those activities that make possible the full development of human social capacities: to guaranteeing the biological and social infrastructure for human development, and to cultivating the human intellect and the human will. And we know as well that the market does not do this, cannot do this, because it has no access to information regarding the impact of various activities on the integrity of the ecosystem or on the development of human social capacities.

This argument is, to be sure, cast in the language of the Aristotelian and Thomistic tradition. But it can be recast in a way that engages humanity's other wisdom traditions. Hindu epistemological debates, for example, closely parallel those it the West (Chatterjee 1954), and my own position is closest to that of the Vedanta schools, which acknowledge not only sensation and inference, but what they call "presupposition," a kind of transcendental argument. The cosmological and metaphysical position that I have outlined represents a rejection not only of modern Western thinking but also of the Buddhist doctrine of dependent origination, which regards everything as dependent on everything else, without recourse to a necessary first cause. (Such a doctrine of dependent origination might, however, be sustained as a doctrine of contingent being, and is rich with wisdom regarding the conditions of life for such beings. And the ethics I have suggested, with its focus on the development of human capacities, is quite compatible with not only a Confucian ethics of self-cultivation but also a Buddhist ethics of "ripening Being.")

Political-Theological Directions

Within this context, the political theology that I am proposing represents an attempt to conserve as much as possible of the modern project—specifically its focus on human creativity and rational autonomy—while avoiding its false promise of divinization by means of innerworldly civilizational progress, whether scientific and technological or revolutionary and political. Rather, it sets civilizational progress and spiritual development in a complex dialectical relationship with each other. The human civilizational project is, like everything material, an attempt at the divine, and always has been. From the earliest intentional burials up through the great pyramids of old, from the mystery cults of Ancient Greece and the meditative traditions initiated by the Upanishads up through the modern cults of technology and revolution, human beings have sought God as we have understood her. And we have, most of the time, sought not only *relationship* with God, but actual divinity. Every single such attempt has, furthermore, failed and brought in its train not only spiritual failure and disillusionment but ultimately profound social crisis.

There have, of course, been numerous authors who have read human civilization in something like this way, and it will be useful here to distinguish my position clearly from theirs. Essentially all of these positions derive from Augustine's claim, in the *City of God*, that there are two different cities: the city of God, ordered to God through love, and the city of Man, ordered to honor and pleasure. Human civilization is, fundamentally, the history of the latter in which the lovers of honor, because they are more disciplined and effective, subjugate the lovers of pleasure and establish a kind of rough justice. The city of God exists within the city of Man and makes use of this order, but ultimately seeks higher ends and does so on the basis of divine grace.

This Augustinian problematic constitutes a whole spectrum of positions which, while more or less optimistic or pessimistic about the prospects for the conversion or transformation of human civilization, regard this change, to the extent that it is possible, as coming from the outside, from God. The tradition is united in condemning as idolatrous the human drive to seek honor, a drive that terminates logically in an attempt at divinization (an attempt made by most great civilizational builders, either explicitly or implicitly).

At one end of this spectrum we have someone like Jacques Ellul. Ellul argues that human civilization itself represents an act of rebellion against a transcendent and loving God, an attempt at self-sufficiency that is not merely misguided but ultimately idolatrous. He thus condemns human civilization as such, and argues that while Christians must live *in* the city, we are not *of* it. At the other end of the spectrum we might place any of a number of American Protestant thinkers from Winthrop and Edwards to H. R. Niehbur who envision the comprehensive conversion of the city of Man through the evangelical and reforming activity of those who have themselves been converted. In between we might place the Catholic Augustinianisms of thinkers like John Milbank who argue for an "other City" based on love rather than desire or self-cultivation and who see that other city as neither a countercultural sect nor an evangelical united front, but rather as an emerging, alternative form of social life, a civilization within a civilization.

A rather distinctive version of this Augustinian theme is represented by Eric Voeglin who reads modern attempts at what we are calling self-divinization as "Gnostic" and thus as a kind of heretical departure from Christianity. What defines Gnosticism is the conviction that esoteric knowledge of some kind (scientific-technological, philosophical-political) can allow one to dissolve the tension between God and humanity that constitutes history and to realize the Good to which history is ordered and in which it participates but with which it is never to be identified.

What is distinctive about the thesis of this work is that unlike all of the above (and unlike all of the other Augustinianisms currently so popular in Christian circles) it fully and enthusiastically affirms the pagan *agon*, the human drive towards self-divinization, which, we believe, is actually *constitutive* of our humanity and of the human civilizational project. To use the mythological language of the Greeks, it is the challenge the gods set for us, a challenge that alone is capable of eliciting the heroic struggles necessary for our full development. It is just that (also like the challenges that the Greek gods set for humanity) it is also a trap that always catches us up (infinitely) short of the mark.

What we are suggesting in other words is that *both* our struggle for self-divinization *and* our failures are spiritually meaningful, part of a dynamic written into the ontological structure of the universe. Understanding God in a certain way (or sometimes rejecting the idea of God altogether, as the Buddhists do, but replacing it with an alternative creative ideal, such as that of the Bodhisattva), we seek that ideal and do so not just individually but collectively, with all of the resources our ecosystem makes available to us, and structure our societies accordingly. These bids for divinization thus define whole civilizational patterns, including not only systems of beliefs and values, but public authorities of various kinds, ways of centralizing and organizing resources, and ways of transforming physical, biological, and social matter into the stuff of civilization (and thus of the divine). And *each* civilization (including modernity) is a real participation in the life of God, revealing and cultivating among human beings some aspect of the divine nature.

The deepest spiritual progress, however, occurs as civilizations fail and we understand both our own limitations and the limitations of our understanding of God. For some, to be sure, the result is despair (deconstructionism), and for others a descent into nihilistic theomachy (neoconservativism and the clash of civilizations). But for others it is a moment in which we realize the mysterious depth of Being and discover a new ideal. And while such insights may well crystallize in moments of solitude and deep meditation, they are almost always gestated in the womb of a society in ferment, through the complex process of collective effervescence. This is how God stretches us, helping us to become more and more human, and more than human, and ultimately but only in an infinitely distant future, divine.

This idea may, perhaps, be conveyed best with an example from the great Hindu epic, the *Mahabharata*. It will be recalled that in this epic the Pandava clan is locked in an ongoing struggle with the closely related Kaurava clan. In the context of this struggle the leader of the Pandava clan Yudhisthir undertakes the great *rajasuya* sacrifice, part of a complex of Vedic rituals that leads ultimately to the divinization of the king. This, in turn, sets in motion a series of events that costs the *Pandavas* their kingdom and leads to a "world war" that brings to a close the third age of humanity.

Throughout this process, the *Pandavas* are advised by Krishna, a minor king allied to them but also an avatar of the god Vishnu, who in this strain of Hinduism is regarded as Brahman himself, the first principle in a fully post-axial sense. Not only does Krishna not advise against these ill-fated actions, he encourages them. And when, at the pivotal point in the epic, Arjun questions what seems to him all this unnecessary killing for what he is beginning to realize are ultimately petty ends, Krishna tells him that he must fight on, and argues his point by demonstrating vividly that Arjun, as he currently exists, his apparent spiritual seeking notwithstanding, is incapable of tolerating, much less actively pursuing, Krishna as he actually is—as Brahman. Furthermore, the social changes that the war brings about—the end of the corrupt third age of humanity—really are worth the struggle, given what they will make possible in terms of civilizational progress and spiritual development.

One cannot, in other words, become a *brahmana* seeker until one has been a *ksatriya* warrior, and perhaps not until one has been a *successful* sacral world emperor, and taken full measure of the limits of this road. And humanity desperately needs those reforming kings who struggle hard to build a just social order even as they seek their own self-divinization. At the same time, it is through just precisely this process that we discover that self-divinization through innerworldly civilizational progress—whether by means of the *rajasuya* or the communist revolution—leaves us far, far short of what we desire. For what we desire is *Esse*, and this we gain only over the course of an infinite history and infinite lifetimes.

In this sense, the fact that humanity is ordered towards transcendental ends has real sociological significance. Being acts (*God* acts) in society, if only as a final cause or lure, at once catalyzing the whole process of civilization building *and* leading us beyond any finite understanding of or civilizational expression of the divine nature (and thus catalyzing the crisis and death of civilizations as well as their birth). And yet everything in society can still be described sociologically, as the work of human beings seeking definite ends under definite material conditions, through definite social structures.

Let us see what this implies for social theory and geopolitical analysis.

Dialectical Sociology

We humans are complex beings, deeply rooted in material reality, but driven by profound spiritual aspirations. We are, on the one hand, animals, whose world is defined, at least to begin with, by what we know with our senses and who strive for ever more diverse and intense sensory experience. It is this desire for pleasurable sensation that motivates us to do what we need to in order to survive and reproduce and ensure the survival of the species. In this sense we are not too different from dogs, who charm us precisely because we share so much in common with them. Unlike dogs, however, we can abstract from the images we garner from the senses and rise to ever higher principles. We can ask what things are and what they mean, and our sensations are thus always meaning-laden—and all the more pleasurable or painful because of this. We want to know what the world means and to understand the significance of our place therein.[7]

These twin aspects of human nature—material and spiritual—come together in the one activity that appears to be uniquely human and that, were we to meet other species that engage in it, would define

---

7. This formulation, which may seem reminiscent of Fromm (Fromm 1947), actually goes much further. For Fromm, human spirituality is rooted in a disharmony in our existence. Unlike the other animals, we are aware of our finitude and isolation, and this gives rise to an existential anxiety that we seek to resolve by various means, some healthy (creative engagement with the world around us) and some not. While Fromm allows for a sort of nontheistic spirituality, he rejects the idea that we might actually be ordered to an end which transcends human development and civilizational progress. My own formulation, on the other hand, treats our animal capacities as the material basis for the development of higher order abilities which are not in conflict with them, but merely transcend them, and takes seriously the reality of the transcendental ends to which we aspire.

them as our close comrades in the cosmic hierarchy: the act of production or creativity. Unlike other animals who merely reproduce, making more of their own kind, and unlike the angels of Catholic doctrine who contemplate God and manage God's creation but do not themselves engage in material creation, we humans are constantly engaged in creating new and more complex forms of organization: new technologies, new relationships and social structures, new forms of art, science, and wisdom. The emergence of this new capacity is partly a result of our materiality and finitude. The earth on which we evolved was already full of organisms that prosper simply by means of rapid reproduction, so that the death of large numbers of individuals is of little concern, and had its share as well of those that exploit narrowly defined niches on the basis of great physical prowess. We humans are neither rabbits nor lions. Big-brained weaklings that we are, we take too long too gestate and grow to maturity for what population biologists call an "r-strategy," centered on rapid reproduction, to be realistic. And yet we could hardly hope to compete with the large carnivores, which best us in strength, speed, agility—and thus the ability to hunt. We *had* to learn how to make things.

But production is also, as we argued above, an intellectual act, and thus never purely material. It involves an understanding of both the raw material and some end or purpose. And even the most rudimentary ends—to help procure food, for example—have a profound spiritual dimension. We seek to escape our finitude and contingency, at least for a while, and to persist in Being. And once our more basic needs are taken care for, we quickly turn to the pursuit of more complex ends that, taken together, amount to civilizational progress and spiritual development. The development of humanity's productive capacities thus involves not only scientific progress, which helps us to understand better the matter on which we work, but also sapiential[8] progress: an ever deeper understanding of the end to which humanity and the universe as a whole are ordered. Civilizations are nothing more or less than the

---

8. I use the term sapiential to include all those disciplines which terminate or claim to terminate in wisdom or knowledge of first principles: religion, philosophy, theology, mysticism, etc. Sapiential progress is progress in wisdom; the sapiential authorities are those authorities whose legitimacy is based on their wisdom: religious leaders but also philosophers, theologians, mystics, and practitioners of connatural or caritative wisdom.

product of our efforts to achieve definite spiritual ends under definite material conditions, by means of definite social structures, and cannot be properly understood without reference to all three types of factors.

1. The *material* basis for the development of civilization is the human organism and the ecosystem or ecosystems it inhabits, which constrain profoundly the range of survival strategies that are open to it and thus the whole pattern of social development.
2. The *formal* cause of human civilization is social structure. Social structure includes:
    2.1. technological structures, i.e., particular ways of reorganizing physical and biological matter,
    2.2. economic structures, i.e., particular ways of organizing human labor and centralizing and allocating resources,
    2.3. political structures, i.e., particular ways of building and exercising power,
    2.4. psycho-social structures, i.e., particular ways of organizing the human psyche to serve the aims of the society in question, and
    2.5. ideological-cultural structures, i.e., particular ways of organizing our experience of the universe, including languages, natural and artificial.
3. The *final cause* of human civilization, as of everything else, is *Esse* or Being as such. But each civilization understands, and thus pursues, this cause differently. The way in which a civilization understands the end to which it is ordered we call its *civilizational ideal*. Thus Chinese civilization historically understood itself as ordered to *Tian* or Heaven, Medieval India to the union of *Brahman* and *atman*.[9]

---

9. This frankly Aristotelian approach is the result of a dual effort to address developments in the sciences that point towards the need to reintegrate teleological thinking into scientific explanation, an argument that I make in outline form in *Knowing God: Restoring Reason in an Age of Doubt* (Mansueto 2002), and will make at much greater length in its sequel, *Knowing God: The Ultimate Meaningfulness of the Universe*, and an effort to reintegrate both ecological and spiritual considerations into dialectical and historical materialism, which, when these are factored back in, *is* Aristotelian.

The lines between material basis and social structure and social structure and teleological ordering are a bit ambiguous. Absolutely speaking the material basis is confined to the ecosystem. Technology and economics are just as much social products as politics and culture. Relatively speaking, however, the whole "built up" infrastructure of a society, including its technological apparatus and the social surplus it can generate, constitute the material foundation on the basis of which political and cultural realities develop. A religious ideology is, similarly, an integral part of the social structure, i.e., the way a particular society is organized, and not itself an end or *telos*, but the objects of which it speaks are such a *telos*. We gain access to the way a society understands its ends, however, by analyzing its ideological-cultural structure. The same is true of the relationship between the various instances of the social structure. Organizing labor and centralizing and allocating resources both involve building and exercising power. Building and exercising power, similarly, generally involves an appeal to fundamental principles and values. This is true even in predominantly secular societies. These categories should thus be used flexibly in a way that serves the purposes of the particular analysis that is being carried out.

As civilizations develop they leave a kind of deposit that is *material, structured*, and *teleologically ordered*. This is often referred to simply as the "built environment," but this phrase fails to capture the extent to which the form of buildings and the structure of cities encodes a civilization's adaptation to its ecosystem, its way of organizing and centralizing resources and building and exercising power, and its way of understanding the end to which it is ordered. Phillip Bess (Bess 2006), who captures this reality better than other theorists I have read, uses the term "formal order," but in the philosophical context of this work this seems to ignore the materiality of the deposit involved. My preference is simply for the term *architectural* organization, both because of its reference to the discipline that studies and creates such global forms of organization, and because of its joining of a term for the end to which the built environment is ordered (*archi-*) to one for the act of building (*-tecture*), though the term must be understood to include the study and creation of entire urban and indeed rural landscapes and not simply single buildings.

The importance of the architectural organization of a civilization cannot be underestimated, because the accumulated architectural record constrains, in the way few other things can, the future direction of civilizational development. However "secular" modern Europe may have become (and we have seen that this term is highly problematic), the presence at the center of essentially every European city and village of a cathedral or parish church, marking a sacral center of meaning, constrains and orders human activity in a way that conserves elements of earlier civilizational patterns. The same is true for the any other ancient civilization. Thus the Communist Parties of the Soviet Union and of China tried to hegemonize the sacred spaces at the center of their polities (St. Basil's and the Kremlin on the one hand, and the sacred complex formed by the Tian-an (Temple of Heaven), Tianamen, and the Forbidden City on the other hand, but were partially hegemonized by them.

But it is not only ancient structures that function in this way. Chicago, for example, is in many ways a high modern city *par excellence*, organized around a downtown of financial and corporate headquarters and high-end shopping, with outlying districts built around factories of various types and sizes. But the people themselves altered this high modern space by placing at the center of their neighborhoods countless churches and synagogues that are the real centers of meaning in the city, and by creating shopping districts that serve the needs of distinct ethno-religious communities (with dietary laws creating distinct economic niches). This Tocquevillian space, as Phillip Bess (Bess 2006) calls it, is perhaps unique to the industrial-era cities of the United States. Dallas, on the other hand, understands itself as an intensely religious city. Dallas Theological Seminary is the intellectual headquarters of dispensational premillennialism. But the public spaces of Dallas are defined by office parks and shopping malls, with churches, no matter how grand, scattered unobtrusively through residential districts, so that they play essentially no role in the way the *meaning* of the city is ultimately defined. These architectural structures mean that it would be nearly impossible for a high modern "secularist" agenda to become hegemonic in Chicago or for a "Catholic" sense of sacramentality to become dominant in Dallas.

When approaching a civilization, it is possible to identify several different levels of analysis: metacivilizational, civilizational, structural, etc. Analysis at the metacivilizational level looks at clusters of civilizations with ideals that share common characteristics. A *metaciviliza-*

tional project is a cluster of civilizations that, while defined by different and even incompatible ideals, nonetheless share certain common characteristics. Broadly speaking it is possible to identify the following metacivilizational projects:[10]

- Pre-axial civilizations, such as the great agrarian sacral monarchic empires of the Bronze Age, regard meaning as unproblematic and are ordered to achieving divinization understood simply as *immortality*, generally only for the king or the aristocracy, by means of sacrificial rituals.

- Axial civilizations accept the fact that meaning has become problematic, are characterized by religious rationalization and democ-

---

10. This represents, to be sure, something of a redefinition of Jaspers's original characterization of the Axial Age (Jaspers 1953) and a departure from the way the term has been used in modern social science (Aronson et al. 2005), which emphasizes the beginning of a process of the disenchantment of the universe, a "disembedding" of the individual from society, the cosmos, and the divine (Taylor 2007, 146–58), and a shift in religious aims from worldly flourishing (to use Taylor's term) to salvation of some kind. Central to the thesis of this book is the idea that, at the deepest level, humanity's aim has always remained the same. It is Being, or God. What changes is the way in which this end is understood and pursued. But simply survival or worldly flourishing, immortality, the union of *Brahman* and *atman*, *nirvana* or bodhisattvahood, the beatific vision, and the modern ideals of divinization through scientific-technological and revolutionary-political progress are all ways of understanding and seeking divinization. Indeed, Protestantism and certain forms of Asharite Islam are unusual in positing ends (a simple paradise for those who submit to God, or everlasting life for those who believe) that do not look much like divinization. In reality, however, these represent simply the carrying over of earlier, pre-axial ideals of divinization into a context in which the idea of God itself has advanced in a way that prohibits humanity from actually seeking what God *is*—infinite power—for the simple reason that (unlike *Esse*) this cannot be shared, and seeking it represents an assault on rather than worship of God.

This redefinition of what happens in the Axial Age will be important to a second claim of this work, namely that modernity does not continue and complete the axial revolution (as Taylor claims in the pages cited above) but rather represents a decisive break with it in the ways outlined in this chapter and explained in detail in those that follow. Taylor is certainly correct that the axial revolutions were incomplete (Taylor 2007, 146, 430–39, 613–14). But this was not simply the result of an equilibrium in which the people pursued pre-axial religious aims and virtuosi post-axial aims. Rather, the forms of popular religion themselves changed. The mystery cult, of which Christianity is the most successful, for example, was a classical example of a post-axial form that democratizes religious aims (divinization understood as immortality) and makes it accessible to the people. And modernity was not the completion of the axial revolution but rather its abandonment in favor of a new ideal.

ratization, and aim at regrounding meaning and at cultivating human capacities by means of rationalized spiritual disciplines. They generally understand human civilizational progress as a real participation in this process of spiritual development, but do not reduce spirituality to civilization building. They seek divinization by means of the cultivation of various spiritual capacities, though the capacities valued and cultivated often differ considerably.

- Modern civilizations claim that meaning can be rendered once again unproblematic by either revelation (in the case of the early modern ideal) or reason (scientific or philosophical) and aim at achieving divinity by innerworldly means (scientific and technological progress or revolutionary political practice).

It is central to the argument of this work that, while the pre-axial and modern metacivilizational projects have proven themselves unworkable, the Axial Age project has not yet exhausted its potential, and indeed represents the main stream of the human civilizational project. Our principal task in the present period is to re-engage this stream and resituate within it the genuine contributions of modernity that are worth conserving, while carrying the project to a qualitatively higher stage.

Analysis at the *civilizational* level focuses on the complex interaction of material basis, social structure, and civilizational ideal. The ideals that constitute civilizations are constrained and shaped by the social conditions (both material basis and social structure) under which they develop. But social structures must be understood as ways of realizing definite civilizational ideals. And civilizational ideals also represent at least a partial grasp of the truth and can thus continue to motivate human action long after the conditions that gave birth to them have vanished. When this happens, the meaning of these ideals inevitably changes, though this may happen consciously, when the ideals constitute a living tradition that values both continuity and change, or unconsciously, as fundamentalists reassert what they imagine to be ancient and unchanging truths but that (even when the words remain the same) are really innovations.

Structural analysis focuses on the way in which societies engage the material environment in order to realize a definite ideal. Several distinctive modes can be identified:

- *Band societies* are found in a variety of ecosystems, and generally have hunter-gatherer technology, a kinship system that only weakly influences the formation of actual groups, and a totemic religious structure that brings clans together for occasional religious festivals.

- *Tribal societies* are also found in a variety of ecosystems, but persist longest on open steppes or grasslands with large populations of ungulates. They have generally developed advanced hunter-gatherer or pastoral nomadic technologies that allow them to exploit these herds, sometimes supplemented with raiding or trading, and have strongly developed kinship systems that largely organize social life, and polytheistic religions often characterized by the emergence of male sky gods with warlike characteristics, such as the Aryan *Indra* or the Turkic *Tengri*.

- *Communitarian societies* are found in ecosystems that make the cultivation of food relatively easy, and have developed horticultural or agricultural technology. Land is generally owned by the clan or village and is often periodically redistributed. A strong kinship system is cross-cut by social forms that transcend kinship ties, such as the village itself and various religious societies. The polytheistic religions of communitarian societies are characterized by a strong emphasis on fertility rituals and are often dominated by a goddess of wisdom and fertility, such as the Keres *Sussistinako* or the universal Mediterranean goddess that forms the background of the cults of *Isis* and *Demeter*.

- *Archaic societies* are found especially but not exclusively in riverine ecosystems and have advanced horticultural or agricultural technologies. Surplus is centralized and reallocated by a temple complex, which may or may not form the center of an urban concentration. The polytheistic religious ideologies of archaic societies are characterized by the emergence of an increasingly well-defined high god concept, often associated with the sun. Evidence for such societies is scant; most were quickly absorbed into emerging tributary empires, but the Anasazi stage of the Puebloan civilization, the Mississippian civilization, and the societies that built Stonehenge and Avebury may all represent an archaic structures.

- *Tributary societies* are often founded as nomadic raiders conquer communitarian or archaic riverine communities and impose rents, taxes, and forced labor, eventually building large urban centers and transforming the religious structure in a way that leads to a predominance of divine monarchs who integrate both warlike and priestly functions, such as the Egyptian *Ra* or the Babylonian *Marduk*.

- *Petty-commodity* societies generally emerge in coastal or oasis ecosystems on the basis of specialized agricultural production. Resources are allocated by a market in goods and services, and political structures, which may vary from relatively democratic city-state forms through large military empires, focus their attention on capturing as much surplus through trade as possible. Religious ideologies undergo a process of rationalization as myth gradually gives way to philosophy and new religious movements emerge with a greater focus on ethical conduct, social justice, and spiritual development. This is the Axial Age described by Karl Jaspers to which we referred above and which we will discuss in greater detail in the next chapter. These ideologies gradually assert ever increasing influence, both by hegemonizing state structures (Confucianism in Han or Sung China, *Dar-Al Islam*) or by building monastic or mendicant communities that become major economic and political as well as cultural actors (e.g., the *Mahayana Buddhist* monasteries of Sui and T'ang China or the Benedictine monasteries of medieval Europe; the *Sufi* orders throughout *Dar-al Islam*, but especially Central Asia, and the mendicant orders in late-medieval and Baroque Europe and in New Spain).

- *Capitalist societies* are defined by the development of industrial technologies, and markets in labor power and capital as well as goods and services. Political organization varies, but generally involves some sort of representative format except in transitional periods, but is strongly subordinated to the market, which it serves. Religious ideologies emphasize submission to a sovereign God who is a reflex of the mysterious imperatives of the market order, or else conceal themselves as secular doctrines that seek transcendence by technical and/or political means.

- In *socialist societies* the state displaces the capital markets as the principal resource allocator, something that generally reflects a teleological ordering to civilizational progress rather than capital accumulation and luxury consumption, although the markets in goods and services, and in labor power, remain. Most socialist societies have insisted on an official atheism in order to guarantee that the drive of the population towards transcendence is focused exclusively on innerworldly means.

The way in which a particular society is structured in turn constitutes a definite complex of *social actors*. We distinguish between primary, secondary, and tertiary social actors. By primary social actors we mean groups defined by their position in the social structure. The most important of these are *social classes*, which are constituted first of all by position with respect to the economic structure, but which also develop their own characteristic forms of political organization and their own ideologies. These may be a refraction of the larger aims of the society as seen from their social location, but if the structure of the society is deeply in contradiction with either their survival or their development, oppressed social classes in particular may develop revolutionary ideologies that at least aim to become alternative civilizational ideals. Class struggles are thus never purely economic—even political-economic—in character. They are always, simultaneously, direct or indirect struggles around fundamental questions of meaning and value.

Peoples are defined by their position with respect to political and cultural structures. They are groups of human beings that, generally speaking, share a common homeland and have a common history and culture. While they may have been incorporated into a larger civilizational complex, they often have distinctive beliefs and values that may be a variant on the dominant ideology of the civilization, but may also reflect an alternative civilizational ideal that has been subordinated to those of the dominant peoples in the civilization. When the oppressed classes and peoples of a civilization cannot resolve its internal contradictions, these contradictions are often resolved for them by invading peoples who impose an entirely new civilizational ideal. This was the role of the Germans and Arabs in the collapse of Roman civilization.

Gender, that is, the meaning that a people or a civilization attaches to sexual difference, is defined by position with respect to the psychosocial structure of the society, its way of reproducing human social beings. This is expressed in the sexual division of labor, in power relations within the family, kinship, and larger social networks, and in the dominant ideology and culture, and can also form a line of demarcation along which fundamental social struggles unfold.

Primary social actors lie behind all social processes, but they are never, as it were, visible to the naked eye. They appear only when one scrutinizes social processes through the lens of social theory. Secondary social actors, on the other hand, are formed on the basis of primary social actors (or alliances of primary social actors) in order to act rationally in the public arena. These are groups that understand themselves as such and appear to others as concrete social actors. They include families, villages, corporations, organizations such as guilds or trade unions, political parties, educational, scientific, cultural, or religious organizations. Secondary social actors may represent the perspective of one primary social actor or they may articulate an alliance or coalition of such interests. Understanding how such coalitions are formed is one of the fundamental tasks of social analysis, as it provides the key to rendering intelligible otherwise opaque and apparently voluntaristic processes.

It is in this context that de Tocqueville's analysis of the "intermediate" institutions of civil society should be situated. Such institutions permit groups of individuals to pursue distinctive variants of the hegemonic civilizational ideal, or even countervailing ideals by means of economic, political, and cultural activity. The scope that exists for such diversity within a society we call its degree of ideological pluralism. At the one extreme, we find *totalitarian* societies in which the institutions of civil society have been extinguished entirely or made instruments of the hegemonic tertiary (political-theological) social actor. At the other extreme, we find societies in which the public arena is *constituted* by deliberation around fundamental questions of meaning and value, and the civilization is constituted not so much by a single ideal as by an open and civil contest between ideals.

Tertiary or *political-theological* organizations are formed consciously and rationally to act on primary and secondary social actors in order to conserve or transform human civilizations. They may act at the level of civilizational ideal, social structure, or public policy, but at least implicitly have the capacity to act at all three levels. They may be informal—ruling-class networks that negotiate aims and strategies through informal interactions in diverse social settings—or formal, like a religious order or political party. Generally speaking, however, informal networks have less capacity for common action than disciplined organizations, and generally represent efforts on the part of ruling classes to conserve the existing structure and manage change, rather than attempts at revolutionary reorganization.

Now human societies develop as human beings pursue the Good as they understand it, given the constraints imposed on their perceptions by the material conditions and social structures. They develop social structures in order to make possible the pursuit of the Good under those material conditions. When those structures begin to hold back their ability to pursue the Good, they challenge and attempt to modify them, sometimes gradually and incrementally, sometimes through revolutionary upheavals. Particular ways of understanding our End or purpose (particular ideologies) can serve either as catalysts for change or as means of social control.

In analyzing the dynamics of human societies it is necessary to distinguish between civilizational, structural, periodic, and conjunctural crises.[11] A *civilizational crisis* takes place when, generally after a succession of structural crises, people actually lose faith in a civilizational ideal and stop pursuing it. A *structural crisis*, on the other hand, arises from a contradiction between the social structure or complex of structures by which the civilization organizes its activities on the one hand, and the underlying material conditions (the ecosystem) and/or the real ends to which people aspire, on the other. Structural crises can be, but are not always, resolved by fundamental structural change. The Anasazi-Pueblo civilization expanded beyond the carrying capacity of the ecological niche it inhabited and responded to the resulting crisis by decentralizing, abandoning large temple complexes of the sort we see at Chaco for the scattered villages that we now see among the Puebloan peoples, a shift that may also reflect changes at the religious level (Stuart 2001), but that also reflects significant civilizational con-

---

11. These distinctions derive from Louis Althusser and his followers (Althusser and Balibar 1968/1970), but have been modified to reflect the larger approach to social theory outlined above.

tinuity. Roman civilization ran into a structural crisis because its basic strategy—using the surplus generated by chattel slavery to buy into the Silk Road trade—ran into insuperable limits. Logistic and ecological factors made further expansion impossible, bringing an end to the wars of conquest that provided a steady supply of slaves. The empire was forced to shift from the use of chattel slaves to the use of settled, dependent peasants known as *coloni* and to significantly increase rates of exploitation. This exploitation was legitimated as service to the common good using Christian religious ideals, something that allowed the empire, but not, perhaps, Roman civilization, to persist in parts of the East, where elements of the old structure served a new ideal. In the West and in the *Masreq* and the *Mahgreb,* this system lacked credibility, and Roman civilization was displaced by the religious civilizations of Christendom and *Dar-al-Islam,* both of which were inspired by ideals radically different from those that shaped Rome.

Both civilizational and structural crises are times of what Durkheim called *collective effervescence* when, unable to live in the old way, people interact more intensely and question more deeply than they otherwise would. As we suggested above, it is out of such moments of collective effervescence that new insights into the mystery of Being, and thus new civilizational ideals, ultimately emerge.

Geopolitical-theological Analysis

We are now in a position to explain what difference our political-theological and social-theoretical innovations make at the level of geopolitical analysis—or what, given the role we have assigned to transcendental ends as real if final causes of social patterns (and following Milbank 2006a), we prefer to call geopolitical-theological analysis.

We begin by recalling some definitions. Geopolitical analysis is, first and foremost, analysis that attempts to specify the balance of forces on a global scale in any given *conjuncture* or *period.* By a conjuncture (Althusser 1965/1977, 1968/1970, 1966–1969/1971) we mean a political moment defined by a precise combination of forces. A period, on the other hand, is defined by a relatively stable alignment of economic, political, and cultural forces.

The principal impact of a political theology or social theory on geopolitical analysis is to select from among the various forces that define the current situation those that are most important, either because they reflect powerful, deeply rooted social trends or because they bear in one way or another on important values. In our case, this means focusing attention on a variety of factors ignored by modern social theory and the geopolitical analysis that derives from it:

1. the nature and integrity of the ecosystem,
2. the operation of secondary and tertiary social actors, i.e., the organizations of civil society and political-theological organizations, treated not merely as agents of primary social actors such as classes and peoples, but also as carriers of (often competing) civilizational ideals *and* the structure of the social space (totalitarian or pluralistic) in which they are operating,
3. the *architectural organization of the society*, which defines sacred and civic space and thus constrains and orders action in the public arena, facilitating, obstructing, or channeling in various ways the development of collective effervescence.

Finally, all of these factors (together with those considered by the various forms of modern social theory, the importance of which we do not negate), are considered in so far as they bear on advancing or constraining the realization of one or another civilizational ideal.

Let us look briefly at what difference this makes in practice. Neoliberal and historical materialist analyses of the current situation focus on the formation of a unified global market in capital, since this is a development that both regard as reflecting deeply rooted social trends and bearing on important values—technological and economic growth and development, even if one regards it as unambiguously positive and the other as something to be transcended. Similarly, interpretive sociological and the more culturalist forms of populist analysis focus on the contradictions between civilizations or between North and South. Conjuncture-defining events such as the collapse of the Soviet Union or the terrorist attacks of September 11, 2001, are read as advancing or beating back one or another of these forces.

Our own dialectical sociology and the global *Convivencia* theology in which it is embedded does not negate the importance of any of these factors, but rather reads them as they bear on the fate of the modern civilizational ideal in both its positivistic and humanistic variants. This will require that we look, first of all, at the current ecological crisis in a way that none of the principal trends in contemporary geopolitical analysis really do. This crisis is the principal constraint on the realization of both variants of the modern ideal. Second, it will require that we read the actions of both the organizations of civil society and of global political theological actors as bearing not *only* on the fate of the global market but on the fate of the modern ideal. This will lead us to identify tendencies that are otherwise invisible to most contemporary geopolitical analysis—the emerging politics and spirituality of meaning and self-cultivation, for example, and to understand others, such as fundamentalism, very differently. Finally, we will need to look at the way both social and architectural spaces are defined and the way these constrain and order responses to the current situation. Is there a *place*, both literally and figuratively, where the collective effervescence can develop and a new ideal can emerge? If so, where is it? If not, how do we create it? This will, as we see, lead to a very different understanding of what is happening in the present period and a very different kind of political-theological strategy.

But before we look in depth at the current situation, we need to consider what this perspective tells us about the broader sweep of human history.

CHAPTER 2

The Human Civilizational Project

All human civilizations have told stories about themselves—about their origin, development, and future prospects. These stories almost always have some basis in fact, but they serve first and foremost to provide a framework of meaning in the context of which the members of that civilization can make sense out of their current situation. For the earliest human societies these stories were, for the most part, epics that told the story of the people through the exemplary stories of its greatest heroes. Thus the *Epic of Gilgamesh*, the *Iliad* and the *Odyssey*. Later, epic histories gave way to salvation histories that recounted God's work of redemption or and/or humanity's ascent to enlightenment—works such as the *Exodus* narratives, or the *Mahabharata* and the *Ramayana*, the Gospels, Augustine's *City of God*, Dante's *Commedia*, or, on the very edge of modernity, Milton's *Paradise Lost*.

Modernity claims to have transcended such storytelling and to have replaced it with a scientific history of the human civilizational project. And there is more than a grain of truth to this claim. The techniques of modern historical scholarship *can*, indeed, ascertain what actually happened in a way that older narrative genres did not even attempt to do. And analyzing what happened by abstracting from particulars to broad sociohistorical structures *is* different from merely telling a story. And yet the *result* of this work remains, whatever else it might be, a *story* about modernity—its origins, development, and future prospects—a story to which members of modern civilization can turn in order to make sense out of their current situation, every bit as much as the *Epic of Gilgamesh* or the *Ramayana*. And to the extent that people buy into that story and see themselves as part of it, the modern project is legitimated and sustained.

This much, of course, is now a common theme of postmodernist critiques of modern "grand narratives." In the previous chapter I have, however, suggested a critique of the modern project that runs much deeper than postmodernism. While acknowledging the rootedness of our ideas in definite social structures and their powerful role in legitimating social interests, this alternative avoids the radical relativism of the postmodernists and suggests that while there may be no "final theory" and that while no story can encompass the rich complexity of the truth, there are better theories and worse, and better stories and worse, both from the standpoint of their capacity to explain reality and from the standpoint of the way in which they order human action. We have also argued that if humanity is to overcome the current crisis we need a new theory (which we began to sketch out in the last chapter) and a new story that can inspire and legitimate a new civilizational ideal. Here we will subject the modernist grand narrative to critical scrutiny from the standpoint of the theoretical framework elaborated in the previous chapter. We will then suggest an alternative account of human history that, we believe, has both greater explanatory power and a greater ability to inspire action to address the current crisis.

If what follows—both our account of the modernist narrative and our alternative reading of history in the light of a dialectical sociology and a *Convivencia* theology—reads a bit like a condensed course in world history that is because it is in two very specific senses. First, methodologically, I became aware of many of these issues when called on to teach a course in Western Civilization to a predominantly *Diné* (Navajo) student body at the University of New Mexico–Gallup in the years between 2001 and 2006. In the process I was forced to subject to critical scrutiny the whole concept of the "West" and the self-understanding embodied in the Western Civilization course, a self-understanding that is reflected in even the best textbooks and anthologies. It is this self-understanding that we have set forth in our account of the modernist narrative. Second, our aim in presenting an alternative narrative is not to write a complete scholarly history of the world—something that would surely require a multivolume work—but rather to present something comparable to the narrative we have criticized, but more adequate, both from the standpoint of its explanatory power and the way it orders human action.

The Secular Messianic Narrative of High Modernity

What, exactly, is the modernist historical narrative? It resides, as much as anything, in a certain periodization or cluster of alternative periodizations and in the way certain critical breakthroughs are theorized. The first of these breakthroughs is the development, on the part of a group of hominids, of the capacity to make tools and thus subdue their environment. This breakthrough is understood as itself just a random, spontaneous variation in behavior. This is important, because in the high modern narrative human beings themselves are the agents of their own divinization, and *agency* as such is confined to humans. Before that, all is randomness and contingency. For thousands and thousands of years this breakthrough amounts to nothing more than an ability to compensate for the fact that these hominids are neither fast breeders nor very strong or very fast and that they do not have claws or fangs or other "built-in" weapons that might make them more effective hunters. Eventually, however, human beings learned how to domesticate plants and animals—the second breakthrough—subduing them and ordering them to human ends. The resulting increase in the social surplus product makes it possible for humans to begin building permanent settlements around which they completely reorganize the pre-existing ecosystem.

The third breakthrough is the development of urban settlements with writing, something that occurs around 3000 BCE in Mesopotamia and shortly thereafter in the Nile Valley, the Indus Valley, and the Huang He (Yellow River) Valley. This is understood as the product of some combination of demographic pressure, technological innovation (agriculture and metallurgy), increased trade, and the emergence of conquest as a strategy for economic development.

The fourth breakthrough is what is generally called the "Axial Age," the period between 800–200 BCE that witnessed the development of mathematics and natural philosophy as well as humanity's root salvation religions—Judaism, the Hinduism of the Upanishads, Buddhism, Confucianism, and Taoism (Jaspers 1953). Modernists, as we noted in the previous chapter, read the Axial Age as fundamentally a step towards secularization in Charles Taylor's sense, the beginning of the "great disembedding" of the individual from society, cosmos, and the divine (Taylor 2007, 146–58) that is completed only in the modern world. The salvation religions are regarded as progressive because they involve an at least partially rationalized (systematized and abstract) content, because they recognize that there is something wrong in the world that needs to be changed, even if the solutions are often otherworldly, and because they encourage systematic rational activity towards an end (Weber 1921/1968). In the older, more purely Eurocentric versions of this narrative, this is, of course, the great "classical era" when humanity took the first steps towards democracy and towards the development of a scientific worldview and produced its first great humanistic works of art.

This brilliant period of rationality and creativity could not, however, be sustained. Liberal theory attributes this to the incomplete character of the disembedding—the people remained immersed in popular religious practices focused on the use of essentially magical means to realize innerworldly goods; historical materialism attributes it to the low level of development of the productive forces. Humanity collapsed back into a long period of darkness and superstition during which the salvation religions—apparently having expended their progressive potential—kept human beings from exercising their rational capacities and extending their control over their environment. In the West, this period is generally refereed to as the Middle Ages ("middle" between the enlightened ages of Classical Antiquity and Modernity), though many students are still taught in school to call the entire period between the collapse of the Roman Empire in the West and the "discovery" of the Americas the "Dark Ages."

This period of superstition ends only when a small minority of intellectuals in the mercantile cities of Italy and the Low Countries rediscover the beauty of classical antiquity and when the Reformation breaks the hegemony of the Catholic Church, which had hitherto maintained a stranglehold on humanity that held back scientific and technological progress. The rediscovery of reason leads in turn to the Scientific Revolution, as humanity finally begins to unlock the secrets of nature and, understanding how the universe works, learns to bring it under rational human control. The Industrial Revolution is essentially just the practical side of the Scientific Revolution, the first step in a systematic reorganization of the natural environment. The Enlightenment extends this process of rationalization into the social and philosophical realm, giving birth first to the democratic revolutions, which sweep away all that is old and superstitious and irrational and, eventually, to the social sciences, which open up the prospect of a rationally organized social structure that, making optimum use of human labor, will be able to carry out hitherto inconceivable civilizational feats.

Liberal and socialist theories both put forward variants of this narrative, but reject none of its major features. At the level of social theory, historical materialism would, for example, put more emphasis on the way in which social structures (modes of production) occasionally became obstacles to further technological progress and either disintegrated or were swept away in revolutionary transformations. Later liberal theory (Hayek 1988), trying to distance itself from historical materialism, would put a bit more emphasis on the role of intellectual developments and might treat socialism as a replay of the old Asiatic empires. And in defining the modern ideal itself there are some nuanced differences. Liberalism has *usually* focused on humanity's ascent to a mastery of nature that points ultimately to divinization by means of scientific and technological progress, and socialism has *usually* focused on elevating humanity, through the medium of the party, to the status of Subject of the cosmohistorical process. But there are liberals who have focused on rational autonomy and democratic citizenship (a kind of subjectivity) and socialists who have understood socialism as primarily a means of unleashing the development of the productive forces.

Where does this narrative end? That is one of the great divides of the present period. For a few, who still believe in it, it extends into a brilliant future in which humanity will, through genetic engineering, vastly extend its lifespan or even conquer death entirely (Wagar 1999), will eventually give birth to still more complex and intelligent forms of organization, and will bring the universe fully and completely under their mastery, becoming, in effect, divine. This is the case with transhumanists like Frank Tipler (Tipler 1994), who argue that the development of artificial intelligence will make it possible to "download" or fully emulate human consciousness and then load it onto microprobes that will then expand out into the universe, exploring and reorganizing, and eventually taking control of its evolution in such a way as to guarantee both the permanent survival and omnipotence and omniscience of life and intelligence. In the socialist version it leads to all this and more—a kind of collective transcendence of contingency in which the "social individual," rationally autonomous and acting through noncoercive networks of cooperation beyond the party and the state, becomes fully and completely the Subject of the self-organizing cosmos, in such a way that the contradiction between existence and essence is resolved and humanity becomes—in the full Thomistic sense of the word—God. This is the variant we have called secular messianism in which the scientist, engineer, and entrepreneur, or the revolutionary intellectuals organized in the Communist Party, lift humanity above finitude and/or contingency into a realm of freedom that can only be called divine.

Others—those who call themselves postmodernist—have recognized that this narrative, its scientific foundations notwithstanding, is simply one of many possible narratives that humanity has produced throughout its history, and seek to deconstruct or at least relativize it, thus undercutting its legitimating functions. Indeed, some, such as Taylor (Taylor 2007), *define* secularity as that point at which *all* narratives are "one among many."

The vast majority of people are, however, in neither camp. Rather, when they think about such things, they wonder what has happened to the dreams of the past five centuries, the future promised in the science fiction narratives on which so many of us grew up. But few question the basic outlines of the modernist narrative. Whether as tragedy, comedy, or melodrama, it is still very much the story we tell about ourselves. And we *must* have a story.

What is Wrong with the Modernist Narrative?

From my point of view, however, it is not enough to say that the modernist narrative is "ideological," that it is at once the product of and a mechanism for reinforcing definite social interests. That, by itself, does not speak to its truth-value one way or another. We have argued elsewhere (Mansueto 2002b, 2005) that the human intellect, however constrained by social location, can in fact aspire to at least a relative and partial objectivity. We must take seriously the claim of the modernist narrative to such objectivity and evaluate it on its merits.

Let us say, first of all, that the modernist narrative does, in fact, point to an important truth: that of progress. We agree with the modernists that humanity represents a real advance over merely animal life and that the human civilizational project represents an ongoing dynamic of growth and development that adds to the complexity and organization of the universe, and thus represents a real value (Mansueto 1995, Mansueto and Mansueto 2005). The difficulty is not with the claim of progress, but with the modernist understanding of progress and of its relationship to humanity's transcendental end.

This is apparent, first of all, in the modernist understanding of scientific and technological progress. Central to the modern ideal is the claim that by understanding how the world works we can subject it rational human control, gradually extending the sphere of human sovereignty. In reality, however, human civilization was dependent from the beginning on certain potentials latent in the physical and biological universe, potentials that we have not so much brought under our control as catalyzed and nurtured. Gradually, to be sure, this process becomes conscious. But throughout most of its history, science was understood as an attempt to understand the latent potentials of matter and technology as a way of tapping into and cultivating those potentials. Reducing science to mechanics and technology to industry, which breaks down existing forms of organization in order to release energy and do work, is a modern mutation and one that, we will argue, may in the long run do more to undermine than to build up the complexity and organization of the universe.

This same misunderstanding of the nature of progress is reflected in modernist political economy. Liberal and socialist theories both share the conviction that progress is best served when the principal resource allocator (be it the state or the market) has full access to the entire social surplus product and allocates that product in accord with rational norms. They simply differ regarding the nature of such an allocation and the best structural mechanism for ensuring it. Liberal theory favors the market and socialist theory the state, in part because the former understands rationality in terms of a purely quantitative growth and the latter in terms of a substantive development of creative capacity. In both cases, however, the expropriation of small producers (peasants, artisans, and the autonomous intelligentsia) is regarded as progressive, and both (capitalism in principle and socialism in practice) make the wage relation the principal means of organizing labor. I argue, on the contrary, that the most progressive periods of human history have been characterized by structures that secured a high degree of autonomy for primary producers, which allowed them to retain a significant portion of the social surplus, and which favored persuasive over coercive means of surplus centralization. This will be reflected in a number of specific differences in historic analysis regarding the origins of urbanization and the reasons for the industrial revolution.

The modernist narrative also errs in confounding rationalization and secularization and in regarding the latter as a condition for democracy and progress. This is apparent in the modernist accounts of the Axial Age and the Scientific and Democratic Revolutions, of which, as we have suggested, we will give very different accounts. Indeed, I will suggest that the very way in which the modernist narrative understands secularization is itself a lie. Specifically, it pretends to have transcended religious concerns in order to conceal a very specific political-theological agenda: the modern ideal of divinization by means of innerworldly (scientific-technological and/or philosophical-political) progress.

Finally, the modernist narrative misunderstands the relationship between innerworldly progress and humanity's transcendental end, and misrepresents the way in which this relationship was understood by the great spiritual civilizations of the Silk Road Era: Christendom, *Dar-al-Islam*, and their Jewish subculture, the Buddhist civilizations of India and Southeast Asia, the Hindu civilization that supplanted Buddhism in India, the Confucian/Taoist/Buddhist civilization of China, and the Confucian/Shinto/Buddhist civilization of Japan. On the one hand, we will argue, there is a fundamental ontological boundary, that between necessary and contingent Being, across which no innerworldly progress can carry us. At the same time, innerworldly progress, because it increases our degree of participation in Being, *does* have real spiritual significance. Modernity, by posing a false alternative between innerworldly civilizational progress and otherworldly spirituality, an ideal it falsely attributes to the civilizations of the Silk Road Era, fundamentally misleads humanity regarding its nature and destiny. It is this latter error, I will argue, that specifically condemned the socialist project, which did not so much misunderstand divinity (as did positivistic modernity) and attempt to achieve a false godhood by means of scientific and technological progress, but actually proposed to put humanity in the place of *Esse* as such. In doing so it sought something that is ontologically impossible and that, the power of historical materialism as a social theory and the civilization-building contributions of socialism notwithstanding, was doomed from the beginning.

With this said, let us now try to formulate an alternative narrative of the human civilizational project—one with both greater explanatory power and greater promise as a guide to our future development.

Civilization and Spiritualization

The Origins of Human Civilization

Emerging Humanity

Our story begins very differently than the modernist narrative, because it is rooted in a fundamentally different understanding of matter—i.e., as ordered to Being and thus to the development of complex organization. What we call the *sapient*[1] form of matter emerges when organisms begin to create new forms of complex organization rather than merely reproducing the biological structures encoded in their genome. Specifically, this means the development of tools, the creation of organized social groups, and the development of semiotic capacities sufficiently complex to create within the human mind, and within the intersubjective reality of human culture, not merely images of the world around us, but also concepts that engage questions of meaning and value. Which of these developments came first, or whether, as we suspect, they came more or less all at once as part of a unified phase transition, we cannot say with certainty.

The first stages of this "phase transition" are already visible to us in the behavior of various animal communities. There is significant evidence that dolphins and possibly even parrots have the capacity for symbolic communication. Canines and other carnivores have a highly developed band organization that permits them to cooperate effec-

---

1. I use the term "sapient" rather than "intelligent" in order to distinguish humanity (and any hypothetical comparable species) from hypothetical intelligent machines that may well match or surpass human beings in their capacity for formal abstraction and formal operations (e.g., mathematics) but which lack the capacity to engage questions of purpose, meaning, and value—questions that are, as we saw in the first chapter, embedded from the very beginning in the creative act.

tively in hunting animals far larger than themselves. And subhuman primates, especially the chimpanzees, have demonstrated the capacity for organization at all three levels: the use of tools, the formation of organized bands, and use of symbolic communication. Rather, what makes human beings distinctive is our insistence on asking "why?" and on discovering, in answer to this question, ever more complex ends to pursue, ends that are finite and contingent reflections of the transcendent end that lures us ever onward.

For some reason, the nature of which remains obscure, sometime around 35,000 BCE the rate of progress began to increase rapidly. There were only five major technological innovations between 4,000,000 and 100,000 BCE and only three between 100,000 and 35,000 BCE. But there were 16.5 such innovations between 35,000 and 10,000 B.C.E., and 15.5 between 10,000 and 7,000 BCE (Lenski 1982: 110). This is especially interesting in that 35,000 BCE also marks, very roughly, the point at which we begin to see rock art and cave paintings, phenomena that many scholars associate with the emergence of religious thought and thus engagement with fundamental questions (Heyd and Clegg 2005). While it is probably impossible to determine with any certainty the purpose of these paintings, this synchronicity suggests a deeply rooted association between the pursuit of wisdom and human progress generally.

Horticultural-Communitarian Societies

The most critical technological innovation in human history was, of course, the domestication of plants and animals. This process of domestication was not so much a triumph of human power over various plants and animals, which humans bent to their will, as it was a kind of symbiosis, which tapped into and extended the evolutionary dynamic that had led to the emergence of human beings in the first place. Recent research regarding both human evolution and the process of domestication has centered on the phenomenon of neoteny. Neoteny refers to the retention by a sexually mature organism of juvenile and even infantile physical and behavioral characteristics. Adult humans look like nothing so much as infant apes, just as domestic dogs resemble young wolves and domestic cattle the calves of their wild bovine ancestors. Neoteny apparently permits the extraordinarily rapid development of new, evolutionarily progressive characteristics. Among the most importance of these are curiosity and a tendency to abandon specialized for generalist behaviors, traits that would otherwise have taken thousands of generations of intentional breeding or millions of generations of random selection to achieve. Many ecologists now believe that the existence of human settlements, with their tendency to clear away wild plants and to accumulate piles of scrap food, in effect created a niche into which opportunistic members of various plant and animal species settled, and which created powerful forces that selected in favor of rapid neotenization (Budiansky 1992: 85–86).

The domestication of plants and animals, and the emergence of the horticultural mode of production, was not, therefore, so much a triumph of human control over nature as it was a development within nature itself of a more complex mode of organization, and one that advanced the survival interests of all of the species involved. Horticulture was part of the self-organizing movement of the cosmos from less complex to more complex forms. It represents the emergence within the cosmos of organisms capable of grasping the latent potential of matter, and working matter in such a way as to release that latent potential.

Humans now established permanent settlements, characterized by an emerging division of labor. Growing surplus permitted an increasingly large part of the population to be relieved from the responsibility to produce food. Specialists in various crafts emerged, as well as a priestly stratum, which organized more complex productive activities, and engaged in protoscientific study of the motion of the sun and stars, the rising and falling of the tides and of rivers, and other aspects of the natural environment that affected their people's survival. This was, in many ways, a remarkably productive period in human history.

> Before the agrarian revolution comparatively poor and illiterate communities had made an impressive series of contributions to man's progress. The two millennia immediately preceding 3,000 B.C. had witnessed discoveries in applied science that directly or indirectly affected the prosperity of millions of people and demonstrably furthered the biological welfare of our species by facilitating its multiplication. (Childe 1951: 181)

Among the discoveries of this period we should note

> artificial irrigation using canals and ditches; the plow, the harnessing of animal motive-power; the sail boat, wheeled vehicles; orchard husbandry; fermentation; the production and use of copper; bricks; the arch; glazing; the seal; and, in the earliest stages of the revolution—a solar calendar, writing, numerical notion and bronze. (Childe 1951: 180).

This rapid development of human social capacities was facilitated by the emergence of new socioeconomic forms, the most important of which was the village community, which gradually displaced the clan and the tribe as the basic units of social organization. The domestication of plants and animals made possible the establishment of permanent settlements that usually, though not always, included people drawn from different clans. This in turn facilitated the development of inter-clan relationships based on something other than marriage. Sometimes these relationships grew out of collaboration in the clearing of fields or the construction of simple public works such as the irrigation systems or ritual centers. At other times it was the need to mobilize the able-bodied adults of the village for warfare that catalyzed the emergence of inter-clan ties. In still other cases it was the religious cult itself that united members of different clans, as in the case of the various religious societies of the Hopi, Zuni, Keres, Tewa, and Towa. Because of the role of the village community in organizing production, we call these societies *communitarian*.

The village community was the effective owner of the land, which in most societies was parceled out to individual families for cultivation and periodically redistributed in order to insure a rough equality. Collective labor was not uncommon, and woodlands and grazing land were generally used, as well as held, in common. Mandel has collected extensive documentation of this phenomenon (Mandel 1968: 32–35).

There is widespread evidence that many if not most early horticultural communitarian societies were matrifocal if not matriarchal. This, at least, was the view taken by the first students of these societies—nineteenth-century theorists such as Bachofen, Morgan, and Engels (Engels 1880/1940). After falling out of favor for some time, this "primary matriarchy thesis" was revived during the 1970s by feminist scholars (Giambutas 1974; Stone 1976) and has been the focus of intense controversy ever since.

The evidence for the hypothesis is threefold. There is, first of all, the archeological evidence. Giambutas, for example, based her claims largely on archeological evidence from sites such as Catal Huyuk in Anatolia and other sites in Southwest Asia and Southeastern Europe. These sights, Giambutas, argues, show relatively little evidence of weapons or fortifications. There are relatively few rich burials and these are as likely to be of women as of men. The most common images, she says, are of pregnant women or of women with exaggerated sexual features. Given the fact that in such societies images are generally made for religious purposes, we can conclude that these are, in fact, statues of goddesses of some kind. And since religious symbols reflect the structure of the society that produced them, this must mean that women were at the very least held in high regard. Indeed, given the paucity of male figures, we might even conclude that they ruled.

Merlin Stone has extended this work by drawing extensively in ancient literary sources. These sources are of two types: mythic texts in which goddesses predominate and legends that speak directly of times and places where women ruled. The pivotal role of goddesses in the myths of Bronze and early Iron Age peoples is well documented. On the one hand, in most such societies there is a well defined male high god: Anu among the Sumerians, Amon-Ra among the Egyptians, or Zeus among the Greeks. On the other hand, it is often as not the goddesses who drive the action or, at the very least, serve as the principal teachers of advocates for humanity. The Mesopotamian Inanna and the Egyptian Au Set (which means "exceeding queen"), for example, seem to have functioned as authentic high gods, bearing titles such as "Great Goddess . . . Queen of Heaven, Lady of the High Place, Celestial Ruler, Lady of the Universe, Sovereign of the Heavens . . ." (Stone 1976: 22). As Ishtar, Inanna was the Morning Star and more generally the Goddess of the whole night sky. Au Set was the cosmic writer, whose pen directs the course of the world, librarian of the gods, a great physician and healer, and the one who established justice in the land (Daly 1984: 118; Stone 1976, 32). In the Epic of Gilgamesh, it is Ishtar who comforts humanity after the war god Enlil causes a great flood.

What is the relevance of these myths, which come from Bronze Age civilizations, for our understanding of the Neolithic? We know that religious symbols reflect the structures of the societies that produced them. We also know that Bronze Age civilizations were overwhelmingly—if not entirely uniformly—patriarchal. The argument is that these myths must have originated in the near Neolithic past of the great Bronze Age civilizations, in a time when women ruled or were at least equal with men.

There is also a whole complex of myths that record the displacement of the goddess by a male war god. Merlin Stone describes the incorporation of the Indo-European god Horus into the myths surrounding Isis.

> Hor, (later known as Horus to the Greeks) was described in various texts as fighting a ritual combat with another male deity known as Set . . . generally identified as the uncle or brother of Hor. The fight symbolized the conquest of Hor over Set . . .
>
> In Sanskrit the word *sat* means to destroy by hewing to pieces . . . It was Set who killed Osiris and cut his body into fourteen pieces. But it may be significant that the word Set is also defined as "queen" or "princess" in Egyptian. Au Set, known as Isis by the Greeks, is defined as "exceeding queen." In the myth of the combat Set tries to mate sexually with Horus; this is usually interpreted as being an insult. But the most primitive identity of the figure Set, who is also closely related to the serpent of darkness known as Zet, and often referred to by classical Greek writers as Typhon, the serpent of the Goddess Gaia, may once have been female . . . perhaps related to Ua Zit, the Great Serpent, the Cobra Goddess of Neolithic times. (Stone 1976: 89–90)

The final form of the myth of Isis and Osiris, in other words, actually encodes the defeat of the original form of Isis (Au Set or Ua Zit) by Horus, the sun god of the patriarchal Indo-European invaders who introduced kingship into Egypt.

Sometimes there is an explicit attempt to rationalize the displacement of the goddess in terms that might be acceptable to the peasantry. Inanna, for example, was said to have lost her royal scepter to Enki, who discovered how to build irrigation canals (Stone 1976: 83). In other cases the transition from a gynocentric to an androcentric pantheon is presented without much comment. In Hesiod, for example, it is Chasm or the Abyss—a vaguely female figure who is "first." She gives birth to Gaia, who in turn gives birth to Ouranos, who becomes her lover. Gaia and Ouranos give birth to Kronos and Rhea, who in turn give birth to

Zeus and Hera. We proceed, in other words, from a single female deity to a female/male pair in which the female has priority, to two male/female pairs, in the latter of which the female (Hera) has been reduced to clearly subordinate status.

We see this same memory of a transition between mother-right and father-right recorded in the *Orestaia*, which wrestles with the contradictions between kinship relations, which seem to have been principally a concern of women and to have been defended first and foremost by the female Furies, and the imperatives of the public arena of the *polis*, which was an exclusively male domain defended by Apollo. And the original statement of the settlement of this conflict, which was foundational for the identity of Athenian society, does not represent a total defeat for the Furies and the mother-right that they represent. On the contrary, Athena says to the Furies:

> Thou art mine elder, wiser then than I.
> Yet Zeus hath not denied me understanding.
> Find out a new race, other soil; yet here
> Your heart will be; I speak this for your warning.
> The tide of Time shall for my people roll
> With ever-mantling glory: thou shalt have
> Thy mansion here hard by Erectheus' house,
> And men and women come with frequent pomp
> And greater laud than the wide world can give.
> (Aeschylus *Eumenides* 848–69)

The Furies are invited to share the land with Athena, in a subaltern role, perhaps, but with honor nonetheless, something that marks the enduring significance of the archaic matriarchal tradition they represent.

Finally, the cult of the goddess plays an important role in the development of philosophy. Plato situates two of his most important dialogues, the *Republic* and the *Timaeus*, at festivals of the goddess, and wisdom, which philosophy serves, is increasingly personified as Sofia, the highest manifestation of the feminine dimension of God.

The legendary material is equally suggestive. Diodorus Siculus is typical in this regard. Writing of Egypt, he says that

> ... it was ordained that the queen should have greater power than the king and that among private persons the wife should

> enjoy authority over the husband, husbands agreeing in the marriage contract that they will be obedient in all things to their wives. (Diodorus Siculus in Stone 1976: 36)

Similarly in Ethiopia,

> All authority was vested in the women, who discharged every kind of public duty. The men looked after domestic affairs just as the women do among ourselves and did as they were told by their wives.... (Diodorus in Stone 1976: 35)

H. W. F. Saggs writes that "the status of women was certainly much higher in the early Sumerian city state than it subsequently became" (Saggs in 1976: 39). Heraclides Ponticus writes of the Lycians that "from of old they have been ruled by women" (in Stone 1976: 46). Indeed, this seems to have been the pattern throughout the Mediterranean basin.

> Among the Mediterraneans as a general rule society was built around the woman, even on the highest levels, where descent was in the female line. A man became king or chieftain only by formal marriage and his daughter, not his son succeeded so that the next chieftain was the youth who married his daughter ... Until the northerners arrived, religion and custom were dominated by the female principle. (Seltman in Stone 1976: 47)

The Amazons of ancient lore may well have been communities of women who banded together to resist the new patriarchal order (Stone 1976: 46).

The comparative ethnographic evidence in support of the thesis is also compelling. A majority of horticultural communitarian societies do, for example, have matrilineal kinship systems. This does not, to be sure, imply by itself that women held power. But the fact is that in many, if not most, of the indigenous societies of the Americas the women also had effective control of the land, which was the principal resource. This is true, for example both of the Iroquois and of many of the Puebloan peoples, especially the Keres, the Hopi, and the Zuni. Among the Iroquois, the women cultivated the land themselves; among some of the Puebloan groups, the men cultivated it and were conceived of as laboring for their wife's clan. While the official leaders of these societies were mostly male, there is some evidence that this may not always have been the case, or that official office may not correspond to effective power. Among the Iroquois, the clan mothers stand behind the men when they sit in council and "advise" them. Among the Aztecs, one of the two highest officials—the chief priest—was known as the "snake woman." While always a man in historical times, the name suggests this office may once have been held by women. Given the fact that it corresponds to the role of cacique or "inside chief" among the Puebloan peoples, it is quite possible that many of the horticultural societies of southwestern North America and Mexico may once have had female priestly rulers (Eggan 1973).

What we know is that these societies, while they were not without powerful male deities, also had goddesses who look suspiciously like the Mediterranean goddesses of wisdom and fertility. Thus, Spider Woman, the great goddess of southwestern North America, is known in Keres as Sussistinako, or "thinking woman," "who thought outward into space and what she thought became reality" (Tyler 1964: 89). In Hopi she is known as *Huruing Wuhti*, or "hard beings woman," and is credited, in some accounts at least, both with creating the universe and with instructing humanity in the arts of civilization (Tyler 1964: 82ff.).

There is, in other words, very strong evidence to support the primary matriarchy thesis. There have, however, been some credible criticisms as well. This criticism has centered on the interpretation of purported goddess images and of the archeological evidence used to support the claim that Neolithic societies were peaceful and egalitarian. Much of this concerns the interpretation of the archeological evidence. Bryan Hayden, for example, charges that Giambutas in particular has been too liberal interpreting various symbols as evidence of goddess worship.

> These symbols encompass a wide range of phenomena, including: oblique parallel lines, horizontal parallel lines, vertical parallel lines, chevrons, lozenges, zigzags, wavy lines, meanders, circles, ovals, spirals, dots, crescents, U's, crosses, swirls, caterpillars, double axes, chrysalises, horns butterflies, birds, eggs, fish, rain, cows, dogs, does, stags, snakes, toads, turtles, hedgehogs, bees, bulls, bears, goats, pigs, pillars, and sexless linear or masked figures. One wonders what is left. Over 10 years ago, I drew attention to this deficiency in methodology (Hayden 1986) and to the fact that at least some of these forms are more generally associated with male deities (pillars, stags,

bulls, snakes). Given this poor quality foundation of the basic data, it is difficult to take Gimbutas' subsequent claims very seriously. (Hayden 1998)

More important, Hayden points out, Giambutas ignores the most important image in the Neolithic societies of southwestern Asia and southeastern Europe: the bull, which is the image of masculine strength *par excellence.*

Hayden also finds fault with the idea that Neolithic societies were peaceful and egalitarian. The Neolithic Pre-Pottery B Culture expanded, he notes, at the rate of one kilometer per year from the Near East towards northwestern Europe—too fast a rate for the expansion to have been peaceful. The arrowheads found at such sites are of quality generally used only in warfare. And Giambutas's claims notwithstanding, many sites have fortifications, weapons caches, mass killings (including human sacrifice), and burials rich in prestige goods (Hayden 1998).

What are we to make of this debate? We should begin by pointing out that Hayden and the other critics of the primary matriarchy thesis are involved in some very significant obfuscation, even if this obfuscation has in some measure been made possible by a lack of conceptual and terminological clarity on the part of the advocates of the thesis. Thus, while Giambutas may well claim images for the goddess that do not really belong to her, Hayden does the same. While there are, for example, *obvious* images of bulls in Neolithic art, there are also many images that could be bulls or could be, for example, a moon above the sun. And we know that even goddesses—Isis for example—sometimes appeared in headdresses that could be described as horned.

Second, while Giambutas and her associates may sometimes have suggested otherwise, the primary matriarchy thesis in no way requires that warfare or even human sacrifice were unknown. On the contrary, the very institution of the year king seems to presuppose both, together with an attempt to limit the gradually increasing importance of warfare as an economic strategy. Part of the difficulty here comes from the insistence that warfare and patriarchy were imported into Europe and the Mediterranean by Indo-European invaders at the beginning of the Bronze Age and imposed on peaceful indigenous societies of non-Indo-European stock. This seems to be a mistake. While it is likely that the Indo-Europeans, coming as they did from less favorable ecological niches, would have been more inclined to opt for warfare and raiding as economic strategies, we would also expect that warfare would gradually have increased in Europe and the Mediterranean as the more favorable niches filled up and competition increased. Indeed, the fact that matriarchal communitarian societies eventually gave way to patriarchy and the tributary mode of production means that we should expect, at the end of the Neolithic, to see evidence of just precisely such a transition.

The primary matriarchy thesis, in other words, has considerable merit. We cannot say with certainty that *all* Neolithic societies were once matriarchal or that those that were were peaceful and egalitarian. What we can say is that there is good reason to believe that women did exercise more authority in these societies than in others—and that later gynocentric myths must be interpreted in this light.

Participation in the village community, matriarchal or not, provided a basis in experience for grasping the universe as an organized totality. Day to day collaboration in the work of bearing and raising children, growing food and producing tools, building the complex social relationships necessary to carry out these tasks, and investigating the latent potential of the various forms of the material universe made the village quite literally a microcosm of the organizing process that constitutes the universe itself. Each of the tasks of daily life provided not only a window on, but an actual means of participating in, the work of the cosmos.

Humanity's emerging vision of the universe as an organized totality was symbolized in countless different ways. Nearly all, however, reflected an ordering to wisdom and to fertility or generativity—and a conviction that these two principles were intimately bound together. It is increasingly the human rather than the plant or animal that provides the symbolism for representation of the divine. Ancestor worship becomes increasingly central, reflecting the enduring importance of kinship ties, but also a marked advanced in understanding kinship as a system of relationships among human beings. It is no doubt also from this period that the memory of "culture heroes" derives—gods, demigods, or rulers who taught humanity the art of civilization: the Chinese Shen-nung for example (Chang 1963), the *katchinas* of the Hopi (Waters 1963), or the Greek Prometheus and the other Titans.

It is interesting to note that while most communitarian societies have some concept of a high god, their operative religious structure is radically polytheistic, with high gods, demiurges, gods of various natural phenomena, and culture heros all participating in important ways in the mythic cycles, and all sharing in the community's worship. As Durkheim suggests (1911/1965) the emerging concept of a high god probably reflects some sort of dawning awareness of other peoples, and thus of a social reality that transcends the tribe. The actual activity of organizing society, however, remains the work of the community as a whole. There is no warlord who alone organizes the society. To the extent that communitarian societies did worship a high deity, this deity was (as we have already suggested) more likely to be a goddess than a god.

What does this tell us about the civilizational ideal of horticultural, communitarian societies? The universe is understood as in some sense the expression of an underlying, organizing principle, often symbolized as a divine creatrix. But it is also a collective process incorporating the diverse efforts of a variety of different kinds of beings. Organization is immanent to matter itself, just as the capacity to give birth to new life is immanent in the Great Mother who gives life to all and does not require the intervention of an ordering power from on high. The hierarchization of the various deities under the mantle of the Great Mother is less a mark of their subordination to her than of their integration into an organized cosmic totality. The task of humans is, quite literally, to participate in the divine by means of their own creative activity, an activity centered first and foremost on understanding and nurturing the creative potentials of matter itself. Thus the link between wisdom and *techne* that is characteristic of these societies.

Urban Civilization

If we understand communitarian societies correctly, their dynamism naturally pointed beyond itself, to systems of villages grouped around ritual centers and eventually to cities, just as the largely oral wisdom traditions of communitarian societies point beyond themselves towards writing. It is just precisely this claim, however, that is contested by modern and postmodern theory alike. For modern social theory, *civilization*, understood in the narrower sense of urbanization and writing, are the product of some combination of demographic pressure, technological innovation, trade, and conquest. While it is generally regarded as a positive phenomenon, it is also regarded as representing a sharp break with the relative egalitarianism of horticultural, communitarian societies, one marked by the emergence of stratification and even exploitation, depending on the particular strain of modern theory in question (liberal or socialist). Bryan Hayden's views are typical in this regard.

> Civilizations and even chiefdoms simply cannot and do not function in an egalitarian fashion. Hierarchical control is their *defining* feature and no amount of philosophical or idyllic reverie seems capable of changing this characteristic in the real world. The topic is too vast to deal with in detail here, but I know of no ethnographic or archaeological examples where any credible claim of a nonhierarchical chiefdom or state exists. In the European Neolithic, fortified sites were often at the top of local settlement hierarchies indicating at the very least the existence of political hierarchies, while their sheer size (up to 300 hectares) and complexity indicates centralized political control by elites (Scarre 1984: 242, 335; Milisauskas and Kruk 1989; Anthony 1995; Demoule and Perles 1993). On the basis of community sizes, settlement hierarchies, wealth discrepancies, and craft specializations, archaeologists do not hesitate to ascribe a chiefdom status to the most important Old European sites described by Gimbutas, and a state level of organization to the major centers on Minoan Crete. These are some of the most certain conclusions archaeologists have established in the past half-century. Describing Neolithic Old Europe as egalitarian and non-hierarchical is simply inconsistent with all the current ethnographic and archaeological data. For an archaeologist, maintaining that complex societies can develop without socioeconomic inequalities or hierarchies or hierarchies is on a par with arguing that the earth is flat or arguing that the world was created without the process of evolution. (Hayden 1998)

Most accounts are also at pains to point out that writing was used, at least initially, largely to keep economic records and had little to do with the pursuit of wisdom or other higher civilizational aims.

Postmodern theory, both "secularist" and religious, is even more critical, ultimately calling into question the value of the human civilizational project itself. This view was especially prominent in the neo-populist socialism of the 1970s and 1980s, which sometimes regarded civilization as itself inherently oppressive, for the simple reason that it involved the extraction of surplus from the countryside (Miranda 1971/1980), an approach that reached its most extreme manifestation in the policy of the Khmer Rouge (and that Miranda himself ultimately rejected). Religious critics such as Jacques Ellul (Ellul 1975) go further, arguing that the city represents humanity's ultimately hopeless and self-defeating bid for autonomy.

Postmodern approaches to the development of writing similarly stress the fact that it creates new structures of oppression. The first such structure is that of logocentrism (Derrida 1967a/1974). Logocentrism is not a product of writing as such, but of a certain attitude towards it, which regards it as a representation of speech. For Derrida and the deconstructionists, this reflects a metaphysics of presence, in which all signs point beyond themselves to a signified, which is their *meaning*, what is really real, and in which all meanings ultimately point towards a transcendental signifier, God or the Logos, which constitutes and governs them. In this context writing becomes a kind of theurgic magic in which the transcendental signifier is captured and manipulated, constituting a technology of domination. This fundamental logocentric structure is reinforced by the constitution of a literate intelligentsia and the fact that writing facilitates the emergence of fixed meanings and thus official, legitimating ideologies. This is by contrast to pre-literate cultures in which everyone participates in creating meanings, which remain fluid as oral traditions pass from one voice to another. Finally, literate societies invariably believe themselves superior to preliterate societies, so that writing becomes yet another way of legitimating conquest and domination.

Finally, there is the fact that even if urban civilization is *possible* apart from conquest and exploitation, most actually existing urban civilizations not only engaged in but were constituted by these practices. What does this mean for our larger argument?

Let us address these arguments in turn, looking first at the question of the *origins* of urbanization and writing, and then at their *value*, and finally at the contributions, if any, of those urban civilizations that *were* constituted by warfare.

With respect to the question of urban origins, two distinctions are in order. First, while urbanization clearly *was* associated with all of the factors that modern theory cites: growing demographic pressure, technological innovations such as the plow and metallurgy, the expansion of trade, and the emergence of conquest as an economic development strategy, there is significant evidence that these processes were layered over another, deeper and more profound dynamic. The principal evidence of this is the existence of societies that were developing towards full urbanization, but largely because of the attractive, organizing power of a ritual center rather than because of demographic pressure or the development of agriculture, trade, or conquest. This form of organization we call the *archaic*, because it reflects an ordering of humanity to a well-defined first principle or *arche*. Villagers provided grain; priests studied the stars and created calendars that told the peasants when to plant and when to harvest. They also stored grain to provide for the people in times of famine, coordinated the construction of irrigation complexes, and—most importantly—provided a framework of meaning and values in the context of which cooperation and the production and surrender of surplus made sense. This appears to have been the structure of the earliest urban settlements in Mesopotamia, the Nile Valley, and the Huang He Valley, as well as later developments in places like Chaco and Stonehenge, which yield very little evidence of fortification, *systematic* violence, or exploitation.[2] It should be noted, furthermore, that at least some of these societies used writing for purposes other than commerce and administration: witness the Chinese oracle bones, used for divination, and the records of astronomic observations at sites such as Chaco.

Second, it is important to distinguish between differences in status, differences in power, and differences in economic position (Weber 1921/1968). It is also necessary to distinguish, when considering economic inequalities, between differences in consumption levels and the existence of exploitative structures. It is true, for example, that social

---

2. The Indus Valley represents a somewhat different case. Here, there is little evidence of warfare or fortification, but also no monumental religious architecture. Either we are missing the religious monuments because they are so different from what we find elsewhere (we do, for example, find tanks or pools, which might have been used for rituals centered on water and on the river) or else we are dealing with what amount to large market towns.

complexity requires conscious leadership, and precisely to the extent that the leaders actually are more capable than the rest of the population, they will attract greater respect. Their work may, furthermore, require greater access to resources. Priests require access to sanctuaries and ritual objects; experts in empirical lore of various sorts (who are often identical with the priests in communitarian societies) will acquire a variety of objects in the course of their researches. Political leaders, in the course of organizing people, also organize their resources to which they inevitably gain some preferential access. All of these leadership activities require some release from the obligation to produce food. In all these ways complex societies are inevitably hierarchical and involve the centralization of surplus. The question is just how the surplus is centralized and just how it is used. Is the surplus extracted coercively or noncoercively? Is it invested in a way that develops broad sectors of the population or is it squandered on warfare and luxury consumption? There is no reason a society could not have existed that was both hierarchal and nonexploitative.

Finally, the fact that many urban civilizations did emerge out of warfare and conquest does not mean that warfare and conquest were the driving force in their development. On the contrary, warfare and conquest are themselves ways of seeking Being. Not all human communities were endowed with a fertile ecosystem that made it possible to generate a significant surplus by means of agriculture. Such societies roamed the steppes with their herds, periodically raiding established settlements. They generally retained a tribal and patriarchal structure, their principal deities taking on increasingly warlike qualities. Indeed, it is such societies that have generally cultivated a warrior ideal in its pure form. Where warfare is the principal source of sustenance, the gods themselves are understood as warriors, and human beings achieve divinity, if at all, on the battlefield.

These tribes must have grown increasingly envious of those who lived in the emerging urban communities. It is in this context that we must understand the rapid spread of warfare and conquest around the year 3000 BCE.

> In the course of a few centuries the villages of the plain fell under the domination of walled cities on whose rulers the possession of bronze weapons, chariots and slaves conferred a

measure of superiority to which no community could aspire.
(Watson 1961 in Lenski 1982)

The story was much the same throughout India, in the Mediterranean basin, and in Africa. As Gerhard Lenski puts it

> For the first time in . . . history, people found the conquest of other people a profitable alternative to the conquest of nature . . . One might say that bronze was to the conquest of people what plant cultivation was to the conquest of nature (1982: 145).

Victorious warlords put the villages that they conquered under tribute, forcing the villagers to perform unpaid labor on their fields or to build temples, palaces, and fortifications. They imposed taxes, or distributed village lands to their retainers, who imposed rents. Warlords, meanwhile, continued to fight each other, with the strongest eventually emerging as monarchs and emperors.

This new form of social organization, which we call *tributary*, represented the only way that the nomadic peoples of the steppes could gain access to—and participate in—the development of human civilization. Its emergence was neither a necessary evil, something required in order to extract surplus from indolent peasants who would otherwise have consumed it, nor a mark of the intrinsic evil of human nature and something that marks the human civilizational project as inherently sinful from the beginning. On the contrary, it represent an organic expression of the underlying drive of humanity towards ever higher degrees of participation in Being, simply under the less favorable conditions created by a difficult ecological niche.

This brings us, in turn, to the question of the value of urbanization and the associated phenomenon of writing. As we noted above, modern theory values urbanization, but largely as a stage along the way in humanity's gradual rise to sovereignty over nature and ultimate technopolitical divinization. Postmodern theory, on the other hand, is anxious to defend the values of the pre-urban and pre-literate, and treats the city and writing both as vain expressions of humanity's drive towards sovereignty and as instruments of domination.

We would like to suggest a very different approach. Both cities and writing add something vitally important to the universe. As we have noted above, the centralization of surplus by cities does not, in and of itself, constitute exploitation. The question is how the surplus is extracted and how it is used. Early urban centers, *even many of those formed by conquest*, provided important services to the peasant populations that supported them, including irrigation systems too large to be managed by a single village, calendars that told peasants when to plant, and a wealth of artistic, scientific, and religious knowledge. And far from representing a bid for human autonomy, cities grew up around temples and other ritual centers that acknowledged their foundational ordering to the divine. If these religious forms do not meet the standards of Protestant critics like Ellul, then the reason is theological and not sociological.

Writing, similarly, represents a precondition for the full and open engagement with fundamental questions that define human beings as *sapient*. More specifically, it is essential to the development of formal definitions and thus to the formal arguments that define a dialectical ascent to the first principle. This is, of course, just precisely the sort of discourse that deconstructionists attack as logocentric. The *existence* of a transcendental signifier is a philosophical and not a sociological question and will be addressed elsewhere. For now, suffice it to say that even if this is a sort of theurgic magic, it does not follow that it is inherently oppressive. On the contrary, the development of formal argument is also the precondition for open public debate around fundamental questions of meaning and value. Writing, in other words, opens the theurgic magic involved in seeking wisdom to wider public scrutiny and eventually makes it a kind of open source code that can be accessed by everyone. While these developments come much later, with the Axial Age (800–200 BCE) and with the extension of literacy in the later Silk Road and modern eras, development of writing represents a critical first step.

Neither the creation of a literate intelligentsia nor the fixing of meanings compromises the positive contributions of writing. On the contrary, the creation of a literate intelligentsia sets the stage for a struggle for access to the full and complete literacy that remains the province and privilege of this intelligentsia, and thus for the multiplication of intelligentsias—priestly, scribal, philosophical, scientific, humanistic, literary, etc.—and the development of a more complex public arena. Precisely because it fixes meanings, writing sets the stage for ideological conflict and thus the emergence of an open, pluralistic, public arena. Finally, writing creates a standard language that permits communication across various dialects, expanding the scope of the public arena. This does not, however, mean that it is necessary to devalue the band, tribal, and communitarian (i.e., preliterate) societies that are thereby brought into the *oikoumene*. On the contrary, nonurban, nonliterate societies not only enrich the diversity of human civilization, but also constitute an ongoing reservoir out of which new pathways of development, urban and literate or not, can emerge.

There is, finally, the question of the distinctive contribution of tributary societies to the human civilizational project. First, this form of civilization cultivated, in a way that more pacific communitarian and archaic structures could not, the virtues of the irascible appetites— our capacity to strive for things difficult to obtain, or to contend with things that are dangerous or harmful. Second, while we certainly reject the more extreme claims advanced by the religions of some tributary societies—e.g., the Aztec and the Aryan—that creation comes about through destruction, the experience of warfare as the foundation of civilization cultivated an appreciation of the creative role of conflict and contradiction and its critical role in clearing away the room necessary for new growth.

These civilizations also developed a very distinct civilizational ideal—one the traces of which endure to this day. If communitarian societies aspired to participation in the creative activity of their gods, tributary societies aspired to actual *individual* divinization—something that is apparent from an examination of an epic like *Gilgamesh* or the funeral practices of the Egyptians. There were, to be sure, real limitations. Divinity was understood simply as immortality. Only the ruling classes, and sometimes only the king himself, could aspire to it. And the *means* by which this divinity was to be achieved was, furthermore, sacrifice—a ritual form of the violence that actually sustained tributary societies themselves. We cannot understand the modern willingness to pursue a scientific and technological utopia at the cost of millions of lives and centuries of brutal exploitation apart from the background of this earlier ideal.[3] Even so, the drive towards divinization, in the sense

3. The tributary societies that developed much later in the Americas—and especially the Aztecs—represent a distinctive variant of this pattern. The underlying instability of their empire lead the Aztecs to believe that permanence was impossible even for the gods. Their civilizational ideal was centered on sustaining, for as long as possible, the ultimately doomed divine economy that sustained the universe, an economy founded

of seeking Being, is itself constitutive of humanity, and bringing it to consciousness represents a real contribution.

This said, it is clear that by sometime between 1500 and 1000 BCE—what is traditionally called the Late Bronze Age—most of the tributary societies of Eurasia had entered a period of crisis. There were a number of factors involved in this crisis. First, tributary structures proved to be a nearly insuperable obstacle to the development of human social capacities. While there is some evidence for the use of bronze to produce plowshares, the supply was always strictly limited. Bronze production depended on the mining of tin, a rare element, the trade of which always remained a ruling class monopoly. Fearful that the peasants would produce weapons that could be used against them, or reasoning that their wealth could be increased more easily through warfare than through investment in agricultural production, the ruling class blocked the extensive development of bronze agricultural technology. This is why the promise that they might someday "beat swords into ploughshares" evoked such powerful passions in the peasants of Israel and Judah.

Indeed, the tributary mode of production put a real brake on technological development in general. The ruling class was able to extract almost the entire surplus product from the direct producers. This had the effect of removing any incentive for innovation on the part of the peasantry, which knew that it would not benefit from its own increased productivity. In many cases, of course, the peasants were ground down below the subsistence level and had neither the time nor the energy to innovate. The ruling class, on the other hand, invested its energies in extensive accumulation through conquest—extending the area subject to its taxing power—rather than intensive accumulation based on improved agricultural techniques. Warriors and priests increasingly held all forms of manual labor in contempt. The two thousand years after the advent of the warlord state

> say from 2,600 to 600 B.C. produced few contributions of . . . importance to human progress . . . They are the "decimal nota-

---

on sacrifice by the *gods* and fed by a steady diet of still beating human hearts (see Brundage 1985). We might call such societies post-tributary. People live the tributary while no longer really believing in its efficacy. This is by analogy with postmodernism, in which people live modernity while no longer really believing in the modern ideal of transcending finitude by means of scientific and technological progress.

tion" of Babylonia (about 2,000 B.C.); an economic method for the smelting of iron on an industrial scale (1,400 B.C.); a truly alphabetic script (1,300 B.C.) and aqueducts for supplying water to cities (700 B.C.). (Childe 1951)

The result was a global (or rather pan-Eurasian) period of crisis and decline that lasted from roughly 1200 to 800 BCE. In some places the collapse was complete—the Mycenaean civilization of Greece, for example, disappeared and along with it both urban life and writing. The Indus Valley civilization seems to have suffered a crisis of similar proportions. In other places the crises were less severe. Egypt and Mesopotamia, for example, simply declined enough to allow a new form of social organization—the revolutionary communitarian society of Ancient Israel (Gottwald 1979)—to emerge in the Syro-Palestinian corridor. And China seems to have suffered little more than a dynastic crisis.

Axial Civilizations

The Axial Age

It is against the background of this crisis that we must understand the Axial Age, which above all represents a revival of the civilizational impulse beginning around the year 800 BCE. We noted above that the modernist narrative treats this period as a kind of early, partially abortive attempt at secularization. We will see that the reality was quite different.

In order to understand why, we need to begin by looking at what was happening at the technological and economic levels. The Axial Age was set into motion, first and foremost, by the emergence of specialized agriculture and crafts production, the development of which continues up into the early modern era. In the Mediterranean Basin this meant, above all, oil, wine, and the pottery in which to store and transport these agrarian products (Anderson 1974; Ste. Croix 1982), though there is some evidence that the Greeks also exported the occasional sophist for the amusement of Indian rulers (Thapar 2002: 178). China produced silk (Frank 1998); India traded in pepper and other spices, teak and ebony, and cotton textiles (Thapar 2002). Southeast Asia entered the system largely as an exporter of spices and specialty woods.

Peripheries such as the Horn of Africa and Southern Arabia exported frankincense. Gold and textiles came from West Africa. Porcelain and tea entered the system later from India and China.

Initially the development of specialized agriculture seems to have taken place under the sponsorship of archaic or tributary structures. In Greece, for example, civilization seems to have revived around tribal and inter-tribal sanctuaries that, because they drew pilgrims for seasonal festivals, also became important market centers (Snodgrass 1980). Elsewhere, where civilization had not collapsed altogether, tributary states sponsored investment in these new products (Thapar 2002, 137–279). But in the long run specialized agriculture meant the emergence of markets—first local, then regional, and eventually "global" (i.e., Afro-Eurasian) in scope. Increasingly, investment decisions were dictated by the complex interplay of supply and demand. Thales of Miletus, for example, who is generally credited with taking the first steps towards the development of an abstract mathematics, also discovered the law of supply and demand. Foreseeing an unusually good crop of olives one year, he secured control of every olive press in his region, and then demanded monopoly prices for their use—though at least one story suggests that having made his theoretical point he relented and let the presses at their "fair" or "natural" price (Turnbull 1956: 79–82). Archaic and tributary structures became subordinated to what eventually, with the completion of the Silk Road around 200 BCE, became a global petty commodity system in which resources were allocated, at least in large measure, by a global market in luxury goods.[4]

---

4. There is a vigorous debate regarding the point at which an integrated "world economy" or "world system" first emerged (Frank and Gills 1993). In its original form "world systems theory" attributed the formation of a world economy to the European conquest of Africa, the Americas, and Asia (Wallerstein 1974, 1980, 1989), a conquest that was regarded as the origin of the current poverty and underdevelopment of the "Third World." Gradually, however, as scholars began to overcome their Eurocentrism, it became apparent that a world system incorporating all of Eurasia and much of Africa already existed long before the European conquests (Abu-Lughod 1989). Andre Gunder Frank, originally a proponent of the view that the creation of a unified world system was a result of the European conquests in the sixteenth century, now argues that the existence of global (i.e., Eurasian) trade networks can be traced back some 5000 years (Frank and Gills 1992) and has argued that the Chinese in fact retained a dominant role in the system until roughly the time of the Industrial Revolution (Frank 1993). He also rejects the notion of "capitalism" as a useful way of distinguishing the modern world system from its predecessors. While I think Frank does a good job of

It is important to be clear what is meant by a petty commodity system. On the one hand, this system must be distinguished from one in which there is trade—even a substantial quantity of trade—but in which resource allocation is still primarily driven by the decisions of some centralizing authority, such as a temple complex or a sacral monarchy. We now know that there were significant trade relations between many of the great civilizations of the Bronze Age—Mesopotamia and the Indus Valley, for example. It is not, however, correct to speak as Andre Gunder Frank now does (Frank and Gills 1992, 1993) of a 5000-year-old world system, in the sense of a market structure, that *regulated* resource allocation. For the most part, resource allocation in these societies took place through the extraction of surplus, through religious or coercive means, from dependent peasant communities, and its redistribution by temple or state structures, not through the mediation of a market in which a large number of producers responded to market forces. It is the emergence of authentic market forces, documented, for example, by Thales's decision to buy up all the oil presses and extract monopoly rents, which marks the emergence of a petty commodity *system*.

Petty commodity production differs from capitalism, on the other hand, in that there is a market in goods and services, but not in labor-power or capital. Once again, this does not mean that there is no wage labor or usury. Certainly there were. But these forms are marginal and secondary. The organization of labor remains either coercive—tributary forms persist, for example and are supplemented by chattel slavery—or else peasant and artisanal, and most borrowing is for the purpose of covering expenses either on the part of the peasantry or on the part of

---

showing the long history of global trade, I also believe that he misses three important transitions. First, beginning around 800 BCE we see the development of local and regional trade networks that actually begin to shape what is produced. This is apparent by the recognition of the laws of supply and demand by thinkers such as Thales of Miletus. By around 200 BCE these networks have effectively linked together all of Afro-Eurasia, from Mali, Iberia, and Britain all the way to China (Bentley 1993). These two transitions represent the advent of local and regional petty commodity production: i.e., a system in which resource allocation is shaped by the existence of a global market in luxury goods. Finally, between 1500 and 1800 we witness the gradual emergence of a new system, capitalism, in which not only goods and services but also labor power itself has become a commodity. The construction of capitalism cannot be said to be complete, however, until the full development of capital markets in the twentieth century, which makes capital a commodity as well.

the ruling classes, and is not a source of capital. This means that while individual producers, large and small, are beginning to engage in an economically rational calculus, they are not dependent on a pool of investors who require that they guarantee the highest possible rate of return on investments.

Politically, this was a period of fragmentation. The Hellenic *poleis* were, first and foremost, sanctuaries become market towns that extracted surplus from their hinterlands by religious means or later by means of exchange rather than by coercion. Debt servitude and chattel slavery were later developments, which depended in part, at least, on the absence of a state structure that could provide effective economic regulation (Snodgrass 1980; Anderson 1974; de Ste. Croix 1982). Small states prevailed in areas that, like China and the Fertile Crescent, had previously been dominated by large empires. Northern India was just undergoing what seems to have been a primary process of urbanization, largely independent of the earlier Indus Valley or Sarasvati Civilization, which in any case did not extend east into the Gangetic Plain, north in to the Himalayan foothills, or south into the Deccan or the peninsula. Some of these states were *gana-sanghas*, a sort of republic in which power was held by the senior lineages of what was still in part a tribally organized pastoral-raiding society that had only partly adopted agriculture. Others were small kingdoms (Thapar 2002: 98–173). Where larger tributary structures persisted they gradually altered their economic strategies, seeking to tax trade rather than direct production and thus to capture for themselves a portion of what was becoming a very healthy commerce.

The emergence of specialized agriculture and crafts production and of petty commodity production offered to humanity an extraordinary new opportunity. By using the principle of comparative advantage it was possible for distant regions to profit from trade with each other, and thus grow rich without the systematic exploitation of either their own populations or their trade partners. Such an outcome, however, required conscious leadership and intervention into the marketplace. The spontaneous tendency was towards rapid economic differentiation, as those with better land and better access to markets grew rich and those less well endowed grew poor. Peasants, who in many places had just been emancipated from tributary exploitation, found themselves falling into debt peonage and losing access to their land altogether.

Nouveau riche elements who cared nothing for the traditional obligations between classes challenged sacral monarchs and priestly elites for power, so that political structures lost their integrity altogether (Anderson 1974; de Ste. Croix 1982; Chaney 1986, 1993).

Life in a market society is, furthermore, alienating as well as liberating. People experience the society—and thus the universe as a whole—as a system of only externally related atoms (individuals) without any obvious ordering to a common end. The result was the emergence of radically skeptical and materialistic ideologies such as Hellenic atomism and Sophism (Collins 1998: 86–89, 145–48), the Indian Caravaka school (Chaterjee 1954: 56–64), and Chinese Legalism (Collins 1998: 148–55), all of which restricted the scope of human knowledge to objects of sense perception, denied the ultimate meaningfulness of the universe and the existence (or at least the actual supremacy) of the gods, and regarded morality as at best a set of conventions necessary for humans to live together and at worst as simply a way of legitimating particular social interests (Mansueto 1998b, 1999, 2000, 2002b). These ideologies effectively disarmed the people, giving them no moral leverage against their oppressors.

This is the common social context of all the "Axial Age breakthroughs." Where the great tributary empires of the Bronze Age had used religious meaning to legitimate exploitation, allowing the people to appeal above the heads of their rulers to the gods those rulers claimed as their patrons, petty commodity production called meaning itself into question, making it the central problem that constituted Axial Civilizations. Humanity's principal wisdom traditions, which all flow out of this period, are simply different ways of approaching this problem: different ways of answering the question of meaning.

This common context led to some common patterns. First, as we have noted, meanings that were previously shared and taken for granted became problematic, partly because trade brought societies with different myths into contact with each other, but more importantly because life in an emerging petty commodity society undercut the basis in experience for shared meanings and engendered atomism and skepticism. But even where skepticism did not dominate, old stories had to be retold in new ways if they were to continue to be meaningful. Thus the transition from myth, for which meaning is taken for granted, to literature, for which it is contested.

Second, Axial Age societies experienced a process of religious rationalization, as imaginative discourse generally (myth but also literature), which approaches fundamental questions through images and stories, was supplemented by philosophy, which uses concepts and arguments. This was also the result of the emergence of petty commodity production, which gave people the experience of society, and thus of the universe, as a system of quantities (prices) and led eventually to the emergence of an abstract mathematics. One sees this in the way the divine was conceived. At the beginning of the Axial Age (e.g., for Homer) the gods are characters in a story, with fully developed personalities. A bit later, for Hesiod, they are personified natural forces. Still later, they appear as natural forces without personification (e.g., in the natural philosophers), and are eventually described by mathematical terms such as the One (Anaximenes) or the Infinite (Xenophanes).

Third, Axial Age societies underwent a process of religious democratization. The much-vaunted democratic revolutions of Ancient Greece, for example, were as much struggles for full cultic participation as they were for political participation. Indeed the two were *inseparable* (cf. Milbank 1989, referring to the French traditionalist Ballenche). Thus, in the wake of these struggles, the *archontes*, who were first and foremost religious leaders, were elected, the secrets of access to deification, originally the province of *eupatrid* families who believed themselves descended from the gods, were now accessible to all through mystery cults, and the business of interpreting religious traditions, historically the work of hereditary priesthoods, was now thrown open to philosophers, poets, dramatists, etc.

Parallel developments, furthermore, took place in India and China. Witness the emergence of Upanishadic Hinduism, Jainism, and Buddhism, which contested establish Vedic norms, took a more abstract approach to the sacred, and opened up full religious participation and even leadership to those who were not Brahmins. And witness the Confucian and Taoist rationalization of Chou religious ideas such as *tian* and divinization texts such as the *I Ching* and the retheorization of nobility as a matter of virtue rather than birth.

From here patterns diverge, yielding distinct civilizational ideals. Israel, which had come into being as a result of a peasant revolt during the crisis of the Late Bronze Age (Gottwald 1979)—a revolt that re-established communitarian and egalitarian social structures—gave birth to a series of prophets who at once called the people back to their revolutionary heritage, but did so using an increasingly abstract language, eventually giving birth to the name YHWH—the causative form of the verb "to be." Some of these movements advocate a return to the structures of the premonarchic period; others argue for a monarchy that is faithful to the revolutionary values of earliest Israel but that can protect the people effectively against foreign oppressors as well. In either case, however, we witness the emergence of a civilization that is ordered to Being as such and seeks being first and foremost in the just act and in the struggle for a just social order (Gottwald 1979; Chaney 1986, 1993).

In China, the principal Axial Age breakthrough also took as its point of departure an earlier uprising at the end of the Bronze Age—the one that had brought to power the reforming Chou dynasty. The movement that eventually became known as Confucianism argued for a return to the principles of that dynasty. Countervailing movements such as Taoism were more skeptical about the possibilities of a "just" monarchy and put forward alternative approaches to fundamental questions of meaning and value. What eventually becomes the dominant Confucian ideal is ordered to realizing the mandate of heaven (*tian*), which is the creative power behind the universe, by means of ethical conduct and harmonious social relationships. The countervailing ideals—Taoist and later Buddhist (see below)—subordinate *tian* or the creative to the unlimited or to emptiness and seek peace in withdrawal, detachment, or nonaction (Gernet 1985; Williams 1989; Yao 2000).

In India, during the early part of the Axial Age, we witness a gradual rationalization of the Vedic tradition as the Vedic gods gradually give way to a more abstract concept of Brahman and as the focus on animal sacrifice yields to a doctrine of ascetic, internal sacrifice. The Brahmin monopoly on religious leadership is challenged by these ascetics, something that leads first to the development of the Jaina and Buddhist traditions and eventually to a popular Puranic Hinduism that allows the Brahmins to find a new place for themselves in a complex, pluralistic tradition that speaks more adequately than the Vedas had to the interests of warriors, merchants, peasants, and even outcastes. The characteristic ideal of Indian society is *moksa* or liberation from the cycle of rebirth, though there are many different ways of understanding what this means. It is variously construed as union with or devotion to Brahman or the creative liberation from matter, or the various Buddhist conceptions of *nirvana* that themselves range from a kind of cosmic compassionate generativity (in certain strains of the Mahayana) to complete extinction (in some strains of the Theravada). Liberation can, furthermore, be sought in many different ways: through meditation and knowledge, through right action and the accumulation of merit, through devotion, or even through Tantric rituals that cultivate detachment *through* the experience of pleasure rather than through asceticism as it is usually understood (Chaterjee 1954; Williams 1989; Kalupahana 1992; Collins 1998; Thapar 2002).

In Greece, finally, we see a rationalization of the old warrior ideal, in which the gods challenged human beings to seek excellence and a divinity that was always just beyond the horizon (as in Homer). Now, however, excellence is not simply martial, but above all intellectual and moral. In its high form this is the *via dialectica* charted by Socrates, Plato, and Aristotle, in which a rational ascent to first principles grounds ethical conduct that in turn cultivates moral virtue. Closely associated with this struggle for intellectual and moral excellence is the ideal of democratic citizenship that we noted in the previous chapter, in which free human beings enter the public arena with rationally autonomous approaches to fundamental questions of meaning and value and engage similarly rational peers in struggle around those questions. Together these ideals constitute what we have called classical humanism.

For the majority of the people, to be sure, the process of religious rationalization was less complete, and democracy meant something different. In the popular form of the Hellenic axial ideal, participation in the rituals of cult made available to the masses the secrets of divinity (understood here as simple immortality) that formerly belonged only to the *eupatrid* elite (Cornford 1952; Vernant 1962/1982; Detienne 1967/1996; Wood 1978; de Ste. Croix 1982; Collins 1998; Mansueto and Mansueto 2005).

This formulation of the Axial Age thesis helps to explain why some peoples had "breakthroughs" and others did not. Those societies whose cultural forms remained mythical rather than scientific or metaphysical were precisely those into which market relations did not penetrate and in which meaning did not, therefore, become a problem. It also allows us to see how distinctive civilizational ideals emerged in response to a common problem: the utter failure of the tributary ideal centered on seeking divinity through sacrifice. Finally, it makes clear the fact that the *problematization* of meaning, the *rationalization* of the ways in which societies seek meaning, and the *democratization* of the public arena do not necessarily mean "secularization" in the sense that modernists have claimed. It does not necessarily require an abandonment of the quest for divinization. On the contrary, they mean a reconfiguration of the religious, which nonetheless keeps religious questions at the center of the social order.

This latter point is especially important in our argument with Taylor, who, we will remember, reads the Axial Age as the beginning of a "great disembedding" of the individual from society, cosmos, and the divine, a disembedding that at this point extends only to religious elites. We can see that both aspects of this claim are erroneous. There is no sense in which *any* of the axial or post-axial religions disembed the individual, even the religious virtuoso. Consider, for example, Buddhism, which he cites as going furthest in this regard (Taylor 2007: 146–58). In what sense can a doctrine organized around the concept of *pattica samupada* (dependent origination) be seen as disembedding anything from anything else? Rather, it *rationalizes* our understanding of this embedding and theorizes it in a particular way (i.e., as something other than a participation in *Brahman*) and thus *problematizes* it, while making the religious ideal defined by it accessible to a much wider range of human beings. And even those civilizational contexts in which "disembedding" seems least advanced (e.g., China) *the problematization of meaning, religious rationalization,* and *religious democratization* in some measure impact the whole population. Even peasants, for example, become aware of the existence of and competition between Confucian *ru,* Taoist priests, and Buddhist *bikkhus* and their academies, temples, and monasteries. While they certainly operate in a universe that is still largely mythological (many people even in advanced industrial or postindustrial societies still do today), in interacting with religious leaders, they encounter and must engage more rationalized concepts. This is easiest to see in the use of concepts such as infinity or unity to define God in Western religions, but the same would have been true of the different way in which post-axial *ru* spoke of the Tao or of *tian,* or the way in which even simple Buddhist *bikkhus* gave discourses on the doctrine of no-self and the origins of suffering. Finally, religious leadership, the status of religious virtuoso, and the higher spiritual ends defined by the axial revolution became accessible to ordinary people in a way that was not true before that revolution. This does not mean that the first in particular was achieved by them as frequently as those from more privileged backgrounds, but history is full of stories of prophets who tended sycamores or worked as carpenters, of *sudra* religious poets and peasants who rose to become great *ru*.

We need now to see how the civilizational ideals that emerged during the Axial Age became the basis for new, world-embracing civilizations.

The Silk Road Era

If the Axial Age was not the period of incipient secularization that the modernist narrative claims it to be, then neither was the period that followed a reactionary era of repression and superstition. There were, to be sure, some profound changes in the way human societies were organized from about 200 BCE on. As specialized agriculture and crafts production spread, it led to rising population density and increased competition. When only a few cities are exporting oil or wine or silk or pepper, they can make a decent living doing so on a local scale. When everyone in the same region gets in on the act, profits decline and economic crisis sets in. The only solution is to find new markets—or else to conquer a wide swath of territory and tax the declining revenue being generated by each of the conquered cities.

This is, in effect, what happened during the period between 400 and 200 BCE. In Greece, for example, prosperity bred population growth and population growth colonization. But the colonies, which spread out all around the Mediterranean and Black Sea basins, engaged in roughly the same economic activities as their mother cities, something that resulted in a major economic crisis during the fourth century BCE. Similar patterns affected India, as the Ganges Basin became increasingly urbanized, and China, as small states competed to control trade and territory.

By 200 BCE, however, a new pattern was emerging. As we have already mentioned, by this point all of Afro-Eurasia was linked together in one unified trade network that reached from Britain, Iberia, and the Sahel in the west to China in the east and south to the Zanzibar and Malabar coasts. Luxury goods circulated throughout this system, with wine, oil, gar, and wool textiles flowing east from the Mediterranean and silk, spices, and eventually porcelain traveling west. Throughout most of the next 2000 years China was the principal economic engine of the system, followed closely by *Dar-al-Islam* during its peak under the Abbasid, Fatimid, and Umayyad Caliphates, and by the spice exporting depots of Southeast Asia and the Malabar coast towards end of the Silk Road Era. The West suffered an enduring balance of trade deficit with China and the rest of the system (Anderson 1974; de Ste. Croix 1982; Gernet 1985; Frank 1998; Thapar 2002)

Politically, this was a period of great empires. These states were, however, different from the old empires of the Bronze Age. Where those states generated most of their revenue by taxing the peasantry directly, the new empires also taxed trade, which they promoted aggressively. Indeed, the whole *raison d'etre* of these formations was just precisely to build roads, protect trade routes, and to centralize revenue on behalf of a ruling class that would otherwise have been in danger of seeing its revenues decline as specialized technologies spread and competition increased.

This being said, it must also be noted that there were significant differences among the imperial formations of the Silk Road Era—and these differences have everything to do with the impact of the salvation religions that emerged out of the Axial Age. Even where, as in the case of the Hellenistic and Roman Empires, Axial Age ideals had little impact on the economic structure, which remained brutally exploitative, imperial structures were ordered to the realization of axial ideals (in the case of Hellenistic-Roman Civilization, the classical humanistic ideal of the free human being and citizen). Increasingly, however, the great empires of this era were forced to look to Axial Age ideologies or their derivatives (Christianity, Islam) for legitimation. And the price of this legitimation was a more progressive political economic strategy. In some cases the change was marginal. Christianity, for example, as it was appropriated by the Roman Empire, legitimated the existence of vast differences in wealth, but it rejected the nearly ontological difference between slave and free that had characterized the Hellenistic and Roman civilization and helped the empire make the transition from slave labor, on which the West in particular had relied, to dependent peasant labor (the *coloni*) at a time when the closing of the *limes* had undercut the supply of slaves (de Ste. Croix 1982; Theissen 1982; Kyrtatis 1987).

In other cases, however, the impact was dramatic. The adoption of Buddhism by King Ashoka of the Mauryan Empire motivated him to carry out radical land and credit reform and to invest heavily in infrastructure and in the monasteries and other religious centers that eventually gave birth to one of the great universities on the planet—Nalanda (Sarkisyanz 1965; Thapar 2002).

In China, the impact varied depending on whether Confucian or Buddhist ideologies were ascendant, but both discouraged exploitation of the peasantry and encouraged investment in human development and civilizational progress. Thus the great reformer Wang Ming (9-23), founder of the short-lived Xin Dynasty, systematically nationalized estates and slaves and attempted to reorganize agriculture on the basis of the Chou-li (Gernet 1985, 149–51). Under the Sui and the early Tang, the ruling classes patronized large Buddhist monasteries that eventually came to control fully 25 percent of the arable land in China and that played a major role in encouraging economic development. Under the Song, the reformer Wang An-shih (1069-76) proposed taxing landlords, imposing price controls, extending low-cost credit to small farmers, and reforming the system of exams to include engineering and science instead of just the literary classics (Gernet 1985: 305-9; Collins 1998: 301-2) Somewhat later Chia Ssu-tao (1213-75) tried to limit land ownership to 500 mu (about twenty-seven hectares) and have the state buy a third of the surplus to support the armies (Gernet 1985: 315).

The most dramatic example of the impact of these ideologies, however, was the emergence of *Dar-al-Islam*. At the very heart of Islam was the aspiration to actually realize—on a global scale—the vision of a just society that had emerged out of Judaism and that Christianity had distorted into a vision of an otherworldly paradise (Crone 2004). Thus the emphasis on establishing a polity that could actually command right and forbid wrong (*al-amr bi'il ma'ruf wa'l-nahy 'an al-munkar*). While this project eventually became bogged down in conflicts between the Sunni and the Shi'a over the relative importance of political-military power (lest Islam become an impotent minority like the Jews) or intellectual and moral leadership (lest it become simply a form of legitimation for an oppressive empire like the Byzantine Christians), there were key aspects of the Islamic system that contributed profoundly to human development and civilizational progress. The most important of these was the *zakat*, a tax on net wealth of 2.5 percent that ensured that taxation fell most heavily on the wealthy and not at all on the poor, that created an incentive for economic development—lest fortunes be taxed away—and that provided a ready stream of income for mosques and *madrasas* and for institutions such as the *Bayt Hikmah* (House of Wisdom) established by the Caliph al-Mamoun in the ninth century, which became one of the planet's principle research centers.

Western Europe during the Middle Ages was simply another variant of this general civilizational pattern. On the periphery of the Silk Road network, Europe beyond the Alps had no history of indigenous urban civilization. The decline of Roman authority in the West, however, and the displacement of slavery by dependent peasant labor (facilitated by Christianity) led to declining rates of exploitation and permitted the development of a cluster of progressive new agricultural technologies: the alpine plow, the three field system, and increased use of water and animal power among them. The result was an increase in agrarian yields from 4:1 in the fifth century to 9:1 in the tenth. This more than doubled the available surplus, which was centralized first by monasteries, which played a critical role in the technological advances of the so-called dark ages, and later by cathedral towns, many of which developed into thriving urban centers (Anderson 1974). The Catholic Church played a critical role in this process. On the one hand, the Church itself was a major landowner, and while as such it frequently engaged in exploitative practices, it tended to put surplus to better use than the warlord elite with which it was in an uneasy tension, distributing alms, supporting religion, science, philosophy, and arts. On the other hand, the papacy and to a lesser extent local bishops served as a kind of counterweight to the claims of the warlord elite, holding them accountable before the court of natural law and opposing policies that were exceptionally exploitative and brutal (Goerner 1965; Gilson 1968; Gleason 1936).

All of this was possible because the ideologies that emerged from the Axial Age breakthroughs all effectively grounded a framework of meaning and values in the context of which material progress was seen not as an end in itself but as a means to even higher spiritual ends. Confucianism and Taoism, Buddhism and Hinduism, Judaism, Christianity, and Islam all approached this problem differently, to be sure, but they all played a critical role in ameliorating oppressive structures and redirecting surplus toward human development and civilizational progress. In the case of what eventually became the dominant Confucian ideal of Chinese civilization, human society was ordered to the realization of the mandate of heaven, which was conceived as pointing to the cultivation of intellectual and moral virtue. In the case of the Buddhist minority tradition in China and the Buddhist societies around its margins to the south and west, human society was ordered to the cultivation of enlightenment, understood as a recognition of the emptiness of phenomenal reality and the radical interdependence of all things, and to the ripening of being. In the case of India, civilization was ordered to the cultivation of union with or devotion to Brahman, or to a radical independence from the material world. In the case of *Dar-al-Islam*, civilization was ordered to the actual realization of the will of God in a just social order. In Christendom, finally, human society was ordered towards the cultivation of both the natural (intellectual and moral virtues) and the theological virtues that prepare human beings for their final end: the beatific vision. The Jewish minority subculture in *Dar-al-Islam* and Christendom, meanwhile, held these civilizations accountable for their forgetfulness of the foundational event in which they both claimed their ultimate origin—the advent of Being in Israel's struggle for justice—and thus played the role of a critical leaven that, in Christendom in particular, eventually helped to shape the emergence of a new critical ideal.

In any case, this broad civilizational impact on the part of the Axial and post-axial religions is further evidence against Taylor's claim that the axial revolution affected primarily religious virtuosos. Through its impact on the great empires of the Silk Road Era, it affected—and improved—the lives of nearly everyone in the vast Afro-Eurasian network.

The Crisis of the Axial Civilizations

Why did this pattern of development not continue, with markets expanding but also being regulated by political authorities at least partially accountable to religious leaders who forced them to limit exploitation and devote an increasing percentage of the surplus extracted to activities that promote human development and civilizational progress, and with humanity's gradually increasing technological capacity being understood as a contribution to the cosmohistorical evolutionary process—and not as a bid for cosmic sovereignty?

We have already noted above the rather subtle differences in ecology and demography that led Europe to focus on the development of labor-saving devices rather than on the exploitation of cheap human labor. This might be enough to explain how Europe was able to catch up and even surpass China, but it not by itself sufficient to explain modernity. At first, the labor-saving devices being developed in Europe were classically alchemical (based on tapping into the existing potentials in matter) rather than industrial (based on breaking down existing forms of organization in order to release energy and do work). And the broader civilizational pattern in Europe—political authorities drawn from the warlord class held accountable by religious leaders rooted in an Axial Age tradition—was in no sense fundamentally different from that in the rest of the world. Rather, I would like to suggest, the European eco-demographic pattern was overlaid by a dynamic of conquest and state building that ultimately transformed European culture—and that coincided with similar developments in China, India, and *Dar-al-Salam* that undermined the vitality of the old axial civilizations.

Christendom, it should be pointed out, was already in part the result of a dynamic of migration and conquest: i.e., of the Germanic migrations that accompanied the decline of the Roman imperial system. The last wave of these migrations, that of the Normans, led to the earliest attempt at the formation of a centralized, sovereign state structure in Europe (England). But developments within Christendom itself re-awakened this dynamic and led ultimately to conquests on a global scale that radically transformed the structure of European society and led to the emergence of the modern world.

Medieval Europe, we have noted, grew rapidly as a result of the new agricultural technologies. This led, by the middle of the twelfth century if not earlier, to land shortages (Anderson 1974). These were not so much *absolute* shortages in the sense that the carrying capacity of the land was being pushed, but rather relative shortages engendered by feudal landholding patterns. The law of primogeniture, followed in varying degrees by most European warlord families, meant that nearly the whole of a lord's land was bequeathed to his eldest son. Dowries were provided for daughters and perhaps for a second son who chose to enter a monastery or who was able to obtain a senior clerical post. The other sons were sent to be trained as knights and to serve as retainers for other lords. They lived in their lord's castle as "knights bachelor" until such time as their lord was able and saw fit to grant them a fief, after which they could settle down, marry, and have children. The difficulty is that as the land under cultivation was extended so too was the land that was already enfoefed. This meant more knights bachelor—and what amounted to a sort of aristocratic gang problem, as these armed, unmarried young men did what such men have always done, preying on women and peasants and generally undermining the social order.

Many aspects of medieval culture can be traced to efforts to address this problem. The codes of chivalry were no doubt, in part at least, an attempt to control armed men by ideological means. But a shortage of land and a surplus of armed men in the long run could only mean one thing: pressure for conquest. This dynamic was already becoming significant in the eleventh century with the beginning of the crusades. These "greater crusades" were eventually extended to al-Andalus (Muslim Iberia), to Africa, to the Americas, and to Asia.[5]

These conquests had two results. First, they gradually improved the position of Europe in the global trade networks and provided the "first installment" as it were in the primitive accumulation of capital, which led eventually to the emergence of an authentic bourgeoisie and to the industrial revolution. Second, wars of conquest helped bring into being strong monarchies that gradually put forward claims to sovereignty that were hitherto unheard of in Europe. Indeed, it is *only* in those regions of Europe that were touched significantly by these conquests that we see early developments in the direction of the sovereign nation-states: England, which was formed by the Norman Conquest of Britain; France, where the monarchy played a leading role in organizing the crusades; and Spain, which was the product of the *Reconquista*. Elsewhere state formation lagged, sometimes well into the nineteenth century.

It was above all the emerging monarchies that catalyzed the emergence of new cultural patterns. On the one hand, the development of

5. The institutional and ideological continuity between the crusades, the *Reconquista*, and the conquest of the Americas is well established. Ramon Gutierrez (Gutierrez 1990) for example points out that the office which financed pacification of the Indians in New Mexico in the seventeenth century was called *la cruzada* and that the Spanish regarded the indigenous peoples of the Americas as "Moors."

sovereign states created the basis in experience for thinking of God as a sovereign unconstrained by the dynamics of natural law. On the other hand, neither the emerging monarchies nor the bourgeoisie really wanted to be constrained by a natural law ethic that required them to act in such a way as to promote human development and civilizational practice. The result was a series of attacks, beginning in the 1270s, on Aristotelian science and metaphysics, led by Stephen Tempier, the Bishop of Paris, who was allied with the emerging French monarchy, and by Robert Kilwardy, his English counterpart. The whole idea of a teleological universe naturally ordered to God was rejected in favor of a mechanistic model in which the universe is the way it is because God made it that way. Teleological explanation gave way to mathematical model building, a shift that, over the course of several centuries, led ultimately to the Scientific Revolution of the seventeenth century. There was also a shift away from the analogical metaphysics that characterized the older Platonic and Aristotelian traditions in favor of a new univocal metaphysics. By an analogical metaphysics we mean one in which the terms for the first principle (God) are used analogically, so that God is not understood to exist in the same way we do, but rather in a qualitatively higher, pre-eminent way. Specifically, in the Thomistic tradition that developed this analogical metaphysics furthest in Christendom, God is Being as such; we simply share in a Being that is ultimately God's. The difference between God and the universe is qualitative, a fundamental ontological boundary that cannot be crossed. At the same time, everything participates in the life of God in a manner appropriate to its development. This in turn points towards a natural law ethics in which the fundamental moral imperative is to cultivate the potential latent in all things, so that they gradually ascend the scale of Being, participating ever more fully in the life of God. In a univocal metaphysics, on the other hand, the terms for the first principle (God) are used in the same sense as they are for other things. The difference between God and the universe is quantitative. God is infinite; we are finite. On the one hand, there is no fundamental ontological barrier that cannot be breached. On the other hand, for precisely this reason, our drive towards growth and development amounts, at least potentially, to a threat to God's sovereignty. This in turn leads to a spirituality of authority and submission and divine command ethics in which things are good because God commands them and wrong because God forbids them. This cultural shift, which we call the Augustinian Reaction, led ultimately, by way of John Duns Scotus and William of Occam, to the Reformation.

At roughly the same time Christendom was beginning its conquests and undergoing the internal structural transformations we have identified, several other peoples were also on the move. The most important of these were the Mongols and the Turks. The Mongols swept across Eurasia during the thirteenth century, dealing a deathblow to the Abbasid Caliphate, the traditional center of high Islamic civilization, and subjecting the civilizational heartland of China to brutal domination. The Mongols were followed by various Turkic groups, who took much of India and the eastern part of *Dar-al-Islam*. Finally, in the far West, in *al-Andalus*, the weak *taifa* states that emerged from the collapse of the Caliphate of Cordova turned to the Almoravids and Almohads for protection, a strategy that ultimately failed as *al-Andalus* fell to the advancing Christian armies.

While all of these groups understood themselves as adopting and conserving the ideals of the civilizations they conquered, they also radically transformed them. The Mongols began the long transformation of Confucian thought from a vibrant, dynamic philosophy centered on the development of human capacities into an ossified system directed at legitimating the authority of a declining elite. The Turks, for their part, showed little interest in *falasafa* and became the patrons of what became the dominant Asharite school of *kalam* that, like Augustinian Christianity, focused on the sovereignty of God and favored a univocal over an analogical metaphysics. The same was true of the new Berber rulers of *al-Andalus*, who joined their focus on divine sovereignty to a conservative Malikite jurisprudence. Indian philosophy during this period developed a new *dvaita* trend that reflected Christian and Islamic ideas of divine sovereignty and that focused more on devotion to Brahman than on union with it.

The Augustinian Reaction was accompanied in Europe by a kind of counter reaction on the part of the "left" wing of the Aristotelian movement. In effect, when the elements in the hierarchy that were allied to the emerging monarchies rejected the accountability of theology to reason, philosophy responded by rejecting the accountability of reason to a higher, revealed wisdom and opted instead for an Averroist hermeneutic in which "revealed" religion was at best an imaginative way of presenting truths that philosophy understands far better to the broad masses who are unable to understand them. In this sense, the spirituality of authority and submission, on the one hand, and the spirituality of autonomous reason on the other represent the twin products of the disintegration of the unified and balanced ideal of the axial civilizations.

It might seem, at first glance, that the result of this fission, at least on the side of the Radical Aristotelians, would yield nothing new. The philosophy of Ibn Rusd himself, after all, was quite sober and even conservative. In rejecting a higher wisdom that transcends human reason, he also limited the scope of any salvation to the identification of the human with the Agent intellect. And this was possible only for a few. He counseled against exposing the masses to philosophy, arguing that the resulting disillusionment would undermine the social order, and alongside philosophy he practiced a conservative Malikite jurisprudence focused in fidelity to the Quran. It is little wonder that there was, essentially, no such thing as Islamic "Averroism."

Things were different, however, in Christendom, where ibn Rusd's ideas encountered a religion that took for granted the possibility of full divinization. Liberating reason from faith and philosophy from theology meant not foregoing the possibility of salvation but rather transposing it to an innerworldly key, a process that is completed only in the works of Hegel, Marx, and their interpreters.

Just how this process played itself out is still somewhat obscure. While Latin Averroism gradually died out as a leading philosophical trend, many of its concerns were translated into the Neo-Platonizing Humanism of the Renaissance. And there was, in fact, a direct line between the Jewish Aristotelianism of Moshe ben Maimon and the rationalism of Benedict Spinoza, who conserves and advances the concerns of this trend in a new ideological context. Recent research has at least begun to untangle this web. Idit Dobbs Weinstein (Dobbs Weinstein forthcoming a, b) has traced out the lineage linking Spinoza to the Radical Aristotelians by way of Gersonides. Yirmiyahu Yovel (Yovel 2001), for his part, has stressed the *converso* milieu as the context that nurtured this tradition. It is not hard to see how the cross-fertilization of Jewish innerworldliness and the Christian focus on divinization would trace a pathway from ibn Rusd through Spinoza to Hegel and beyond.

It is, furthermore, clear that Spinoza, despite his fascination with the results of the scientific revolution, had deep roots in the medieval Aristotelian and specifically Averroist tradition. Spinoza frames the question of God not quantitatively, as perfect being, in the manner of Descartes, but rather qualitatively, in terms of the problem of substance, which for Spinoza is that which can exist on its own—i.e., Necessary Being. At the same time, he makes a very subtle move that opens up the way for a modernist transformation of the Aristotelian tradition. Human beings are but modes of this one substance, the product of intersecting networks of relationships. Our only hope for beatitude consists in identification with the whole, that is, with God. This can be read in the manner of a very sober philosophical spirituality in the manner of Maimonides or ibn Rusd, for whom human beings found fulfillment in identification with the Agent Intellect, simply adapted to the realities of a post-Copernican cosmology, in the context of which the idea of the Agent Intellect no longer made much literal sense. But it can also be read as a challenge: to develop to—or at least towards—the point at which we *are* in fact identical with the single substance.

For both an inner core of Radical Aristotelians and a broader periphery of thinkers working in other traditions (e.g., the Neo-Platonism that became prominent during the Renaissance) the developments of the late medieval and early modern era—the scientific revolution and later the democratic revolutions—are read as actually raising humanity to a higher ontological level. At first this is simply a new spin on the old Radical Aristotelian soteriology, which terminates (when we understand fully how the sublunar realm works) in identity with the Agent Intellect. But ultimately it pointed, by way of Spinoza's more ambiguous doctrine of the intellectual identification with Nature=Substance=God, toward the Hegelian doctrine of innerworldly divinization. Because the specifically Averroist form of this doctrine gradually disappears, and because it is increasingly characterized by a focus on innerworldly human civilizational activity, we will henceforth refer to this trend as "humanistic."[6]

---

6. Philosophically informed readers will no doubt be asking whether or not the Averroist Counter-Reaction *also* abandoned an analogical for a univocal metaphysics. This is a good question. Spinoza's metaphysics, for example, with its tendency to identify God with the whole, seems univocal; Hegel's, I would argue, because of his focus on questions of freedom and necessity, probably is not. But this is a question that will require further investigation.

These twin developments, the Augustinian/Asharite Reaction and the Averroist/Humanist Counter-Reaction, place us on the cusp of the modern world.

Modern Civilization

A Spirituality of Authority and Submission

As in the case of the "medieval" Silk Road civilizational pattern, what we are calling "early modern" civilization is a global, or rather pan-Eurasian, phenomenon. Its defining feature is its ordering to the ideal of *sovereignty*. What sets it apart from high modernity is the conviction that it is not humanity that is sovereign, but rather God, with human beings acting as His vice-regents. And this early modern ideal, which we will call the *spirituality of authority and submission*, was quite powerful. In its moderate forms, it drove Mongol and Manchu China, the Mughal Empire in India, the Ottoman Empire, and many of the *ancien regime* states of Europe, from Russia to Spain. In its more radical forms, it drove the English and Dutch colonial projects and was the founding ideal of North American civilization. And it has enduring power even in the present period: it is this ideal that is being revived by most Christian and Islamic fundamentalisms.

This being said, early modern Europe *was* different from the rest of Eurasia, in a way that medieval Europe had not been. Five factors were in play here. The first, which we have already noted, was the contingent fact of its ecological and historical disposition to low population and high wages, which encouraged investment in labor-saving devices. This tendency was reinforced by the Black Death at just the time when Europe had begun to develop more "normal" demographic patterns. Second, Europe's conquests were of more distant and less technologically advanced peoples than those of the Berbers, Turks, and Mongols. This led to the development of a new type of colonialism in which, rather than simply expanding civilizationally and exploiting conquered regions, colonies were plundered and the new wealth repatriated and invested, something that fueled the primitive accumulation of capita. Third, European nation-states were smaller, something that made it possible to realize the ideal of sovereignty to a degree of which far-flung empires could only dream. (Colonies needed only to be raped and pillaged, not systematically controlled). Fourth, the Reformation radically democratized the concept of human vice-regency, so that it was not only the King or Sultan or Son of Heaven who ruled in God's name, but every single one of the elect. The gradual increase in literacy that accompanied the development of advanced handicrafts and the expansion of trade led to a similar development on the humanistic side, as ordinary artisans and merchants began to aspire to a degree and kind of sapiential literacy and political participation that had hitherto been reserved for a handful of scholars. Finally, both Protestantism, as Weber noted (Weber 1920/1968), and humanism placed new value on innerworldly civilization-building activity, even if they understood both that activity and its significance in very different ways. For Protestants it was a probable sign of election while for humanists it was a step on the way towards innerworldly divinization.

For precisely this reason, the spirituality of authority and submission was unable to sustain its hegemony for very long. We will explore the reasons for this in greater detail in the next chapter, by way of a case study—that of the United States. For now it will suffice to say that the ideal is marked by a profound internal contradiction. This turns on the question of who is elect or who (in the Islamic context) is the legitimate vice regent of God. The Reformed churches soon divided between liberals, who regarded as elect those who were most useful to the community, a turn that increasingly favored those engaged in the high modern projects of industrialization and capitalist development, and evangelicals, who insisted on a personal conversion experience. Meanwhile, continued scientific and technological progress, the gradual emergence of capitalism, and the democratizing impulse embedded in the Reformation itself, which helped catalyze political revolutions, all gave more and more people the experience of actually sharing in sovereignty. This undercut the spirituality of authority and submission, favoring liberal readings of the Protestant tradition and strengthening the hand of the humanists. Little by little the ideal of human vice-regency gave way to that of innerworldly divinization by means of scientific-technological progress, Enlightenment, and political revolution. The early modern ideal of divine sovereignty, in other words, soon gave birth to the high modern ideal of human sovereignty—to what we call the *secret religion of high modernity.*

The Secret Religion of High Modernity

It is customary to associate modernity with secularism, and to understand secularism as involving a diminishing influence of religion, or at least a banishing of religion to the private realm. We have, throughout the course of this work, been gradually arguing towards a very different understanding of modernity. If by religion we understand a cluster of beliefs, values, and practices that grapples with fundamental questions of meaning and value, then clearly *every* worldview is ultimately religious and the whole concept of secularism becomes meaningless. But modernity, we would like to suggest, is religious even by a much narrower definition. It does not so much reject the drive towards transcendence that characterized earlier civilizations but rather, as we have said, transposes it into an innerworldly key. Indeed, modernity does not even reject—as some religions such as Buddhism do—the concept of God. It simply sees God as something to be built rather than something to be worshiped.

This secret religion was, as we have seen, the product of two originally very different impulses. On the one hand, the Augustinian Reaction led to a repression of Aristotelian science and a shift in the way we did science from teleological explanation, which ultimately served philosophy and theology, to mathematical model building, which focused on understanding *how* the world works and which was ordered to technological and economic progress. This impulse was applied in both the technological-economic and the political-ideological spheres, resulting in the industrial revolution, capitalist development, democratic revolutions, and the Enlightenment. On the other hand, the humanist counter-reaction set about finding a strategy that would allow human beings to become, at the very least, identical with the Agent Intellect and perhaps even to achieve a sort of divinity. The modern revolutions seemed to provide the means for this, though from the beginning the humanistic trend tended to cast a critical eye on actually existing modernity, asking whether or not industry, capitalism, democracy, and science really offered the transcendence they promised. This ultimately led to the emergence of the socialist variant of the modern ideal, the final, or at least the latest, heir of the Averroist/Humanist Counter-Reaction. Let us look at each of these dynamics in turn.

Industrial technology is a fairly straightforward expression of the Scientific Revolution. Where earlier technological regimes tapped into existing dynamics of growth and development, industry instead breaks down existing forms of organization in order to release energy and do work. Indeed, the very concept of "Work" is defined by the new physics in a way that points directly toward industrial concepts of efficiency. If W is work, f force and s distance, then:

$$W = f * s$$

Efficiency can then be measured by the work done per unit of time, energy, or money. It is the birth of this *forma mentis* more than any specific invention, such as the steam engine or the assembly line, that defines modern industry. Rather, these particular technologies just apply that *forma mentis* to the production process. Engines break down existing physical matter by combustion and harness the energy to work. The assembly line breaks down existing forms of social organization—the village and the guild—in order to harness raw human labor power to a production process guided from the outside.

In this sense the defining feature of modern economies is neither the market nor rational, bureaucratic planning systems, but rather the wage relationship. It is the wage relationship that allows the employer—whether a private capitalist or the state—to maximize both overall productivity and surplus extraction. Capitalism and socialism (at least in the sense of actually existing, modern, "scientific" socialism) have both insisted on this. Where they differ is around the question of just what structure is most effective at allocating the surplus extracted: the market (especially capital markets) or the state.

It was, of course, capitalist structures that predominated, at least at first, in the European homelands of modernity, though the role of the state in promoting industrialization and capitalist development should not be underestimated, even in England and the United States, but especially in France and countries that followed one or another version of the Prussian Road, in which state purchase of arms create a protected market for local capital (e.g., Germany, Japan, Russia). Socialism as a real historic movement emerged out of a triple dynamic. On the one hand, peasants and artisans actively resisted the new, more intense forms of exploitation that modern industrial capitalism made possible.

On the other hand, capitalist structures seemed limited in their ability to realize the modern ideal, especially in late industrializers that lacked colonial empires to use as a basis for the primitive accumulation of capital. Where the local ruling classes understood this and rationalized state structures in order to promote capitalist development (Prussia, Japan) revolution was avoided. But where they did not, powerful but internally contradictory movements that joined antimodernist peasants with modernizing intellectuals (and small groups of artisans and industrial workers ranged in between) came to power with the dual charge of at once humanizing and accelerating the modernist project. Theorizing the whole project, however, were humanistic intellectuals for whom the socialist revolution had aims that were nothing short of metaphysical. They aimed at elevating humanity, through the medium of the Communist Party, to the status of Subject of the cosmohistorical evolutionary process, i.e., to the status of God.

Modern "secularism," I would like to suggest, simply serves to conceal the real nature of the modern project from both the large population who continue to practice premodern or early modern religions, and who would never embrace the high modern ideal if they understood what it entailed, as well as from line practitioners of the ideal who might question it if it were to be honestly articulated. This concealing is not intentional. Indeed, there have been and continue to be open advocates of technological "god-building." Consider the Bolshevik godbuilders, including the novelist Gorky and the critic Lunacharsky (Rowley 1987) or Frank Tipler (1994) who has proposed reorganizing the whole fabric of the universe in order to build God. Rather, it is more a matter of a "self-deception" made necessary by the fact that modernity ran into contradictions very early on. In the case of the positivistic, scientific-technological variant of the modern project, this took the form of scientific results that called the viability of that project into question: Malthusian demographics, the Second Law of Thermodynamics, the Poincaré recurrence theorem, Darwinian evolution, modern standard cosmology, etc. In the case of the humanistic, socialist variant, it took the form of a contradiction between the rational autonomy that defines subjecthood and the *realpolitik* of revolutionary practice. Organizing and directing human history required a disciplined form of political organization that left little room for dissent. And rapidly modernizing backward states proved easier and more attractive to postrevolutionary elites than the hard work of figuring out what an authentic collective democratic subject might look like. It is hard to live a spirituality one knows is false, even if the short-term return, individual and collective, is enormous. These disillusionments merit more detailed analysis.

Towards a Civilizational Crisis

The humanistic current that flowed into high modernity was always conscious of its limitations. This is apparent, for exampl, in the work of Immanuel Kant. Kant recognized that both the rationalist and empiricist variants of modern philosophy were running into dead ends and set himself the task of regrounding science, religion, and ethics. He soon found, however, that the unaided human intellect (at least as it was understood in the wake of the Scientific Revolution, as providing formal organization for sense data) is not only unable to rise rationally to first principles; it cannot even grasp things in themselves. Science, for Kant, became simply a way of organizing our experience in accord with the intellect's innate forms of intuition (space and time) and the categories of the understanding (quality, quantity, relation, and mode). It is only in the moral realm that we can grasp the principles of things (because we choose those principles). And conduct in accord with reason does not necessarily transform the external world of nature. The idea that the universe is organized in accord with a rational moral principle (God) is at best a postulate of practical reason.

These initial misgivings notwithstanding, however, most members of the humanistic trend celebrated the achievements of modernity and simply argued that they needed to be completed in some way. At the economic level this generally meant bringing the rapidly developing capitalist economy under some measure of democratic control, or else transcending capitalism entirely. This impulse was especially strong among the vast networks of guilds, *compagnonages* (journeymen's associations), Masonic lodges, and other secret societies that played such an important role in the democratic revolutions up through the middle of the nineteenth century and in the revolutionary socialist organizations that were they successors, and that understood modernity, first and foremost, as a radical democratization of the Axial Age ideal. This understanding of socialism as economic democracy was given voice in the works of the early Marx, who criticized capitalism not for holding back the development of the productive forces, but rather for alienating human beings from the products of their labor, and thus from nature and each other (Marx 1844/1978). Eventually, however, members of this trend became disillusioned with actually existing socialism as well, precisely because it conserved the wage relation and thus instrumentalized human labor in service of technological and economic progress, and constituted a kind of internal opposition within the socialist and communist movements.

Democracy presented similar problems. The sort of revolutionary democratic movements that engaged masses of newly literate artisans and Enlightenment intellectuals in a world transforming practice that might satisfy their innerworldly metaphysical aspirations seemed inevitably to disintegrate into revolutionary terror and reactionary dictatorship. This was the pattern established by the French Revolution and sustained by later socialist transformations. Even so, an entire section of the humanistic intelligentsia continued to support these movements well into the twentieth century, usually operating as a kind of subaltern strain within Leninism. Thus Lukacs, who endowed the Communist Party with functions that can only be regarded as metaphysical (it was to be the "unique subject-object of human history"), and Gramsci, for whom it was a vast network of organic intellectuals rising from the working class to "organize and direct" the course of human history. Moderate liberal democracies did a better job of respecting individual liberties and thus the humanistic ideal of rational autonomy, but they tended to exclude the people from full political participation and, in any case, were rarely world transforming. We can actually hear the disillusionment in the work of the music of Beethoven, whose late style, Adorno points out, reflects the crisis of the ideal of the rational, autonomous subject (Subotnik 1976).

It was modern science, however, which presented the greatest challenge for the humanistic trend. Hegel responded to Kant's critique of the limits of science by proposing that *Vernunft*, a higher reason, could complete it, layering over its formal, mathematical models a rational explanation of the structure of the universe and the course of human history. Engels attempted something similar in his *Dialectics of Nature* (Engels 1880/1940). The difficulty was that modern science was increasingly generating results that called the modern ideal itself into question. Thomas Malthus (Malthus 1798), for example, argued as early as 1798 that technological progress, far from liberating humanity from want and need, would in fact exacerbate the poverty of the masses. This was because, while food production grows arithmetically, population grows geometrically, making it essentially impossible for humanity to achieve food self-sufficiency. Even if the details of Malthus's argument are subject to question, his work represents an early recognition of the limits of technological progress. Similar results soon began to accumulate in the physical and biological sciences. The discovery of the Second Law of Thermodynamics, for example, demonstrated in another way that there were limits to technological progress. It is impossible, it turns out, to build a perfect heat engine—i.e., one that recycles all of the energy that it uses. Heat dissipates; systems tend towards disorder. And worse still, the universe, which high modernism theorizes as a kind of vast heat engine, will eventually wind down as heat dissipates and matter becomes ever more randomly dispersed. Heat death, not technological godhood is, according to this view, the ultimate future of humanity. The Poincaré Recurrence Theorem, which demonstrates that a closed system of particles will eventually return to its initial state after an arbitrarily long period of time, had similar implications for high modern ideals about progress. And even when science continued to theorize progress—e.g., in Darwinian evolutionary theory—it increasingly understood this as a brutal process by which the less fit were weeded out and only the best survived.

The dominant tendency within the humanistic trend was to conclude that real human divinization was impossible and that meaning and purpose were human products that lived and that would ultimately die with human civilization. Thus, strictly speaking, Lukacs's "unique subject-object of human history" and Gramsci's "organizer and directory of human history" are not divine. They are more like a sociologized agent intellect. The more spiritually sensitive practitioners of this dialectical tradition have attempted a serious engagement with science (Harris 1965, 1991, 1992) that regrounds belief in the existence of God, while taking seriously the results of modern science. These efforts have flowed together with developments within the liberal Protestant and Catholic traditions and significantly inform the perspective of this work. But their broader civilizational impact remains very limited. Critical theory remained faithful to the socialist ideal of rational autonomy and increasingly tended over the course of the twentieth century towards a negative dialectics that analyzes and exposes the causes of alienation but lacks a strategy for transcending it, resulting ultimately in a postmodernist pessimism. This is certainly true of Adorno and Horkheimer, but it is implicit as well in the work of Fromm and Marcuse.

Outside the humanistic trend the reaction to the contradictions of modernity was even more profound. Romantic critics began to question modern industry and modern scientific rationality as early as the late eighteenth century. By the middle of the nineteenth century we witness both a wholesale re-assertion of Reformation theology in the works of Kierkegaard, as well as the much darker vision, which prefigures postmodernism, in the works of Nietzsche, who treats the universe as a kind of global and ultimately losing struggle for power. Kierkegaard, Nietzsche, and their philosophical offspring set the tone for much of the twentieth century, which witnessed the protracted death of the modern ideal in the long global war that reached, with only a few breaks, and with the last chapter fought by proxy, from 1914 to 1989—and in the Shoah, in which the modern West's drive towards divinization finally revealed its demonic core.

We will address these developments in a later chapter in greater detail. For now, though, we must examine the principal reason why the crisis of modernity has been so protracted, and the modern ideal so resilient: the very distinctive history of modernity's second homeland: the United States of America.

CHAPTER 3

An Imperfect Union

INTRODUCTION

In the previous chapter, we analyzed the emergence of modernity globally and defined the nature of the modern civilizational project. The present period is, however, defined as much as anything by the dominant position of one particular modern society: the United States. And the United States has a very peculiar relationship with modernity and presents distinct challenges and opportunities as we struggle to come to terms with the crisis of the modern ideal. On the one hand, the United States is, in many ways, the planet's most modern and most capitalist country. Born with little or no residue of older "feudal" social formations, it would seem to be a pure expression of the liberal version of the modern ideal. An early industrializer, according to historical materialist theory it ought to have developed a strong, independent workers movement early on, and to have been one of the pioneers in the transition to socialism. And yet the United States is not only among the most religious countries in the world; its religion has an intensely conservative streak. According to one recent survey, 61 percent of the population believes in a literal second coming of Jesus and 44 percent in the so-called rapture, in which the elect will "go to meet the Lord in the air," while those who have not accepted Jesus Christ as their personal Lord and Savior will be "Left Behind" (Sheler 1994). The United States, furthermore, has been uniquely resistant to socialism. But it is not only liberal and socialist theories that have had a hard time understanding "America." According to functionalist secularization theory, which ties religious belief to the presence of traditional communities bound together by shared beliefs and values—what Durkheim called "mechanical solidarity"—the United States, with no tradition of village communities and its extraordinary ethnoreligious pluralism, ought to be the most secular of countries. And from the standpoint of Weberian interpretive sociology it is a simple impossibility: a society as pluralistic as the United States ought to have descended into an ethnoreligious war of all against all long ago. And yet the much-vaunted "culture wars" notwithstanding, the United States has developed such a strong culture of ethnoreligious pluralism that—even while engaged in what many on both sides regard as a war on Islam—it is regarded by many Muslims, for example, as a much better place to live than European countries that have criticized this war.

This difficulty in understanding the United States should, however, come as no surprise. Most modern social theory, whether liberal or socialist, was formed in a European context. Much of it, in fact, represented an attempt by Germans to understand why their country was not following the same road to modernity as France or England, or represented a response to nationally specific Church/State struggles.[1] As such, it strains to understand the specificity of even the various European national experiences, and often generates gross misconceptions when applied to Asia, Africa, or Latin America.[2] But "America" is something else. Perhaps because it is so inextricably bound up with the principal ideological divisions that have affected the planet for the past hundred and fifty years, it has been difficult for either partisans or opponents of the "American way of life" to approach the question of American exceptionalism with anything like real insight. And yet that,

---

1. This was certainly true for Marx, for example, whose *German Ideology* was first and foremost an attempt to come to terms with the fact that Germany had not followed anything like the French revolutionary democratic path of development (Marx 1846/1978). Durkheim's work is best understood as a thoughtful reflection on some of the costs of French secularism—and a proposal to ameliorate them—while Weber's can be understood as an attempt to argue that Germany's imperial ambitions would be better served by following a more nearly Anglo-American development strategy, rather than the strategy of authoritarian "modernization from above" pioneered by Bismark.

2. Consider, for example, the Weberian claim that Asian religions such as Buddhism, Confucianism, and Taoism are incapable of sustaining action aimed at innerworldly transformation (Weber 1921/1968). Committed Weberians have every bit as much difficulty understanding Japanese industrialization or Burmese Buddhist socialism as committed Marxists do the United States' resistance to socialism (Bellah 1957; Sarkisyanz 1965).

precisely, is what is necessary if we are to understand a current situation in which the United States plays a globally dominant role

This chapter is an attempt to do just that. I begin by situating the American ideal in the context of Western modernity, identifying two distinct "founding" traditions: a complex ideological ensemble deriving from Puritanism and a moderate variant of humanistic modernism that we will call Deistic Republicanism. The first of these gave birth, through a complex series of transformations that we will trace out in detail, to both liberal and evangelical Protestantism. Liberal Protestantism, in turn, gave birth to a gospel of scientific, technological, and economic progress (the uniquely American variant of positivistic high modernism) and to the Social Gospel. Evangelical Protestantism gave birth to both socially engaged postmillennial strains that focused on building the reign of God on earth and more pessimistic fundamentalist currents that looked forward to the end of history. Deistic Republicanism, because it did not have to confront a Catholic *ancien regime*, and because it crystallized before the disappointments of the nineteenth century, lacked the critical, revolutionary democratic, and ultimately socialist edge of its European counterparts. I show how the contradictions within and between these tendencies forced the creation of a new kind of polity—one that brought together in a common public arena advocates of fundamentally different variants of the modern civilizational ideal. This sort of society was rendered possible by the development of a network of what Tocqueville and his followers have called intermediate or mediating institutions, in between the family and the state that not only tempered individualism but also brought together people from different social classes and ethnoreligious communities and different political and theological orientations. The result was not to render the United States as a society immune to secular messianism, but rather to render the American *polity* so resistant, rescuing the United States from totalitarian experiments whether theocratic, positivistic, or humanist.

Both of the American variants of the modern ideal were disappointed during the nineteenth century—Deistic Republicanism by the changes that accompanied western expansion, and Puritanism by the failure of the Civil War to finally create a utopia of social justice and Protestant piety. What emerged instead was an industrial capitalist power with imperial ambitions and objectively ordered, even when it did not want to be, to the high modern ideal of transcending finitude by means of scientific and technological progress. Even so, the opportunities that the United States offered made the country attractive to continuous waves of immigrants who, only half consciously, have been renewing and enriching the "real" Tocquevillian form of the American ideal. This ideal conserves the democratic and pluralistic American commitments of modernity, but rejects the drive towards divinization by innerworldly means, instead creating a polity in which partisans of diverse ideals can build institutions and pursue the good as they understand it. The United States, in other words, is not a modern society in the strict sense of the word (i.e., one clearly ordered to either the positivistic or humanistic variants of the modern ideal) but rather a society in which diverse ethnoreligious communities have used the space opened up by modernity to create something new—a society in which the constitutive ideal is the contestation of ideals. Elites on both the right and the left as well as the United States' admirers and critics around the world have had enduring difficulty understanding the possibilities of this new way of understanding what it means to be "American."

I conclude by arguing that the United States is at a crossroads. I show that the "end of history" (Fukuyama 1989) and "clash of civilizations" (Huntington 1993) theses are no more appropriate for understanding the United States than they are for understanding the world. Postmodern, Neo-Marxist, and Radical Orthodox theories do no better. Rather, as high modernism has lost its appeal, the country is increasingly caught between reaction—trying to enforce the hegemony of early modern (Protestant) or high (positivistic) modern ideals on a world that no longer wants them—and embracing its authentic Tocquevillian identity, which would make it a model for a new kind of polity that is at once democratic and pluralistic, but that also takes principles and values seriously, and that is *constituted* by deliberation around fundamental questions of meaning and value. Only such a polity can conserve the contributions of Western modernity while creating a context for the emergence of a new civilizational ideal.

Situating "America" in the Context of Western Modernity

In the previous chapter we outlined the complex process by which the modern ideal first emerged. The United States developed along with and under the impact with this modern ideal in a way that sets it apart from the modernizing societies of Asia, Africa, and Latin America—or even Europe. But that does not make it modern in the sense in which that would be understood by most modern social theory. Rather the American identity has been shaped by two competing variants of the early modern ideal—the Puritan variant of the Protestant ideal and a moderate variant of humanistic modernity associated in the popular imagination with "Jeffersonian" democracy that we will call Deistic Republicanism. And these ideals collided not just with each other but with the complex material and political economic processes involved in creating a new society on a new continent to create something quite different from either liberal or socialist modernity.

It is to this story that we now turn.

The Formation of the Puritan Ideological Ensemble

Understanding Puritanism and its role in the larger project of modern civilization is, of course, a *locus classicus* for modern social theory. Our own approach does not reject Weber's Protestant Ethic Thesis out of hand. Unfortunately, however, Weber and his successors lacked the in-depth understanding of the internal dynamics of Protestant Christianity generally, and English Calvinism in particular, that would have been necessary in order to comprehend the complex interaction between Puritanism and modernity.

The Protestant Reformation was essentially just an extension of the Augustinian Reaction that we discussed in the previous chapter. This reaction was, as we noted, a product of the emergence of sovereign national states and of generalized commodity production. The existence of sovereign states provided a new model for understanding God—as an absolute divine sovereign. And neither absolute monarchs nor the emerging bourgeoisie wanted to be held accountable before the court of natural law, a possibility that was at least implicit in the earlier analogical metaphysics of the high Middle Ages. As a result, the emerging monarchs and later the bourgeoisie itself supported theologians who, like Stephen Tempier, John Duns Scotus, and William of Occam, mounted a sharp attack on Aristotelian philosophy and theology, charging that it undermined the sovereignty of God, and in the process gave birth to a new univocal metaphysics in which the difference between creator and creature is understood as quantitative rather than qualitative. God is, in effect, an absolute and arbitrary sovereign to whom we must either submit or be damned. It is merely God's free decision to love and offer salvation that defines Christian morality as one of self-sacrificial love, and it is only because of Christ's sacrifice of Himself on the cross that we are even aware of God's offer.

Initially this encouraged a spirituality centered on the struggle to emulate Christ's self-sacrificial love—something typical of the Franciscan tradition in particular. Luther extended the Augustinian Reaction by arguing that we cannot actually emulate this kind of self-sacrificial love, and that we cannot, therefore, merit salvation, even with the help of divine grace. Justification is a free gift of a sovereign God. He also rejected the idea that either reason or revelation have anything to say about the social order. Any attempt to build a just social order will dilute the gospel's core message of forgiveness. Any extension of the ethic of forgiveness into the social arena will give aid and comfort to a still largely unredeemed humanity desperately in need of the repressive power of the state.

Luther's doctrine reflected the ideological needs of the emerging monarchies, which were given a mandate to build strong states that could restrain the sinfulness of an unredeemed humanity and were liberated from accountability to either natural law or the radicalism of the ethics taught by the Jesus of the synoptic gospels. Calvin's doctrine, (Calvin 1536/1993), on the other hand, reflects the situation of the emerging bourgeoisie and allied groups. Calvin taught that grace not only assured salvation to those who received it, but also transformed them into instruments of God's work in the world. While God chose, "before the foundations of the world" (Eph 1:4) those who would be saved, there were, in fact, signs that indicated whether or not one was among the elect. These might include a "godly walk" especially usefulness to the community and/or personal conversion experience.

Weber (Weber 1920/1958) argued that Calvinism created an ideological and psychological situation uniquely favorable to industrialization and capitalist development. On the one hand, Calvinism regarded all useful work, not just specifically religious work, as an expression of God's will in the world. On the other hand, the fact that such work was a probable—but only probable—sign of election created a profound psychological tension that favored hard work, investment, and accumulation. If I work hard, then I *might* be among the elect; if I am lazy I know I am damned. If I save and invest, so that my work serves the common good, I *might* be among the elect; if I consume what I produce then I know that I am damned...

Weber's analysis has much to commend it, but drawing as he did on a single text by a middle-of-the-road English Calvinist, Richard Baxter, he misses the internal diversity within the Calvinist tradition around the question of just how, precisely, one knows whether or not one is among the elect. Broadly speaking, Calvinists divided on this question between those who stressed "usefulness to the community"— something that some, in turn, understood to mean productivity in the economic arena and others to mean a concern for religion and social justice—and those who stressed the need for a convincing narrative of a personal conversion experience. The New England Puritans were marked by, among other things, the requirement that such a narrative of personal conversion be presented to the existing members of the church as a condition for admission to membership, something that in the Massachusetts Bay and New Haven colonies was in turn a condition of suffrage. It is not possible in this context to trace out in detail the complex internal struggles of the Holy Commonwealths.[3] Suffice it to say that after the English Revolution in 1640, radical Puritans were more inclined to stay home, where the action was, and that the children of the original colonists, as well as many newcomers, saw the colonies first and foremost as commercial ventures and were more interested in making money and in advancing their social position than they were in building Holy Commonwealths. Many of the children of the early colonies' leading lights were unable to fulfill the requirement that they give a convincing narrative of their conversion experi-

---

3. This account of Puritanism, of the development of New England society, and of the impact of Puritanism on the larger American project is indebted to, among others, Rutman 1965; Walzer 1965; Moore 1966; Lockridge 1970; Nash 1970; Hill 1972; Ahlstrom 1972; Boyer and Nissanbaum 1974; Hatch 1977; McLoughlin 1978; Marsden 1980; Conforti 1981; Geissler 1981; Bryant 1983; and Dayton 1983.

ence, and were thus unable to qualify for membership in the church and thus for the franchise. The result was the "Half-Way Covenant," which admitted the children of church members to baptism and thus to the franchise, though not to communion, and eventually, the reorganization of Massachusetts Bay as a royal colony. Accompanying this gradual process of secularization was the strengthening of what eventually emerged as "liberal" Calvinism, which stressed usefulness to the community rather than personal conversion as evidence of election. At its far end, liberal Protestantism gradually evolved away from many of the historic tenets of Christianity, including the divinity of Jesus, and gave birth to Unitarianism.

Liberalism did not, however, mean abandoning the sense of "election" that had characterized the founders of New England. It is just that being among the elect now meant a sense of moral superiority based on greater productivity (and thus prosperity) or on a sense that the new society being forged in the Americas was free of many of the social injustices that characterized old England and especially the Continent, rather than a radical conversion experience.

The Great Awakening of the 1730s was, first and foremost, a response to this growing liberalism and to the growing wealth and privilege of those who espoused it. The poor, especially in the more remote regions still focused on subsistence agriculture, could not give any great evidence of their "usefulness to society," especially when this was interpreted to mean productivity and wealth; but they could provide a convincing narrative of personal conversion. North American Evangelicalism was, in other words, from the very beginning, a movement of those who had been "left behind" by modernity. At least to begin with, this "evangelical" trend in American Protestantism did not reject the struggle to build a better society. It was, rather, anxious to point out the hypocrisy of the liberals, many of whom were involved in the slave trade or in grabbing land from the Indians, and who were in general more concerned with enriching themselves than with advancing God's work of redemption. Indeed, up through the Civil War, most evangelicals upheld what is known as a postmillennial eschatology, which teaches that Jesus will return only *after* the millennium, that is, only *after* humanity, by means of personal conversion and social reform, has created a just social order. Very early on, however, the evangelical trend itself began to experience differences between those who stressed the purely subjective character of the conversion experience, and placed relatively little emphasis on transformed personal conduct or social reform, and those who, such as Jonathan Edwards and his followers in the New Divinity movement, regarded ethical conduct as the natural consequence and best indication of authentic conversion and who were actively engaged in efforts to combat the evils of American society, such as slavery and land speculation (Heimart 1966; Hatch 1977; Bryant 1983; Dayton 1983).

By the middle or end of the eighteenth century, in other words, New England Calvinism had developed from a relatively compact ideology into a complex ideological ensemble containing at least four distinct trends. There was, on the one hand, a liberal trend, which was less and less focused on historic Christian doctrine and regarded usefulness to the community as the best indicator of election. The liberals in turn were increasingly divided between those who regarded economic prosperity as the best evidence of usefulness to the community and those who focused on efforts at social reform. These two tendencies eventually gave birth to the Gospel of Wealth and the Social Gospel, both of which remain important poles in the liberal Protestant spectrum. The evangelicals, on the other hand, while united in stressing the importance of personal conversion, were, in turn, divided between the high Calvinists (and especially the New Divinity movement) who believed that conversion had to bear fruit in ethical conduct and social reform and what was originally a relatively small group of backcountry revivalists who stressed a more purely emotional conversion experience—and, for the most part, gradually abandoned, at least in practice, their adherence to Calvinist distinctives such as limited atonement and double predestination.

Anyone who is familiar with the political and religious history of late colonial North America, or with the period during and immediately after the Revolution, knows that these various trends despised each other and saw themselves locked in what many regarded as mortal combat over the soul of the new "nation." What they all shared in common, however, was the idea that they were building something qualitatively new and fundamentally superior to anything that existed in Europe or elsewhere. They had united unquestioningly in supporting England, which they regarded as the capital of True Christianity, in her struggle against "papist" France during the Seven Years War, but they saw themselves as building something nobler and purer than old England could ever hope to be. Freed from the bonds of tradition and the accumulated weight of medieval corruption and tradition, they would build a society that was truly capable of advancing God's work in the world, whether that work was understood as personal conversion, social justice, or capitalist accumulation—or some combination of all three. They were intensely aware of the moral failings of the new nation, especially the guilt of slavery, but regarded this consciousness of guilt as itself a mark of election, something that set them apart and promised to bear fruit in a future more glorious than that of the planet's grandest empires. It would be the last and the best empire, and while some understood this literally and others more figuratively, it would be the empire of Jesus Christ.

Deistic Republicanism

The second of the broad traditions that contributed to the formation of the American identity is the Deistic Republicanism that finds its purist expression in the thought of Benjamin Franklin and Thomas Jefferson, but that influenced many of the American founders in both the Federalist and Democratic-Republican Parties. This Deistic Republicanism is, I would like to argue, a moderate variant of humanistic modernism. While it upheld the existence of a divine creator, it granted to humanity an almost complete autonomy in governing the universe. And while it was deeply interested in the progress of science and technology, its principal focus was on democratizing the Axial Age ideal of the philosopher, making both the pursuit of wisdom and active participation in the public arena accessible to ever-wider sectors of the population. In its classical Jeffersonian and Franklinian forms, this was to take place by making small landownership or artisan-entrepreneurship essentially universal, creating a society of yeoman farmers and small businessmen who would enjoy sufficient prosperity and leisure to set aside time for study and civic engagement.

This humanism did, to be sure, *understand itself* as classical—that is, as a revival of the ideal of rational autonomy and democratic citizenship that had been born in Greece and that inspired Hellenistic Roman civilization. Indeed, like many other democratic revolutionaries, the American Founders modeled their Constitution, like their buildings, on an imagined classical past. But this claim cannot be taken at face value. Classical humanism never seriously aspired to extend the ideal of rational autonomy and democratic citizenship to the whole society. And while American democracy was dependent from the beginning on slavery and other forms of exploitation, it was never fully comfortable with this. Most important, however, is the conviction, shared with the Puritan ideological ensemble, that the American Revolution had global, salvific significance.

We call the American variant of humanistic modernism moderate, nonetheless, because, on the theoretical side, it avoided the more radical claims of thinkers like Hegel and Marx regarding the deification of humanity (Hegel) or the displacement of God by humanity as the conscious subject of the cosmohistorical process (Marx), and, on the practical side, because it believed, at least initially, that it would have the luxury of simply carving a new type of the society out of the wilderness rather than engaging in revolutionary struggle against the aging social forms of Europe. It was also eclectic and was not attached to any one philosophical trend. What united it was the conviction that "America" would be a land of universal opportunity in which everyone would have a chance, and the best would naturally rise to the top, forming a sort of natural aristocracy, while all participated in decision making through the structures of democratic citizenship. This was reflected in its interventions in the religious arena, in which the harsh anticlericalism of the Continent gave way to efforts to "revise" Christianity in some very un-Protestant ways. Jefferson, for example, produced his own version of the New Testament that completely excised Paul and that made Jesus into a moral teacher fully compatible with Enlightenment Deism (Jefferson 1991). Franklin took a frankly Averroist approach to religion, regarding it as good for the cultivation of virtue, and probably maintaining belief in a divine creator, but eschewing most of the dogmatic structure of historic Christianity. In many places it was associated with Masonry, though American Masonry was also more moderate than many European, especially Continental variants.[4]

4. The role of Masonry in the American Revolution is a disputed question that has been much confused both by conspiracy theorists anxious to expose what they see as a dark secret and the reluctance of serious scholars to affirm, even if in a very different context and with considerable qualifications, any proposition that conspiracy theorists have ever put forward. For good accounts of this question, see Bullock 1998; Tabbert 2005.

It is important to recognize the distinctive difference between this early Deistic Republican ideal and later variants of the American dream that also invoke Jefferson or Franklin. For Jefferson especially, widespread access to education and especially to the new public university that he founded was to be the *result*, not the *cause* of widespread prosperity, enabling the best sons of yeoman farmers to gain a liberal education and join the enlightened elite that would guide the rest of their communities. This is very different from later Republican and Democratic Party platforms that made education simply a means to economic growth and upward mobility.

This Deistic Republican ideal was the guiding vision of what became the dominant wing of the Democratic-Republican Party, and echoes of it can still be heard, in updated form, in the rhetoric of the Democratic Party to this day.[5]

An Imperfect Union

It is not possible in this context to consider in detail the factors that led what became the United States to seek independence from Great Britain. Suffice it to say that one after another the various sectors of North American society came to believe that membership in the British Empire was more an obstacle than an aid in realizing their own distinct versions of the American ideal. Their reasons included: a seigniorial reaction on the part of the English aristocracy that, after the middle of the eighteenth century, began to assert rights to quitrents and other privileges that they had formerly ignored; restrictions on migration beyond the Appalachian Mountains to regions reserved for the Indians and out of the reach of the British Crown; threats to abolish or limit the slave trade; new taxes and tariffs meant to help pay for the long struggle with "papist" France; a continuing failure to grant the colonies representation in parliament; and the threat to appoint an Anglican bishop,

---

5. Another wing of the party was dominated by evangelicals such as Nathaniel Niles, who derived from their Calvinism a radically democratic ideology that stressed the struggle for social justice and that sought to hold the rich accountable for the sins of the new nation. This wing of the party was led by Aaron Burr who was bound to it by blood, being a descendant of Jonathan Edwards, and was discredited after he was marginalized from political life (Heimart 1966).

and thus to call the question on the status of New England's dissenting but non-separating established Church (Heimart 1966; Nash 1970).

Broad sectors of the North American people did, in other words, have reason to support independence, but they were not the *same* reasons, nor was there any shared vision of just what kind of civilization they hoped to build. The thirteen colonies represented thirteen very different societies, themselves often divided regarding directions for the future. The option for the somewhat stronger central government permitted by the U.S. Constitution as against the looser structure envisioned under the Articles of Confederation was simply an arrangement on the part of the ruling classes to keep open their options regarding future economic development and to protect themselves—as much against internal rebellions as against renewed pressure from Great Britain. The result, however, created a public space that was unique in history—one that brought together representatives of distinct cultural traditions in common deliberative bodies and engaged them in debate around fundamental questions.

This point is vitally important if we are to understand correctly the unique "American" settlement of church/state questions. Among the founders were moderate representatives of both the Puritan and Deistic Republican ideals, and among those they represented were more radical advocates of these ideals. Left to their own devices some would have opted, if not for a holy commonwealth then at least for a polity that took for granted its roots in the traditions of Anglo-American Calvinism. Others would, no doubt, have preferred something like the French solution, in which traditional Christianity gave way to a Masonic spirituality centered on reason.[6] But neither tendency had the weight to impose its will on the other, and both were divided against themselves. The result was a polity that was neither confessional nor secular but rather pluralistic. It was taken for granted that people would enter the public arena formed by their own specific ideological tradition, be it religious or "secular,"[7] and advocate policies that were rooted in their

---

6. Masonry may have originated in England and Scotland, but it played a major role in revolutionary movements on the Continent, serving as the locus for revolutionary organizing and the original site of the cult of Reason, which the Jacobins tried, ultimately unsuccessfully, to make the official religion of France.

7. I use quotation marks because of the fact that, as we noted in the previous chapter, the pretended secularity of the modern ideal in fact conceals a secret religion

own distinctive principles and values. What was excluded was any attempt to establish one particular tradition as constitutive of American identity and the authoritative reference point for public policy.[8]

Two texts from the early years of the Republic capture this almost accidental creation at the moment of its birth. The first is the *Federalist*, written to garner support for the new constitution, and especially *Federalist* 10, written by James Madison. A reader literate in modern social theory, and especially in historical materialism, is struck by just how close Madison's understanding of politics is to that of Marx or Lenin. Popular governments, as he calls them, have always been plagued by faction. This problem can be addressed either by extirpating its root causes—the aspiration of Rousseau and the French republican tradition—or by ameliorating its symptoms. While faction has its most immediate roots in ideological differences, these differences themselves are based first and foremost in differences in the amount and type of property. Madison differs with Marx only in regarding differences in property as based in ability—and in the fact that he wants to preserve these differences rather than abolish them. He thus opts for ameliorating the symptoms of faction. Now minority factions can be controlled by the principle of majority rule, but the faction of the majority (the poor) cannot. He argues, however, that the structures created by the new constitution have the effect of preventing the formation of a unified party of the poor. Representative rather than direct democracy, a federal rather than a unitary republic and (he might have added) ethnoreligious differences, all but guarantee that the American poor will never be able to unite.

Madison was *trying* to create a polity in which political democracy never came to mean economic democracy. That he *succeeded* has had enormous costs for the United States, holding it back from pursuing as progressive a civilizational strategy as it otherwise might have. But in the process he *also* created (probably inadvertently) a polity in which political democracy could never come to mean either popular theocracy or secular totalitarianism. Just as the politics of representation, the existence of local and state identities, and ethnoreligious differences

---

centered in divinization by innerworldly means.

8. It is true, to be sure, that establishment at the level of the individual states was still not excluded. But the individual states soon became too pluralistic themselves for establishment to be a realistic option.

cut across class lines, local and class identities cut across ethnoreligious identities and prevent the formation of either fundamentalist or secularist parties capable of maintaining a stable majority. And for that we should be eternally grateful.

The second text that captures the unique character of the United States at the moment of its birth is Alexis Tocqueville's *Democracy in America* (Tocqueville 1835/2003). A French aristocrat who is probably best located philosophically on the center left of the traditionalist movement, Tocqueville was, in many ways, profoundly critical of the social forces he saw at work in the United States. He was, first of all, at best skeptical about democracy as such. On the one hand, democracies, because they vest authority in the people as a whole, tend to promote "the welfare of the greatest possible number," while aristocracies "concentrate wealth and power in the hands of the minority." But aristocracies "are infinitely more expert in the science of legislation than democracies ever can be," and specifically tend to have more long-term vision (Tocqueville 1835/2003: I.1.14). He was, however, especially concerned about the tendency of democracy to promote individualism. Aristocracies, he thought, embedded people in a community extending "from the peasant to the king." Democracies cut people off from their past, from their neighbors, and even from their own descendants. (Tocqueville 1835/2003: II.2.2).

At the same time, Tocqueville was also fascinated by the fact that American democracy had not resulted in the descent into violence that had characterized revolutionary France. He was also impressed by the ability of the United States to temper its radical individualism with effective civic engagement. He attributed this success to the existence of a network of voluntary organizations between the family and the state that brought people together and cultivated collaboration for the common good. Indeed, he thought that participation in civil society made ordinary Americans act "in just the same way as a man of high rank" (Tocqueville 1938/2003: II.2.5).

Of particular note to Tocqueville was the fact that, unlike democratic France, the United States had proven itself especially hospitable to religion generally and to Catholicism in particular. He rejected the Enlightenment claim that religious faith would decline more or less automatically with the advancement of freedom and knowledge. The United States, he said, was among the freest and most enlightened societies on the planet, but also among the most religious. He attributed this to the separation of church and state (Tocqueville 1835/2003: I.1.17).

Religion, furthermore, was critical to combating the problems of democracy. This is because it gives people a sense of meaning and direction, focusing them on some good higher than material consumption, and because it promotes a sense of community and solidarity (Tocqueville 1835/2003: II.1.5).

Democracy, Tocqueville notes, promotes its own distinctive religious tendency, what he calls pantheism (Tocqueville 1835/2003: II.1.7). At the same time, he argues, some very different Christianities contribute to the democratic character of the United States, benefit from the conditions it creates, and help to heal its internal contradictions. He characterizes Puritanism as a "democratic and republican religion" but one hostile to equality. Catholicism tends, on the other hand, to foster obedience but also to put all human beings on the "same level" (Tocqueville 1835/2003: I.17).

What we see here is, in effect, an alternative account of the underlying nature of American democracy and indeed of democracy in general, one that is deeply at odds with both Protestant and humanistic modernism. This account is, to be sure, still incipient and not fully developed. But all the key elements are present. Democratic societies, if they are to succeed, must be neither confessional nor secular. They must rather be founded on a rich network of intermediate institutions that order human activity toward the common good. And at the center of this network must be religious communities. These communities must, on the one hand, reject establishment, which only pits them against dissenting minorities and, by involving them with the state, puts them at odds with the democratic aspirations of the people. But they must also be vigorous in ordering citizens towards higher ends and indeed must be the means by which citizens promote their own vision of what it means to be human.

John Winthrop (or Jonathan Edwards) and Thomas Jefferson (or Benjamin Franklin) may have been the *conscious* architects of the twin variants of the American ideal, but it was Madison (and the other architects of the Constitution) who were the unconscious architects of the American polity and Tocqueville who was its best theoretician. While the Constitution provided a framework in which competing variants of the modern ideal—and later other civilizational ideals as well—could contend with each other without seeking hegemony, the network of intermediate voluntary organizations provided a framework in the context of which advocates of those competing ideals could *both* carve out enclaves in which they could, at least to some degree, live out their ideals even without persuading the majority *and* collaborate with each other around questions affecting the community as a whole.

The result has not been to make the United States as a society immune to secular messianisms. On the contrary, both Puritanism and Deistic Republicanism as well as later variants of the American ideal share, in varying degrees, in the modern project of divinization through innerworldly civilizational progress. It has, however, made the American *polity* resistant to secular messianisms—just as it has to successful attempts at theocratic restorationism.

We need now to see what happed to the competing variants of the American ideal and to the accidentally pluralistic America that emerged from the Revolution.

From Republic to Empire

The Crisis of "Old America"

The Crisis of Deistic Republicanism

As might be expected, Deistic Republicanism initially had greater popular appeal than the Puritan ensemble, if only because its political program consisted in promoting widespread land ownership and entrepreneurship. This, however, proved to be its undoing. Partly because he wanted to expand opportunities for land ownership, and partly out of a desire to help his ally Napoleon, Thomas Jefferson agreed to acquire the Louisiana Territory and then to commission the Lewis and Clark Expedition that eventually opened it up to settlement. But the land in question was not, of course, uninhabited, nor were all those who sought to "settle" it prospective yeoman farmers on the Jeffersonian model. It was Indian land, and those pressing most strongly for westward expansion were the slave-owning planters of the South, where expanding cotton cultivation was rapidly depleting the soil and where access to new land was a powerful economic imperative (Genovese 1988), or else land-hungry settlers with powerful anticivilizational impulses. The result, of course, was to link the democratic-revolutionary (and the Deistic Republican) project both to westward expansion at the expense of the indigenous peoples of the Americas (i.e., to *imperium*) and to the interests of the Southern landed elite and anticivilizational settlers. Deistic Republicanism was thus at once diluted and discredited as a vision for social reform.

This tendency for the Deistic Republican tradition to become discredited was overdetermined by the fact that the United States (contrary to what we are all taught in elementary school, and what we relive every time we sing the Star Spangled Banner) was on the *losing* side of the War of 1812, which was part of the broader geopolitical struggle between the revolutionary French and the reactionary English and Russians. Indeed, the violence of the French Revolution had already done a great deal to discredit Deistic Republicanism as a revolutionary ideology and the war itself was the occasion of America's first great Red Scare, the Bavarian Illuminati scandal, in which Federalist politicians and Calvinist ministers from New England, most of whom opposed the war and some of whom advocated secession, attempted to associate the Democratic-Republican Party with a conspiracy of French-style revolutionaries, Masons, and Jesuits to undermine true religion and the "American Way of Life" (Hatch 1977).

These developments did not kill the Deistic Republican tradition in the United States. Indeed, Democratic Party politicians still invoke both the name and the vision of Jefferson as one foundation for the party's ideological tradition, with one or another new mechanism of upward mobility replacing land ownership as the economic engine for realizing his vision. But from the War of 1812 on, Democrats always had to be at pains to prove their loyalty to an "America" increasingly defined by Anglophile and macro-Puritan tendencies and to deflect suspicion that they were "soft" on foreign revolutionary and religious ideologies. And the Democratic Party—especially when it has been successful—has more often been "Jacksonian" than "Jeffersonian," promoting widespread upward mobility without worrying too much about whether or not the specific pathways towards upward mobility actually helped realize the Deistic Republican ideal of an informed citizenry actively engaged in self-cultivation and deliberation regarding the common good.

This is what happened to the rural, Jeffersonian variant of the radical Enlightenment tradition in the United States. What about its urban, freethinking, and crafts variant? The cities have always been more resistant to hegemonization than the countrysides in the U.S., and urban radicalism in the United States has, even today, not so much been decisively defeated or hegemonized as it has been marginalized and rendered irrelevant. It seems, however, that the United States passed through a critical juncture—that of the industrial revolution—rather differently than did many European countries. In Europe, and in France in particular, craftsmen's organizations, especially the *compagnonages* or journeymen's associations, an outgrowth of the medieval guild system, played a critical role in both the resistance to industrialization and capitalist development and later in the emergence of a mass socialist movement (Sewell 1980). In the United States, which had no history of guilds, craft organizations of this sort were weaker. "Mechanics" and laborers were regarded as a dangerous element, and generally lived in their master's household under his discipline and supervision. To the extent that craftsmen organized at all outside the churches and political parties, they did so through clubs of the Masonic type, which carried an ideology that valued labor and spiritual excellence, but that also included numerous local businessmen and thus, being cross-class, were not really autonomous centers of artisanal organization like the French *compagnonages*. The Industrial Revolution, which began to affect the United States in the 1820s and 1830s, gradually broke down this pattern and created, for the first time, large concentrations of workingmen who were not under the direct supervision of their employers—who, in turn, were becoming increasingly wealthy and socially distant from those they employed. Taverns in particular emerged as centers of an autonomous working class culture, at just the time when the use of alcohol was becoming increasingly incompatible with productive employment.[9] Johnson (Johnson 1978) has shown that the Industrial Revolution, the advent of temperance movements, and the Second Great Awakening all occurred at roughly the same time in cities like

---

9. Prior to the Industrial Revolution it was not unusual for the employer himself to roll out a keg of rum around mid afternoon to carry his workers through the final hours of their work day. Industrialization, which involved the use of fast-moving, dangerous equipment, made this impossible.

Rochester in western New York that were among the most important new centers of industrial development.

What the Second Great Awakening did was, in effect, to hegemonize at least a part of the emerging industrial working classes—that drawn from English stock and from older immigrant groups that had been more completely assimilated. It did so by means of an ideology that could no longer be called classically Calvinist. Gone was the emphasis on predestination. Salvation was open to anyone who chose it. Along with this went a commitment to perfection—both personal and social—that at once tended to draw workers away from taverns and other centers of autonomous working class culture and channel working class political energy into bourgeois reform projects. The Second Great Awakening was, it should be noted, closely aligned with the Anti-Masonic movement and with the anti-immigrant Know Nothing Party.

The Puritan elite was, meanwhile, at work in other ideological institutions as well. Universal public education was an integral part of the Deistic Republican program and was hardly something that the New England Calvinist elite, with their tradition of a literate laity and a learned ministry, could oppose. But they also did not want the schools to become agents of what they regarded as an anti-Christian ideology, as they threatened to become in France. This is the origin of the peculiar character of the United States educational system—far more extensive, far earlier than most European systems, but uniformly mediocre. It is possible to read in the debates in state legislatures during the early and middle decades of the nineteenth century just how this happened. Schoolteachers were not, under any circumstances, to be drawn from among the graduates of elite universities where they might be exposed to foreign ideological influences, but from normal schools where they would learn what they needed in order to train a literate populace—but no more. The minister, not the schoolteacher, was to be the sapiential leader of the local community. And these normal schools would be kept away from the great cities where foreign influences might creep in. The curriculum, kept closely under the control of local elites, was to assimilate the people, and especially the waves of new immigrants, to an American (read macro-Puritan) identity. This is why every child in "America" grows up believing that his or her ancestors came over on the Mayflower, seeking religious freedom, when in fact the Mayflower brought only a tiny group of dissenting Puritans who even the founders of Massachusetts Bay thought extreme (Lasch 1995; Brouilette 1999).

All of these developments had the effect of putting Deistic Republicanism in the United States on the defensive. Where in Europe similar trends gave birth to revolutionary democratic and eventually to socialist impulses, Deistic Republicans in the United States were kept busy defending their Americanism and trying to hold constituents who might otherwise be lost to the Second Great Awakening, usually by promising them cheap land, and thus pandering to anticivilizational impulses.

The Crisis of the Puritan Ideological Ensemble

This whole complex of developments, which seemed to so favor the Puritan over the Deistic Republican variant of the American ideal all came to a head in the middle of the nineteenth century as a growing section of the bourgeoisie moved gradually into the antislavery camp. North and South had longstanding differences over questions such as tariffs and state expenditures on infrastructure, both of which were essential to the emerging industrial economy of the North and both of which threatened the South's position in the global economy as an agricultural exporter. And the northern bourgeoisie had never been entirely comfortable with slavery. But for a long time, these tensions with the South were balanced by the need for cheap cotton. Gradually, however, industry developed to the point that its need for free workers and an internal market loomed larger than its need for cheap raw materials, and the northern bourgeoisie gradually came to the view that slavery, one way or another, would have at least to be contained, and preferably come to an end.

The result of this process was the formation, under the aegis of the new Republican Party, of a broad alliance of industrial capitalists, commercial farmers in the old Northwest (what we now call the Midwest), and part of the urban proletariat and petty bourgeoisie (the part hegemonized by the Second Great Awakening) on a platform of commitment to containing or ending slavery, expanding access to land for prospective yeoman farmers, high tariffs, and state investment in infrastructure and education. Thus, by the time of the Civil War, the more modernized part of the rural population, as well as a significant part of the urban population of the United States, was firmly bound to the industrial bourgeoisie, and its principal hopes for upward mobility linked firmly to the imperial project of westward expansion. All of this was articulated through a rhetoric that linked the concerns of liberal Protestants and (postmillennial) evangelicals in a way that was inspiring to both. One need only think of the Battle Hymn of the Republic to understand the power of this vision.

But as was the case with other "bourgeois revolutions," the full promise of the Republican program of 1860 was never realized. A complete capitalist transformation of the United States would have involved not only an end to slavery but expropriation and redistribution of the lands of the southern plantation owners. This was, in fact, the program of the Radical Republicans, who represented the emerging steel and railroad industries, but the proposal won only thirty-seven votes in the House of Representatives. The older section of the bourgeoisie based in the New England textile industry was still too deeply dependent on cheap cotton to liquidate entirely the southern plantation system. Indeed, after 1876 the Union withdrew its troops from the South and allowed the southern landed elite to reconstitute itself on the basis of tenant rather than slave labor. Between 1876 and 1908 the industrial bourgeoisie ruled, in effect, in coalition with the southern landed elite in what Barrington Moore has called an American version of the Prussian alliance of iron and rye (Moore 1966: 141–55). The United States emerged from the Civil War as a dynamic, rapidly industrializing contender for great-power status and effective control of the entire middle section of the North American continent. And it soon developed imperial ambitions that extended to Latin America and Asia. But it was a far cry from the Holy Commonwealth envisioned by its Puritan founders.

One way of capturing the change that took place is by analyzing the transformation of the North American university. Up until the Civil War, North American universities were mostly small liberal arts colleges founded by churches to train clergy. They had, somewhat reluctantly, taken up the auxiliary task of training a broader literate elite. A few public institutions such as the University of Virginia and the University of Pennsylvania aspired to make a liberal arts education accessible to the broader natural aristocracy that Jefferson and Franklin had hoped would emerged from the yeoman and artisan classes. Central to the

Republican program of 1860, however, was the establishment of land-grant universities. The Morrill Land Grant College Act of 1862 set aside some 30,000 acres of federal land for each state for each Senator or Congressman that represented it in Congress. This land was to support the establishment of agricultural colleges, which eventually became the cornerstone of the state university system. These universities had from the beginning a very different mission from the old liberal arts colleges: they were to be drivers of economic development, carrying out research and development and training the intellectual workers necessary for a technologically, advancing economy. New private universities (Johns Hopkins was the first) developed with a similar mission, modeling themselves on the German research university. The effect was nothing less than to shift the intellectual center of gravity of the North American university system from the liberal arts and sapiential disciplines to science and technology, and to reorder them from service to the Protestant or humanistic to the positivistic variant of the modern ideal.

The disillusionment that resulted from the failure of the bourgeoisie to complete the promised redemption of the "nation" cannot be underestimated. As we noted above, most American evangelicals up until the Civil War were postmillennialists and regarded the creation of a just social order as the essential precondition of the second coming of Christ and thus an integral part of God's work of redemption. The struggle against slavery was seen as the leading edge of that process. God really was sifting out the nations beneath his judgment seat—and the Union armies were to be the agents of that judgment. When the promised redemption failed to take place, the old Evangelical United Front began gradually to dissolve, with some drifting towards the liberal gradualism that eventually became the Social Gospel movement and others abandoning their postmillennial eschatology in favor of what eventually emerged as modern fundamentalism (Marsden 1980). This new, fundamentalist evangelicalism was based on a dispensational premillennial eschatology. According to this view, God deals differently with humanity during different periods. The ministry of Jesus, up until the time of his crucifixion, was part of the dispensation of the Law, and Jesus's moral teachings with their profound social implications are essentially part of a superceded Judaism. Humanity is living now in the age of grace, when salvation is by faith, not works. What is more, rather than leading naturally to moral uplift and social reform, personal conversion has no really visible moral or social effects. Far from looking forward to the creation of a just society, the new fundamentalism expected the world to get worse and worse until Jesus came to "rapture" the elect and redeem it.

This new fundamentalism had a social base very different than that of the old Evangelical United Front. While evangelicalism had always spoken to those who were "left behind," it did so at least in part because it promised a better world, and not only in the beyond. Evangelicalism had been, in other words, an ideology of those who hoped to make America keep its promises. In this regard, it overlapped very substantially with liberal Protestant reformism. Now, increasingly, it spoke to those who recognized that high modernity (they never said "America" or "capitalism") had no use for them and their way of life and who felt, furthermore, that the proposals of liberal reformers and socialists, far from offering a more humane modernity, simply promised a more vigorous effort to extinguish their way of life.[10] For broad layers of the rural population in the South and West and for the petty bourgeoisie and even small capitalists of the smaller cities and towns, "progress," whether understood in the capitalist or the socialist sense, meant only further attacks on their way of life. And so they dug in their heels and resisted and waited for Jesus. They are still waiting.

The one politically significant exception to this pattern was the African American people who, alone among the members of the old Evangelical United Front, have retained both their evangelicalism and their commitment to social reform. Black evangelicalism has, to be sure, always been different from its "white" counterpart. As Eugene Genovese pointed out long ago, African Americans never really bought into the doctrines of original sin and double predestination (Genovese 1974). The Black community has, however, always had a deep sense of the degrading effects of oppression on personal morality. Personal con-

---

10. There were, to be sure, exceptions to this pattern. Oklahoma and North Texas, for example, gave birth during the first decades of the twentieth century to a mass socialist movement with strong roots in the Pentecostal churches (Burbank 1976; Green 1978; Bisset 1999). Such movements of resistance to capitalist modernization were, however, rejected by both the Socialist and Communist Parties, on the ground that socialism was, first and foremost, about realizing the modern ideal. This successfully alienated the marginalized rural population and drove them into a more pessimistic fundamentalism once and for all.

version in this context means getting your act together and learning to live productively and creatively in "the world as it is" while struggling to create "the world which could and should be."[11] The result has been that African Americans, while more than willing to point out the shortcomings of the United States are, perhaps more than any other group in the country, true believers in "America," and are so in more nearly the classical Puritan sense than any other ethnoreligious community. As anyone who has attempted to organize in the African American community has discovered, it is one thing to call "America" to task for her sins; it is quite another to attack the American ideal. It is interesting to note, however, that when African Americans *have* called the American ideal into question, this has usually involved an explicit break with Christianity, something that could be made fully explicit only by opting for another, and historically opposed, religion—Islam.

In other words, well before the end of the nineteenth century the American Dream, as it had been understood by both its Puritan and Enlightenment advocates, was dead. The United States would be neither a Holy Commonwealth the Christian commitments of which would be reflected in a just social order nor a petty bourgeois utopia of self-cultivation in which yeoman farmers and master craftsmen studied the arts and sciences and philosophy in the evening and sent their sons to public universities that allowed the best the rise to the top while permitting everyone to develop as far as they could. It was, rather, a developing industrial capitalist power with a continental empire—and a voracious appetite for cheap labor.

Immigrants and "America"

This might well have been the end of the American ideal, and proof that the America seen by its global critics—a rapacious empire the religious and humanistic ideals of which are merely an alibi for exploitation—is and always has been the only America. But something happened. Its very real shortcomings notwithstanding, the United States still offered to the dispossessed of Europe—and many other parts of the

---

11. The phrases "world as it is" and "world as it should be" are part of the stock-in-trade of the Industrial Areas Foundation, an organizing institute that challenges people in oppressed communities to take seriously the need to build power. The language seems ultimately to derive from Nietzsche.

world—what seemed like unprecedented opportunities, and became a magnet for peasants displaced by the penetration of capitalist relations of production into the countryside, as well as for religious minorities—especially Jews—escaping persecution. These immigrants, furthermore, brought with them civilizational ideals that were, in many cases, fundamentally different or even in conflict with both the Puritan and Deistic Republican ideological ensembles. And yet they also seemed to understand intuitively the potential of the authentic Tocquevillian America far better than the old Puritan and Deistic-Republican elites. And because of this they were able to renew and reinvigorate American civilization in ways that allowed it to once again participate creatively in the larger human civilizational project.

There were, broadly speaking, four new currents introduced into the United States by immigration during the nineteenth century. The first was a more moderate, liturgically oriented Protestantism, including especially the German and Scandinavian Lutheran and German Reformed Churches. In some cases these churches reacted strongly against the Puritanism they found in the United States, giving birth to Catholicizing movements such as the Mercersburg Theology (Schaff 1964; Nichols 1966; Ahlstrom 1971; Nevin 2000), a German Reformed movement that stressed the incarnation over the crucifixion and that moved towards a more liturgical form of worship, something that has shaped profoundly the evolution of the modern United Church of Christ, which brings together English and German Reformed churches in the United States. These churches founded colleges that, in many cases, have remained more faithful than their Puritan—or Catholic—counterparts to the old liberal arts ideal of cultivating free human beings and citizens with a commitment to serving the common good. This immigrant Protestantism was reinforced by trends in the English Protestant tradition, including both Methodism, with its focus on cultivating moral excellence, and Anglo-Catholicism.

Second, the United States, which was founded by deeply anti-Catholic English Protestants, became home to a growing Catholic minority.[12] These immigrants brought an extraordinarily diverse range of different expressions of the Catholic tradition, from Irish and Polish

---

12. For a good general account of the history of the Catholic Church in the Untied States, see Dolan 1983, 1985, 2003; Fischer 2002; Orsi 2002.

Catholics for whom Catholicism was a defining mark of national identity, and who thus identified strongly with their hierarchy and clergy, to anticlerical Sicilians who brought a rich tradition of popular religion but little commitment to the Catholic Church as an institution. And while essentially no one in the American Catholic Church—from members of lay confraternities with only the loosest connections to their local parishes, much less to Rome, up through the great prelates—saw themselves as providing a beachhead for papal power, Catholicism *did* bring a very different political theology to American shores: one that recognized the autonomy of civil society and the ordinary political authorities, but that regarded the Church as a guardian not only of humanity's transcendental vocation but also of natural law. And despite numerous missteps, the American Catholic Church, both as a hierarchical institution and as a complex of ethnoreligious communities, found far more effective ways to act on this political theology than they had it Europe. The European Church did little to build an infrastructure of parishes in emerging industrial working class communities. It fought democracy for a long time and entered the democratic public arena through the mechanism of Christian Democratic or Social Christian political parties and mass organizations (trade unions and peasant organizations) that, while often the carriers of highly innovative public policy initiatives, functioned for their sponsors more as levers against secularist liberal, socialist, and communist parties than as vehicles for a distinctive vision of social justice. In the United States, on the other hand, immigrant communities built strong local parish structures, both ethnic and territorial, which at once helped conserve a distinctive ethnoreligious identity and mediate between the immigrants and the larger American society that they had joined. Movements like Catholic Action worked through local parishes, forming grassroots leaders with a strong Social Christian outlook, which was then brought into the larger political arena primarily through nonconfessional (though often congregationally based) community organizations, as well as labor unions and the Democratic Party, ensuring that a broad agenda for social justice rather than clerical interests predominated. Indeed, it was the American Catholic example, as interpreted by Belgian sociologist Francois Houtart (Houtart 1952) that inspired the innovative pastoral strategy of the Latin American Bishops in the 1960s and 1970s.

Third, Jews, who had always had a presence in the United States, became its first significant non-Christian ethnoreligious immigrant minority.[13] The country's first Jews had been anglicized Sephardic Jews who came from Spain by way of England. The second wave was composed of German Jews strongly influenced by the Enlightenment, and who founded the Reform movement that, especially in its early years, borrowed on the forms of liberal Protestantism. But towards the end of the nineteenth century the United States became home to millions of Jews escaping persecution in the Pale of Settlement, and who brought with them both the traditional rabbinic and Hasidic forms of Orthodox Judaism and revolutionary national movements such as Bundism (a trend that sought cultural autonomy within Western societies), territorialism (a trend that sought an independent Jewish state in Eastern Europe or North America), and Zionism, all three of which were laced with socialism. As was the case with Catholicism, Jews brought with them a very different political theology—in this case, one centered on struggling for justice within a society they could never hope to (and did not aspire to) dominate. Both in its more assimilated Reformed version and in its radical Orthodox and nationalist forms, Judaism brought to the U.S. public arena the critical leaven that Christian Europe was purging from itself.

Finally, immigrants from throughout Europe brought with them more intense expressions of the humanistic variant of the high modern ideal, specifically in the form of a vigorous socialist movement. These ideals were carried at first by refugees from the failed uprisings of 1848, many of them German, who played a critical role in founding socialism in the United States, but by the end of the century, these intellectuals were joined by millions of artisans and workers (many of them highly literate autodidacts) who hoped that the United States would prove more hospitable to their revolutionary agenda than had their countries of origin.

Often these tendencies were woven together with each other into a rich and complex tapestry. Among Italian immigrants, for example, we find a loose synthesis between the populist socialism of the displaced peasantry, which was primarily a means of *resisting* capitalist

---

13. Good histories of American Judaism include Cutler 1996; Diner 2004; Eisen 1995; Glazer 1988; Sarna 2004.

modernization, and the socialism of the literate artisanate inspired by the humanistic modern ideal of rational autonomy and democratic citizenship and determined to resist the alienation engendered by the wage relation. This socialism found its base in the mutual benefit societies formed by the immigrants on the basis of old village networks that were gradually transformed into the cells of immigrant socialist organizations such as the old *Federazione Socialista Italiana*. These organizations were ideologically diverse but for the most part reflected a combination of peasant popular religion and Masonic and freethinking craft traditions. Thus, in the Italian socialist periodical *Parola del Popolo*, articles about the *Gesù socialista* ran side by side with columns by writers using pseudonyms like *Lucifero*. Anticlericalism was nearly universal, but anything like a full-blown atheism was rare. This was a socialism better understood using the categories of Durkheim, Gramsci, or even the Russian *Narodniki* than those of Marx, Engels, Kautsky, or Lenin. On its periphery, this Italian immigrant socialism met with the diverse ideologies of the Jewish community, with whom they shared a common concentration in the garment trades.

This mixture of popular Judaism and Catholicism and Masonic and Socialist rationalism made the immigrants a nativist's nightmare. But the immigrants did not see themselves as engaged in a frontal assault on the American way of life; rather, they understood America precisely as defined by a pluralism that at once admitted to the public arena even ideologies fundamentally at variance with the historic consensus (such as socialism) and that not only permitted but actually encouraged the development of distinct subcultures. Thus socialists of my grandfather's generation saw no conflict between their socialist commitments and their love for "America." On the contrary, it was precisely because the United States allowed them to advocate socialism openly and struggle for it by peaceful and democratic means that they loved it so deeply. Jewish territorialists (a tendency within the Jewish socialist movement that supported the establishment of a Jewish homeland, but did not believe that that homeland needed to be in Israel) even imagined that U.S. federalism might allow them to create a Jewish socialist state within the larger framework of the U.S. polity, and efforts in this direction were undertaken in New Jersey (Eisenberg 1995).

The immigrant culture that developed in the great industrial cities of the U.S., in other words, engaged the "America" actually created by the founders rather than any of the Americas the founders had intended. They often struggled actively against aspects of this "actually existing America,"—i.e., its capitalist economic structure. But other aspects—the possibility of a polity *defined* by debate around fundamental questions of meaning and value, and thus of a democracy far more profound than that envisioned by either liberals or socialists in Europe—they transformed into a conscious ideal.

How did their efforts fare? In one sense, they fared very poorly. The immigrant communities themselves were unable to conserve their traditions sufficiently to realize the full promise of the Tocquevillian pluralism that they envisioned. This was due partly to the failure of the principal global institutions with which the immigrant communities interacted and to which they looked to help them advance their visions and conserve their traditions—the Roman Catholic Church, Judaism, and the international socialist and communist movements—and partly to the Second World War and the profound social transformations that followed.

The Catholic Church in the late nineteenth century was not of one mind as to how to contend with the ethnic differences that divided the immigrant church in North America. Many felt that the most important task for the Church was simply to maintain, or in the case of the Italian communities to gain, the institutional loyalty—and thus to "save the souls"—of the immigrants, and advocated the establishment of national parishes, often drawing on religious orders based in the old country, to establish a religious environment in which the immigrants would feel comfortable (Shanbuch 1981).

Increasingly, however, the "Americanizing" wing of the hierarchy was gaining influence over the North American Church. These Americanizers were profoundly impressed with the accomplishments of American civilization, which they attributed in no small part to the vigor and individualism of American culture, and they were sensitive to accusations that Catholicism was "un-American," which they believed had to be answered effectively if the church was to have a future in this country. And, with the exception of the immigrant clergy themselves, even those ecclesiastics not associated with the "Americanist" tendency had little commitment to preserving the religious traditions of the immigrant communities themselves, and tended to see the national parishes more as a temporary expedient for gaining a foothold in the communities than as a permanent institution. And the Vatican, while more than a little suspicious of "Americanism," both as a theological tendency and as a way of life, was profoundly suspicious of the institutional pluralism and relative autonomy from diocesan control that the national parish system tended to give the immigrants.

In 1915 matters finally came to a head. A new code of canon law was promulgated that made the territorial parish the legal norm, from which departures were possible only by exception (Shanbuch 1981: 163). Promulgation of the code was accompanied in Chicago by the appointment of Mundelein as archbishop. Mundelein had little taste for cultural pluralism and declared an immediate moratorium on creation of new national parishes (182). Those already existing, provided they were self-supporting, would be transformed into vital links in an aggressive program of Americanization (172–73). Those that could not support themselves—this included most of the Italian American parishes—would be closed (163).

Of critical importance to Mundelein's program of Americanization was the parochial school system. Initially, many Italian-American and other immigrant clergy had hoped that the parochial schools, attached to national parishes, would be the first line of defense for immigrant culture, assuring that the children of the immigrants were taught in their parents' languages, and that English was taught only as a second language. Such, however, was not to be the case. James Jennings, Mundelein's school superintendent, wrote in 1916 that it was his purpose to

> thoroughly Americanize the Catholic school system in Chicago. We propose to teach our children that there shall no longer be Irish-American, German-American, or Polish-American in our city but only real Americans. In other words we intend to take the hyphen out of the parochial school system in Chicago. (187–88)

All subjects, with the exception of foreign languages—as the native tongues of the immigrants were now called—were to be taught in English. Italian children were rarely taught by Italian sisters, but rather by Irish or French Americans. It was not unheard of for Italian children to be segregated during mass, being made to sit in the back of the church with the African Americans (Vecoli 1969: 233).

For Jews, the issues were somewhat different. American Judaism had always been torn between more assimilationist Reform Jews, mostly from Germany, and those from the Pale of Settlement who sought to conserve their ethno-religious distinctiveness, whether they understood this in Orthodox or modern nationalist or socialist terms. But Jews were different enough, and "America" still Protestant enough, that there was little danger of Judaism loosing its critical edge through assimilation. It was, rather, the establishment of the state of Israel that changed the terms on which American Jews engaged the American polity. And even here the effect was far from complete. The effect, rather, was to divide the (very substantial) energies of the Jewish community between the promotion of a pluralistic, just social order in the United States and the protection of the state of Israel. Gradually, as Israel's geopolitical alignment changed, this pulled some American Jews to the right and into an alliance with fundamentalist Protestants who saw the state of Israel as a sign of the end times. Even so, the Jewish presence in the United States remains overwhelmingly a force for pluralism and social justice.

It is, however, the role of the international Left in undermining immigrant identity that is most surprising. The old Socialist Party was dominated largely by Anglo, German, and to a lesser extent Irish workers drawn from the skilled crafts and organized in trade unions, and these workers looked down on what they saw as unskilled foreigners who had to be assimilated to "American" culture before they could become real participants in the public arena. Many Socialists—though by no means as many as in Europe—also supported participation by the United States in the First World War. Not surprisingly, therefore, immigrants from Southern and Eastern Europe gravitated to the newly formed Communist Party. But this party did not understand their socialism any better than the "American" social democrats. In 1922, only 10 percent of the party's members belonged to the English-speaking section, and by 1925 this figure had grown to only 14 perdent (Glazer 1961: 40). The party was, furthermore, organized around the semi-autonomous language federations. The leadership, however, did not understand what it had achieved by conquering for itself the allegiance of the immigrant working class. Indeed, in 1925 the party expressed its recognition of the contributions of the immigrants by undertaking a campaign of "Bolshevisization" designed to "raise the level of organization, political, and ideological discipline." At the center of this campaign was the liquidation of the language federations, which were the carriers of the immigrant socialist traditions, and the reorganization of the party around a system of factory nuclei—in spite of the fact that some immigrant groups, the Italians in particular, tended not to work in factories. English classes were to be mandatory for all comrades who were not already fluent in the language, and leadership cadre were to be drawn from among the "American" comrades (Glazer 1961: 47–52, 56). "Strengthening ideological discipline" meant that the orthodox atheistic position of the communist movement on the religious question was much more in evidence, and religious propaganda of the sort promoted by the FSI was out of the question.

This campaign had disastrous results. Membership dropped from 14,037 to 7,215 in the space of *one month*, between September 25 and October 25, 1925, as immigrant workers resisting the new line left or were purged from the party. Worse still, the party lost its precious roots in the popular communal institutions and the popular religious traditions of the immigrant working class—roots it has never been able to rebuild.

The liquidation of the language federations had two critical results. First, liquidation of the language federations deprived the immigrant communities of the institutional apparatus they needed to conserve their own cultures while engaging the broader pluralistic public arena. Second, the party sent a strong and clear message to the immigrant communities that the struggle for socialism had nothing to do with them or their traditions. On the contrary, it meant the destruction of their institutions and the devaluation of their traditions. Not surprisingly, most immigrants abandoned socialism once and for all, significantly undermining the ideological pluralism of the American public arena (Mansueto 2002a).

It was, however, not the strategic decisions of religious and political institutions but rather external pressures that did the most to undercut the immigrant reading of American pluralism. And here the ideological salience of the struggle against fascism played a central role. Where at least many of the European workers who joined the resistance fought against fascism under the banners of the Communist Party (and even those who did not fought alongside Communists), workers from the United States fought under the banners of "America." Indeed, it would not be too much to say that the war took the sons of Italian, Sicilian, Polish, Jewish, and Irish workers and made "Americans" out of them. Certainly the women of the immigrant communities felt the change. As one woman told me, "the boys were somehow *different* when they came back. It is like we couldn't talk to them any more. Like they were no longer one of *us*" (Oral Testimony, Italians in Chicago Oral History Project).

It is conceivable that, had the returning soldiers been re-integrated into their old communities, something more of their ethnic identities might have remained, but shortly after the war they began moving out of the cities in large numbers, populating newly developed suburban communities, something that utterly disrupted the social patterns that made it possible to create and sustain distinct ethnic identities in the first place (Bess 2006). Rather than spending the evening sitting on the stoop chatting with neighbors or paying a visit to the barbershop to discuss the affairs of the day, people camped out in front of their television sets. Rather than getting their news from *The Jewish Daily Forward* or *Parola del Popolo*, they got it from the newly formed networks, something that represented an unprecedented concentration of the media of social communications in the hands of Capital. And of course the most important function of the media was not to interpret the world, but rather to change it, by feeding to viewers images of the good life that centered more or less exclusively on consumption. The GI Bill gave those who had served in the armed forces unprecedented access to higher education, albeit of a rather diluted variety. As the postwar generation entered the professional middle class their commitment to trade unionism declined, and even those who remained pro-union were rarely active members.

When, in the 1950s, Joseph McCarthy unleashed his campaign against Communism in the United States, he faced little real opposition. But more was at issue here than simply purging a discourse around socialism from public life. McCarthy's campaign resonated deeply with earlier witch-hunts going all of the way back to the Bavarian illuminati scandal and perhaps further, to the literal witch-hunts of the Puritan era, and made allegiance to one or another version of the Puritan variant of the American ideal (usually the "secularized," high modern variant) the condition for participation in the public arena.

This said, the wave of immigrants that came to the United States between 1870 and 1924, together with their descendants, left an important legacy. They demonstrated once and for all that it is possible to be an "American" without subscribing to either the Puritan or the Deistic Republican variants of the American ideal—and that in fact Tocqueville understood America far better than any of its founders. They also laid the groundwork for a new understanding of the public arena, as at once pluralistic but value based, as indeed *constituted* by deliberation around fundamental questions of meaning and value—an understanding that will become increasingly important as the larger modern ideals (including its distinctly American variants) are called ever more profoundly into question.

An Empire in Crisis

The United States emerged from the Second World War as the leading representative of capitalist high modernity and as an imperial power with a reach the scope and depth of which was unprecedented in human history. It also found itself immediately locked into a pitched battle with the leading representative of socialist modernity, the Soviet Union, and with a diffuse but growing alliance of movements and newly independent states that understood themselves as not only resisting imperialism but also as seeking a road to development that would allow them to recover and conserve their traditional cultures. China moved back and forth between these two poles, sometimes embracing socialist modernity, sometimes interpreting its socialism in a way that represented a significant break with modernity or even with civilization as such.

The identification of the United States with capitalist modernity was, meanwhile, challenged from within by a broad array of movements beginning in the 1960s. The most important of these was the Civil Rights movement, which was first and foremost a movement *within* the established framework of "American" political discourse (indeed within its most authoritative variant, the old evangelical social reform variant of the Puritan ideological ensemble), and a movement to gain for those who were still excluded, especially African Americans, access to what other Americans already enjoyed. There was also a new wave of the women's movement that, while it certainly developed a more radical wing, was for the most part also firmly embedded in the

"American tradition." Indeed, this wave was first and foremost a response to the development of effective artificial contraception that gave women increased control over their bodies and opened up for them new possibilities that, however, required some modest changes in law and custom if they were to be realized. What was being demanded, however, was simply what every liberal society claims it accords its citizens anyway—equal access to careers and public office on the basis of talent. Both of these movements, precisely because their demands could be accommodated within the context of capitalist modernity and within the context of the dominant political culture, had a significant impact on U.S. society, even if they fell short of their more ambitious aims.

The youth and student movement was more complex and ambiguous in its social character. At its base, this was a movement of the petty bourgeois intelligentsia resisting proletarianization—resisting transformation, in the words of the popular sociology of the day, into "organization men." This gave the movement a radical edge and an ability to see some of the contradictions of modernity that had been missed even by the communist left—the problems of bureaucratic organization, for example, and the danger of ecological devastation. And because of the profound connection between capitalist modernity and the "American" way of life, it also gave the young rebels an impetus to question the role of the United States in the world and to develop a sense of solidarity with popular struggles in Asia, Africa, and Latin America. This push was intensified by the fact that the youth/student movement was also, first and foremost, a movement against the war in Vietnam. All of these factors led some critical theorists to regard the youth movement as the single most important constituency for social transformation (Marcuse 1962).

And yet even this movement did not lead to a global, generational break with or transformation of American identity. On the contrary, the most radical elements in the student movement simply self-destructed. Here there were two principal trends. The first became involved in an ultimately hopeless effort to build a new communist party[14] to replace the broken remnant that had survived McCarthyism and that was now

---

14. For a more traditionally historical materialist account of the new communist or party building movement see Elbaum 2002.

denounced as hopelessly reformist. This party would ultimately give to the petty bourgeois intelligentsia the capacity to organize and direct the cosmohistorical evolutionary process and thus the divinization it had always craved. Another wing embraced a postmodern politics of permanent revolution that has only lately been adequately theorized by philosophers like Badiou (Badiou 1988, 2006) as a politics beyond the party that seeks to redefine the underlying ontological structure through "events" not only in the realm of politics, but also in art, science, and love.

The more moderate elements, on the other hand, were reabsorbed into the larger fabric of American society. There was, after all, a long-standing tradition of anti-imperialism *within* the liberal Protestant and evangelical social reform traditions, going back to Whig resistance to the conquest of Mexico, and most of the resistance to the Vietnam War and to later adventures in Central America remained within this framework. Most of those who went beyond anti-imperialism to genuine solidarity with movements of national liberation did so on the basis of a shared Catholic religious identity with those prosecuting those movements, an identity that was undercut when the Vatican began its campaign against the theology of liberation in the 1980s.

Ultimately the youth/student movement reflected the underlying weakness of its social base. It is not that, as classical historical materialism has argued, the petty bourgeoisie is incapable of developing a powerful movement for social justice—that is what the guilds were all about, and earliest socialism was first and foremost a movement of petty bourgeoisie *resistance* to capitalist development. It is that *this* petty bourgeoisie was weak. Partly this is because it was not really much of a petty bourgeoisie at all. While elements in the movement were drawn from old petty bourgeois families that were, ironically, experiencing *both* increased prosperity *and* proletarianization, as members of the liberal professions were gradually turned into "organization men," most were the grandchildren of immigrant workers and the children of physicians, attorneys, or more often of engineers, accountants, schoolteachers, nurses, or social workers, who had attended the university on the GI Bill. They believed that expanded access to higher education was an invitation to join the ranks of the autonomous liberal professions, and when they found out that instead it was a mechanism for training a new intellectual proletariat, they balked. They lacked, however, a petty bourgeois tradition that might actually have sustained real resistance. As we have seen, the postwar generation grew up in a suburban environment that had all but destroyed the rich network of institutions and traditions that had nurtured immigrant socialism. Rejecting the "American" way of life meant rejecting the traditions of the old "American" petty bourgeoisie—i.e., the traditions of liberal Protestant, evangelical, or Deistic Republican social reform. And so their resistance more often than not took the form of pure self-indulgence: sex, drugs, and rock and roll. And when they realized that their pleasures cost money, and that, the apparent prosperity of their youths notwithstanding, their parents were very far from being able to endow them for life, they cried "uncle" and were reborn as the "yuppies" of the 1980s and 1990s—organization men (and now organization women as well) even more pliable than their parents because they were even more addicted to prosperity.

The broad global resistance to "capitalist America," meanwhile, underwent its own crisis. On the one hand, the socialist variant of the modern ideal was gradually losing its appeal. This led to the decline and eventual collapse of the Soviet Union, which was the principal strategic reserve of the national liberation movements, and undercut the authority of ex-colonial states that had attempted to modernize while conserving elements of their traditional culture, under the guise of African, Arab, Buddhist, Gandhian, or Islamic socialisms. We will consider this crisis in more detail in the next chapter. On the other hand, the internal dynamics of capitalist development, and specifically the emergence of a unified global market, forced on national liberation movements and ex-colonial states a stark alternative: an essentially premodern autarky or creative engagement with the global market. The first alternative was, furthermore, made particularly difficult by the fact that the premodern demographic balance had already been upset by the introduction of new foods from the Americas and by the impact of modern medicine. Radical attempts at autarky (China during the Cultural Revolution, "Democratic" Kampuchea) led to holocaust and civilizational decline; moderate attempts (Tanzania, Myanmar) led to stagnation. Engagement with the global market, on the other hand, meant effective abandonment of socialism, in either its populist or modernist variants.

It was, ironically, this same development—the global victory of capitalism—rather than any of the popular movements that ultimately began to undermine the strength and call into question the identity of capitalist "America." Already in the 1960s this dynamic was beginning to have an impact. Capital flowed out of the United States into low wage countries, especially in Asia, gradually undermining the competitiveness of U.S. industry. First textiles and clothing, then steel, and eventually even automobiles all succumbed to this dynamic. Meanwhile, the very measures that had helped stabilize U.S. capitalism during the underconsumption crisis of the 1930s—income transfer programs, regulated collective bargaining, and federal deficit spending—now simply exacerbated the problem. Income transfer programs and collective bargaining led to wage increases that, due to the export of capital, were no longer supported by rising productivity, while deficit spending raised interest rates and undercut capital formation (Davis 1986; Galbraith 1988).

After a long period of trying to avoid serious structural changes during the 1970s, the U.S. moved sharply to break with the old social liberal model during the 1980s and 1990s. This change took place in two stages. First, the Republican government of the 1980s moved sharply against an already weakened trade union movement and instituted a program of social austerity that undercut the upward pressure on wages. Then, in the 1990s, the Democratic government undertook a serious effort to reduce deficits and increase capital formation. The result was a period of renewed growth that lasted until roughly 2001.

Neither measure, however, was able to address the underlying structural issue facing capitalist "America": namely, the fact that the long-term tendency of globalization is to drive wages down to world market levels, with only those who are able to capture monopoly rents on skill and innovation able to prosper. Modest investments in education, mostly at the community college level, come nowhere near addressing this question. As a result, a growing segment of the U.S. population feels more and more "left behind," a dynamic that is accentuated by the fact that even those who continue to enjoy high and even rising incomes are constantly threatened with lay-offs and outsourcing. As we will see, it is this sense of being left behind that lies behind the rise of the Religious Right, in the United States and around the world.

Others, meanwhile, who are prospering from globalization[15] embrace an increasingly cosmopolitan identity that deepens the divide with the "left behind." And globalization has brought to the United States a new wave of immigrants—Muslim, Hindu, and Buddhist, as well as Mexicans who have renewed the tradition of popular Catholicism—who will not be so easily assimilated.

What does America Mean?

What does this analysis imply about the United States and its larger contributions to the human civilizational project? Clearly, the United States *cannot* claim to be the Holy Commonwealth or the Republic of Virtue that its Puritan and Deistic Republican founders hoped it would be. Both of these ideals were compromised from the very beginning by their complicity in the process of imperial expansion and capitalist modernization. Nor can the ideal of a scientific high modern "Capitalist America," promoter of free markets, formal democracy, and a secularized consumer culture, expect to have much salience in a world where the modern ideal is increasingly being called into question even by the privileged, and where the vast majority who are not privileged associate it with brutal exploitation and the destruction of their traditional way of life.

On the other hand, our analysis suggests that it is also difficult to claim that "Capitalist America" is the *only* America or, to put the matter differently, that the United States is the true "Evil Empire"—and nothing more. As we have noted above, no single variant of the modern project ever gained hegemony in the United States. Indeed, large sectors of the population—mostly immigrants—dissented from significant aspects of the modern ideal as such, even when they affiliated with modern political movements such as socialism.

This creates a distinctive opportunity as we enter a period of civilizational crisis. On the one hand, modernity has been good enough to the United States, and all three variants of the modern ideal (Protestant, humanistic, and scientific) influential enough, that we are unlikely to see any violent antimodernist upheavals. The United States can play

15. Those sectors of capital centered in the finance, information, and technology sectors, together with those workers—mostly highly educated—able to capture monopoly rents on skill or innovation.

the role of one of the conservers of the authentic achievements of modernity. Both the Protestant social reform traditions (liberal and evangelical) and the distinctly American variant of humanistic modernism, which I have called Deistic Republicanism, are likely to be part of this mix. On the other hand, there is a way of understanding America—as the homeland of cultural pluralism *par excellence*—that opens up exciting new possibilities in a period in which the modern ideal is increasingly being called into question. This way of understanding America is, furthermore, supported by key aspects of our political structure and historical development. The U.S. polity may not have been *conceived* as a locus for dialogue around fundamental questions of meaning and value, a space neither confessional nor secular in which we can engage questions of ends before we address questions of means, but it is structured in such a way as to make that kind of dialogue not only possible but inevitable. This potential is, furthermore, supported both by the strong tradition of intermediate voluntary organizations and by the waves of immigrants who have come to the United States—both those who came before 1924, and those who have come since, so that our public arena is not just Jewish and Protestant and Catholic and humanistic, but also Islamic, Hindu, Buddhist, Confucian, and Taoist. Each of these traditions brings its own understanding of what it means to be human and its own distinctive political-theological perspective.

The possibilities of American pluralism are, to be sure, still constrained by the changes in social patterns that took place during the post-WWII period. Mediating institutions have declined, especially among the descendants of older generations of immigrants, as the United States has become suburbanized and privatized. Newer waves of immigrants are establishing institutions that will allow them to conserve and practice their own traditions. But in some cases these institutions are not especially well adapted to mediating functions. Hindu priests and Buddhist monks, for example, often still have very weak English skills and are not, in any case, trained for debate in a larger pluralistic public arena the way most Jewish, Christian, and Islamic clergy have been. And not all immigrant communities have traditions of institution building. Mexican immigrants, for example, bring an experience of the Church as a colonial institution, which often defended them against exploitation but that was essentially provided for them. There is thus much less internal financial support for or ownership of parish communities by Mexican Catholics than there was among earlier Catholic immigrant communities. Secondary institutions that bring together people with mixed identities are few and far between. And there is certainly a danger that those left behind by globalization will opt for reaction—for an attempt to reassert early modern macro-Puritan patterns—as a way of conserving identity and protecting backward economies. We will look at both of these issues in the next chapter.

These problems notwithstanding, the road forward for the United States lies clearly in building on its pluralism. The result will not be the Holy Commonwealth or the Republic of Virtue, the "last, best hope for humanity" that various founding fathers envisioned, but it may be something far better: a society that realizes that precisely because humanity is so varied and creative, there *is* no last best hope, but only an ongoing search for meaning and an ongoing struggle for excellence. If the United States can bequeath this to humanity, it will have more than justified its existence.

CHAPTER 4

An Era of Civilizational Crisis

We have now reached the crux of our argument. We explained in the introduction and the first chapter why we believe the principal alternative analyses of the current situation—as well as the modern and postmodern social theory behind them—are wrong. We have elaborated a new theoretical framework that joins the kind of structural analysis characteristic of modern social theory with a commitment to taking seriously the distinctive *ends* or *ideals* that different civilizations seek. We have demonstrated the power of this framework in making sense out of the human civilizational project generally and modernity in particular. And we have examined in some depth the distinctive way in which modernity unfolded in the United States. In this chapter we will make in greater depth our case for the claim that we are entering a period of civilizational crisis and show how this thesis sheds light on the current situation.

The Idea of Civilizational Crisis

Political Theology, Social Theory, and Geopolitical Analysis

Political Theology

It may be useful to begin by recapping in some detail our argument up to this point. The alternative analysis that we are proposing is based on very different philosophical and political-theological foundations from those of modern social theory. Like dialectical and historical materialism, we uphold a moderate realism tempered by recognition of the role of social structure and social location in shaping the way we think

(Mansueto 2002b). Also like dialectical materialism (Engels 1880/1940; Bogdanov 1928/1980), we regard the universe as a self-organizing system that develops towards increasingly complex levels of organization (Mansueto 2005: 43-64).[1] Like functionalism and interpretive sociology, we take seriously the ideas that constitute societies and give meaning and direction to human action, and we regard politics as, at the highest level, a struggle around fundamental questions of meaning and value. Unlike all of these theories, however, our perspective recognizes that the cosmohistorical evolutionary process generally and the human civilizational project in particular are ordered towards a transcendental end. Everything in the universe seeks Being, in proportion to and in accord with its nature and specific characteristics (Mansueto 2005).

What this means is that human beings and human societies seek God, not just in the sense of a *relationship* with the divine, but in the sense of seeking actual divinization in so far as, and in the way in which, they understand it. Everything we do, from the most basic activities necessary to survival—which is a struggle to persist in Being—to the most complex products of our civilizations, shares this common end. It is just the way in which we understand the divine and the means by which we seek it that changes.

Theologically, we understand this struggle for divinization as fundamentally positive and constitutive of our humanity. It is what first stretches us and calls out the best from us. But it is also a struggle doomed to failure, for the simple reason that the boundary between

---

[1]. In Christian circles this view is often associated with Teilhard de Chardin, but he is hardly the only thinker to have upheld this view over the course of the past two centuries, and his work is notable in *not* confronting the difficult scientific and philosophical issues involved in this claim: i.e., whether or not modern science really supports a doctrine of cosmic evolution toward increased levels of complexity and if not (and I believe that it is ambiguous on this point if simply because the claim involves judgments of value that modern science does not make) whether or not a philosophical argument can be made for the claim, which takes modern science seriously while engaging its limitations. This is what I have done in a brief way in *Spirituality and Dialectics* (Mansueto 2005: 43-64) and do in an extended way in *Knowing God: The Ultimate Meaningfulness of the Universe* (Mansueto forthcoming a). For other approaches, see Bohm 1980; Gal-Or 1986; Prigogine et al. 1977, 1979, 1984, 1989; Barrow and Tipler 1986; Tipler 1994; Lerner 1991; and Harris 1964, 1999, 2000. Teilhard's work is best understood as a Catholic theological reflection on the religious meaning of cosmic evolution and has much to commend it from this point of view, but cannot be taken as a demonstration of the claim that such evolution is taking place.

contingent and necessary being simply cannot be crossed. Every attempt at divinization—and every civilization constituted by such an attempt—thus ends in failure. And yet it is just precisely in such failures that we discover a deeper knowledge of the divine. The horizon of our failures defines a beyond into which we are irresistibly called, becoming more human, and more than human, finding new meanings and the charter for a new epoch in the human civilizational project.

Social Theory

This has profound implications for the way in which we do sociology, because it means recognizing not only that some individuals and societies *understand themselves* as ordered to transcendental ends, and that this makes a difference—something that interpretive and functionalist sociology already do—but that all individuals and societies *really are* so ordered, whether they understand themselves to be or not. Thus our frankly Neo-Aristotelian tripartite model of social organization, that I have argued is determined by the material conditions under which a society develops (i.e., its ecosystem) various social structures that represent an adaptation to those material conditions, but also a way of realizing transcendental ends. Human beings and human societies, in other words, pursue Being under definite material conditions and using definite social structures.

This innovation has allowed us in turn to introduce the new concept of *civilizational ideal*. A civilizational ideal is a particular way of pursuing Being and represents the conscious aims of a civilization. It is more fundamental and enduring than a structural pattern such as capitalism or socialism. Human societies thus pursue Being under the guise of a particular civilizational ideal. They do this under definite material conditions and by means of definite social structures.

When a civilization is unable to realize its ideals using a particular structure it undergoes a crisis. Our framework allows us to distinguish between three very different types of crisis: a *crisis of regime*, a *structural* crisis and a *civilizational* crisis. The *crisis of regime* occurs when a long established set of policies no longer allows people to realize their aspirations, but where the contradictions are not so profound as to require a change in social structure. A *structural crisis* occurs when it is no longer possible for a society to pursue its civilizational ideal within the context of the existing structure. A *civilizational crisis*, on the other hand, takes place when, generally after a succession of structural crises, people actually lose faith in a civilizational ideal and stop pursuing it.

Finally, we distinguished between three different *metacivilizational* projects: pre-axial, axial, and modern. In pre-axial civilizations there is a common set of meanings that is taken for granted. The civilization is generally ordered towards the divinization of its rulers by means of sacrificial rituals. Axial civilizations are characterized by the problematization of meaning, by religious rationalization, and by religious democratization and are ordered toward the cultivation of human capacities, and especially human spiritual development, in a way that includes but transcends innerworldly civilizational progress. Modern civilizations, finally, seek divinization by purely innerworldly means, scientific-technological or philosophical-political.

Geopolitical Analysis

As we noted in the first chapter, the principal impact of a political theology or social theory on geopolitical analysis is to select from among the various forces that define the current situation those that are most important, either because they reflect powerful, deeply rooted social trends or because they bear in one way or another on important values. We do not negate the structural factors emphasized by modern social theory but identify others that we believe to be equally important. Specifically, our analysis of the current situation will, first of all, take into account the nature and integrity of the ecosystem, and especially the developing ecological crisis. Second, in considering structural factors we will look not just at the ability of various economic structures (capitalism and socialism) to realize the modern ideal and at the balance of forces between primary social actors, but also at the operation of secondary and tertiary social actors, i.e., the organizations of civil society and political-theological organizations, treated not merely as agents of primary social actors such as classes and peoples, but also as carriers of (often competing) civilizational ideals *and* the structure of the social space (totalitarian or pluralistic) in which they are operating. One particularly important manifestation of this, too little studied, is the architectural *organization of the society*, which defines sacred and civic space and thus constrains and orders action in the public arena, facilitating, obstructing, or channeling in various ways the development of collective effervescence. Finally, we will take into account the viability of civilizational ideals themselves, treating the current situation as a real debate around fundamental questions of meaning and value in which a strategic assessment is always also a political-theological claim.

The Current Situation

This framework has allowed us to understand the current crisis in a new and more profound way. Specifically, by thematizing the concept of civilizational ideal, we have been able to understand more accurately just what modernity is about—and thus why humanity has been so disappointed by its failure. Far from representing a global abandonment of humanity's transcendental aim, modernity, like all other civilizational ideals, represents a specific way of understanding and achieving those aims. In its dominant form, modernity is founded on a univocal metaphysics that understands the first principle as infinite or unlimited and specifically as infinite or unlimited knowledge and power. Thus the tendency among modernists not only to *characterize* but actually to *define* God as omniscient and omnipotent and thus as *sovereign*, i.e., as exercising effective control over the universe and its constituent elements. Early (Protestant) modernity recognized the existence of such a divine sovereign and sought for humanity a kind of subaltern sovereignty as his vice-regent. Positivistic high modernism, on the other hand, was skeptical about the existence of such a God precisely because it sought the full measure of divinity for human beings and sought to achieve this by means of scientific and technological progress—including progress in the social sciences and social engineering. If high modernity was generally hesitant to admit this goal even to itself (though there have always been, as we pointed out in an earlier chapter, "god-builders" and "transhumanists" of various kinds), it is because modern science began early on to generate pessimistic results such as the Second Law of Thermodynamics that called radically into question the viability of that goal. And yet it could not abandon it completely, because it is what legitimates the sacrifices that modern social structures, both capitalist and socialist, have required of humanity. Humanistic modernism, finally, retained the analogical metaphysics of *Esse* that was dominant in most post-axial civilizations, but sought to transcend *contingency*, and thus implicitly to attain divinity, by means of a philosophical wisdom and revolutionary political practice that elevated humanity to the state of the unique subject-object of the cosmohistorical evolutionary process.

Both positivistic and humanistic modernism are *secular messianisms* in that they seek the redemption once promised by Christianity *in this world* and *by innerworldly means.*

In what follows, we will argue that modernity is in crisis for three principal reasons. First, the pursuit of the modern ideal (and specifically of the positivistic modern ideal), far from liberating humanity from finitude and materiality, seems to be generating an ecological crisis of unprecedented proportions—one that may threaten the actual habitability of the earth. This is because modern industrial *techne*, rather than tapping into and nurturing existing dynamics of growth and development, dissolves such dynamics (generally by combustion) in order to release energy and do work. We are quite literally burning up the planet and suffocating in the resulting smoke.

Second, neither of the two principal economic structures associated with modernity nor the modern sovereign nation-state have been able to realize either the positivistic or humanistic variants of the high modern ideal. Both capitalism and socialism are characterized by a way of mobilizing labor—the wage relation—that results in profound alienation, undercutting the humanistic modern ideal of rational autonomy. And both are characterized by internal contradictions that ultimately lead to crisis and stagnation, thereby undercutting the scientific and technological progress that would be necessary to carry humanity beyond finitude by innerworldly means. Capitalism redeploys capital to low-wage, low-technology activities and drives down wages, undermining both capital formation and effective demand. Attempts to ameliorate these problems require high levels of state spending, which either leads to high deficits and rising interest rates, further undermining capital formation, or to high taxes, undercutting attempts to support effective demand. Socialism, while it has demonstrated its effectiveness at carrying out basic development tasks such as ensuring food self-sufficiency and first and second stage industrialization, and at centralizing resources for civilization building, leads to rising worker incomes coupled with shortages of consumer goods, something that leads inevitably to declining productivity and eventually to permanent stagnation. The modern sovereign nation-state, meanwhile (or its proxies, such as the Communist Party), to just precisely the extent to which it has attempted to become the vehicle for making humanity or a section thereof into the "unique subject-object" of the cosmohistorical process, has in fact undermined the most basic conditions for the cultivation of rational autonomy and democratic citizenship. To the extent that it has not aspired to such high ends, it has been largely an instrument of capital in developing national economies and as such simply a stage along the way in the development of global parastatal structures that show little signs of being democratic.

Third—and most importantly—the modern ideal itself is flawed. Ultimately this flaw is rooted in bad metaphysics. The univocal metaphysics at the core of the Protestant and positivistic variants of the modern ideal understands God as the infinite or the unlimited. This leads either to a spirituality of *authority and submission*, with humanity acting as God's vice-regent, or to an attempt to actually *build* God through scientific and technological progress. In either case, the results are profoundly unsatisfying. This is because what beings actually seek is neither childlike submission nor the "bad infinity" of endless existence and unlimited power, but rather ever fuller participation in the creative power of Being itself. Scientific and technological progress can certainly be such participation, but modern *techne*, with its effort to consume and combust the earth, and modern science, which always and only serves such *techne*, are both ultimately counterfeits. It is not just that modern efforts to build God have failed, but that God cannot be built. God *is*; the divine within us—individually and collectively— must be cultivated.

Humanistic modernism presents different problems entirely. This trend, which has its roots the Radical Aristotelianism of the High Middle Ages, found its highest expression in Hegel and Hegelian Marxism. Unlike Protestant and scientific modernism, it largely conserves, as we have noted, the analogical metaphysics of the Silk Road Era. What it seeks to transcend is not so much finitude as contingency. For Hegel as for Hegelian Marxists, philosophical wisdom rooted in democratic and/or revolutionary practice allows us to *identify* with the Idea, or with the historical process, becoming, as the early Lukacs put it, "the identical subject-object" of the historical process (Lukacs

1922/1971). In this sense it is very much in continuity with the more mystical strains of Aristotelian and Thomistic philosophy, such as those represented by Meister Eckhardt. The difficulty, of course, is that we are, in fact, contingent, and no deepening of philosophical wisdom and no extension of democratic citizenship or revolutionary political practice can overcome that. Lukacs already partly acknowledged this when he argued that it is the *class* (read the Communist Party) and not the *individual* that is the authentic subject-object of human history (Lukacs 1922/1971). But of course the proletariat and its political party, even if we argue that they enjoy a certain ontological privilege in virtue of their rootedness in humanity's core activity of creating, are also contingent. Thus humanistic modernism fades over into the urbane despair represented by the Frankfort School and thinkers like Adorno, an attitude that is very close to postmodernism.

This said, there *are* aspects of modernity worth conserving. From scientific modernism, we need to take away a deepened insight into *techne* as a real participation in the self-organizing activity of the cosmos. From humanistic modernism, we need to conserve the ideal of rational autonomy and democratic citizenship, and to remember the sane roots of humanistic modernist politicism in the Jewish identification of *da'ath 'elohim* (knowledge of God) and the just act.

Finally, we will devote significant attention to phenomena that developed in the modern era but that are not, properly speaking, governed by the modern ideal: the emergence of rich networks of intermediate institutions ordered to diverse civilizational ideals and the emergence in the United States first, but perhaps with growing global migration elsewhere as well, of a polity that is pluralistic but that takes questions of meaning and value seriously.

The Unfolding of the Crisis

The foregoing analysis tells us why, fundamentally, modernity is in crisis. But it does not capture the profoundly traumatic nature of that crisis or the way in which it has unfolded. Broadly speaking, it is possible to identify three overlapping stages in the crisis of modernity:

1. early disappointment of regarding the outcome of the democratic and the first socialist revolutions, which can be traced back to as

far as the end of the eighteenth century, and which dominated most of the nineteenth, leading to Romantic reaction, the first "postmodernism";

2. the "long war" and the trauma of the twentieth century, which began in 1914 and extended up through the collapse of the Soviet Union in 1989; and

3. the present "late modern" or "postmodern," period, which began to take shape after the Second World War, and which has been fully formed since 1989.

Revolutionary Disappointments and Romantic Reactions

Revolutionary Disappointments

Modernity, in both its positivistic and humanistic forms, was, in effect, stillborn. The positivistic variant of the modern ideal promised to divinize humanity through the conquest of nature, the humanistic variant by creating a collective subject that would liberate humanity from contingency and make history the conscious expression of the rationally autonomous will. But the realities of modernization were very different. This was partly a result of industrialism, which transformed labor, historically a creative act that tapped into the latent potential of matter and brought it to perfection, into a series of repetitive, meaningless tasks, making human beings—as the popular *Matrix* suggested, into little more than batteries. But partly it was also a result of the wage relation. Marx analyzed the reasons for this in his *Paris Manuscripts* (Marx 1844/1978). The wage relation transforms human labor, which is the expression of our species being and binds us to nature and to other human beings while at the same time being an autonomous expression of our individuality, into simply a means of survival. This alienates us from ourselves, from the natural world, and from the rest of humanity.

Democracy, meanwhile, turned out to have its own contradictions. In order to understand this, we need to distinguish between two variants of modern democratic theory.[2] There is, on the one hand, the

---

2. There is a third variant of democratic theory associated with the Thomistic natural law tradition which rejects the concept of sovereignty altogether and regards legislation as a matter of interpreting natural law rather than of either protecting rights or

liberal democratic tradition that emerged out of the Anglo-American experience, which understood democracy primarily as a way of protecting and supporting pre-existing natural or traditional rights and institutions. This is the vision of Locke. It is also, with some modifications, the vision embodied in *The Federalist* and in the expanded Tocquevillian understanding of democracy that we discussed in the last chapter. Generally speaking, this tradition only very reluctantly embraced universal suffrage and focused on restraining the state rather than on using it as a vehicle for social transformation. On the other hand, the radical democratic tradition that emerged out of the French Revolution, and that was inspired above all by Rousseau, understood democracy as above all popular sovereignty—the capacity of the people collectively to remake the world in that they live.

It was this latter vision of democracy that was taken up by humanistic modernity as its vehicle for liberation from contingency. The difficulty, of course, is that a party or state that is effective at global social transformation, and can thus function as the subject of the historical process, is unlikely to be characterized by significant internal democracy. Liberal democracies, on the other hand, which did much better at conserving the conditions for authentic rational autonomy and democratic citizenship, are rarely good vehicles for revolutionary social transformation. The humanistic modern intelligentsia, in other words, was faced with a choice between repression and marginalization, and the humanistic project itself was more or less permanently stalled.

The internal contradictions of the humanistic modern project, finally, extend to the cultural realm. Indeed, it is here that many cultural theorists working in the critical tradition believe the crisis of their project first manifested itself. Theodor Adorno, for example, argued that the abandonment of the sonata-allegro form,[3] which he reads as

---

making laws *ex nihilo*, as it were. This theory is democratic in that regards the capacity to participate in such interpretation as, at least to some extent, shared by all human beings in virtue of their reason. See Maritain 1951.

3. Sonata allegro form, characteristic especially of the music of Haydn, Mozart, and Beethoven, begins with one or two initial themes or musical subjects, which it then modulates to a different key (usually one fifth higher, or in minor key compositions one fourth lower) and then develops extensively, driving towards a recapitulation in which the original subjects are reinstated in the original key but in more complex form. Adorno reads this as a metaphor for the self-unfolding of the rational, autonomous subject, which derives its content from itself and grows in complexity without dependence on anything outside itself.

the musical trace of the ideal of the self-unfolding of a rational, autonomous subject, in Beethoven's late style, in favor of the external form of the Catholic mass or the more static theme and variations, reflects a double disillusionment, first with the Revolution, as a result of its termination in Napoleon's dictatorship, and second with the Restoration that followed his defeat (Subotnik 1976). Lukacs has made a similar point about the modern novel, which reflects the struggles of the critical modern subject in a world in which meaning has become radically problematic (Lukacs 1916/1974).

Ultimately all these contradictions were rooted in the very nature of the humanistic modern project itself. Seeking divinization by elevating humanity to the status of the unique subject of the cosmohistorical process makes meaning into a social product and human beings its authors. But this is the same thing as saying that meaning is simply a product of power struggles, and leaves the humanistic project itself ultimately ungrounded.

Socialism was, from the very beginning, an attempt on the part of humanistic intellectuals to salvage their variant of the modern ideal from the contradictions of industrial capitalism and liberal democracy. It was the hope of the early Marx that socialism would transcend the wage relation, and the socialist movements of the 1840s, for which he sought to provide a vision and a strategy, shared this aspiration. They were, on the one hand, movements of resistance on the part of the artisanate to capitalist modernization and specifically to proletarianization, and they drew significantly on the old guild tradition (Sewell 1980). On the other hand, they were not *only* movements of resistance. On the contrary, they reflected an effort on the part of the artisanate to transform itself into a kind of mass auto-didact intelligentsia, using what was left of the guilds and *compagnonages* as well as the emerging network of Masonic lodges and revolutionary organizations as a kind of popular university. It was this culturally rich and politically engaged world that made it possible for Marx to imagine a socialist future in which people would engage in creative manual labor in the morning, write philosophy in the afternoon, and paint or compose in the evening.

It was, however, just precisely this socialism that was defeated in the struggles of 1848, even if its echoes lived on for another hundred and fifty years. Partly this was simply a result of the immanent process of capitalist development and specifically of proletarianization, which gradually liquidated the artisanate and the humanistic intelligentsia that made up the principal constituency for humanistic modernism —though as late as the 1980s and early 1990s I knew manual laborers with no formal education who continued to embody the old autodidact ideal. Partly, however, it was a result of the displacement of the humanistic-artisan alliance by a new alliance between sectors (primarily the scientific technical intelligentsia and the industrial proletariat) whose principal criticism of capitalism was that it held back economic development, and the effective abandonment of the humanistic in favor of the positivist variant of the modern ideal. The mature Marx to some extent, but more especially Engels, became the theorists of this trend, a shift already apparent in the *Communist Manifesto*, published in 1848, and that was fully developed by the time *Capital* was published in 1867. What this meant practically was that actually existing socialism, whether reformist or revolutionary, never really attempted to transcend the wage relation and thus to overcome the alienation that was at the heart of the humanistic critique of capitalism. Partly, finally, it was a result of mixed motives of the humanistic intelligentsia itself, for which socialism was not simply a strategy for unleashing human potential, but first and foremost a strategy for human self-divinization. This is what first drew Hegel to his doctrine of the State as the embodiment of the Idea, and it is what eventually drew much of the humanistic intelligentsia away from its creative engagement with artisans and workers and into the Leninist project, of party building. Finally, socialism, far from addressing the implicit groundlessness of meaning in earlier variants of the humanist project made this groundlessness explicit, rejecting Hegel's philosophical theology in favor of Feuerbachian and Marxist anthropology.

Romantic Reactions

For the dialectical and historical materialist tradition, 1848 marks the point at which capitalism ceased to be progressive. Georg Lukacs (Lukacs 1953/1980), for example, notes that this is the point at which the bourgeoisie abandoned the direct apologetic for capitalism (i.e., the argument that it would actually make possible the realization of the modern ideal) in favor of what he calls the "indirect" apologetic, the argument put forward by thinkers as diverse as Kierkegaard, Nietzsche, and Heidegger that the human condition being what it is, *nothing* will make human beings happy, and that capitalism is the best we can do. There is, no doubt, considerable truth to this claim. But our analysis suggests that more was in crisis than capitalism. And indeed, what Lukacs calls the "direct apologetic" has in fact returned periodically, for example in the neoliberal theory of the present period (Hayek 1988). Rather, we would like to suggest, what was in crisis was the modern ideal itself, and especially its humanistic variant, the contradictions of which had already been sufficiently revealed to compromise the support of sections of the humanistic intelligentsia and to open the tradition up to criticism from the outside—and most especially from the heirs of the Augustinian Reaction.

It is in this context that we must understand the Romantic reaction of the nineteenth century. Romanticism brought together a broad spectrum of tendencies from humanistic intellectuals disillusioned by the productivist turn in the socialist movement and/or with the groundlessness of meaning that the socialist project implied to neo-Augustinians, religious and atheistic, who were hostile to the humanistic modern project from the very beginning. The result was a complex dynamic that created odd bedfellows. Traditionalists and objective idealists such as Schelling, who were fundamentally concerned to reground meaning and were willing to compromise humanistic principles if it was necessary in order to do so, rubbed shoulders with protoexistentialists who read the failure of the humanists to ground meaning as a victory and began to assert openly that meanings and values were a function of power, whether divine (Kierkegaard and the religious existentialists who followed him) or human (Nietzsche and Weber).

Many aspects of this Romantic reaction were benign and even drew attention to aspects of Europe's spiritual heritage that had been effaced by the Enlightenment. We have already mentioned the important contributions of Ballanche in analyzing the religious component of the democratic project and of Tocqueville in pointing out the importance of a vigorous civil society to the success of that project. We might add to this the broad spectrum of post-Enlightenment religious thinkers from the American Transcendentalists to the Russian Orthodox revival represented by Soloviev, Bulgakov, and Berdyaev. But other aspects of the Romantic movement were more troubling. Specifically, it signaled a shift in the balance of forces between the *national* and *democratic* and *socialist* elements in the modern revolutionary movement. Where previously democratic and protosocialist revolutions (such as the French revolutions of 1789, 1830, and 1848) were articulated across the space of a nation-state first constructed by absolute monarchs now *ethnic nationalist* movements undertook the task of state building directly, appealing to national myths that claimed to be *given* and *contingent*, even though national identities were *always* constructed. Thus the Italian *Risorgimento* drew on the myth of a *Terza Italia* (Lovett 1982), the various national movements in the Balkans on Catholic or Orthodox identities set over and against Ottoman multicultural imperialism, and, most ominously, the emerging German nation on a deconstruction of the Latin/Celtic/Germanic synthesis on which Western Christendom had been built in favor of a (constructed) purely German identity. These movements were not, to be sure, entirely without democratic or even socialist aims, aims that once again came to the fore as the movements extended to the colonized Americas, Africa, and Asia in the twentieth century. But ultimately ethnic nationalism was a mechanism for building a modern state at a time when the humanistic project had been compromised. It could serve as a means of liberating colonies from imperial hegemons, but also, as we will see, as a means by which late entrants into the imperialist game could build the internal support they needed for a policy of austerity, militarization, and conquest. And sometimes, when the colony was itself a former imperial hegemon, such as China or *Dar-al-Islam,* the line between these two phenomena was not always clear. And in either case, because the humanistic ideal of rational autonomy had been compromised, the resulting states rarely paid more than lip service to either liberal or democratic principles.

The Long War and the Trauma of the Twentieth Century

The revolutionary disappointments and romantic reaction of the nineteenth century, however, represented only the first stage of a much deeper crisis. It was only in the twentieth century that the really profound problems of modernity would become apparent. On the one hand, beginning with the First World War, it became increasingly apparent to an ever-broader sector of humanity throughout Asia, Africa, and Latin America that capitalism would be unable to fulfill the full promise of high modernity, at least for them. Marx and Lenin identified the reasons for this long ago. Since surplus is generated by human labor, as an economy becomes more technologically advanced, the rate of profit declines unless it is artificially held up by monopoly rents on innovation. In response, capital is redeployed to low-wage, low-technology sectors, holding back the development of the productive forces. Furthermore, to the extent that technology does advance commodities become cheaper, driving down the value of labor power and creating profound underconsumption tendencies (Mandel 1968; Amin 1979/1980). Both of these contradictions can be significantly ameliorated. The state can subsidize high technology sectors, something that has usually, but need not, take the form of arms purchases, and it can support demand by means of minimum-wage laws and transfer payments. Regulated collective bargaining can also ensure that wages increase with productivity. This is essentially the model adopted by the advanced capitalist countries in the wake of the Great Depression and the Second World War. But it is not available to countries that lack colonies, much less to countries that are themselves colonies that, if and when they develop, do so only as low-wage entrepots that generate surplus but enjoy few of the benefits of modernity. In order to ensure their access to colonies, the imperial powers either occupy and govern their colonies directly or form alliances with local landed elites, large merchant capital, and later with local capitalists using low-wage labor to produce goods for export who then form repressive client states that stifle the democratic aspirations of the people. Free expression is smothered, and with it the formation of a culture that values science and rational autonomy.

Thus the long war. Historical materialists, especially those working in the Leninist tradition, have generally regarded the First and Second World Wars as inter-imperialist conflicts: i.e., as a struggle between capitalist powers to gain or maintain the colonial empires that they needed in order to resolve the internal contradictions of capitalist development. The military expenditures necessary to secure these colonies subsidize high technology sectors at home, sustaining technological and economic progress, while the profits repatriated from colonies make it possible to subsidize higher rates of consumption on the part of the working classes, ameliorating the underconsumption tendencies. Eventually imperial powers come into conflict with each other over the division of the world, leading to great global conflicts like the First and Second World Wars (Lenin 1916/1971). Defenders of the Soviet variant of historical materialism understood the Cold War in a somewhat different light—as an attempt on the part of the premier capitalist power, the United States, to secure for capital the liberated zone create by the Soviet Union and its allies. Advocates of Mao Zedong's Three Worlds Theory, on the other hand, regarded the Cold War as an interimperialist conflict and treated the Soviet Union as just another imperial power scrambling for colonies.

There is considerable merit to the idea that the World Wars were inter-imperialist conflicts, and the question of the nature of the Soviet Union and its relationship to its Third World allies is an empirical question that is not essential to our argument here. As with most historical materialist analysis, however, it tells only part of the story. Specifically, it misses the implications of this *structural* conflict for the fate of the scientific modern *civilizational* ideal.

I would like to suggest, first of all, that the First World War represented the maturation of the crisis of the capitalist form of modern civilization. In this sense the Leninist analysis of that war was very much on the mark. It had become impossible for capitalism to continue to make progress towards the realization of the modern ideal without colonies—without exporting its internal contradictions to places that were, as a result, largely excluded from further civilizational progress.

The results of the First World War left those countries that had either lacked colonies going into it or had very few (Germany, Italy, Spain, Portugal) in an even weaker position: even more desperate to defend and expand their empires and even less able to do so. At the structural level, fascism represented fundamentally an attempt on the part of these countries to militarize their societies in order to expand and/or defend a colonial empire. At a civilizational level, however, fascism represented a mobilization and radicalization of ideologies developed during the Romantic reaction of the nineteenth century to legitimate a policy of austerity, militarization, and conquest. Specifically, the fascist parties all argued, in one way or another, that modernity—and especially humanistic modernity—had failed and had made the West (or at least parts of it) weak, and it was time to return to one or another older civilization ideal, generally much misunderstood and reconfigured in such a way as to allow it to legitimate the militarization of society that fascism as a *political-economic strategy* required. For Portugal and Spain this meant an ossified, authoritarian version of Counter-Reformation Catholicism; for Italy it meant an idealized Roman Empire; for Germany it meant an imagined Aryan Pagan past. In all cases the result was a reversion to a spirituality of authority and submission.

The horrors of fascism and the Second World War not only discredited it as a solution to the emerging civilizational crisis; it also discredited, at least in Europe, the idea of a recovery of earlier civilizational ideals. The effect was to leave Europe profoundly wounded. Postwar Europe was, in this sense, "postmodern" from the very beginning, in the sense that it continued to live modernity without actually *believing* in the modern ideal—or, for that matter, in any alternative ideal. The economic success of postwar Europe made this "nonsolution" to the civilizational crisis look attractive for a while. Europeans were able to consume the products of earlier civilizational endeavors without creating anything authentically new. It is only as globalization has begun to threaten European economic prosperity and immigration and expansion into the former Soviet bloc has flooded Europe with partisans of other civilizational traditions (Islamic, Conservative Catholic, Orthodox) that the limitations of the European solution are beginning to become apparent.

The other way for countries that lacked colonies to modernize was, as we have said, to break with capitalism and use the state as an engine for primitive accumulation and technological and economic development. Under the circumstances, it should come as no surprise that socialism, in one or another form, proved itself very attractive to the masses of Asia, Africa, and Latin America.

Socialism, however, has its own problems. Socialist countries have proven themselves quite successful in addressing basic development tasks, however they have defined them. Thus, the Soviet Union was able to make itself a major industrial power in a matter of a few decades; China was able to restore basic food self-sufficiency in a fraction of that time (Bettelheim 1976; Amin 1981/1982). And this won them the loyal support of the generation that they led out of poverty. The question has been what to do next. Having secured the basic welfare of its people and built an industrial apparatus adequate to its security needs, the Soviet Union decided to invest in civilization building along classically modernist lines and by the 1960s had an artistic, scientific, and cultural apparatus second to none. The difficulty was that the vast majority of the people, while comfortable by the standards of their parents, saw little or no expansion of consumption opportunities. Ruble bank accounts grew, but there was nothing to spend them on. A close examination of party documents from the early 1950s suggests that the party expected people to eschew consumerism and become junior participants in the great scientific and cultural achievements of the period, taking evening classes and engaging in artistic and scientific creativity. But formation as a factory worker does little to prepare one to participate actively in artistic creation or scientific research. And the ideological dynamics of secular socialism were insufficient to motivate the people to expend their lives in service to a future neither they nor their children would likely enjoy. The result was growing absenteeism and declining productivity, something that left the system in a state of profound crisis from the late 1970s on.

China, meanwhile, read the socialist project very differently. It would be easy to read the Maoist experience as an example of socialist resistance to capitalist modernization: as the limitations of the Soviet "high modern" model became apparent, the Chinese began to emphasize the conservative elements of the socialist project, focusing on radical land reform and food self-sufficiency. And this may have been true up until the early 1960s. But the experience of the Cultural Revolution makes this reading impossible. Mao and his associates went well beyond resistance to capitalist modernization; they unleashed a deeply rooted anticivilizational impulse. This was rooted partly in the experience of an oppressed and exploited peasantry that had long born the burdens of civilization without enjoying many of its benefits, but it also reflected the standpoint of displaced youth anxious to advance their own interests rather than mastering the disciplines of civilization building. Thus the appeal of a politics that, as we have suggested in an earlier chapter, allowed individuals and small groups to quite literally play God, constantly redefining, through a permanent and ongoing revolution, the very terms that define reality.

The Soviet and Chinese experiments together suggest that like capitalism, socialism has its own distinctive crisis tendencies. At least one of these is what we might call the "scissors tendency," after the "scissors crisis" of the 1920s in which Soviet peasants, enjoying the results of land reform and lacking outlets for their increased incomes, reduced production to subsistence levels, nearly starving the cities and creating the pretext for the forced collectivization that followed (Bettelheim 1976). More generally, a scissors crisis occurs when a socialist economy, following its internal logic, both substantially frees workers and enterprises from market pressures and invests surplus rationally in civilization-building activities. Workers and enterprises do not need to produce in order to survive, and have no outlets for their increased incomes, and so reduce their activity or investment levels, resulting in economic stagnation. Thus the slow collapse of the Soviet system; thus the ability of the Chinese to avoid a similar collapse only by fully exposing workers to global market pressures and entering the world market as a low-wage entrepot—i.e., just specifically the fate socialism was supposed to help them escape.

None of this, however, should be read as affirming the neoliberal triumphalism of the period since 1989. On the contrary, we must be clear that capitalism was able to survive and prosper in the West only because imperialism allowed the advanced capitalist countries to export their contradictions and because Keynesian economic policies shored up internal demand. The difficulty is that "actually existing Keynesianism" has its own contradictions. While strict Keynesian doctrine calls for counter-cyclical fiscal policies, with deficits during recessions balanced by surpluses during periods of growth, this is politically very difficult to implement. The result is a tendency for deficits and state indebtedness to accumulate, something that drives up interest rates and undermines capital formation in the long run. Keeping wages high, meanwhile, creates opportunities for competitors in low-wage regions to capture first, lower technology, but eventually essentially all sectors of the economy. Only high-end strategies focused on constant innovation are really viable for a high-wage economy, and even these are difficult to sustain as newly industrialized countries climb up the technological ladder (Wright 1978; Amin 1979/1980; Davis 1985). The result has been a gradual loss of the West's comparative advantage in high-end sectors, coupled by intense competition from the developing world in low and medium technology activities.

Neither capitalism nor socialism, therefore, has been able to make a credible bid at realizing the high modern ideal. This failure is particularly acute for the so-called "baby-boom" generation that came of age in the 1960s believing that by the turn of the century interplanetary travel and space colonization would be routine and that this same technological prowess could be used to address deep-rooted needs at home, vanquishing hunger, replacing polluting fossil fuels with clean, renewable alternatives, and rebuilding our cities in a way that made slums and traffic jams a thing of the past. These were the years of the New Frontier and the Great Society—years when it really seemed that scientific innovation and civic responsibility would at long last triumph over humanity's millennia of ignorance and egoism. The aspirations of the period were perhaps best captured by the popular science-fiction series *Star Trek*, which depicted a society in which not only had poverty and hunger been vanquished and racial and national contradictions overcome, but everyone performed useful, challenging labor. The only hierarchies were those based on ability, and even these were remarkably fluid. James T. Kirk, the 34-year-old starship captain, was a kind of cosmic Jack Kennedy, grouping around himself the expertise he needed to complement his own decisive (if sometimes reckless) leadership. For those of us who grew up in the 1960s, society on the model of *Star Trek* seemed not only possible but inevitable. It was only a matter of time.

This was, however, not to be. By the end of the 1960s the internal contradictions of the postwar, Keynesian settlement were already becoming apparent. Long years of stagnation through the 1970s and early 1980s were followed by a period of renewed growth, but not by renewed hope in the full form of the modern ideal. Economic growth had been reduced to a means of increasing individual consumption. On the other hand, movements with their roots in the romantic and conservative reaction of the later nineteenth century, and that pretended to reject modernity in favor of a return to older civilizational values, when they briefly gained the upper hand in the middle of the twentieth century, had demonstrated a degree of brutality hitherto unknown in the history of the planet, using modern techniques to carry out systematic genocide and to prosecute a program of world conquest. The result was to discredit both traditional and modern civilizational ideals, resulting in a global weariness with the entire human civilizational project. It is this weariness that defines the postmodern condition.

The twentieth century, in other words, became the long century of disillusionment. Intellectual and moral leaders, in both the West and the Soviet bloc, lost confidence in their civilizational ideal and in their strategies for realizing that ideal. This, in turn, had a further effect.

At just the moment when our civilization most needed teachers who could pass on the deep civilization-building capacities that humanity had accumulated over the course of five millennia—the ability to make and evaluate arguments and especially to seek meaning, and the ability to order one's life in a way that allows one to actually seek the end so discovered—our teachers stopped teaching. The academy became, increasingly, the preserve of specialist scholars and systematically excluded nearly all whose work attempted to address fundamental questions. Furthermore, as the academy expanded to accommodate the need of capital for skilled intellectual workers, traditional liberal arts curricula were watered down and university-level credentials granted to those who had not mastered even the skills that, in a previous era, would have been necessary to graduate from high school. No longer did a university degree signify the ability to make and evaluate arguments across disciplines, and especially regarding fundamental questions of meaning and value. And without these capacities it is quite impossible to embrace or reject a civilizational ideal, to pursue or combat one, much less to participate in giving birth to a new one. Thus our current atmosphere of nihilism and despair and the seemingly ever-present miasma of dangerous stagnation.

These flaws were already apparent in the so-called "greatest generation" (Brokaw 1998), which, after the trauma of the antifascist struggle and Second World War, largely settled down to enjoy the postwar prosperity. No longer really believing in anything, they lost the will to pass on the core capacities of their civilization. My own generation, the baby-boomer generation, unsurprisingly concluded that the previous generation had nothing to teach and stopped listening even when they *did* have something to say. And each generation since has experienced further generational alientation.

The Present Period

The Ecological Crisis

The crisis of the modern civilizational ideal has, then, been a long time coming. What makes the present period so distinct? First, the gradual degradation of the ecosystem as a result of the industrial-technological regime is finally beginning to make its effects felt. This regime is centered on combustion, i.e., on breaking down existing forms of organization in order to release energy that can then be used to do work. Combustion, by its very nature involves 1) the destruction of the underlying fuel source, and 2) the production of by-products that alter the ecosystem in important ways.

This means, first of all, that unless significant progress is made very soon in developing renewable and thus fundamentally nonindustrial energy sources, we will eventually deplete the fossil fuel sources on which the industrial regime depends, undermining its material basis. This point was, in fact, made rather rigorously and definitively some time ago by M. K. Hubbert (Hubbert 1956), who showed that, assuming a finite supply of any mineral, production will increase rapidly after discovery, peak, and eventually fall off very sharply, with the change in production being described by the derivative of the logistic equation. Estimates of just when production of any given fossil fuel will peak and when all sources will be depleted are complicated by the ongoing discovery of new sources, economic factors affecting the rate of exploration and exploitation, etc. Thus some early estimates (Hubbert 1974 predicted that production would peak in 1995) have proven inaccurate, but the underlying argument is valid, and there are current estimates that production may well peak in 2010 (Campbell 2007).

The same principle applies to all of the other mineral inputs required by an industrial civilization.

It also means that the by-products of industrial production are significantly altering our ecosystem. The most important such effect is the climate change induced by increasing carbon dioxide levels, the most important direct effect of combustion. According to the Intergovernmental Panel on Climate Change,

> Warming of the climate system is unequivocal, as is now evident from observations of increases in global average air and ocean temperatures, widespread melting of snow and ice, and rising global average sea level ... Eleven of the last twelve years (1995–2006) rank among the 12 warmest years in the instrumental record of global surface temperature (since 1850). The updated 100-year linear trend (1906–2005) of 0.74 [0.56 to 0.92]°C is therefore larger than the corresponding trend for 1901–2000 given in the TAR of 0.6 [0.4 to 0.8]°C. The linear warming trend over the last 50 years (0.13 [0.10 to 0.16]°C per

decade) is nearly twice that for the last 100 years. The total temperature increase from 1850–1899 to 2001–2005 is 0.76 [0.57 to 0.95]°C. Urban heat island effects are real but local, and have a negligible influence (less than 0.006°C per decade over land and zero over the oceans) on these values. (Intergovernmental Panel on Climate Change 2007: 5)

Furthermore,

For the next two decades a warming of about 0.2°C per decade is projected for a range of SRES emission scenarios. Even if the concentrations of all greenhouse gases and aerosols had been kept constant at year 2000 levels, a further warming of about 0.1°C per decade would be expected. (Intergovernmental Panel on Climate Change 2007: 12)

These averages are deceptive. Climates are complex, nonlinear systems and even small fluctuations can have large effects. Some analysts, for example, have claimed that melting of the polar ice caps, for example, could desalinate the Atlantic Ocean, undermining the Gulf Stream and depriving Europe of its mild climate (McGuire 2003).

The panel believes that

Most of the observed increase in globally averaged temperatures since the mid-20th century is *very likely* due to the observed increase in anthropogenic greenhouse gas concentrations. This is an advance since the TAR's conclusion that "most of the observed warming over the last 50 years is *likely* to have been due to the increase in greenhouse gas concentrations". Discernible human influences now extend to other aspects of climate, including ocean warming, continental-average temperatures, temperature extremes and wind patterns. (Intergovernmental Panel on Climate Change 2007: 10)

Resource depletion and climate change are, furthermore, only two dimensions of the emerging ecological crisis. There is broad evidence that the pollution of the environment and food supply with the by-products of industrial production is contributing significantly to rising cancer rates and other health problems. Far from allowing us to transcend the limits of material finitude, industrial civilization may well bring us crashing up against those limits in an unprecedented way.

Political-Economic Contradictions

The second factor that makes the current situation unique is the crisis of socialism. This has shaped the current situation in two ways. First, up until 1989 socialism played a role in global politics that softened the impact of the long crisis of modernity. On the one hand, in its high forms, dialectical and historical materialism presented an alternative modernist ideology that offered an explanation of the failure of capitalism to realize the modern ideal and a strategy for so doing. On the other hand, at the popular level, especially among the marginalized peasant and proletarianized peasant masses of Asia, Africa, and Latin America, socialism continued to serve as a vehicle for resistance to capitalist modernization. More specifically, religious ideologies, whether the millenarian ideologies that motivated peasant movements in the nineteenth and early twentieth centuries, or modernizing religious ideologies like liberation theology or Islamic or Buddhist Socialism, became ways of linking the antimodernist masses to the modern project. This, coupled with memories of the debacle of fascism, made full-blown rejections of high modernism rare. The crisis of socialism and the collapse of the Soviet Union, coupled with the turn of China towards integration into the global market, changed all this, undercutting the role of socialism as both an alternative, more humane modernity and as a sink for popular resistance to modernity as such.

Second, partly as a result of the immanent dynamics of capitalist development, and partly as a result of the collapse of the Soviet bloc, and the strategic reserve it offered to those resisting capitalist modernization and the penetration of market relations, we are finally witnessing the completion of the capitalist project: the formation of a unified global market not only in goods and services and in labor, but also in capital, in which resources can be re-allocated almost instantaneously from one activity to the other. This has meant a more intense exposure to market pressures and thus to the rationalizing dynamics of high modernity, and specifically its scientific-technological form—now shorn of the utopian hopes once attached to them—than has hitherto been the case anywhere on the planet.

In the present period these tendencies are beginning to push us towards an irreversible and irresolvable impasse. Specifically, the formation of a unified global market has, on the one hand, made it increasingly difficulty to sustain an effective global intellectual property regime. And even where such a regime prevails, it takes only one engineer and two lawyers to find a way around it, as the Apple Corporation discovered to its dismay. Monopoly rents on innovation will thus be increasingly difficult to sustain, undermining investment in new technologies and resulting in global stagnation.

At the same time, and perhaps more importantly, technological development is gradually driving the value of labor power towards zero. We are probably still a long way from being able to completely or even almost completely automate routine production functions, but we can automate enough of it that the value of labor power is simply well below the levels at which it is currently being reimbursed in the U.S., Europe, Japan, and other developed countries. And the development of a unified global market means that downward pressure on wages is inevitable, something that will be intensified by demographic pressures in places like China and India, where it is possible to reimburse labor at a rate below its value because there is such a large surplus population waiting in the wings. And this phenomenon is not confined to manual labor but extends as well to even highly skilled intellectual labor. And yet it is just precisely the high wage levels in the advanced capitalist countries that have driven the global economy for the past sixty years.

It would be nice to think we could resolve this contradiction by implementing the political program of the center left—a global "New Deal" that extended the benefits currently enjoyed by, say, French or Swedish citizens to everyone on the planet. This is, however, quite impossible. First, at the economic level, high wage rates in the advanced countries were always based on a combination of shared imperialist superprofits from abroad and actually higher rates of productivity. Globalization of the first privilege was always impossible, and with global information exchange and capital flows we are rapidly reaching a situation in which productivity levels will be more or less uniform on a world scale. Second, implementing such a global New Deal would require effective action on the part of the working class on a global scale, the existence of a global political arena in which such action was meaningful, and an effective global political authority that could carry out the resulting reforms. All three requirements entail organizing and institution-building tasks of well beyond anything humanity has yet achieved.

All of this could, of course, be taken to mean that Marx was simply premature in his predictions and that the "final conflict" was at long last approaching and a new, more authentic socialism on the agenda, as thinkers such as Hardt and Negri, Arrighi, and others have suggested. But this is unlikely for a number of reasons. First, the crisis of socialism is real and, as we have noted, socialism has its own, fundamental, internal contradictions. Second, the emergence of a global market and the intensification of market pressures have not been bad for everyone—or even for all of the working classes. On the contrary, globalization has had an extraordinarily uneven impact that has cut across classes, sectors, and regions, raising up and cutting down without respect to the predictions made by earlier forms of social theory, liberal or socialist.

Among those who have benefited from globalization, we can cite the following disparate economic sectors:

1. high-end innovators, especially in the information and technology sectors, who have been able to draw more or less uninterrupted monopoly rents, and who benefit from access to a global market for the goods and services they produce;

2. high-end luxury producers across sectors (housing, clothing, consumer goods, food, etc.) who cater to those in the previous category; and

3. middle and low technology producers and service providers who can produce goods and provide services of quality comparable to those produced and provided in the most advanced capitalist countries, but at a fraction of the cost, while still increasing the living standards of the profoundly impoverished populations of their countries.

These benefits, furthermore, extend across classes. They accrue, that is, to workers as well as capitalists in each of the sectors mentioned—even to low-wage workers for whom their superexploitation by capital represents a liberation from rural stagnation and the oppression of premodern social forms.

Among those who have suffered from globalization or who are threatened by it, we can cite the following equally disparate economic sectors:

1. middle and low technology producers and mid- to low-end service providers in the advanced capitalist countries;
2. those in sectors and economies that have been relatively sheltered from market pressures, including
   a) those protected by socialist or populist regimes or by trade unions, which find it increasingly difficult to maintain their policies and positions in the new situation; and
   b) those in economic sectors who have historically enjoyed quasi-monopoly power but are threatened by the rise of new sectors of capital that may force rationalization (energy, especially petroleum globally; health care and insurance in the U.S.); and
3. those lacking the most minimal social conditions for even low-wage economic development.

Between these two poles there are, of course, broad middle layers: the humanistic, as opposed to the scientific-technical, intelligentsia, those elements of the scientific-technical intelligentsia working in less favored or "cutting edge" fields, those elements of the petty bourgeoisie whose market niche falls somewhere between the chic and favored on the one hand, and the backward and declining on the other.

It should already be apparent that the process of globalization is creating strange bedfellows. The most progressive sector of the bourgeoisie and petty bourgeoisie, together with the information-technological intelligentsia, finds itself allied with low-end manufacturing interests in the Third World that have highly exploitative labor practices. Historically socialist or populist regimes and movements find themselves aligned with petroleum producers and the more backward sectors of capital in the advanced countries.

Matters become still more complex, however, when we begin to factor in geographical patterns. Neoliberalism has meant greater mobility primarily for capital. While migration is increasing, barriers to the mobility of labor remain and likely will for some time. And it turns out that there are some very specific things that help a region to profit from the neoliberal regime—and very definite things that mean that it will probably never be able to profit from that regime. Specifically, I would like to suggest, the old distinctions between "First World" and

"Third World," between "developed," "developing," and "underdeveloped" regions, "center" and "periphery," while still relevant, have been layered over by and are rapidly giving way to a distinction between "metropoles," specifically understood as "world cities" or "world city candidates" and "hinterlands." Such cities can be identified in any number of ways, but the most economically relevant classification has been developed by the Globalization and World Cities (GaWC) Study Group and Network at Loughborough University in Leicester in the UK. Their classification is based on corporate service criteria in accounting, advertising, banking, and the law. One might add to these economic criteria others, such as serving as a "great power" capital or headquarters for a major international organization, or cultural criteria having major research universities or media outlets, but even so, the results are striking. Of the cities ranked as "Alpha" or full-service corporate centers, North America has three, Europe four, and East Asia three. Africa, Latin America, India and *Dar-al-Islam* have none. Of cities ranked as "Beta" or major centers, North America has two more, Europe three more, the former Soviet bloc one, Latin America two, and East Asia and Oceana one each. Still nothing in India, *Dar-al-Islam*, or Africa. Of cities ranked as "Gamma" or minor centers North America has another eight, Europe another thirteen, and East Asia eight. Latin America picks up two and Africa one. There are three cities at this level in *Dar-al-Islam*, but only one (Istanbul) in the heartland and that is in an historically secularist state. The other two (Jakarta and Kuala Lampur) are in East Asia. It is only when one looks at "emerging" world cities that one finds a significant number of centers in the heartlands of *Dar-al-Islam* and India. And here India performs much better than the Islamic world, having two cities with relatively strong evidence of world-city formation (Mumbai and New Delhi) where *Dar-al-Islam* has only cities with "some" and "minimal" evidence of world-city formation (Beaverstock, Smith, and Taylor 1999).

We still need to do more research to understand what underlying factors allow such "world cities" to emerge, but their distribution gives us an excellent map of where people are finding ways to profit from globalization and where they are not. And it must be remembered that in major metropolitan centers of the sort we have described, it is not only those with capital or high order skills who benefit; the vast sums of wealth concentrated in these areas open numerous opportunities for small business development (boutiques, restaurants) that generate income at a level comparable enterprises in lesser centers cannot.

What this means is that in addition to cleavages along sectoral lines, the political landscape in the present period will be characterized by cleavages along geographical lines—and not just on the largest geopolitical scale. Large polities such as the United States, China, India, Russia, Brazil, and even Mexico will be sharply divided between metropoles linked to the global market and profiting from it, and hinterlands largely cut off from the global market and increasingly resistant to globalization. This is especially apparent in the United States, where these divisions, furthermore, often correspond to older regional cleavages. Note that the World Cities map includes only four minor centers in the southern part of the U.S. (Dallas, Houston, Atlanta, and Miami), only one of which (Atlanta) is unambiguously in the cultural "South." There is only one emerging center (Richmond). There are no centers, actual or emerging, in the mountain states. This division corresponds at least roughly to current U.S. voting patterns, as the results of the 2004 presidential election indicate. The clearest pattern in the election was not based on class, ethnicity, or even religion, but rather geography. Kerry carried only big cities (60 percent). He split smaller cities (49 percent) and lost all other types of communities to Bush. Kerry votes were, furthermore, concentrated in the Northeast, the upper Midwest, and the West Coast. Exceptions to this pattern correspond to either "Third World" (i.e., never developed) regions or minor civilizational centers. Thus Kerry carried the Rio Grande Valley, San Antonio, Northern New Mexico, and the San Luis Valley—all historically important Latino regions. He also carried parts of the Indian Country and the Mississippi Delta and swaths of territory through the Deep South (historically African American). Of particular interest, however, is the fact that he also carried much of the upper Mississippi Valley in Minnesota, Illinois, and Iowa, as well as a swath of territory extending west into Iowa along Interstate Highway 80. These are largely Scandinavian, German, Belgian, and Luxemburger regions with an unusually strong continuity of cultural institutions—Benedictine Monasteries, small Catholic and Lutheran colleges, etc.[4] We see a similar pattern in India, where the

---

4. Results from the 2008 General Election suggest similar patterns, albeit with a shift towards the Democrats.

high-tech South is pluralistic and tolerant, while the North is a hotbed of sectarian strife and the headquarters for the Hindu Fundamentalist *Bharatiya Jana Sangh.*

In other regions, such as Europe, characteristics we have identified as "metropolitan" are widely diffused, but are layered over by social-democratic protections that reduce incentives to compete on a global scale. The fate of regions such as this will depend very largely on their ability to remain sufficiently innovative, or to conserve historic monopolies on traditional luxury goods (wine, cheese, olive oil) to attract the monopoly rents necessary to sustain *both* high incomes and social democratic protections.

Finally, it must be noted that the formation of a global market and the imposition of a rigorous neoliberal regime have tended to undermine one of the principal bases of historic socialism: movements of *resistance* to capitalist modernization on the part of intact but threatened traditional (especially peasant) communities. Indeed, the crisis of socialism as a mass movement and the emergence of various religious fundamentalisms as the principal form of resistance to capital is largely a product of this change. While socialism was able to capture and hegemonize the resistance of largely intact premodern communities to the destruction of their way of life by the penetration of capitalist relations of production, fundamentalism taps into the despair and disorientation of communities that are in the process of disintegrating or that have already dissolved. In this sense we disagree with Milbank that the revival of religion in the present period is primarily a mark of *resistance* to the "enclosure of the sacred" (Milbank 2006a). It is, rather, a reaction to the *successful* enclosure of the sacred that, precisely because of that enclosure, has been forced to embrace early modern forms. The only real exception to this pattern is in Latin America, where a populist socialism informed by popular religious traditions and articulated through the theology of liberation remains a significant factor.

The net result of these developments is that modernity has no way forward. Both capitalism and historic socialism are at an impasse. Whatever comes next will need to be very, very different.

Political-Theological Cleavages and the Emerging Civilizational Crisis

The foregoing analysis makes it possible to explain the complex political-theological cleavages in a way that the principal alternative analyses cannot. On the one hand, precisely because there *are* sectors of the population that are still benefiting from capitalist modernization and more specifically from the global market, we still find significant reservoirs of residual high modernism, especially in the planet's principal metropoles. These take two principal forms. First, there is the officially dominant neoliberal consensus that free markets, democracy, and secularism are, in fact, winning out and that current conflicts represent the death throws of reactionary resistance to modernity. As noted above, radical elements within this neoliberal trend (Tipler 1994) still uphold the hope that modernity will not merely lead to a better life for everyone, but that it will allow humanity to gradually transcend the limits of finitude. Within the neoliberal camp, there are sharp divisions between those who argue for state-led investment in order to promote and maintain competitiveness (Reich 1992) and radicals who argue that market forces should be left to operate on their own (Hayek 1988). This division seems to derive ultimately from differing degrees of dependence on "big science" and the information industries, both of which generally favor a more interventionist economic policy. Geopolitically, this trend is associated with the "end of history" thesis put forward by Francis Fukuyama (Fukuyama 1989).

Second, in spite of the crisis of socialism, there are still regions in which socialist modernism retains a constituency. These locations are mostly in rapidly developing regions in the Third World, and the socialism in question is far from orthodox. The most important such center is China, where the Communist Party continues to think in historical-materialist terms, even when it makes the judgment that the marketplace can still play a progressive role in economic development. The position of the party remains that the level of development of the productive forces is still too low to sustain fully socialist property forms, but that such forms may become appropriate in the future. More to the point, while allowing China to develop as a market economy profoundly integrated into global exchange networks, the party is leveraging vast resources for projects that the market itself would not support: building a hundred new Green cities, with a hundred new universities for example. The party is also showing increasing sensitivity to the impact of globalization on the working classes, moving to strengthen trade unions in order to ensure that China does not permanently remain a low-wage export entrepot. Socialist modernism also retains some salience in Southern India, especially Kerala, where the land reform and education policies of the Communist Party of India (Marxist) have helped create the conditions for high technology development, and in emerging world cities in Latin America where it has provided a base of support for a new left committed to engagement with the world market coupled with investment in promoting human develop and creating the conditions for authentic popular participation in increasingly higher-end economic activities. This is distinct from the populist left represented by Hugo Chavez, Manuel Lopez Obrador, and Evo Morales (Castenada 2006), which we will consider shortly.

There are also, as we noted, broad layers of the population who occupy an ambivalent position with respect to the global market: the humanistic intelligentsia, those on the peripheries of the information-technology sectors, and the new "boutique" petty bourgeoisie that has grown up to service the needs of the newly enriched infogenrty and technogentry. This has provided a large constituency for two alternative ideological trends: postmodernism and the religious left. Postmodernism largely accepts both the modern critique of earlier religious ideologies and the death of the modern ideal itself and argues that we need to learn to live *without* a unifying civilizational ideal. Such an existence, of course, will be attractive only to those who are materially comfortable enough to find their consolations in this life and too dulled by patterns of modern life to ask enduring questions of meaning and value.

Those opposed to the neoliberal regime of accumulation are similarly sharply divided—in this case between proponents of various fundamentalisms and a cultural-populist/socialist trend.

The nature of fundamentalism has, of course, been one of the principal topics of recent socio-religious analysis. End of history theorists regard fundamentalism as merely a last-ditch resistance to the inevitable, all the more irrational because it is desperate and doomed. Clash of civilizations theorists interpret it as evidence that one or more major civilizations may be holding out against Western modernity. Radical Orthodoxy interprets it as a form of resistance to the enclosure of the sacred. What they all share is the conviction that fundamentalism represents a *rejection* of modernity. I would like to argue that this is not really accurate, and that fundamentalism is, in fact, a reassertion of *early modern ideological tendencies*. Let me explain.

As we have seen in earlier chapters, Medieval Europe and the Silk Road civilizations with which it was linked all valued reason very highly. These civilizations also tended towards what philosophers call an *analogical metaphysics*. God was understood as *Esse*, the power of Being as such, in which all created things have a share and participate to the extent of their ability, as the *tathagatagarbha*, the Buddha-nature that gives all things the potential for enlightenment, or as *T'ai Chi*, the Great Ultimate that all things seek. The moral imperative was to promote the development of human capacities; spirituality was understood not as opposed to but as the summit of human creative potential.

This ideological pattern legitimated a system in which markets were allowed to operate—and indeed did so on a grand global scale—but were also constrained by moral norms that prioritized human development. These norms were enforced partly by the state (especially in China and *Dar-al-Islam*), which used taxation to redirect surplus in ways that promoted human development (the best example being the Islamic wealth tax or *zakat*), but also by religious institutions themselves (temples and monasteries and *waqfs* that centralized surplus and invested it in the arts, sciences, philosophy, and religion).

It was only in the late-medieval and early-modern periods that this consensus gave way—in Europe and *Dar-al-Islam* especially—to a *univocal* metaphysics in which a divine sovereign, who differs from us not in nature so much as in power, presides over a universe from which he demands nothing so much as submission: the God of Calvin, but also of the Asharites and especially the Wahabis. One can even detect similar tendencies in the *dvaita Vedanta* that provided the philosophical underpinning for the theistic *bhakti* (devotionalist) movements that became so influential in late-medieval and early-modern India. This happened because the emerging modern state and later the bourgeoisie felt constrained by the moral imperatives deriving from the older metaphysics. It was against *this* god that modern secularists later rebelled, pointing out, quite correctly, that greater (even supreme) power is not a legitimate basis for authority. Their intent, however, was simply to liberate the bourgeoisie from its erstwhile ally, the absolute monarchies, not to reground an analogical metaphysics and a natural law ethics that might have ordered human society to a higher end. The "people," acting through either the market or the state, simply replaced God as the supreme sovereign.

State and market have competed ever since as agents of modernization, with the state generally favored by those who are behind and the market by those who are ahead. But backward sectors of capital face a particular difficulty. They need to rein in the market—and especially the global market—without calling capitalism fundamentally into question. Fundamentalism offers them a way to do just this. On the one hand, by privileging particular identities, it sanctions at least partial withdrawal from the global market. On the other hand, it cultivates a spirituality of authority and submission that at once discourages resistance to exploitation and stakes identity on something other than cutting-edge creativity. It is, in other words, a way to legitimate the use of force to make up for the fact that one's society, whether through poor ecological endowments, internal structural problems, bad decisions, or external oppression, has fallen terribly behind and lacks the will to invest in cultivating real creativity. In the United States, fundamentalism has been mobilized to build a mass base for a global military empire that will secure the position of the most backwards sectors of the U.S. economy. In *Dar-al-Islam*, it is being used to mobilize support for what would presumably be an Islamic state partially delinked from the global market, except for its ability to extract petroleum rents from those regions that had not seriously invested in alternatives. A Eurasianist Russia—having established itself as Europe's principal supplier of petroleum—would undoubtedly attempt something similar. It is a strategy that smacks of fascism—whoever attempts it.

The second trend in the opposition to the global market is the populist socialism that has experienced a rebirth in Latin America and that is represented by leaders like Hugo Chavez, Evo Morales, and Manuel Lopez Obrador on the electoral front and movements such as the *Zapatistas* in the political-military arena. Much of the neocommunist movement in the former Soviet bloc (as opposed to the "reformed" parties that have governed places like Poland and Hungary with some success) falls into this camp as well. This trend differs from the modernist socialism of the Brazilian Workers' Party or the Communist Party of India (Marxist) [CPM] in that it is primarily a vehicle for *resistance* to the new wave of capitalist modernization—and to what Milbank calls the "enclosure of the sacred" represented by the neoliberal regime of accumulation. This trend is strongest in countries that have a tradition of state-led industrialization and state protection for the working classes. In many cases these countries also have a very significant base of petroleum or other mineral rents that they can use to subsidize the poor without large-scale redistribution. Other formations on the Left, such as the World Social Forum, incorporate elements from both the modernist and the populist left and are simply united in their rejection of *pure* neoliberalism—something that has made it difficult for them to develop a coherent vision and strategy.[5]

Standing somewhere between modernist neosocialists and the cultural/populist left, we find the religious left—or, as I prefer to call it, the party of meaning and hope. This trend includes all those who accept the humanistic modern ideal of critical, rational autonomy and at least some aspects of the socialist critique of capitalism but have rejected the hope of divinization by means of revolutionary political practice, and draw on axial and post-axial spiritual traditions and spiritual practices

---

5. Readers may be wondering where a trend such as the theology of liberation, which was so important in the 1970s and 1980s, fits within this analysis. It is necessary, first of all, to distinguish between liberation theology as a popular movement (here it is more accurate to speak of the popular church) and of liberation theology as a theological trend. The popular church, especially in its alliance with the Marxist left, is a classic example of what was fundamentally a movement of resistance to capitalist modernization (or as Milbank would say, to the "enclosure of the sacred") entering into alliance with what was still, primarily, a modernist socialism, with varying degrees of concession to peasant and populist concerns (Lancaster 1987). This alliance was all but broken by the crisis of the Soviet bloc, but is re-emerging, albeit in a somewhat divided form, with more traditional sectors gravitating towards the populist left and more modernized sectors towards the modernist left. Indeed, some sociologists have argued that liberation theology in places like Brazil has become a movement of the upwardly mobile middle strata.

Liberation theology itself, as I have argued elsewhere (Mansueto 2002a) represents a type of left Augustinianism—essentially a *reprise* of the old Franciscan Spiritual tradition. This is documented by the fact that liberation theology, like essentially all postconciliar Catholic theology (left, right, and center), takes a profoundly Christocentric turn. The only exception to this pattern, and it is only a partial exception, is the theology of Juan Luis Segundo. Politically, liberationists opted for an alliance with the Marxist left in much the same way that the Franciscan spirituals opted for an alliance with the Holy Roman Emperor and against the pope. Today, like their popular base, liberationists are divided between the populist and (humanistic) modernist left.

in a effort to reground meaning and the struggle for social justice (Pew 2008).

We should note that those who lack the minimal social conditions to engage the global market at all, even as low-wage, low-technology manufacturers or mineral or agricultural exporters, are not, for the most part, currently organized in any of the above trends. They provide, rather, a recruiting ground for guerilla movements of the sort we have witnessed throughout Africa in recent years, which, even when they use the language of the Left or of a religious tradition, rarely rise above the level of social banditry and often sink beneath it, into genocide and land grabbing of the kind we have witnessed in Rwanda and Darfur.

Finally, I should point out that the political-theological cleavages identified above are not, for the most part, hard and fast, but have rather soft edges. Thus neoliberal high modernism shades easily into postmodernism, especially among those among the information sectors with a humanistic rather than scientific formation for whom the ideal of scientific and technological divinization has lost much of its credibility. Postmodernism shades on its right wing into neoconservative theomachy and neoconservative theomachy into full blow fundamentalism. Most modernist socialism has, as we have noted, been productivist and technicist for some time and when it is not it shades gradually into the liberationist religious left and then into populism. And the alignment of each sector changes somewhat with its changing fortunes. Petro-rentiers, for example, are less likely to retreat into neoconservative, fundamentalist, or Eurasianist isolationism or belligerence when the price of oil is high and the resources available to diversify their economies: witness recent developments in Russia, or the effort of the United Arab Emirates to build a "knowledge society."

A New Period?

To what extent do the economic crisis and the election of Barack Obama require a modification of the forgoing analysis? In the broad outlines, not at all. On the contrary, it would be best to regard the events of the past two years as fundamentally a playing out of the dynamic analyzed in the previous section. This "playing out" has, however, brought us to the beginning of a fundamentally new period.

This is true at three levels. First, neoliberalism is dead, if not as an ideology then at least as a regime of accumulation. The long wave of growth and development set in motion by the development of new information technologies in the 1980s and 1990s and by the U.S. victory in the Cold War, which led to the creation of a unified global market in capital had already come to an end in 2001. Growth was sustained through the early years of the war with *Dar-al-Islam* largely by using easy credit (money borrowed from the Chinese) to prop up consumption.

But the significance of the crisis runs deeper than this. What has defined the West historically, to the extent that anything has, is a commitment to providing a large part of its population with a high standard of living and the leisure to purse life as free human beings and citizens. This is what we have called the classical, as opposed to the modern, humanistic ideal. Hellenistic-Roman Civilization did this by enslaving captives from its wars of expansion. The modern West did it partly by exploiting its colonies but partly also by achieving high levels of productivity that supported high wage rates for its skilled workers.

Obviously only the latter strategy is sane and healthy, and unfortunately, as China and India have mastered industrial and information age technology, it is increasingly no longer available to us. This is why the Right opted (as dying empires always have) for a strategy of military conquest. But our current position is not unlike that of the Roman Empire during the years of its long decline—militarily powerful but crippled by a long-term balance-of-trade deficit with India and China.

What this means is that not only the *modern* ideal in both its positivistic and humanistic variants, but classical humanism as well, is threatened, not because of a *cultural* conflict with other civilizations, but because its economic base is disappearing. Indeed, it has been threatened for some time. This is because the high-wage regime of the postwar period came along with a relative decline in leisure time, and thus in the time necessary for members of the working classes to function effectively as democratic citizens. Perhaps this is the reason for the cultural pull of the East beginning in the 1960s. Those who wanted to live lives devoted to something other than *production* increasingly found the active life of a democratic citizen closed off to them. Even the academy has become a locus of specialist research rather than global civilizational leadership. Instead they began to take refuge in the spiritual disciplines of China and India.

At the political level, the change that defines our movement into a new period is less dramatic than it may seem at close range. In terms of both voting patterns and campaign contributions, the change from 2004 to 2008 was significant but basically incremental. There has, to be sure, been a shift within the ruling classes themselves, away from the rapacious strategy of the past eight years. This is reflected in campaign finance data that shows that several sectors that supported the Republicans in the past two election cycles have shifted their allegiance to the Democrats, including defense (especially defense electronics), health care, mortgage bankers, automobile manufacturers, and clothing manufacturers. Similar shifts have occurred among some sectors of the petty bourgeoisie, including physicians and the clergy. The Republicans retain much of their base in commercial banking, the extractive sector, and most low-wage, low-technology manufacturing.

At the level of constituencies, there has, similarly, been a significant but basically incremental shift. As in the past two elections, the biggest single determinant of voting patterns is urbanization, reflecting the enduring polarization between those who are able to engage the global market and those who are "left behind" and who represent the core of the Republican base and the principal objects of Republican strategy. Indeed, Obama *lost* some ground among white rural voters in Appalachia and the Upper and Middle South by comparison with Kerry and Gore. And where he gained—among Catholics, Latinos, suburban voters, etc.—the gains were solid but incremental rather than dramatic and transformational. In short, the *numbers* do not point to a dramatic realignment.

But unlike established patterns, turning points are difficult to analyze quantitatively. Or, to put the matter a bit differently, campaign finance data and election results suggest a continuous metric; the actual outcome of elections, and especially of turning point elections like those in 1860, 1932, and 1980, are quantum in nature.

So what makes this a turning point at all?

First, the incremental shifts both in financial support from various sectors of capital and the petty bourgeoisie and in the election results themselves, *in combination with the current economic crisis*, suggest as we have already indicated that neoliberalism and especially its most rapacious variants and the neoliberal-social conservative alliance that has governed for most of the past thirty years are both spent, and that broad sectors of both capital and the people are looking for a new alternative.

Second, both in terms of the political perspective of its leadership and its political strategy, the Democratic *campaign* represented something fundamentally new. The new President himself represents a political tradition that is only now beginning to articulate itself and emerge into the public arena. While recent Democratic standard-bearers have not been the militant secularists that their Republican opponents claimed them to be, but rather believing and practicing Catholics and Southern Baptists, their *politics* was essentially a moderate secular neoliberalism. Concern for social justice was part of a larger ethical imperative to do good. Barack Obama, on the other hand, represents an emerging politics of meaning *rooted in* America's diverse religious communities. This politics is not in any sense confessional. It takes pluralism for granted. But it embraces a theology of liberation in the very broadest sense that it meets God first and foremost in the struggle for justice. And President Obama comes from a very specific wing of this movement. Formed politically as an organizer on Chicago's South Side, he brings an understanding of how justice is won that is more Tocquevillian than either liberal or socialist. It is the work of local communities, informed by diverse values, and organized in local congregations, civic organizations, trade unions, and other organizations of civil society—not the work of *either* the market *or* the state. Markets form the seemingly unavoidable context in which this work is carried out, and the state plays a critical role in facilitating it (through regulation and through centralizing and allocating resources for activities that the market and private philanthropy will not or cannot adequately support), but both are, in the end, secondary players in the human civilizational project.

The Democratic campaign strategy itself can best be summarized as follows:

1. Aim the main blow against nihilism and despair.
2. Organize, using both traditional door-to-door and emerging internet tactics, and mobilize, tapping into the best traditions of the civil rights movement.

What this strategy has done is to energize, mobilize, and organize vast layers of the population that were either passive participants or abstainers (or even trended Republican) in the several two election cycles. These sectors can, of course, be described demographically: the young, ethnic minorities (immigrants as well as African Americans and Latinos), Euro-American industrial workers, etc. But they are best understood as those who have, in many ways, been left behind by globalization because they lack the specific (financial and technological) skills favored by the global market, but whose identity—and indeed whose understanding of what it means to be American—is foundationally cosmopolitan, and who were thus immune to fundamentalist-social conservative cultural politics. Many of these people *did* vote Democratic in the past two elections, but Obama moved enough of them to not only win but to begin to redefine the political landscape.

These are just precisely the forces most likely to demand and benefit from a serious engagement with the ecological crisis, investment in green and other infrastructure that will support wage levels, restriction of the law of value to allow support for self-cultivation outside the wage relationship (the "redistributionism" that drew such attacks from the Right during the election campaign), a principled realism in foreign affairs, and a rupture with the secular/fundamentalist polarization of the past three decades—without the sort of statist turn that will re-energize the Right.

The impact of the Democratic victory, furthermore, extends beyond an electoral realignment; it is a redefinition of what it means to be an American and of the way the United States is regarded abroad. Specifically, the election affirms the emerging American identity as a multiethnic polity in which diverse traditions can pursue their own, distinctive civilizational ideals within the common framework of an open, pluralistic, and engaged civil society and in which the public arena is *constituted* by deliberation around fundamental questions of meaning and value. It also renders far less credible the common view throughout Asia, Africa, and Latin America that America is *merely the* Evil Empire and suggests that the relationship between the North American people, the United States as a political formation, and what the Leninist tradition has called imperialism is far more complex than the global Left has hitherto acknowledged.

So why is this less significant than it seems? For the simple reason that it comes so late—too late, perhaps, to alter than main course of events. The already critical character of the ecological crisis, not just the magnitude but the basic contours of the economic crisis, the enormous budget and trade deficits faced by the United States and many other Western powers, all leave President Obama with a very limited scope for action. And so this man Barack will not be our Moses or our Solon, our Ashoka or our Duke of Chou. Such spirits have already risen in this republic and have already fallen. He is, rather, more like our Marcus Aurelius, the worthy bearer of a worthy ideal who will fight hard for what he believes and perhaps buy America another century and the world time to find a new ideal and new structures, but who in the end cannot save the civilization he leads.

Put in more prosaic terms this means that the United States will rejoin the rest of the world in looking for effective ways to resolve the ecological crisis and shore up capitalism, perhaps paying a bit more attention to the needs of the poor and displaced in the process. But Obama cannot save modernity or the West. Indeed, the most radical thing about him is that he may not really want to.

This brings us to the third change, and the most significant represented by the election. True believers in modernity have been hard to come by for the past forty or fifty years, and most leaders, especially but not only in the West, have focused on pragmatic problem solving rather than secular messianism. This is what makes them postmodern. But Barack Obama goes one step further. He believes in something *other than* modernity. He is an authentic, believing Christian (probably a moderate liberationist theologically). While called to lead in the political arena he does not believe that politics is the sole or even the principal locus in which humanity is working out its destiny. He is the first Western leader in a long time to regard humanity as authentically ordered to higher spiritual ends *for whom this makes a difference in the way he leads.*

And so the neoliberal period ends not in a way that will save modernity, as at least some of the Left had hoped, but with the first steps into a future that transcends both modernity and postmodernity.

Just what will that future hold?

A Tentative Strategic Estimate

Four Scenarios

Humanity faces a period of great uncertainty. But certain broad contours of our future are gradually becoming visible. On the one hand, the crisis of modernity is only just emerging into consciousness. It is only in the period since 1989 that it has become a *theme* of political discourse and has begun to affect the dynamics of global politics. The current situation is still dominated by the intra-modern contradiction between those who are benefiting from globalization and those who are not—the new cosmopolitans, liberal and socialist on the one hand, and the fundamentalists and cultural populists on the other. On the other hand, at a deeper strategic level, the crisis of modernity is profound and the aspirations for something new are building every day. Just how this situation unfolds depends in part, at least, on how we respond. But breaking with modernity means, among other things, recognizing that the historical process is not, never can be, and ultimately should not be, under our control.

There are, broadly speaking, four ways in which the situation can unfold. The first is a *transition by reform.* Under this scenario, the core constituencies for a progressive break with modernity are successful in articulating a new civilizational ideal and building an institutional infrastructure to support it, while advanced elements in capital and the remaining socialist states, perhaps in alliance with leaders of traditional religious institutions, recognize the gravity of the crisis and move forward vigorously to address the ecological crisis, social injustice, and nihilism. These two currents form an alliance that results in a gradual transition that conserves much of modernity while setting it in a new context. This is, of course, the transition we should hope for and work for, and the strategic line proposed in the next chapter is intended to maximize its likelihood even while preparing for less favorable alternatives. We must note, however, that such transitions have been rare—the displacement of classical civilization by Byzantine Christendom in the eastern part of the Roman Empire, for example—and have not always been the most progressive in the long run. For such a scenario to be realized, progressive elements in capital and in the socialist countries (chiefly China) would need to regain the upper hand (in this regard the results of the 2008 U.S. general election are hopeful) and undertake a serious effort to address the ecological crisis, especially climate change, and to ameliorate the economic contradictions of globalization, while entering into dialogue (and providing growing access to the levers of power) with those who are charting the next steps in the human civilizational project.[6]

The second possibility is a *transition by revolution*. Under this scenario, enlightened elements in capital and the socialist states lose out either to radical neoliberals or fundamentalists (or both in different places), and the impending ecological crisis, economic dislocations, and nihilism get worse. Popular sentiment swings towards a clean break with modernity and, at least in significant parts of the planet, a new leadership representing a new civilizational ideal comes to power, whether through the electoral process or armed struggle of some kind, and begins a vigorous process of social re-organization.

This sort of transition also has precedents in the past: the advent of Islam is probably the clearest example. In the civilizational short run of several centuries it proved quite progressive, but ultimately serious problems that can be traced to the civilization's revolutionary origins emerged: the legacy of realizing the will of God by means of armed struggle. We should also point out that in the present period we would be looking for a "revolution" led not by a compact, disciplined, new religious movement, but rather by a pluralistic coalition engaged internally in debate around the most fundamental questions, something

---

6. We already see possible examples of such dialogue today in such institutions as the Alliance of Civilizations, an organ of the United Nations established at the initiative of Turkey and Spain to counter the politics of civilizational conflict, and in the numerous intergovernmental (UNESCO's Intercultural Dialogue Section) and nongovernmental (e.g., the World Parliament of Religions and the United Religions Initiative) interreligious dialogues. The danger is that such initiatives will be used by high modernists to simply *contain* and *integrate* not only fundamentalists (at who they are aimed) but also those advocating a creative re-engagement with the Axial Age project, and thus merely shore up a bankrupt neoliberal or socialist scientific high modernity. Nation-state initiatives, such as the United States Commission on International Religious Freedom and the corresponding office in the Department of State's Bureau of Democracy, Labor, and Human Rights, have similar potentials and present similar dangers, though under rightist governments they have sometimes become instruments in the politics of civilizational conflict. Our *task* is to engage such initiatives, unlocking their potential to become sites in an emerging global public arena constituted by deliberation around fundamental questions of meaning and value.

that seems difficult if not impossible to imagine. A revolutionary transition could, in fact, easily by hijacked by radical fundamentalist or populist forces. The result could look more like fascism than we care to imagine.

The third possibility is a *transition by decadence* (Amin 1978/1980). Under this scenario, neither progressive elements in capital and the socialist states nor the emerging "new civilizational" leadership are able to respond adequately to the developing crisis. Stopgap measures (e.g., severe restrictions on the use of fossil fuels, serious social reform in China, a variety of new religious developments) prevent total collapse, but the overall trend is towards a protracted decline of modern institutions, with a new civilizational ideal, and new institutions to support it, emerging only slowly out of the ruins. This is clearly the most likely scenario given a broader historical perspective. It is, after all, what happened to the West after the decline of Roman authority. And even with a progressive alliance in power, it is possible that it is too late to address the ecological and economic contradictions of modernity—or that the political conditions for doing so (witness the resistance faced by the Obama government to its first tentative efforts at reform) simply don't exist.

Finally, there remains the possibility of a real *civilizational collapse*. We distinguish this from a transition by decadence in that it describes a situation in which the conditions for modern urban life largely disappear and, while the knowledge of previous civilizations may be preserved, humanity must largely rebuild from scratch. Previous such collapses include the crisis of the late Bronze Age, and the collapse of several pre-Columbian American civilizations—the Maya, the Anasazi, the Mississippian, etc. The most likely cause of such a collapse would be ecological dislocations due to global warming, new epidemics, or nuclear warfare.

In such a situation strategic thinking is of limited usefulness. Survival comes first and what works and gains ground is often nearly random. Fortunately, the extensive character of the modern infrastructure makes such total collapse unlikely, at least on a global scale.

This said, and understanding that the future of humanity is not and never will be under our control, let us turn to the question of charting, in so far as possible, the next steps in the human civilizational project, and to ascertaining ways to maximize the likelihood of a transition by reform or revolution, to minimize the likelihood of civilizational collapse, and to find ways through and beyond a transition through decadence.

The Balance of Forces

In order to do this, we need to take stock of the current balance of forces and what they tell us both about the likelihood of each of the above scenarios and the resources on which we can draw in promoting a transition through reform or revolution.

The Impact of the Ecological Crisis

We should note, first of all, that the building ecological crisis represents a background constraint that cannot simply be ignored. Because resolution of the ecological crisis requires a break with at least scientific-technological modernism, this factor works very much in our favor, but only in a negative way. It rules out a long-term victory for our adversaries; it does not guarantee a victory for the party of meaning and hope or even constitute a strategic reserve on which we can draw. Total civilizational collapse remains, after all, a real possibility.

Structural Factors

With respect to the underlying balance of class forces, we must acknowledge the overwhelming and continuing hegemony of global capital and of the political-theological tendencies that articulate its vision of the future: neoliberal high modernism and neoconservative theomachy. Nearly all of the world's economic resources, state structures, and military forces and most of the cultural apparatus, especially the media of social communication, are controlled by various sectors of global capital. And however much the United States and other great powers may fret about the weapons of mass destruction falling into the hands "terrorists" or "rogue states" (admittedly unpleasant prospects) the arsenal of such weapons possessed by the United States and other states effectively controlled by capital renders the insurrectional and *guerilla* strategies employed with some significant effect by socialist and national liberation movements during the last hundred and fifty years effectively impotent.

Global capital is, however, far from being a unified bloc. Two sectors in particular represent powerful, deeply rooted—and opposing—social dynamics. On the one hand, the information and high technology sectors, because they will continue to generate new innovations, will be able to capture, at least for a time, monopoly rents on creativity, strengthening their economic position and thus their political power and cultural influence. As we have noted, these sectors are, in general, more sensitive to the ecological crisis, more dependent on widespread economic prosperity, more cosmopolitan in their outlook—and more open to an alliance with the party of meaning and hope. But internal contradictions within this sector, especially between the United States, Europe, China, and India, and between this sector and more backward extractive interests, have been sufficient to prevent it from fully implementing its agenda, as the recent collapse of the Doha round of world trade talks suggests.

There are, on the other hand, good reasons to believe that the extractive and especially the petroleum sector will exercise continued and perhaps growing influence. While the run up in petroleum prices during 2008 may well have been due in large part to speculation, the gradual depletion of petroleum and other mineral resources *will* lead inevitably to rising prices, enriching and empowering those who live off of mineral rents. This sector is naturally allied with the aerospace and defense sector, for the simple reason that mineral wealth is wealth in land, and land must be protected.

The information/high technology and extractive/defense-aerospace sectors constitute poles within capital between which the other sectors are arrayed. Finance capital remains independent of and superior to all other sectors of capital, which are simply items in a shifting portfolio of interests. While in general finance capital will prefer to invest in those sectors with longer-term prospects for growth, and thus tends to ally itself with the information and high technology sectors, it is a fickle partner and always hedges its bets (indeed, an entire subsector of finance capital is defined by this practice of *hedging*). Lower technology manufacturing and service sectors, commerce, and agriculture are, on the other hand, at this point very much junior partners in alliances dominated by one or the other of the principal players.

It is also, finally, important in analyzing the various sectors of capital to note the relative autonomy of what we might call philanthropic or charitable capital—i.e., the large private foundations—from the sectors from which their endowments originally derived. This will be important in our analysis of the autonomous organizations of civil society, which are largely funded by charitable capital.

Property forms turn out to make much less difference than the larger structural framework (in this case the global market) into which they are inserted. This means that the planet's principal socialist power, China, cannot be expected to behave much differently from a capitalist great power. It will concern itself primarily with achieving an optimal positioning within the global market and its socialism will be expressed primarily in making more rational and productive use of the surplus it is able to generate and capture: addressing serious ecological issues and ameliorating the polarizing effects of capitalist development. It will, in other words, play a somewhat more progressive role than its basic economic character as a low-wage manufacturing entrepot with only emerging high-technology sectors might lead one to believe, but it will still behave like a *capitalist* power, for the simple reason that it is a power in a capitalist system.

The various fractions of global capital, like all primary social actors, are also the carriers of particular civilizational ideals and the struggle between them is a struggle between those ideals. The information and high-technology sector, as we have noted, remains the principal social base of scientific-technological high modernism, though usually in a chastened form that, especially for the information sector, shades gradually into postmodernism. But as we noted above, the Obama government, which draws its principal financial support from this sector, suggests an openness to alliance with the party of meaning and hope. This is even more true for philanthropic capital. While private foundations do, of course, reflect a diversity of ideological tendencies and programmatic interests, the large private foundations have developed a broadly common set of funding priorities that reflects at least some recognition of the deepening crisis of high modernity, albeit also a desire to resolve that crisis within the bounds of the global market. Hence the focus on sustainable development, microlending, strengthening civil society and rule of law, promoting religious pluralism, etc.

The extractive and aerospace/defense sectors are, on the other hand, the principal social base for neoconservative and fundamentalist tendencies. Saudi Arabia is probably the purest expression of this tendency, though we see variants of it in the Republican Party in the U.S. and in Putin's Russia. But this sector has, at certain times and in certain places, pursued very different strategies: witness the populist redistributionism of Hugo Chavez or the effort of the United Arab Emirates to re-invent itself as a "knowledge society."

By comparison with the various sectors of capital, all other social classes are more radically disempowered than they have been since the beginning of the democratic revolutions. This does not mean that there are no pockets of privilege. Those sectors of the "new petty bourgeoisie," concentrated mostly in the information and high-technology sectors, which are able to draw monopoly rents on skill, and those in the "traditional petty bourgeoisie"[7] who cater to them and to the bourgeoisie proper, enjoy high incomes and a range of consumption choices unprecedented in human history. And even many low-wage workers in Asia, Africa, and Latin America may experience their superexploited condition as an economic and social advance over near-starvation in rural regions devastated by capital centuries ago.

On the other hand, the classes that formed the traditional alliances that made socialism a real force for one hundred and fifty years have been devastated by the process of globalization and the neoliberal project. The humanistic intelligentsia has suffered almost total proletarianization. Of those in the academy, a small elite enjoys privilege and comfort at a handful of research universities; they do so only at the price of abstaining from true sapiential leadership. The rest teach at colleges and universities that are under ever increasing pressure to

---

7. By petty bourgeoisie we mean those who live by selling the products of their labor rather than their labor power as such (as does the proletariat). The traditional petty bourgeoisie consisted of artisans, shopkeepers, merchants, and independent professionals such as lawyers, physicians, architects, and others with private practices. The new petty bourgeoisie is distinguished by its formal subordination to the wage relationship, but under conditions that allow it to escape exploitation (the wage paid is equal to both the necessary and surplus labor performed) and retain substantial control over the way in which work is performed. Both sectors can be either very privileged, capturing surplus produced elsewhere (through rents on skill or the skillful use of comparative advantage in trade), effectively proletarianized (retaining only the equivalent of the necessary labor they perform and being subject to intensive control of their work processes), or somewhere in between.

train skilled intellectual labor rather than to cultivate free human beings and citizens. Nearly half teach at community colleges, without the traditional protections and privileges of university membership, while an ever larger percentage labor as adjuncts, often earning less than manual laborers. Outside the academy, the concentration and capitalist rationalization of publishing and journalism have all but eliminated the traditional means of livelihood that sustained generations of public intellectuals.

The industrial working classes in the advanced developed countries, who never fully embraced socialism to begin with, are very much on the defensive and feel as threatened by low-wage immigrant workers as they do by global capital. Not a few gravitate toward the fundamentalist or nativist parties of the "left behind." And even where this industrial working class has retained its traditional social democratic commitments, its traditional organ of struggle—the trade union—and its traditional strategy—the strike—have been rendered impotent by globalization. Workers in Asia, Africa, and Latin America are beginning to take up the struggle, but as we noted above their conditions, bad as they are, are often an improvement over life in the villages. And they, too, operate under the limits imposed by globalization: the threat that a strike will result in redeployment of capital to a still lower-wage entrepot. Few of these workers, finally, enjoy the social space to organize freely.

The penetration of capitalist relations into the countryside, meanwhile, continues to liquidate the peasantry. This does not mean that there are no intact village communities left anywhere on the planet. But conditions in the countryside are very different from those that sustained the Mexican, Russian, Chinese, or Vietnamese revolutions that Eric Wolf analyzed so ably decades ago (Wolf 1969). And ironically, where such conditions have been sustained or recreated, it has often been with revenue redistributed either by migrant workers or by the state from the surplus generated by enterprises fully integrated into the global market. This is the case with much of rural China, which has seen a renaissance of temple building and religious festivals even as its people march off to the great coastal cities to find work.

Finally, one of the symptoms of the emerging civilizational crisis is just precisely the discrediting of the humanistic modernism, and specifically its socialist variant, that linked these classes together in a powerful alliance that effectively challenged global capital for one hundred and fifty years, often in conjunction with linking ideologies such as liberation theology. Increasingly, rather, the humanistic intelligentsia is drawn to postmodern pessimism, newly urbanized populations to Evangelical Christianity and other religious movements that provide newly literate populations with a sense of meaning and community in a fragmented and disorienting social landscape, and intact peasant communities to *indigenista* populisms that eschew any engagement with Western modernity.

There are, to be sure, some exceptions to this pattern. Populist socialist parties have recently come to power in Venezuela, Ecuador, Paraguay, and Bolivia and Bengal and Kerala remain Communist strongholds. But there are limits to what these parties can do. In general, they are forced to choose between resisting the further penetration of capitalist relations of production (the enclosure of the sacred) or leveraging comparative advantages in a way that is favorable to the working classes. Neither amounts to a real vision for the next steps in the human civilizational project or a global strategy for realizing it.

Sacred Enclosures

Thus far our assessment of the balance of forces would seem to be rather bleak. But it is also incomplete, because it has considered only primary social actors, and principally social classes, as they are defined by and situated in relationship to each other by the hegemonic economic structure and as they engage each other in the political arena. But human beings are not just batteries, nor are individual and collective identities wholly defined by class position. On the contrary, human beings of *all* social classes are ordered to transcendental ends. This ordering impels them to creative, civilization-building activity, to seek wisdom and do justice, as they understand it, and to form organizations the purpose of which is to realize these ends. It is in these dynamics and the organizations to which they have given rise that we find our most powerful strategic reserves.

For the most part, these dynamics remain incipient and the organizations to which they have given rise remain at the level of secondary social actors: they pursue their aims within the context of the existing social structure and, even where they may reflect a competing civilizational ideal, they pursue it within the space afforded them by the hegemonic civilizational pattern. Such initiatives, generally speaking, have limited rather than global aims. Broadly speaking they fall into the following categories:

- organizations dedicated to conserving the integrity of the ecosystem, whether by developing new ecologically friendly technologies or by affecting public policy;
- organizations that seek to empower those marginalized economically by globalization and the penetration of capitalist relations of production, whether by catalyzing the formation of small businesses (e.g., microlending) or by organizing for improved wages and working conditions;
- organizations that seek to encourage active civic engagement, especially on the part of those historically excluded and marginalized, whether through formal electoral mechanisms or through extra-electoral means such as direct action, grassroots lobbying, etc., or that support the empowerment of women; and
- organizations that seek to promote the spiritual development of their members, whether traditional religious institutions or new organizations formed to promote new visions or engage new conditions.

These organizations, which make up the emerging nonprofit/nongovernmental sector, or what is often called civil society, are characterized by broad, interclass participation. At the same time, because the bourgeoisie and the most privileged sectors of the petty bourgeoisie can generally realize their interests through corporate or state structures, and because the working classes make up the vast majority of the population, they currently represent the principal form of organization of the working classes and have, in many ways, replaced the old coupling of the socialist or communist party and the trade union or peasant league as their principal forms of organization. While, on the one hand, this can be read as a retreat from the global aims of the old international workers movement, which sought a structural transformation of society, to the more limited vantage point of seeking partial reforms, it can also be read as a decision by human beings that they no longer want to be reduced to the status of batteries, realize that socialism can no more liberate them from that fate than capitalism, and have simply not yet advanced to the point of advancing a global vision and strategy for the future. Civil society, in other words, is where the work of civilizational building and spiritual development continues within the context of a crumbling modernity.

There is one characteristic of the dynamics of civil society in the present period that is especially important for our analysis and for the strategy that we will outline in the next chapter. This is what we call the movement towards *sapiential literacy*. By sapiential literacy we mean the capacity to evaluate arguments made by others regarding fundamental questions of meaning and value and decide independently where they stand in those debates. This dynamic is, of course, an old one: it reaches back to and in a certain sense is definitive of the Axial Revolution. But up until now it has reached only limited sectors of the population and in most cases it has been articulated within the context of a particular religious tradition: it is an aspiration to constitute a literate *laos* that shares ownership of the tradition with its particular *cleros*. But increasingly, as humanity is drawn into a single unified global public arena, these literate laities are coming into contact with each other and aspiring to a sapiential literacy adequate to this new global context. Largely because of the marginalization of the sapiential intelligentsia and its deformation into a body of hermeneutic specialists, this *laos* has tended to seek instruction from often poorly prepared evangelical, fundamentalist, or New Age popularizers. But the fact remains that the underlying aspiration is sound—indeed it represents an extension and realization of the Axial Age project of religious rationalization and democratization and a redemption of the humanistic modern aspiration towards rational autonomy and democratic citizenship—and is thus foundational to our entire project.

This said, the organizations of civil society are far from being fully autonomous. On the contrary, they are largely funded and in some cases directly controlled by two sectors that occupy an ambiguous position with respect to capitalism and late modernity: what we have called charitable or philanthropic capital and traditional religious institutions. Financial support from the large private foundations usually means that the aims of the organizations funded are limited by what is acceptable to the more progressive sectors of capital—the information/high-technology and allied financial sectors or, less often, some other sector that has established a charitable endowment. But it can also pull these sectors of capital in new and interesting directions. Financial and institutional support by traditional religious institutions can affect organizations in many different ways, depending on the religious institution in question. There has, however, been a tendency for religious institutions, with the exception of Liberal Protestantism (which is already modern) and Buddhism (which is not philosophically threatened by modern or postmodern philosophies), in recent years to pull away from engagement with modernity, and especially humanistic and socialist modernity, and to reassert a more traditional or even fundamentalist reading of their traditions. This is most apparent in the case of fundamentalist Islam, which has made the sponsorship of nongovernmental organizations a central part of its strategy, but it is also true of some Hinduism, especially in Northern India, and of the Roman Catholic Church. In some cases this pulls the organizations in question towards the fundamentalist or at least neoconservative pole; in other cases it simply limits their ability to articulate a new global vision, something that presupposes a full and open engagement with humanistic modernity and the critical resources it provides. At the same time, the direct engagement of clergy with pastoral responsibilities in the organizations of civil society is one of the most powerfully creative dynamics imaginable. On the one hand, it roots them in the struggles and aspirations of ordinary working people and inoculates them against initiatives whether of the Right or the Left that would harm or instrumentalize their constituents. On the other hand, it brings to the struggles of ordinary working people a voice that can articulate and draw attention to the larger meaning and transcendental ordering that already latent in those struggles.

Finally, we should note that while there is a wealth of civilization building activity and spiritual ferment at the level of civil society, that there is a real dearth of *tertiary political actors or political-theological organizations*: those that are organized for the purpose of defending or advancing a civilizational ideal as such, rather than just carrying out specific activities that support it, and of making the structural social transformations that that idea requires. To be sure, such organizations do exist: religious orders and other institutes of perfection, for example, in the Catholic Church and their equivalents in other traditions as well as the remnants of the communist movement. But these are largely carriers of older civilizational ideals and remain creative precisely to the extent that they realize that significant adaptation, at the very least, is necessary. There are also many organizations—research and organizing institutes and think tanks—that aspire to be tertiary social actors but have not yet developed either the coherent vision or the complex articulation with the popular organizations of civil society needed to actually be effective at this level. *The absence of political-theological organizations capable of exercising conscious leadership in charting the next steps in the human civilization project is one of the principal strategic weaknesses of the party of meaning and hope.*

All social actors—primary, secondary, and tertiary—take the field, so to speak, in a social space that is defined by varying degrees of openness, pluralism, rationalization, and engagement with questions of meaning and value. There has as yet been very little formal analysis of this aspect of social structure, and it is one of the contributions of our approach to point out the need for it. A society can, for example, be liberal without being pluralistic, for the simple reason that relatively few traditions are represented in the population. This was true of many European countries before the recent wave of immigration began. A country can also be pluralistic while having a relatively low level of engagement with questions of meaning and value. This is the phenomenon that Marcuse called "repressive tolerance" (Marcuse 1964) in which nearly any belief is tolerated for the simple reason that none makes any difference. And it is possible to have a high degree of openness, pluralism, and engagement without rationalization, i.e., without a developed practice of resolving questions of meaning and value by means of rational deliberation.

This is one factor regarding which global analysis is quite impossible. Conditions vary not only from country to country but from city to city and village to village. It is, however, possible to specify some of the factors that must be taken into account in any tactical analysis of the political-theological terrain. The *liberalism* or openness of a social space will depend in large part on:

- legal protections for free expression;
- state structures that can enforce those protections;

- a political culture that values free expression; and
- historic definitions of identities, especially national, but others as well, and the way they articulate with the actual ethno-religious composition of the population.

At issue here is not only the situation within the state, but also the situation within universities, religious institutions, and other cultural institutions that shape public debate.

The *pluralism* of a social space will depend on:

- the degree of ethno-religious diversity;
- the internal structure of ethno-religious communities, and especially minorities, and specifically whether or not they cultivate leaders whose work includes engaging those *outside* the community; and
- the distribution of the economic resources and social capital necessary for diverse ideological trends to make themselves heard in the public arena.

The degree of *rationalization* of any social space depends on:

- the existence of a common philosophical language in which debates between various political-theological trends can be carried out;
- the extent to which the *laos* has been formed in this language to the degree necessary to participate meaningfully in such debates, or at least make informed personal decisions regarding political-theological questions; and
- the existence of a *cleros* that has been formed in a way that puts a premium on rational deliberation (as opposed, for example, to textual exegesis).

The degree of *engagement* with questions of meaning and value will be shaped by factors such as:

- the electoral system;
- the geospatial distribution of different ethno-religious communities;

- the presence or absence of tavern, café, and barbershop cultures; and
- the way in which urban structure and civic and religious monumentalization define public spaces.

Party list systems, because voters select ideologically defined parties, rather than individual candidates, tends to foster a more ideologically charged politics. Ethno-religious communities engage each other most when they have enclaves that allow the formation of distinctive merchant communities and social and religious institutions, but when these enclaves are in close proximity to each other or are even interpenetrating, as in a city such as Chicago. Segregation of ethno-religious communities in distant urban districts reduces engagement, while segregation in separate regions of the country can lead to separatist movements and ethno-religious violence. Tavern, café, and barbershop cultures, which characterized most of modern life, provide an autonomous locus for the development of a working-class culture. Thus the loss of these venues contributed enormously to the bureaucratization and ultimately to the demise of an authentic humanistic socialism. Virtual spaces such as the internet represent a new venue for public deliberation, at least for those who are computer literate, and may turn out to be important in national and global mobilizations, but they do not replace face-to-face contact. In order to fully engage each other as rational animals ordered to transcendental ends, people must have *places* where they actually meet face to face, places that they control and that are structured, intentionally or unintentionally, in a way that focuses attention on questions of meaning and value and that fosters deliberation. Analysis of the impact of urban structure and religious monumentalization is, as we noted in the first chapter, especially important in this regard.

What this—admittedly schematic—analysis suggests is that although global capital currently enjoys undisputed hegemony and although public debate is currently dominated by the contest between residual neoliberal high modernism and neoconservative and fundamentalist theomachy, the party of meaning and hope does have significant resources on which to draw. Human beings are not batteries and will not be treated as such. And even when they are they insist on finding outlets for their creativity and ordering to transcendental ends.

They struggle to protect the earth, to make work the creative expression it should be, and to participate fully in deliberation around not just questions of public policy but also fundamental questions of meaning and value. And they build countless organizations the purpose of which is to advance these ends. While most of these organizations remain at the level of partial aims, seeking to engage in civilization building and spiritual development within the existing civilizational pattern, some are beginning to ask questions about the next steps in the human civilizational project, laying the groundwork for organizations that exercise conscious political-theological leadership. The social spaces in which these organizations operate differ dramatically in their degree of openness, pluralism, rationalization, and engagement, but there are many places, including the United States, that perform well against at least two or three measures. And the more progressive sectors of global capital seem to flourish best within, and thus encourage the development of, such spaces. The long history of human civilization, finally, has left layers of urban structure and religious monumentalization that—even if in the past they served to legitimate one or another aspiring god-king—today serve as reminders of humanity's transcendental vocation. And as global populations migrate and create their own sacred spaces, our cities are increasingly characterized by the juxtaposition of monuments to competing ideals, creating a dialogue in stone, as it were, between spiritual and civilizational ideals. Finally, the 2008 U.S. general election has brought to power a president who is himself almost certainly a member of the party of meaning and hope, even if he leads an alliance dominated by the more progressive sectors of capital.

The question, of course, is how we draw on these resources to make possible a transition by reform or revolution, or failing that, to weather a transition by decadence and avoid civilizational collapse. It is to this question that we now turn.

CHAPTER 5

Between Cathedrals and Starships

In the forgoing chapters we have shown that the principal alternative analyses of the current situation (and the larger social-theoretical and political-theological perspectives in which they are embedded) are inadequate. We are not approaching an end of history in which the modern project will be finally and definitively realized in either a neoliberal or a socialist utopia. Nor is a clash of civilizations imminent. We do not need to live without a civilizational ideal, nor is the contemporary revival of religion simply a form of resistance to the enclosure of the sacred, the defense of an older and truer way of life. We are, rather, in the early stages of a civilizational crisis in which the various forms of the modern civilizational ideal are increasingly called into question, without anything to replace them. This civilizational crisis has been catalyzed by the deepening degradation of the ecosystem by modern industry and by the fact that neither capitalism nor socialism has shown itself capable of realizing the modern ideal, but its roots are, ultimately, much deeper. They lie in bad metaphysics. Humanity cannot escape finitude and contingency by means of innerworldly activity, be it scientific and technological progress or a revolutionary political practice guided by philosophical wisdom. Indeed, our finitude and contingency are permanent and ineradicable. This does not mean that seeking divinization is inherently wrong. On the contrary, it defines our humanity. But such divinization as is open to us depends on the spiritual discipline to learn from inherent contradictions and limitations of all human attempts at God and to be stretched by our failures, as much as by our successes, towards full humanity and beyond.

This said, we have also seen that the early stages of this crisis are unfolding in a political context that is still dominated by distinctly modern struggles—and especially by the struggle between those who have found a way to profit from the global market and those who have not. The first have, for the most part, rallied to defense of modernity, capitalist or socialist. The latter have gravitated either towards fundamentalisms that, we have shown, represent a return to early modern spiritualities of authority and submission, or towards a populist socialism that seeks withdrawal from the global market and an equality achieved by redistribution rather than growth. In between, those who find prosperity but no real opportunity for leadership in the global market, gravitate towards a postmodern rejection of the need for any civilizational ideal whatsoever.

Just how this crisis will play itself out remains unclear. The hegemonic position of global capital, the various fractions of which constitute the principal base of support for neoliberal high modernism and neoconservative and fundamentalist theomachies, is overwhelming. At the same time, we noted, deeply rooted social forces are working in favor of an emerging party of meaning and hope. The building ecological crisis, which has its roots in high modernism, means that a long-term victory for high modernism is ruled out. The economic crisis that began in 2008 has demonstrated the neoliberal regime of accumulation is largely spent. The 2008 U.S. general election points to a new politics of meaning and hope. And human beings of all social classes, but especially the working classes, refusing to be turned into batteries, continue to engage in creative activity and spiritual self-cultivation. In the process they have created a rich networks of organizations—what has come to be called civil society—which continues the work of civilizational building in the midst of the current civilizational crisis. Of particular import, from our perspective, is the growing demand on the part of the people for sapiential literacy—for the ability to make and evaluate arguments regarding fundamental questions of meaning and value—and thus to decide independently where they stand on these questions.

Given this balance of forces, it is unclear whether or not the next steps in the human civilizational project will involve a transition by reform, revolution, or decadence, or a complete civilizational collapse.

In this chapter we will analyze just how best to tap into the latent potential represented by the civilizational and spiritual ferment that is taking place in the midst of the current civilizational crisis. We will begin by arguing that we need to re-engage the main stream of the human civilizational project—and more specifically the Axial Age project. This will allow us to discern clearly what can and should be conserved from modernity and what should not. We will then draw out the structural implications of our vision. What kind of technological, economic, political, and cultural forms are necessary if humanity is to continue to grow and develop? Finally, we will look at what sort of strategy is adequate to the task of building these structures.

Re-Engaging the Axial Age Project

At the outset of this work, we set forth the basic philosophical and theological parameters within which it has been undertaken. At the philosophical level, we affirmed a moderate realism enriched by the contributions of neuropsychology, cognitive development theory, and the sociology of knowledge; a teleological cosmology that takes the results of modern science as something that still need to be *explained* and that point toward a universe that is ultimately meaningful and ordered to a transcendental end; a dialectical metaphysics of *Esse* enriched by dialogue with the results of modern science and humanity's diverse wisdom traditions; and a radically historicized natural law ethics. At the political-theological level, I argued that humanity and human civilization are defined by a drive towards divinization, a drive that, while frustrated in each and every specific instance, nonetheless stretches through this frustration towards and beyond full humanity.

These philosophical and theological foundations in turn grounded a revision of dialectical social theory to take into account the ordering of humanity to transcendental ends and a reading of the human civilizational project that follows from this theory. Specifically we have argued that while the pre-axial and modern metacivilizational projects have proven themselves unworkable, the Axial Age tradition has not yet exhausted its potential, and indeed represents the main stream of the human civilizational project. Our principal task in the present period is to re-engage this stream and resituate within it the genuine contributions of modernity that are worth conserving, while carrying the project to a qualitatively higher stage.

What does this mean? If we look at the larger Axial Age project, it is possible to identify two distinct stages of development, as well as a third incipient stage the unfolding of which was aborted in the late Middle Ages. There is, first of all, the Axial Age itself, which was characterized by localized or regional breakthroughs that took place in isolation from each other: the Zhou revolution, Upanishadic Hinduism, Jainism, and Buddhism in India, the emergence of Israel, and the emergence of Greek philosophy. At this stage of development, while there is an attempt at religious democratization, religious rationalization remains an elite phenomenon. The masses gain access to the cult through mystery religions or remythologized popularizations. Axial Age traditions, furthermore, remain largely marginal to the public arena. Second, there is the great Silk Road Era (200 BCE–1800 CE), during which we see a series of partial dialogues between the various axial civilizations: China with India, India with Islam, and Islam with Christendom. The development of universities and other comparable institutions extends rationalization to a broader elite that then attempts to hegemonize the great empires that, however, remain the principal political-economic institutions during this era. Finally, during the high Middle Ages we see an incipient movement towards full globalization, as Christendom entered into direct contact with China and India, and all of the empires began explorations that would eventually have led them to the Americas. The spread of literacy reaches a critical mass and broad layers of the population (though still far from a majority) begin to demand full participation in the public arena. This is the dynamic that was cut short by the Mongol, Turkic, and Norman conquests and that survived, but only in distorted form, in humanistic modernity. It is also the dynamic that we must re-engage in the present period.

Another way of getting at this matter is to note that both pre-axial and modern civilizations regard meaning as unproblematic. In pre-axial societies meaning is embodied in a shared mythos that has not yet been questioned. In modern societies, it is taken for granted that reason can resolve all questions of meaning definitively. In this latter regard, Charles Taylor, as we have noted, profoundly misunderstands the modernist dynamic. The Axial Age metacivilizational project is defined by *both* the recognition that meaning has become problematic *and* the conviction that this problematization enriches, rather than circumscribes, our search for meaning, which now gradually penetrates the entire population. It is ordered toward the creation of a public arena that is neither sacral and confessional nor secular, but that is *constituted* by deliberation around fundamental questions of meaning and value, with space for both those who find meaning and those who do not. And it insists that all activity, even the mundane activity of production, has spiritual significance, while rejecting the one-dimensional modernist spirituality of innerworldly progress.

It is the vocation of the present period to make the axial dialogue *global*, and to engage the *whole people* in deliberation around fundamental questions of meaning and value and in work that is creative and meaningful in the light of whatever principles they rationally embrace. This means, first of all, bringing all of the various axial traditions—Taoism and *dao xue*, Hinduism, Jaina, Buddhism, Judaism, Christianity, Islam, and the dialectical tradition—into dialogue with each other. It means extending what we call sapiential literacy—the ability to make and evaluate arguments regarding fundamental questions of meaning and value and thus to participate in public deliberation around ends—to the entire population. It means developing a new political economy that cultivates creativity and autonomy in service to the common good. And it means retheorizing and reconfiguring the way in which we produce as an alchemical cultivation of the properties latent in matter, physical, biological, and social, rather than as a means of building God or consuming finite resources for our own pleasure.

Just what sort of civilizational ideal will emerge out of this process remains to be seen. Civilizational ideals are not, after all, simply *written*. It is, however, possible to make an informed conjecture. Imagine a global dialogue between the great Axial Age traditions and the principal variants of modernity. And imagine that the participants in that dialogue want to conserve the achievements of modernity while rejecting its key metaphysical error: the univocity of being. Now there have, historically, been two very different ways of rejecting metaphysical univocity: the analogical metaphysics of *Esse* that developed in Christendom and *Dar-al-Islam*, and that, as we have seen, had correlates in India and China, and the analogical metaphysics of *pattica samupadda* that developed in the Buddhist world. The first metaphysics is analogical in the sense that the phenomenal world of contingent beings is regarded as participating in (but only participating in) the Necessary Being that grounds the system as a whole. The second metaphysics is analogical in the sense that because everything depends on everything else, *nothing* exists Necessarily in the sense of the Avicennist Necessary Being or Thomistic *Esse*, but participates in the interconnected totality (what the Hua-yen call the "jewel net of Indra") in much the same way that contingent beings participate in *Esse* as such in a Thomistic metaphysics.

While these two metaphysical traditions are diametrically opposed to each other on what is, in a sense, the most fundamental question—that of Necessary Being—they both regulate the way in which other fundamental questions can be answered, and constrain those answers in strikingly similar ways. For example, both the metaphysics of *Esse* and the metaphysics of *pattica samupadda* at once affirm reason as the first and ordinary way of approaching fundamental questions of meaning and value, and recognize its limits and the possibility of a higher knowledge (prophetic and/or mystical) that builds on reason. Knowledge of the first principle is the logical terminus of the dialectical ascent, and yet this first principle is, itself, beyond comprehension. We cannot say what Being *is*. Nor, for that matter, for most Buddhist traditions, can we really say what *sunyata* or emptiness is. And for both traditions there is a higher sort of knowledge that transcends dialectics, while building on it—a knowledge that is experiential and nonconceptual and rooted in the practice of justice or compassion on the one hand and contemplative or meditative practice on the other.

Similarly, both the metaphysics of *Esse* and the metaphysics of *pattica samupadda* acknowledge a limited meaningfulness for the phenomenal universe. For the metaphysics of *Esse*, contingent beings participate in Being as such in proportion to their essential natures, by conserving form, by nutrition, growth, and reproduction, by sensation and locomotion, and by intellect and will. For the metaphysics of *pattica samupadda*, contingent beings participate in *sunyata* by gradually evolving towards an Enlightenment that permits them to live with joy and actually help ripen other beings. Both steer clear of the twin dangers of god-building and radical acosmism.

Finally, both metaphysical traditions embrace a kind of natural law ethics focused on ripening or cultivating being, even if they understand this ethics somewhat differently. The moral imperative is, in each case, determined by a correct understanding of reality (and not simply, as in modern ethics, by divine command or by an attempt to ground order in a world without God). In both cases, that imperative consists in cultivating intellectual and moral capacities and in building a social structure that does the same.

The next steps in the human civilizational project will, we would like to argue, be focused on a new ideal of cultivating or ripening being, and characterized by a vigorous debate regarding just what that means. The metaphysics of *Esse* and the metaphysics of *pattica samupadda* constitute, in effect, two poles and two starting points for that discussion. In between lie the diverse alternatives presented by Chinese and Hindu metaphysics—the former, as we have argued elsewhere, actually very close to the metaphysics of *Esse*, but informed and moderated by a direct dialogue with Buddhism, the later a conscious step back from Buddhist otherworldliness. The next civilizational ideal will, furthermore, be defined by a *global* debate. It will no longer be possible, in other words, to write Thomism without engaging Buddhist as well as Augustinian critiques. It will no longer be possible to write *dao xue* without engaging *nyaya* and Asharite critiques. And more will be debated than simply principles. Thus the tradition of sharp polemics between clearly defined theoretical alternatives that defines the public arena in the West (here understood to include *Dar-al-Islam*) and *sometimes* China as well, will be challenged by the Hindu and Chinese models of pluralism. In the Hindu tradition, alternative *darshanas* or perspectives are regarded as partly competing and partly as working out a division of labor in which one excels at logic and epistemology, another at cosmology, and still another at metaphysics. Alternative religious aims—*moksa* (liberation), *dharma* (right conduct), *artha* (wealth and power), or *kama* (pleasure)—are accepted as appropriate to different individuals with different callings or levels of spiritual development. And for those who seek *moksa*, there are many different paths open: *jnana* or knowledge, *dharma* or right conduct, *karma* or service, and *bhakti* or devotion. In the Chinese tradition various philosophical and theological schools are integrated into a higher synthesis using the Chinese Buddhist practice of *p'an chiao*, with each regarded as representing a partial truth appropriate to beings at a certain stage of spiritual evolution (Williams 1979; Collins 1998).

This new ideal of seeking wisdom and ripening being in a radically pluralistic context will, to be sure, leave plenty of room for those who do not find meaning. Doubt is fundamental to the axial project and respect for those who remain in doubt is the condition of any real progress beyond it. Nor will advocates of the various forms of the modern ideal simply vanish, any more than traditional Hindus or Confucians did in the modern era. But the overall tenor of the society will be very different. Let us see how.

The Structural Dynamics of Ripening Being

Human civilizations pursue their ideals under definite material conditions and using definite social structures. Civilizational ideals do not determine structures, but they do constrain them and, more specifically, define a certain social-structural problematic in the context of which struggles around social structure unfold. The development of these structures is also constrained significantly by what remains from earlier civilizations. The structural dynamics of the next steps in the human civilizational project thus depends significantly on which of the potential scenarios we have identified actually unfolds.

This being said, it is possible to describe in broad outlines the likely structural characteristics of humanity's next civilization. We can do this by reasoning from the constraints under which those structures are likely to emerge. On the one hand, humanity will either be struggling to contain and rectify a profound ecological crisis, or else emerging from a civilizational collapse engendered, at least in part, by an ecological crisis it was unable to contain. Harmony with the ecosystem is thus likely to be a fundamental criterion by which social structures are judged. On the other hand, the next steps in the human civilizational project are likely to be characterized by an ongoing search for meaning and a focus on "ripening being," as well as by vigorous debate regarding just what that means, with a spectrum of interpretations reaching from a Jewish, Christian, or Islamic metaphysics of *Esse* to a Buddhist metaphysics of *pattica samupadda*.

What follows may seem to some to be utopian. It is not, at least in the sense in which that term has been used in the dialectical tradition. It is not, in other words, simply a vision of a world that "ought to be" based on a certain set of ethical presuppositions. It is, rather, a real resolution, or rather a set of parameters for a set of possible resolutions, to the crisis of modernity. As such, while we will not make any claims on behalf of its inevitability (total civilizational collapse *is* possible), it has powerful social forces behind it, forces that will constrain and channel the course of history and shape, if not determine, the next steps in the human civilizational project.

Neoalchemical and Synergistic Technologies

We have already noted that one of the most profound dimensions of the current civilizational crisis is the contradiction between industrial technology and the integrity of the ecosystem. This should have come as no surprise. Industry is based, as we have noted above, on breaking down existing forms of organization to release energy and do work. The result will, therefore, almost inevitably be resource depletion as we use up first fossil fuels and then fissionable fuels (what Buckminster Fuller called our planetary trust fund) and global warming and pollution as the waste products accumulate and undermine the integrity of the ecosystem.

This developing ecological crisis has given rise to a number of responses, many of which are merely reformist (Baxter 1974)—suggesting better regulation of industrial technologies—and others that can only be called antihuman. "Deep ecologists," for example, call for reducing the human population planet to essentially Paleolithic levels, on the premise that the planet cannot sustain a higher human population without inevitable damage to its overall ecological viability (Naess 1989). Reformist proposals of the first sort, while they may help stave off crisis until more profound solutions can be developed, fail to address the underlying problem; "deep ecology," on the other hand, is based on an incorrect understanding of all life as essentially equal, a position that is inconsistent in privileging life, but not its more complex and creative forms, and is static, privileging one stage in the evolution of ecosystems over all others.

There is, however, an alternative: a return to an alchemical *techne*, one that cultivates the existing potentials in matter rather that dissolving them to release their energy.

We are not, to be sure, advocating a revival of the specific theories and techniques of medieval alchemy, any more than we argue for a restoration of the specifics of Aristotelian physics. Above and beyond the changes in cosmography that have taken place in the past several hundred years, which we regard as basically valid, humanity has discovered that growth and development take place in the system as a whole, and not just in individual organisms. Thermodynamics, complex systems theory, evolutionary biology, and dialectical sociology have all also pointed to the critical role of chaos, struggle, and disintegration in the evolutionary process. This changes somewhat the way in which we understand the aim of cultivation and alchemical transformation. Rather than seeking a "philosopher's stone" that can confer on all things the incorruptibility of the divine, we seek rather to help each system not only realize its latent potential, but also—perhaps through a process that involves considerable struggle and even death—to transcend the limits of its essence and to become something new and still more beautiful.

What will this look like in practice? As with all dimensions of social structure, the next technological regime will be characterized by struggle within a new problematic rather than by any one uniform pattern. One tendency will build on and extend the internal dynamics of late modern science, especially those disciplines that challenge the mechanistic paradigm of high modernity, such as relativity, quantum mechanics, complex systems theory, and evolutionary and developmental biology, until it creates a technology that is more alchemical than modern. Another will delve deeply into and attempt to revive the premodern scientific and technological disciplines of many different cultures and extend them using methods and resources that (even when they deny it) will owe much to modernity, discovering, for example, just how Chinese and Ayurvedic medicine work and perfecting new techniques drawing on what seemed the dead end of medieval Christian and Islamic alchemy. In between these two tendencies, there will grow up an entire spectrum of new technologies that, like R. Buckminster Fuller's synergetics, integrate modernist elements with ancient (in his case Pythagorean) traditions.

At the beginning of this transition there will appear to be a profound tension between those who "still" want to build starships and those who prefer to tend herb gardens in the shadow of some great cathedral, with only a visionary few understanding that these are and always have been just two dimensions of a single task: that of ripening being. But as the transition proceeds new ways of creating will emerge that break down these barriers. Our road to the stars will turn out to have more to do with the shadow of that old cathedral than we ever imagined, while the new cathedrals we build will be enriched by our journeys to the stars and become true monuments to humanity's evolving participation in the creative life of God.

The Political Economy of Self-Cultivation and the Common Good

The economic arena will also be characterized by sharp tensions. Because of its focus on ripening being, the next civilizational ideal will, to a very large extent, require that economic decisions be justified in reference to the common good: by the promotion of complex organization generally and the cultivation of human capacities and civilizational progress in particular. We will ask, in other words, not "does this structure or policy contribute to economic growth and thus to the (usually hidden) aims of building God by scientific and technological means or of elevating humanity to the level of Subject of the cosmohistorical evolutionary process?" but rather "does this structure or policy contribute to ripening being, individually and collectively?"

Concretely, our break with modernity will be a break with *both* the generalized commodity production *and* centralized bureaucratic planning (although both will likely persist for some time). The rejection of generalized commodity production follows naturally from a recognition of the contradictions of capitalism that Marx identified long ago: the alienation engendered by the wage relation and the fact that markets lack any way to access information regarding which activities serve the common good. The rejection of bureaucracy follows from a recognition of the limitations of actually existing socialism (especially the tendency towards a scissors crisis), as well as of the way bureaucracies function (or rather don't) within capitalist societies.

The question, of course, is what will replace generalized commodity production and state planning. At the broadest level, we can expect to see a return to regulated petty commodity production, a system in which there are diverse ways of organizing labor and diverse forms of property that interact freely in an open marketplace, but in which the commodification of labor and capital are restricted and the operation of the system as a whole is regulated in order to promote human development and civilizational progress.

Within this context we can expect to see at least five different ways of organizing resources for production. First, we can simply decentralize the use of what has long been humanity's principal mechanism for centralizing resources for investment in human development and civilizational progress: taxation. While there are, undoubtedly, projects that are so large that they will require an essentially global taxing authority (e.g., space exploration), and while we may want to require that all communities fund certain basic needs and invest in institutions essential to human development, there is no reason why the centralization and allocation of resources by means of taxation cannot be radically decentralized. This is especially true given the relative decline of nation-states vis-à-vis cities as the defining units of the global economy. If the principal taxing authority rested with cities, rather than with nation-states, there would be far greater diversity in the way resources were deployed.

It is also useful to mention, in this regard, one of the principal economic achievements of the older civilizational tradition we hope to re-engage: the *zakat*, the tax on wealth that forms one of the five pillars of Islam. Because it is a tax on wealth, the poor pay very little, while the rich are compelled to invest their resources in a way that produces growth, lest their patrimonies gradually be taxed away.

A second way to ensure that resources are used in a way that serves the common good without promoting bureaucratic centralization is to endow educational, scientific, charitable, and religious organizations with claims on the surplus generated by particular economic enterprises. This is, of course, already common under capitalism and it was also common in most Silk Road societies, but it is worth considering how the wealth of the nonprofit sector might be expanded. It is important, to be sure, to find ways to protect those who labor for such enterprises. There is no guarantee that a university or a religious institution with claims on the surplus produced by a group of workers will not become exploitative. But this approach does ensure that the surplus will be used in a way that promotes human development and civilizational progress.

Third, we can change the way in which we write corporate charters. We currently require that nonprofit corporations use their resources in a way that serves the "exempt" purpose of the organization. There is no reason why for-profit charters could not gradually be rewritten to contain similar requirements. This means, of course, understanding that the mission of a corporation is to produce some useful good or service, not to make profits for stockholders. The result would be a gradual phasing out of dividend payments, reduction of executive salaries, and so forth, and ultimately the end of the financial markets and the market in capital generally. Banks would be transformed into something more like private foundations. This does not mean, however, that the corporations would fall under state control. Rather, they would be governed as nonprofit corporations are currently governed, with significant leeway as to the way in which they allocate their resources, as well as the right to form strategic alliances, and so forth. Private stockholding would essentially disappear, and corporations would be owned and controlled by their workers, subject to the regulations specified above. We call this the "social charter" system.

These last two approaches are a way to accommodate the likely persistence of larger enterprises in the economy, while encouraging greater social responsibility without bureaucratic centralization.

Fourth, we can re-build the guild system, which linked what was, essentially, the private ownership of small enterprises with collective self-regulation of quality, prices, training, and working conditions. The guild system had the advantage of limiting competition based on price and forcing competition based on quality, something that contributed significantly to helping backward medieval Europe enter the Silk Road economy as an exporter of high-end manufactured goods. This approach has potential not only in traditional artisanal sectors that have experienced a renaissance in recent years, but in information economy and high-technology activities that are characterized by a large number of small firms.

Finally, in some regions and some sectors of the economy (or in the event of a transition by decadence or civilizational collapse, rather than by reform or revolution) still less centralized options exist. Neocommunitarian and neomonastic forms (with or without fully communal living) may be attractive options under certain conditions: a highly productive, intensive agrarian, handicrafts (including "custom high-technology crafts"), and/or service economy (e.g., a residential school) coupled with an intact village or intentional community. The aim here is not complete autarchy. The community provides goods or services to the larger economy, and its charter forbids luxury consumption. It may even pay a tax in cash or kind. And in order to develop, the community would undoubtedly need goods and services from the outside. But because it approaches self-sufficiency, it retains an even greater autonomy in decisions about resource allocation than state or corporate systems, albeit on a much smaller scale.

What we need to keep in mind is that while all five of these structural options centralize and allocate resources for human progress, they will lead to very different trajectories of development. Consider the question of energy sources. Full development of safe fusion energy is likely only under a system with significant state centralization of resources for research and development. Neocommunitarian or neomonastic systems, on the other hand, are likely to favor development of solar energy, because of the greater independence it affords. Social charter systems, or the social charter sector in a larger system, while freed from the market pressures that favor continued use of fossil or fissionable fuels, might tend to be a bit more opportunistic, each organization favoring whatever energy source helped it carry out its own mission. State-centralizing systems make space exploration possible; at least with current technologies neocommunitarian structures do not—but they do conserve social fabric and provide a rich context for certain forms of artistic, scientific, philosophical, and religious development. On the other hand, there is little reason why either the state or small communities ought to, or would want to, be involved in making heavy machine tools. Clearly we need some combination of all these systems, and different regions will likely opt for somewhat different combinations. The choice between these different options depends in large part on forces over which we will have at best very limited control: the relative weight of the various social classes within the civilizational bloc, and the conditions under which we are organizing the transition. A revolutionary or reformist transition clearly favors the use of taxation, though there is no reason why it cannot conserve significant social space for the social charter and neocommunitarian options. A transition through decadence and renewal clearly favors the social charter and neocommunitarian options—the latter more strongly the deeper and more rapid the disintegration. Even so, any form of organization will require the existence of some institution that exercises at least minimal political functions: the administration of justice and the defense of the realm, as well as institutions that provide intellectual and moral leadership.

A Public Arena Constituted by Deliberation Around Fundamental Questions of Meaning and Value

The third arena in which humanity will be breaking with distinctly modern structures is that of political authority. This break will occur along two principal axes. First, there will be a global rejection of the sovereign nation-state. Sovereignty is, as we noted above, in many ways the constitutive relation of modernity, and in rejecting the modern ideal we reject sovereignty as well. In the place of sovereign states we will see, instead, the emergence of complex interpenetrating and overlapping networks of political authority. The most important level of authority will, increasingly, be cities. This is because the city—with its hinterlands—is the natural unit of human civilization and is increasingly the principal unit of the global economy as well. We have already discussed the importance of recognizing for cities the right to tax the way sovereigns currently do. Cities will also play the leading role in developing public educational and cultural institutions. Larger political units—if they are to be relevant at all—will increasingly be collaborations among cities around ecological, technological, and economic projects, while nation-states, rendered culturally heterogeneous by global migrations and economically heterogeneous by globalization, will become increasingly irrelevant.

This said, we will also witness the emergence of supranational political entities, and especially of an increasingly effective international political authority. This will not be a "world state," and even regional entities like the European Union are likely to become less rather than more state-like. Rather, this political authority will have two principal functions: 1) to address issues and undertake projects that, such as the ecological crisis or space exploration, simply cannot or should not be handled at the local level, and 2) to serve as a final political guarantor for peace and human rights. It will, in effect, establish certain minimum standards that city-states must meet, without telling them how to meet them, and will undertake global projects that smaller jurisdictions cannot handle.

Second, we will witness a fundamental change in the way in which we understand democracy. Up until now, democracy has been primarily a debate about means—about how to realize the modern ideal. Increasingly it will become a debate around ends, centered on fundamental questions of meaning and value. This doesn't mean that policy-level debates will disappear, but rather that we will witness the emergence of a new layer of public discourse. This dynamic will be intensified by global communications and global migrations. The result will be to render essentially impossible a polity that is either secular or confessional, for the simple reason that there will rarely be a majority that accepts either a single religious tradition or one or another variant of secular modernity. It will become necessary, if public discourse is to be meaningful, to address the prior questions—questions about what it means to be human—which even now lie behind public policy debates and render them often unproductive.

This second change will reinforce the first. While the radical pluralism of the emerging civilizational project will inhibit any trend towards theocracy or the sacralization of political authority, it will become increasingly clear that the most important leaders are precisely those who lead public deliberation around fundamental questions. Such leaders will not replace political leaders as we currently understand them—those who focus on building power or on policy questions—but the effect will be to inhibit the formation of *any* sovereign authority. Building and exercising power will become increasingly complex and will require serious engagement with fundamental questions.

A Spirituality of Meaning and Self-Cultivation

The final structural characteristic of humanity's new civilizational project will be the emergence of a spirituality of meaning and self-cultivation. This represents a sharp break with the principal spiritual options presented by modernity: either submission to a sovereign God or the pretense that spirituality is unimportant, *passé*, or even delusional, either as a cover for modernist immanentism and self-divinization or as a result of authentic despair. And it represents a real re-engagement with the spiritual traditions of axial civilizations—but with a powerful difference. In early stages of the axial project, sapiential literacy was limited to a small sector of the population. Even where people aspired to full participation in religious life, this was not a real option for them, and ordinary religious leaders became, in effect, mediators between the elite engaged in axial breakthroughs and the masses that could not really assimilate or understand them. As a result, even traditions that held reason in high respect—dialectical philosophy, Confucianism, Catholicism—often became quite authoritarian.

Today this situation is already changing. Increasingly ordinary people are insisting on making their own decisions regarding fundamental questions of meaning and value. Often, because we have yet to achieve anything like authentic widespread sapiential literacy, this has meant that people become attracted to movements that promise cheap grace (Evangelicalism) or cheap wisdom (the New Age). But this simply presents those of us who are the custodians of humanity's spiritual heritage with a new challenge. We must find a way to lead effectively under radically new conditions. And this means, first of all, cultivating real sapiential literacy—an ability to make and evaluate arguments regarding fundamental questions of meaning and value—among the people. It also means respecting the right of people to make their own choices in the spiritual realm.

This need not—indeed must not—entail a derogation of spiritual authority. On the contrary, it demands that spiritual leaders function at a fundamentally higher level of sophistication. It also means that if they can meet this challenge, their influence will, as we suggested in the previous section, expand very significantly. But it does mean that they must actually have something to offer. They must actually lead rather than simply demand deference.

If these conditions are met—if we can cultivate real sapiential literacy among ever broader sectors of the population, and if we can identify and train spiritual leaders who can lead a literate *laos*—we will soon find people turning away from movements that offer cheap grace and cheap wisdom, gravitating instead to those institutions that are most demanding but that because of this have the most to offer them. It is just precisely such institutions, I would like to suggest, that will lead the coming transition.

A Strategy for Civilizational Renewal

Strategic Paradigms

The Principal Alternatives

Each of the principal political-theological and social-theoretical perspectives we analyzed in the first chapter of this book implies its own distinctive strategic paradigm. Positivistic high modernism stresses the role of the underlying process of modernization generally and of scientific, technological, and economic development in particular. The role of political action is simply to remove structural obstacles to this process. In its neoliberal variant, according to which the underlying civilization-building process is essentially spontaneous, this means careful negotiation to remove obstacles to trade and to the flow of labor and capital across borders. This may occasionally require the exertion of political or even military pressure, but the great campaigns are, from this perspective, new large-scale investments, and victories are measured in terms of growth in gross global product, not in cities taken or governments held. Neoliberals differ among themselves regarding the role of the state in creating capacity, with radicals such as Hayek (Hayek 1988) arguing for a pure free-market strategy, and moderates such as Robert Reich (Reich 1992) arguing for intensive investment in research, development, infrastructure, and education. This is the perspective currently associated with the "end of history" thesis (Fukuyama 1989).

The historical materialist variant of positivistic high modernist strategy differs largely in its conviction that state planning is superior to the market as an engine of growth. The social democratic trend has historically argued that as industrialization proceeds, the working class will grow and eventually come to power by means of electoral struggle, which constitutes the main tactic in a strategy that like neoliberalism actually emphasizes scientific and technological progress (Engels 1880/1940). Those who read Lenin in a scientific high modern vein (most of those in the broader Soviet tradition, including Trotskyists and Bukharinists as well as Stalinists) argue that the socialist transition will not take place spontaneously and that, even where the underlying conditions for socialist construction are not yet present, it is preferable for the working class to hold state power so that capitalist development can be guided in ways that best serve the interests of socialist construction and of the modernist project in the long run. This is why Leninists focus on identifying weak states in which global capitalism is holding back and/or distorting development. In such contexts they tap into both the modernizing ambitions of the intelligentsia and the anti-modernist resistance of the peasantry in order to achieve state power. Strategic analysis is fundamentally a matter of defining classes and class fractions with respect to their position in the relations of production and then determining their stand with respect to the principal contradiction of the period and conjuncture. Tactics may vary from electoral struggle through insurrection and popular war, depending on the local conditions. This strategic perspective may have suffered a setback with the collapse of the Soviet bloc, but it must be remembered that in its broad outlines at least it still dominates the strategic thinking of the dominant technocratic wing of the Communist Party of China, which leads a quarter of humanity.

The humanistic variant of modernism, on the other hand, has generally stressed the cultivation of rational autonomy and the construction of a collective Subject of the cosmohistorical evolutionary process, whether that is the state, as for Hegel, or the party as for Marx, Lenin, and their interpreters. The critical difference between liberal and socialist humanisms lies, on the one hand, in the recognition by the latter of the alienating impact of general commodity production, which undercuts the formation of rational autonomy. On the other hand, this difference is also based on a clearer definition of what rational autonomy entails—that is, understanding "the conditions, line of march, and ultimate general result" (Marx 1848/1978) of the cosmohistorical evolutionary process, and thus a tendency to increasingly restrict full participation in that autonomy to a revolutionary elite: the Communist Party. Liberal humanisms have emphasized the wide diffusion of liberal arts education and the cultivation of active civic engagement; socialist humanisms have coupled party building with various mechanisms for linking the party to "the masses" who are not expected to fully understand either what socialism is really about or why it is necessary. The classic expression of this strategy is Lenin's (now read humanistically), who argued for both the creation of a vanguard party (Lenin 1905/1971) and for engaging the masses through what he called "transitional demands" (Lenin 1920/1971), i.e., demands that are accessible to the masses (e.g., "land, bread, and peace" or in later variants, national liberation and land reform) but that the bourgeoisie cannot deliver, either because it is too weak in its relations with colonial powers and landed elites or because it has developed in a distorted way due the country's particular pathway of capitalist development.

The interpretive sociological approach to grand strategy is based on the conviction that human social existence is fundamentally a struggle for power between competing civilizational ideals. This is, essentially, the strategy of the neoconservative and fundamentalist "clash of civilizations" theorists in both the West and *Dar-al-Islam*. According to this view, civilizational ideals are held largely on nonrational grounds and even when regarded as in some sense true, double as ways of legitimating power. Ideological and political military struggle dominate. Economic development is important first and foremost because it serves as the basis for projecting military power and demonstrating the viability of ideals. Whether political-military or ideological struggle is more important depends largely on the strategic position of the political actor in question. Thus the Bush government committed the United States increasingly to a strategy centered on holding militarily regions deemed strategically vital (especially those with vital petroleum resources), while actively promoting the "American Way of Life" not, as in past administrations, in the form of consumerist capitalism, but as a conscious ideology designed to counter fundamentalist Islam. Efforts to build local economies, to strengthen civil society and democratic institutions, and to understand and engage local cultures, while they have become increasingly important—consider, for example, the new counterinsurgency strategy developed by General David Petraeus or the Human Terrain System pioneered by the Office of Foreign Military Studies at the U.S. Army's Training and Doctrine Command (Kipp et al. 2006)—largely support an effort to take and hold terrain militarily. Those without the ability to project military power on a global scale concentrate instead on the ideological struggle. This is vitally important to our understanding of fundamentalist Islam and other antisystemic movements. While it is "terrorism" and popular guerilla war that attracts the media attention, most of these movements concentrate their efforts on promoting their ideologies through networks of schools and community organizations, using military action in a supporting role.

Populism, finally, grounds its strategy in the transformative power of collective effervescence to generate both new ideals and the solidarity necessary to sustain struggle on their behalf. Classic Russian populism for, example, tapped into the solidarities of the traditional *mir*, or village community, to create a basis in experience for socialism. More recent populisms have tapped into popular religious ideologies in order to resist the penetration of capitalist relations of production and the "enclosure of the sacred" (Milbank 2006a).

Each of these paradigms functions as a kind of pole between which actual strategies are located. There is, for example, a spectrum of opinion between neoliberal triumphalism and neoconservative theomachy, as there is between positivistic and humanistic socialism. Humanistic socialism, furthermore, over the course of the twentieth century tapped increasingly into populist dynamics, using "linking ideologies" such as liberation theology to join peasants and recently proletarianized workers to the socialist project (Gramsci 1949c; Portelli 1974, 1975; Laclau 1977; Lancaster 1988). Maoism, finally, stands somewhere between humanistic socialism, poor peasant populism, and a left postmodernism that treats politics as a contest between ideals. It tends to cut ideological struggle loose from its moorings in underlying social processes, so that politics drives ontology rather than ontology politics, and taps into the collective ferment and traditions of the peasant masses not so much to legitimate a stable party structure led by humanistic intellectuals as to call permanently and continually into question all authorities—and their metaphysical grounds—including that of the party.

Ripening Being

Our analysis has already shown why all of these approaches, though they capture part of the truth, are ultimately inadequate. To be sure, we not only recognize but insist on the dynamic and limiting role of the material base (both the ecosystem and the economy) and its role in defining primary social actors. And it should be clear by now that I regard struggle around fundamental questions of meaning and value (ideological struggle) the very substance of politics. We regard the struggle for rational autonomy as an enduring contribution of the Axial Revolution, and recognize the role of collective effervescence in catalyzing the emergence of new ideals and the solidarity to sustain them. But unlike all of the principal alternative theories, modern and postmodern, we regard the human civilizational project as a whole (technology, economic, politics, and culture) as really ordered to transcendental ends—i.e., as a participation in *Esse* as such. Economic development and class struggles in other words, while certainly bearing substantially on technological development and power relations, are also fundamentally about Being. And because production is an intellectual act they are always ideological struggles from the very beginning. Struggles between civilizational ideals, on the other hand, precisely because they are struggles between different ways of Being, are also always struggles about ways of building and exercising power and struggles about ways of organizing resources and of producing. And because they are struggles about the nature of a common reality, they can be advanced by means of rational deliberation. Claims about Being (including claims that claim to be beyond Being) are subject to rational adjudication, both through rational dialectics and through the practical dialectic that unfolds as individuals, communities, peoples, and civilizations try to live them out. Collective effervescence, finally, does not so much *generate* ideals as catalyze new insights into Being, showing to those who experience it something that, however partial, is also *real*.

This has already been reflected in the strategic analysis that we set forth in the previous chapter. Rather than simply identifying potentials for or obstacles to material progress or real or potential ideological power blocs or defining social classes and class fractions in terms of their position in the relations of production or in terms of their potential participation in power blocs, we have identified potential pathways and obstacles to human development, understood as an ordering to transcendental ends, and theorized political and ideological struggles as an ongoing deliberation regarding fundamental questions of meaning and value that, if never resolved, actually generates real insights.

What this means is that while we retain key elements from earlier strategic paradigms, these elements take on a radically new significance in the context of our larger political-theological and social-theoretical perspective. For example, we retain from the humanistic socialist/populist axis, out the self-criticism of which our own perspective has emerged, a commitment both to cultivating conscious leadership (what we have called tertiary social actors or political-theological organizations) and to tapping into the wisdom embodied in the popular religious traditions of the people, especially those who have resisted the "enclosure of the sacred." But in the context of our theory, the political-theological organization is no longer the collective Subject of the cosmohistorical evolutionary process and a mechanism for self-divinization, but rather simply a higher expression of the teaching, governing, and sanctifying office that has been carried out by most religious institutions throughout history—an expression that has assimilated the fruits of historical criticism and critical rationality, including the contributions of modern social theory—but that does not aim to displace or hegemonize traditional religious institutions or achieve a unitary monopolistic status. Similarly, we regard the wisdom embodied in popular religious traditions as real wisdom and valuable as such and not merely because it provides a means of linking peasants and other preliterate and semiliterate populations to the project of the humanistic intelligentsia.

The same is true of the way we regard scientific-technological progress and political-theological struggle. Both are a real part of civilizational progress. But scientific and technological progress are not a means of divinization, but rather a participation in Being, and thus in the creative life of God that are to be valued but not idolized. And we must look critically at technologies and the forms of economic development associated with them to ensure that they conserve the integrity of the ecosystem and the social fabric and actually promote human development. This means that they cannot be regarded as spontaneous drivers of civilizational progress, the obstacles to which need only be removed. Rather, this Earth is our garden, and we must tend it, encouraging complexity and innovation while ensuring that they remain ordered to transcendental ends.

Finally, political-theological struggle—struggle around competing civilizational ideals and the variants of those ideals—is constitutive of the post-axial social order we envision. But this struggle must be treated as a real deliberation and our interlocutors as human beings with honestly (if not always rationally) held convictions from whom we can learn even when we continue to disagree. History, in other words, is not a theomachy, but rather a *gran disputa*, and we must engage it strategically as such, framing questions and listening to as well as proposing answers.

The overall impact of this retheorization of grand strategy is nothing less than a break with modern politics, whether conservative or revolutionary, and a return, albeit on a more conscious basis, to a strategic paradigm more familiar during the great Silk Road Era, in which religious elites, often organized in orders or schools, made a conscious effort to promote their vision and transform society both through scholarship, teaching, and public debate and through engaging existing institutions (including the dominant political and religious authorities) and building new ones,political, economic, and technological as well as religious—without aiming for or expecting to achieve anything like hegemony.

Operational Imperatives

Given what we have said about the current strategic position of the party of meaning and hope, we face two principal strategic challenges in the present period. We must, first of all, re-constitute the core disciplines of human civilization—those that order a civilization towards transcendental ends, which we call the *sapiential disciplines*—and re-build the sapiential institutions and sapiential intelligentsia that cultivate them. More specifically, we need to organize, out of the many institutions of civil society currently engaged in the work of civilization building, political-theological organizations that can exercise conscious leadership in the next steps in the human civilizational project. Second, these organizations must then both engage existing institutions and build new ones—institutions that foster a spirituality of meaning and self cultivation, a new public arena constituted by deliberation around fundamental questions of meaning and value and a political economy that is not only in harmony with the ecosystem and with humanity's fundamentally creative nature, but that actually taps into and cultivates the latent potentials of both.

Re-constituting Sapientia

Fundamental to changing the terms of public discourse is the task of reconstituting the disciplines, institutions, and intelligentsia that lead public discourse. We have already noted that modernity largely destroyed the sapiential disciplines, institutions, and intelligentsia of the Silk Road Era. Philosophy, which had hitherto functioned as a unified and unifying architectonic discipline that included and built on the sciences and that regulated theological discourse, found itself under attack by theologians for whom analogical metaphysics represented an assault on their new ideal of the sovereignty of God. The hermeneutic disciplines, formerly an auxiliary to theology concerned with the interpretation of sacred texts, contributing to but not determining theological judgment, became, in the context of Reformation Christianity (and Asharite Islam), essentially the whole of a theology that understood itself as, purely and simply, the interpretation of the revealed word of God. Those who rejected this theology took refuge in the interpretation of the texts of earlier and other civilizations, now reimagined as "secular." These two developments together constituted something called "the humanities," a science of meanings that can be rationally investigated and interpreted, but embraced, if at all, only on nonrational grounds.

The sciences, meanwhile, abandoned teleological explanation, which had served as a propadeutic to rational metaphysics, in favor of mathematical formalization, which was the precondition for understanding how the universe worked and thus bringing it under rational human control. Philosophy was reduced to what Roy Bhaskar has called "underlaboring" (Bhaskar 1989, 1993) for other disciplines: investigating the conditions of their possibility, clarifying linguistic confusions, etc. Authentically and organically premodern religious traditions, meanwhile, tended for the most part to regard the extension of modern education as a threat, and turned inward, relying for support on largely preliterate, premodern constituencies. With the exception of a few dissenters operating on the margins of traditional religious institutions (Thomism) or the socialist and communist movements (critical theory), humanity was left without intellectuals capable of leading reflection around fundamental questions of meaning and value.

Our task with respect to this situation is complex and multidimensional. On the one hand, we need to reconstitute philosophy and theology as architectonic disciplines that rationally investigate fundamental questions of meaning and value, drawing on the results of the sciences and the hermeneutic disciplines, but subjecting those results to the scrutiny of a higher rationality focused on questions of ends and purposes. This new philosophy and theology cannot, however, operate any longer within the context of a localized civilizational tradition or even in the context of dialogue with neighboring civilizations. They must, rather, be authentically global in character, with Thomists, as we suggested above, engaging critiques advanced by Hua yen Buddhists and practitioners of Advaita Vedanta answering the objections of practitioners of *dao xue* and Hanafi *fiqh*.

But there is more at stake here that simply restoring the status of philosophy and theology as intellectual disciplines. We must heal the wounds created by the Augustinian Reaction and the Averroist Counter-Reaction, which gave birth to the Protestant and humanistic modern ideals respectively and thus led to the marginalization of philosophy and theology in the first place. This means restoring the mutual respect that dialectics on the one hand and supra-rational wisdoms on the other hand owe to each other. No spiritual claim can be legitimate if it contradicts human reason, but there *are* truths that transcend rational demonstration, and when reason denies this it either forgoes the possibility of divinization, which is our true end, or else falls into the trap of delusional, purely innerworldly strategies for transcending contingency, strategies that always lead to disappointment.

Reconstituting the sapiential disciplines means reconstituting the sapiential institutions and intelligentsia. Historically, the highest levels of the sapiential intelligentsia have been organized by three principal types of institutions: the monastery or religious order, the revolutionary party, and the university. All three offer useful models but all three also suffer from serious defects. Monasteries and religious orders have recognized the ordering of humanity to transcendental ends and understood correctly their own identity as communities of those seeking perfection. There has been a tendency, however, greater in the case of monastic than of mendicant communities, towards withdrawal from rather than transformation of society. The celibate character of most such communities, in particular, means that they have not been able to offer the people as a whole a credible model of spiritual excellence, which is inevitably pit against worldly engagement and civilization building. Revolutionary parties, on the other hand, have been world transforming but have denied humanity's transcendental vocation and often failed to cultivate intellectual and moral excellence among their members. And of course the ideal of immanentist self-divinization that defines the communist ideal is part of what this work is rejecting.

Universities represent a rather different problem altogether. They are not, strictly speaking, political-theological organizations—tertiary social actors that aim at conserving or transforming a civilizational ideal—but rather institutions of civil society, and more specifically collections of guilds *some* of which *historically* cultivated disciplines that by their very nature (philosophy, theology, and to a lesser extent politics and law) conserved and/or transformed civilizational ideals. From the very beginning, the university was always in danger of treating the special rights of the professoriate (those associated with academic freedom) as ends rather than as means to even higher goods essential to the human civilizational project. And universities have, as we have seen, largely fallen from their historic vocation and become specialized research and training institutions serving the needs of global capital. At the same time, universities *do* offer something that neither the religious order nor the revolutionary party ever had: a culture of ideological pluralism and debate.

As we rebuild the sapiential intelligentsia we will need to find new forms of political-theological organization appropriate to the next steps in the human civilizational project. It is not possible to specify in advance what such forms of organization will look like, but only to identify some broad characteristics. They will, first of all, recognize humanity's ordering towards transcendental ends, though they may understand those ends very differently. Second, they will recognize the contributions of both humanity's ancient spiritual traditions (pre- and post-axial) *and* of modernity (both modern science and modern critical humanistic scholarship) and will, therefore, be located and act not so much *within* particular wisdom traditions as in relation to all of them, even when they advocate a specific political-theological position. Third, they will join goals of spiritual perfection and civilizational building, of personal regeneration and revolutionary transformation (though perhaps in varying measures). At least some will attempt to show what it means to seek perfection while living in the world, and will thus include not only as full members but among their highest level leaders individuals who are married as well as those who are single or celibate. While passionately advocating for their own perspectives, they will avoid political monopolism and hegemonism. Finally, they will conserve the best traditions of both religious orders and the communist movement: conscientious study, service to the common good, a careful balancing of unity and principle, close ties to the people, and the practice of criticism and self-criticism.

Where will these organizations come from? Some may emerge out of the adaptation to traditional religious orders or (less likely) communist or paracommunist organizations. Something like the Turkish-based Gulen movement, for example, seems to be moving in this direction, though it is still far from having all of the characteristics identified above. Others will develop out of research, education, and organizing institutes that also become real religious communities. This is the hope for my own organization, *Seeking Wisdom*.

The members of these organizations must, we should note, not merely *claim* to be humanity's intellectual and moral and therefore spiritual leaders. They must actually be so. This means that the minimum point of entry must be a demonstrated ability to make and evaluate arguments regarding fundamental questions of meaning and value and to make their principles and values effective in the public arena.[1] They must also soon learn to teach others to do so—to function as effective teachers and organizers. The highest level leaders must actually contribute to humanity's ongoing deliberation regarding fundamental questions and/or be authentic institution builders. Members must also have a real commitment to ongoing spiritual development and follow a spiritual path that they have chosen thoughtfully and on basis of both rational conviction and a developing understanding of their own distinctive strengths, weaknesses, and spiritual needs.

Together, these organizations will define the true *universitas* of the new era, partly displacing existing universities from their position of global intellectual leadership and partly challenging them to rediscover their deeper calling. This is critically important. The new generation of political-theological organizations that we envision must scrupulously avoid the sectarian competition that characterized both traditional religious orders and, especially, the communist movement. On the contrary, they must model a form of engagement that is at once principled and passionate but also respectful of the many ways of wisdom. And, above all, they must avoid the illusion that by establishing hegemony

---

1. This does not mean that they must hold university degrees. We must aim to revive the tradition of autodidact working-class intellectuals and draw from the ranks of community-based liberal arts programs as well as those of college and university graduates. And we must always respond with reverence when we find in our midst a true *tzadik* or *bodhisattva*, who may or may not have any formal education, but nonetheless demonstrates a heroic level of wisdom and justice.

and "organizing and directing the cosmohistorical evolutionary process" they can somehow find a shortcut to transcendence.

It is only in the context of such political-theological organizations and the new *universitas* that they constitute that a new sapiential intelligentsia can emerge. It will be among the principal tasks of these new political-theological organizations to identify, recruit, and cultivate humanity's most promising sapiential leaders, providing them with rigorous training in the liberal arts, social theory, and the art of politics, philosophy, and theology, as well as the spiritual discipline they need to develop into compelling leaders. Those of us who are building these organizations, and who for the most part have had to cobble together our own sapiential and spiritual formation, need to look to each other for the discipline and nurture that existing institutions have failed to provide.

Engaging and Rebuilding Civil Society

Partly because our strategic estimate is uncertain—we cannot tell whether or not a transition by reform is still possible—and partly because our public credibility depends on a willingness to work for reform even when it seems difficult and unlikely, we must pursue what have traditionally been called "dual tactics," at once engaging and transforming the existing institutions of civil society and rebuilding civil society where and as it decays and collapses. This term is somewhat misleading because the imperatives in question are not tactical but rather operational—they don't bear on how our forces are arrayed on the field of battle or on specific methods of struggle, but rather on our principal campaigns in the theatre of civil society.

In the present period, engaging and transforming the institutions of civil society means, fundamentally, a strategic alliance with procivilizational elements in the bourgeoisie and the traditional religious hierarchies, since it is they who currently control these institutions. This alliance is strategic because we share with these sectors an interest in conserving the integrity of the ecosystem, the social fabric, and humanity's civilizational traditions, including both the authentic contributions of positivistic and humanistic modernity and those of pre-axial and post-axial traditions, and in furthering civilizational progress and spiritual development, even if we are guided by different civilizational ideals. The difficulty, of course, is that different elements in the bourgeoisie and religious hierarchies often support different aspects of this agenda. While both are increasingly clear on the need to confront the ecological crisis, the progressive sectors of the bourgeoisie (information, high technology, and allied finance) are more clearly committed to investing resources in developing human capacities (research, education, etc.), and generally respect and defend the value of an open, and pluralistic (if not always engaged) civil society. The religious hierarchies and, to a lesser extent, the conservative sectors of the bourgeoisie understand the need to conserve the integrity of the social fabric and provide support for conserving older civilizational traditions. In general, alliances with the former will be easier than with the latter, but in places where conservative sectors of the bourgeoisie are trying to transform themselves from an extractive to a knowledge-based economy (e.g., the United Arab Emirates), or in situations where religious hierarchies have joined to their concern for the integrity of the social fabric and the conservation of meaning a passion for social justice and a willingness to challenge the market allocation of resources, new and interesting strategic options open up. Our watchword must be careful analysis of the local situation and the changing balance of forces and the flexibility to pursue different alliances in different places, or even in the same place simultaneously.

Substantively, engaging and transforming the institutions of civil society means:

1. Promoting socially responsible investment and social entrepreneurship, while strengthening trade unions, peasant leagues, and other organizations that make "low end" ecologically and economically exploitative strategies less attractive to capital.
2. Active engagement in the public arena, including
    2.1. participation in electoral politics, supporting or forming alliances with the parties most aligned with (and most likely to advance) the principles of the strategic alliance outlined above;
    2.2. extra-electoral participation in public life through lobbying, direct action, etc., to advance the same ends; and
    2.3. working to reshape public debate and create a public arena *constituted* by deliberation around fundamental

questions of meaning and value by helping value-based organizations become effective in the public arena through formats such as interfaith congregation-based organizing and by creating public fora in which debate around public policy is explicitly linked to deliberation around the fundamental philosophical and theological questions that lie behind those debates.

3. Working within the institutions of civil society to transform them in a way that reflects our emerging civilizational ideal. This means:

   3.1. working to transform schools and universities so that they make an authentic liberal arts education—one that cultivates free human beings and citizens capable of making and evaluating arguments regarding fundamental questions of meaning and value and public policy—accessible to everyone; and

   3.2. working to transform religious institutions so that they can creatively and effectively meet the spiritual needs of a sapientially literate laity in a postcritical globalized civilization, accepting the authentic contributions of modern science and critical humanistic scholarship as well as the *fact* and the *value* of engagement with spiritual questions in a way that is not only respectful of but actually draws on the wisdom of humanity's diverse civilizational traditions.

Rebuilding civil society, on the other hand, means building new institutions that link our emerging political-theological organizations to the working classes in a way that effectively engages them in the work of civilization building. This is important even in the event of a transition by reform, because it is what will give us a mass base of support and thus sufficient weight within the procivilizational alliance advance our emerging civilizational ideal. In the event of a transition through revolution, decadence, or civilizational collapse it will give us the nucleus of a new society. Here several distinct forms of activity stand out:

> *We need to build our own enterprises and our own economic base of ecologically sound enterprises that engage ordinary workers in creative labor that provides economic self-sufficiency and sufficient leisure to permit civic participation and intellectual, moral, and spiritual self-cultivation.*

The range of economic activities is potentially limitless, but might usefully be divided between traditional agricultural and craft activities that provide new opportunities to create and capture value in the global economy and emerging high-technology activities to which our political-theological organizations can bring a distinct new emphasis. Examples of the first might include fair-trade coffee, tea, and herb production, ethnobotanicals, or organic truck gardening near major urban centers to supply high-end culinary markets. Examples of the second might include software and game development that services humanistic and social science academic markets or that tells traditional and emerging stories embodying our civilizational ideal in new ways. In between lie the construction and culinary fields to which many immigrant workers bring extraordinary skills.

> *We need to create a public arena constituted by deliberation around fundamental questions of meaning and value.*

This means creating *places* where people from diverse traditions can meet and engage each other around fundamental questions and public-policy debates as well as the social space for such deliberation to take place. As I noted in the foregoing analysis, there is significant diversity around the planet with respect to the openness, pluralism, and engagement that characterizes civil society. This is shaped by everything from legal frameworks and political culture through ethno-religious demographics and urban structure and religious monumentalization. As we are engaging the diverse spaces that already exist, we need to create new ones that are characterized by the highest possible degrees of openness, pluralism, and engagement, and populate them with organizations that provide the people with the ability to engage in real deliberation around fundamental questions. Such spaces will be easiest to create in places with a legal framework that protects free expression and with high degrees of ethno-religious diversity, but even in these settings there remains the difficult work of catalyzing real engagement—an issue we will look at in the next section, which addresses tactics. For now it will suffice to say that we need to create physical spaces where people can come together face to face as well as virtual spaces where they can meet across significant distances. Those spaces need to be structured in a way that promotes dialogue, deliberation, and debate, and be dominated by symbols that mediate our emerging civilizational ideal. It also means actually *organizing* deliberation through individual relational meetings, grassroots programs in the liberal arts and interreligious and intercultural dialogues, and linking this deliberation to action both within and outside existing political structures.

> *We need to build religious congregations of a new kind that are adapted to a sapientially literate and globalized laity or at least to a laity evolving in this direction.*

I have noted before both that people increasingly aspire to sapiential literacy—to making informed, independent decisions regarding fundamental questions of meaning and value—and that they address these questions in a way that engages not only their "native" spiritual tradition but others as well. Congregations rooted in particular traditions will not disappear, both because large sections of the people have not undergone such a transformation and because many who have find their spiritual path and spiritual home within the disciplines of a traditional religious community. But ever-broader sections of the population seek a *community* in which they can study and fashion a spiritual path that draws on the wisdom of more than one tradition. On the one hand, these communities will be more intellectually focused than earlier types of congregations. On the other hand, people will demand from them what they have always demanded of local shrines and congregations: devotional space, public liturgy, rites of passage, etc.

Tactics

The question, for course, is just how one goes about carrying out these tasks. In a certain sense, this is a question that cannot be answered meaningfully in a book that hopes to provide direction on a global scale. Circumstances vary, requiring vastly different approaches. In what follows, however, I offer some basic tactical principles and techniques, centered around one of the fundamental practices of axial civilizations—*dialectics*—and show how this practice can help build the network of relationships we need in order to carry out the tasks identified above. Specifically, I want to argue that the practice of dialectics, while not the only weapon in our tactical arsenal, should be the principal tactic in all of the tasks I have identified: building political-theological organizations capable of leading the next steps in the human civilizational project and engaging and rebuilding civil society. I also want to show how the practice of dialectics, which during the modern era came to divide the revolutionary intelligentsia from the workers and peasants it organized, can become a means of authentic engagement with the people as a whole.

Socratic Dialogue

Let us begin by exploring dialectics as practiced by the founder of the discipline: Socrates. There are many places where we can watch Socrates in action, but none is more fruitful for our purposes than the opening passages of the *Republic*.

Plato opens the *Republic* with a scene that situates the dialogue in its concrete political context. Socrates is returning from the feast of the Goddess Bendis, a Thracian huntress deity associated with a women's revolt at Lemnos that left all of the men on the island dead, at Piraeus. This is a suggestive reference to the cult of the *Magna Mater* with which Socratic philosophy has a profound affinity. It also suggests that far from eschewing engagement with religion, the dialectic in fact *begins* with popular religion—i.e., with the ways in which ordinary people are engaging fundamental questions of meaning and value. He is detained by a group of rich young men who insist that he accompany them home (a reference to the arbitrary power of the rich in Athenian society and to the precarious position of the philosopher in the bourgeois city). Once there he engages his host, a rich man of the older generation, and several of the young men who had detained him in a debate regarding the nature of justice. He disposes handily of the traditional view, represented by his host Cephalus, that justice is merely a matter of paying one's debts, a view that reflects the *mores* of a society in which market relations have begun to emerge but have not yet eroded traditional norms of reciprocity. Socrates rejects this position, showing that it fails to address the vitally important question of what people actually *ought* to have. Thus, it is hardly just to give a mad man a weapon, even if it was borrowed from him before he went mad and would ordinarily have been returned as a matter of course (Plato *Republic* 327a–331d).

This insistence on a substantive ethics already challenges existing norms. Socrates then goes on to answer three positions that were quite common in Athens at the time. First, he addresses the predominant view among the wealthy Athenians of his day: the idea that justice means helping your friends and hurting your enemies. The difficulty with this is that the worst thing you can do to someone is to make them a worse human being, in which case they would undoubtedly do even more harm to you than they had done before. He then turns to the radical sophistic position—that justice is just the will of the stronger, or that conversely, injustice is more profitable than justice. This view he undermines by showing that the stronger do not always know what is in their best interest, and by showing that justice is an art, and that like all the other arts it is devoted not to its own good but to promoting some end outside itself. Finally, Plato addresses the moderate sophistic view, that justice is merely a (necessary) social convention (Plato *Republic* 331e–354c). This position he addresses at much greater length by engaging his interlocutors in an analysis of just what sort of conventions or laws they would establish for a city were they to found one. In the process they discover that they cannot frame laws without reference to some higher principle, some substantive doctrine of the Good in terms of which they evaluate proposed legislation—an argument that absorbs the next several books of the *Republic*.

At each stage of the argument Socrates uses three specific tactics. First, he begins with people where they are—with their actually existing beliefs and values. Philosophy does not "enter" the city, as if from above, but emerges from within it. Second, he asks what organizers call agitational questions—questions that stir up thought, even at the cost of seeming a bit odd or a bit irritating. Indeed, he all but tells Cephalus that he is on death's door! Third, he reinterprets what his interlocutors say in a way that helps them to see it in a new light. He is not concerned with teaching a doctrine but with cultivating the capacity of his interlocutors to achieve wisdom themselves.

Dialectics in Practice

The question, of course, is how one engages in Socratic dialogue—how one practices dialectics—in a fragmented late modern society in which deliberation around fundamental questions of meaning and value has been pushed out of the public arena. I would like to suggest that Socrates' starting points remain valid. First, human beings possess, indeed are defined by, intellect, and this universally shared intellectual capacity extends beyond instrumental reason (*techne* or *phronesis*) to reasoning around fundamental questions of meaning and value (*sophia*). We are, in other words, not just *homo faber* but first and foremost *homo sapiens*. Second, meaning emerges through dialogue, either direct or indirect, spontaneous or conscious. The meanings we spontaneously find in things are challenged and deepened in our encounters with others, who draw out implications (sometimes implications we would rather avoid) or point out contradictions, and push us towards a higher synthesis. This latter process is, quite simply, the dialectic, and everyone practices it, though most do so without realizing it and generally do not do it very well.

This said, there is clearly something more to the practice of dialectics than the spontaneous process of ordinary conversation. Nor can we simply set up a soap box in some dusty inner-city square, or accost people in that late modern *agora*, the shopping mall. We must find ways to engage in intentional conversations that catalyze reflection—and action—around fundamental questions. It is here that I would like to call attention to three practices that, each in its own way, make the dialectic conscious and use it to engage and cultivate the capacities of the people.

The first practice to which I would like to call attention is that of oral history and in-depth interview research. Ordinarily understood as a qualitative research method rather than as a political practice, the in-depth interview explores a question and attempts to sustain a thesis (generally one involving the meanings that the subjects attach to their experience) by engaging ordinary people in a lengthy, open-ended, but nonetheless directed conversation. Among the most important examples of such research in recent years, we would include Robert Bellah's *Habits of the Heart* and *The Good Society* (Bellah et al. 1985, 1991).

Like Socratic Dialogue, in-depth interview research presupposes that ordinary people seriously engage fundamental questions of meaning and value. It also presupposes that meaning emerges in dialogue with others. What it does, in effect, is to *accelerate* the process by which meaning emerges, make it *conscious*, and *direct* it by posing a definite set of questions. The interviewer, to be sure, uses a flexible protocol and formulates questions in response to what the subject has to say, always avoiding leading questions. But the very presence of the research question itself shapes the results and creates meaning that would not otherwise have emerged.

In-depth interviews are generally recorded, indexed, and transcribed. Usually an analysis accompanies each interview and the archive of interviews is made available to scholars researching similar issues. But the principal investigator or investigators also, usually, produce a monograph based on the study, which makes conscious and explicit the meanings that emerged in the process of the study, while offering further interpretation or explanation.

The key difference between Socratic Dialogue as Socrates practiced it and oral history or in-depth interview research turns on the question of reinterpretation. Humanistic researchers try at all costs to avoid imposing their meanings on those they are studying. And certainly no study would be taken seriously if an interviewer mimicked Socrates' leading questions. On the other hand, the very act of framing and posing a question shapes the way in which an interlocutor interprets his or her experience. Questions are more or less leading; they are never meaning or value neutral. And, of course, there are no "pristine" research subjects. The meanings our subjects attach to their experience are in significant measure the result of the conscious or unconscious interventions of others. And we are not outside this system of cultural actors that shape the way they create meaning; rather, we are participants in that system, catalyzing the emergence of yet a new layer of meaning.

It is thus possible to understand oral history or in-depth interview research as a form of Socratic Dialogue. It simply refrains from explicit reinterpretation with the aim of understanding the meanings the subject attaches to his or her experience at the moment of the conversation, and allows the dialogical process itself to carry out the work of deepening reflection. But we would be fooling ourselves (and denying ourselves access to a powerful tool) if we pretended that it is not a transformative practice, both for the individual interviewed and for the community that is the subject of such a study. Both become conscious of their meanings and their history and thus potential political subjects in a way that was not previously possible. Both cultivate the capacity to engage questions of meaning and value and thus the intellectual virtue of wisdom, which is at the center of the spiritual aims of the dialectical tradition. And the process is even more transformative for the interviewer, who overcomes the common assumption that ordinary people don't think deeply about questions of meaning and value, and who cultivates the capacity both to question and to listen. Participation in this kind of study prepares the ground, as it were, for other practices that demand more and that would be resisted without this preparation.

From a tactical standpoint, large-scale oral history and in-depth interview projects that engage broad layers of the population in conversation around the way in which they approach fundamental questions of meaning and value should constitute the first step in the organizing process. On the one hand, such research would give us a much better picture of where the people actually are. On the other hand, they would catalyze broad-based reflection around fundamental questions of just precisely the kind our strategy demands. Our longer-range aim should be nothing less than to engage *the whole population* in this way. The most interesting and promising subjects can be recruited as interviewers, igniting a process of profound critical reflection on a mass scale.

The second practice to which I would like to call attention is the *individual relational meeting* developed by the congregation-based organizing movement founded by Saul Alinsky and developed further by such organizations as the Industrial Areas Foundation, the Gamaliel Foundation, and the Pacific Institute for Community Organizing (Wood 2002). This is the principal method used by interfaith community organizations to identify potential leaders, but also serves as the first step in cultivating leadership potential. Interfaith organizers generally begin with clergy, as it is under the leadership of their clergy that most people in our society engage fundamental questions of meaning and value, and it is clergy who can most often point us to those with real leadership potential.

As taught by the Industrial Areas Foundation, the individual relational meeting involves the following steps:

1. Begin the conversation with something you know or suspect is of interest to the person.
2. Pose an agitational question. By this is meant a question that provokes real thought and reflection. It can be as simple as "Why?" or "What do you mean by?"
3. Get the person's story. What people have done tells us more about who they are and what they value than what they say.
4. Probe for more meaning. Use each story as the starting point for deepening the conversation and drawing out new insights and interests.
5. Reinterpret experience in a way that leads to action. It is at this point that the individual relational meeting differs most clearly from the in-depth interview. Where the humanistic researcher tries to limit the impact of the interview on the subject, the organizer—who aims at action—will question the way someone sees the world, and especially challenge understandings of the world that lead to passivity.
6. Respect the iron rule. Never do something for someone that they can do for themselves.

An individual relational meeting generally results in a *self-interest map* of the potential leader. This map is essentially an analysis of the person's principal interests and relationships and allows the organizer to assess the person's leadership potential. Potential leaders are generally classified as follows:

- *Primary leaders* are interested in principles and values (e.g., Judaism, Islam, or Democracy) and build or maintain the institutions (a religious institution or political party) that promote those principles and values.[2] They have broad networks that include other primary and secondary leaders. Because of their high level of responsibility, they will generally be cautious about acting, but

---

2. This should not be taken to imply that primary leaders must have a great deal of formal education. I have known strong primary leaders with little or no formal education, though they were invariably extremely curious, often autodidacts, and "learned" in popular religious traditions even if they had no real engagement with the high tradition.

can bring significant resources to the table when they do act. Those with sufficient philosophical, theological, and political formation will constitute the core of our political-theological organizations, though we must remember that there will always be important primary leaders who will choose to remain outside such organizations. That choice, which is essential to the openness and pluralism of the public arena, must be respected.

- *Secondary leaders* are interested in issues (abortion, world peace) and build social movements (pro-life, antiwar) that address those issues. They have networks of other secondary leaders and of tertiary leaders. Secondary leaders are action oriented, but tend to go through cycles of hyperactivity and burn-out as their movements wax and wane. This can be combated by channeling them into long-term engagement with the institutions of civil society, either transforming existing institutions or building new ones that bear on the resolution of the issues important to them. Many evolve in this direction spontaneously, leaving behind protest movement politics for grassroots lobbying and electoral politics or work with nonprofits that development and implement solutions to ecological, economic, political, or cultural problems.

- *Tertiary leaders* are interested in concrete problems (a principal who discriminates against Mexican students) and take individual isolated actions (meeting with the principal, participating in a school boycott) to address them. What makes them leaders is the fact that they can turn out significant numbers of people who also care about the problem in question and motivate them to act.

The individual relational meeting, it should be apparent, is structured in much the same way as the oral history or in-depth interview. The principal difference is that unlike the oral history or in-depth interview there is explicit reinterpretation of the interlocutor's responses. In this sense, individual relational meetings represent a second step, which should also be implemented on a mass scale, directed at identifying leaders and drawing them into the capacity-building activities and the forms of political engagement that are essential to building a new civilization.

One way to engage the people in conversation and action around fundamental questions of meaning and value is, of course, simply to share with them what we have found in the course of our interviews or individual meetings. This is standard practice in both oral history and community organizing. But such a conversation—and the scope of any action arising from it—will invariably be limited. Another way, however, is to include them in humanity's ongoing conversation regarding fundamental questions of meaning and value. This, of course, is the traditional task of a liberal arts education. It may be that some of our interlocutors will already have mastered the liberal arts. Many more, however, will not, or will have done so only in a rudimentary and inadequate fashion, either because their educational aims were primarily vocational, or because the institutions they attended (like most) no longer offer such an education. We must make it possible for everyone who is willing and able to cultivate the liberal arts.

It is at this point that our way of engaging people begins to bear profoundly the mark of our commitment to the Axial Age ideal. Other political-theological trends recruit, train, and deploy. We regard the cultivation of human capacities as a strategic end in itself and as the precondition for the work in which we are inviting people to engage. And so, as we identify potential or emerging leaders we need to engage them in cultivating their ability to make and evaluate arguments around fundamental questions of meaning and value. For some this will mean enrollment in colleges and universities, but for others it will mean community-based programs. And our efforts should not be restricted to those with little or no training in the liberal arts. As we noted above, we need to engage pastors, public intellectuals, and organizers in deepening their mastery of the sapiential disciplines as well as of the methods of social analysis and political strategy necessary to effective action in the public arena. And we need to draw scholars into public intellectual leadership, bringing them into dialogue with pastors, public intellectuals, and organizers, so that both learn from each other. It is in this way that we will most profoundly impact existing institutions and build the networks necessary to found new ones.

Whether it takes place within a traditional academic setting or in community-based formats, liberal arts education ought, as I have argued elsewhere, to be organized around fundamental questions (Mansueto 2006), with classical and contemporary texts used to illustrate the principal ways in which humanity has answered these questions, and thus as conversation partners for our students. This approach—which is essentially the *quaestio* method used in medieval universities—has the added advantage of allowing us to include in the conversation sources from all of humanity's wisdom traditions without forcing students to master an unwieldy list of texts. And, of course, it represents a further extension of the dialectic.

～

Our tactical plan, in other words, is centered on a careful, context-sensitive practice of dialectics. We begin by asking questions and by listening, catalyzing reflection around fundamental questions of meaning and value, and the ways in which people are engaging those questions under their concrete material conditions. We continue by reinterpreting, challenging people to see their lives and struggles in a broader perspective. From there, individuals can be invited to participate actively in the next steps in the human civilizational project, at a level appropriate to their own calling and their own conditions, engaging the existing institutions of civil society or building new ones. Throughout this process we must put an emphasis on a continued deepening of philosophical and theological reflection, whether it is with workers and peasants in a grassroots liberal arts program or senior leaders in a seminar that challenges them to rethink their most basic commitments or retheorize their practice.

Under no scenario will this be *enough*. In the case of a transition by reform, the leaders we identify and cultivate will need to be deployed most especially in efforts to engage the existing institutions of civil society, including electoral politics. In the case of a transition by decadence (or complete civilizational collapse), they will need to be deployed primarily in building new institutions as the old ones decay. In the case of a transition by revolution, these tactics will probably be joined by some measure of political-military action, though as we pointed out above, such action can *only* be tactical. This is because, on the one hand, our strategic aim is not one that can be achieved by means of political-military action, which is adapted to struggles for sovereignty rather than to civilization-building and, on the other hand, the weapons of mass destruction controlled by global capital would, in any case, render any such strategy impotent. Political-military struggle should be primarily defensive, creating the social space for identifying and cultivating leaders and transforming and building institutions, and political-military leaders should always remain subordinate to political-theological leaders—though it is, of course, possible to be both.

We face a long and difficult transition. Even under the most optimistic scenarios humanity will, during the next one hundred years, face profound ecological disruptions and economic dislocations. The vast majority of the resources on the planet—as well as weapons of mass destruction, which render traditional revolutionary strategies impotent—will continue to be in the hands of people who are committed to a dying civilizational ideal or—worse still—to no ideal at all. And there is a real danger that, with the collapse of socialism, which linked humanistic modernism to movements of resistance to capitalist development, movements of the latter type may take a profoundly anticivilizational turn, something we already saw in the twilight of the socialist era with the *Khmer Rouge* and *Sendero Luminoso*, and continue to see with both fundamentalist movements and the plethora of "insurgencies" that fail to rise above the level of tribal warfare or organized crime. At times it will seem like everything has been lost. We must remember, however, that everything that *is* participates in Being. Everything that *is* seeks Being, even when it does so in distorted and unproductive ways. In the long run this deeply rooted love of Being will win out. Humans will not live forever under structures that hold back their development. We will not forever consent to be mere batteries. Rather, even if gradually and unevenly and with many reversals, they will find once again that steep and gloriously difficult path that, by means of reason and virtue, leads them towards God. We, who are even now beginning to uncover that path and to resume our ascent, invite you to join us.

BIBLIOGRAPHY

Abu-Lughod, Janet. 1989. *Before European Hegemony: The World System AD 125-1350*. New York: Oxford University Press.
Aglietta, Michel. 1976. *A Theory of Capitalist Regulation: The US Experience*. Translated by David Fernbach. London: Verso.
Althusser, Louis. 1965/1977. *For Marx*. Translated by Ben Brewster. London: Lane.
———. 1968/1970. *Reading Capital*. Translated by Ben Brewster. London: New Left.
———. 1966-1969/1971. *Lenin and Philosophy, and other Essays*. Translated by Ben Brewster. New York: Monthly Review.
Ahlstrom, Sydney. 1972. *A Religious History of the United States*. New Haven: Yale University Press.
Aldaraca, Bridget, et al. 1980. *Nicaragua in Revolution: The Poets Speak*. Minneapolis: Marxist Educational.
Alighieri, Dante. 1300-1318/1969. *Commedia*. Translation of *The Divine Comedy* with commentary by John D. Sinclair. New York: Oxford University Press.
———. 1300-1318/1969. *De Monarchia*. Indianapolis: Bobbs-Merrill.
Amin, Samir. 1978. *The Law of Value and Historical Materialism*. Translated by Brian Pearce. New York: Monthly Review.
———. 1979/1980. *Class and Nation, Historically and in the Current Crisis*. Translated by Susan Kaplow. New York: Monthly Review.
———. 1981/1982. *The Future of Maoism*. Translated by Norman Finklestein. New York: Monthly Review
———. 1988/1989. *Eurocentrism*. Translated by Russell Moore. New York: Monthly Review.
Anderson, Perry. 1974. *Passages from Antiquity to Feudalism*. London: New Left.
Anselm. 1077-78/1970. *Proslogion*. In *A Scholastic Miscellany*, edited and translated by Eugene Fairweather. New York: Macmillan.
Aristotle. c. 350 BCE/1946. *Politics*. Translated by Ernest Barker. Oxford: Clarendon.
———. c. 350 BCE/1952. *Metaphysics*. Translated by Richard Hope. New York: Columbia University Press.
———. c. 350 BCE/1973. *Physics*. In *Introduction to Aristotle*, translated by Richard McKeon. Chicago: University of Chicago Press.
———. c. 350 BCE/1973. *De Anima*. In *Introduction to Aristotle*, translated by Richard McKeon. Chicago: University of Chicago Press.
———. c. 350 BCE/1973. *Ethics*. In *Introduction to Aristotle*, translated by Richard McKeon. Chicago: University of Chicago Press.
Aquinas, Thomas. c. 1260/1963. *In Boethius De Trinitate*. In *The Division and Methods of the Sciences: Questions V and VI of his Commentary on the De Trinitate of Boethius*. Translated by Armand Maurer. Toronto: Pontifical Institute of Medieval Studies.
———. 1272/1952. *Summa Theologiae*. Chicago: Encyclopaedia Britannica.

Augustine. 426/1972. *The City of God.* Translated by Henry Bettenson. New York: Penguin.

———. c. 386/1969. *Contra Academicos.* In *Medieval Philosophy: From St. Augustine to Nicholas of Cusa,* edited by John F. Wippel and Alan B. Wolter. New York: Free Press.

———. c. 395/1969. *De libero arbitrio.* In *Medieval Philosophy: From St. Augustine to Nicholas of Cusa,* edited by John F. Wippel and Alan B. Wolter. New York: Free Press.

Arendt, Hannah. 1958. *The Human Condition.* Chicago: University of Chicago Press.

Arrighi, Giovanni. 2001. *Adam Smith in Beijing: Lineages of the Twenty-first Century.* London: Verso.

———. 1997. *The Long Twentieth Century: Money, Power, and the Origins of our Times.* London: Verso.

Barrow, John, and Frank Tipler. 1986. *Anthropic Cosmological Principle.* Oxford: Oxford University Press.

Astin, Alexander, et al. 2005. *The Spiritual Life of College Students.* Los Angeles: Higher Education Research Institute.

Badiou, Alain. 1988. *L'Etre et l'événement.* Paris: Seuil.

———. 2006. *Logiques de mondes.* Paris: Seuil.

Baxter, William. 1974. *People or Penguins: The Case of Optimal Pollution.* New York: Columbia University Press.

Beaverstock, J. V., R. G. Smith, and P. J. Taylor. 1999. "A Roster of World Cities." *Globalization and World Cities Network Research Bulletin* 5. Online: http://www.lboro.ac.uk/gawc/rb/rb5.html

Bellah, Robert. 1957. *Tokugawa Religion: The Values of Pre-Industrial Japan.* Glencoe, IL: Free.

———. 1970. *Beyond Belief: Essays on Religion in a Post-industrial World.* New York: Harper.

———, editor. 1973. *Durkheim on Morality and Society.* Chicago: University of Chicago Press.

Bellah, Robert, et al. 1985. *Habits of the Heart: Individualism and Commitment in American Life.* New York: Perennial.

Bentley, Jerry. 1993. *Old World Encounters: Cross Cultural Contacts and Exchanges in Pre-Modern Times.* New York: Oxford University Press.

Bess, Phillip. 2006. *Till We Have Built Jerusalem: Architecture, Urbanism, and the Sacred.* Religion and Contemporary Culture. Wilmington: ISI.

Bettelheim, Charles. 1976–1978. *Class Struggles in the U.S.S.R.* 2 vols. Translated by Brian Pearce. New York: Monthly Review

Bhaskar, Roy. 1989. *Reclaiming Reality: A Critical Introduction to Contemporary Philosophy.* London: Verso.

———. 1993. *Dialectic: The Pulse of Freedom.* London: Verso.

Bissett, Jim. 1999. *Agrarian Socialism in America: Marx, Jefferson, and Jesus in the Oklahoma Countryside, 1904–1920.* Norman: University of Oklahoma Press.

Bogdanov, Alexander. 1928/1980. *Tektology.* Translated by George Gorelik. Seaside, CA: Intersystems.

Bohm, David. 1980. *Wholeness and the Implicate Order.* London: Routledge & Kegan Paul.

Bosteels, Bruno. 2005. "Post-Maoism: Badiou and Politics." *Positions* 13:575–634.

Boyer, Paul, and Stephen Nissanbaum. 1974. *Salem Possessed: The Social Origins of Witchcraft*. Cambridge: Harvard University Press.
Brokaw, Tom. 1998. *The Greatest Generation*. New York: Random House.
Brouilette, Matthew. 1999. "The 1830s and 1840s: Horace Mann, the End of Free Market Education, and the Rise of Government Schools." Mackinac Center for Public Policy.
Brundage, Burr Cartwright. 1985. *The Fifth Sun: Aztec God, Aztec World*. The Texas Pan American Series. Austin: University of Texas Press.
Budiansky, Stephen. 1992. *The Covenant of the Wild: Why Animals Chose Domestication*. New York: Morrow.
Bullock, Steven. 1998. *Revolutionary Brotherhood: Freemasonry and the Transformation of the American Social Order*. Chapel Hill: University of North Carolina Press.
Burbank, Garin. 1976. *Grass Roots Socialism*. Baton Rouge: Louisiana State University Press.
Bryant, M. Darrol. 1983. "From Edwards to Hopkins: A Millennialist Critique of Political Culture." In *The Coming Kingdom: Essays in American Millennialism and Eschatology*, edited by M. Darrol Bryan and Donald Dayton. New York: Rose of Sharon.
Calvin, John. 1536/1993. *The Institutes of the Christian Religion*. Translated by Henry Beveridge. Grand Rapids: Eerdmans.
Campbell, Colin. 2007. "The General Depletion Picture." *The Association for the Study of Peak Oil and Gas Newsletter* 76 (April).
Caputo, John D. 1982. *Heidegger and Aquinas: An Essay on Overcoming Metaphysics*. New York: Fordham University Press.
———. 2006. *The Weakness of God: A Theology of the Event*. Indiana Series in the Philosophy of Religion. Bloomington: Indiana University Press.
Castañeda, Jorge G. 2006. "Latin America's Left Turn." *Foreign Affairs* 85:3 (May–June) 28–43.
Chaney, Marvin L. 1986. "Systemic Study of the Israelite Monarchy." *Semeia* 37:53–76.
———, editor. 1993. "Bitter Bounty: The Dynamics of Political Economy Critiqued by the Eighth-Century Prophets." In *The Bible and Liberation: Political and Social Hermeneutics*, edited by Norman K. Gottwald and Richard A. Horsley. Maryknoll, NY: Orbis.
Chang, Kwang-chih. 1963. *The Archaeology of Ancient China*. New Haven: Yale University Press.
Chaterjee, Satischandra, and Dhirendramohan Datta. 1954. *An Introduction to Indian Philosophy*. Calcutta: University of Calcutta.
Childe, V. Gordon. 1951. *Man Makes Himself*. Mentor 64. New York: New American Library.
Collins, Randall. 1998. *The Sociology of Philosophies: A Global Theory of Intellectual Change*. Cambridge: Belknap.
Conforti, Joseph A. 1981. *Samuel Hopkins and the New Divinity Movement: Calvinism, the Congregational Ministry, and Reform in New England Between the Great Awakening and the Revolution*. Grand Rapids: Christian University Press.
Cornford, F. M. 1952. *Principium Sapientiae: The Origins of Greek Philosophical Thought*. Cambridge: Cambridge University Press,
Crone, Patricia. 2004. *God's Rule: Government and Islam*. New York: Columbia University Press.

Cutler, Irving. 1996. *The Jews of Chicago: From Shtetl to Suburb*. The Ethnic History of Chicago. Urbana: University of Illinois Press.

Davis, Mike. 1986. *Prisoners of the American Dream: Politics and Economy in the History of the US Working Class*. London: Verso.

Dayton, Donald W. 1983. "Social Concern in Nineteenth Century Evangelicalism." In *The Coming Kingdom: Essays in American Millenialism and Eschatology*, edited by M. Darrol Bryant and Donald W. Dayton. New York: Rose of Sharon.

Derrida, Jacques. 1967/1978. "Violence and Metaphysics" and "From a Restricted to a General Economy: For an Hegelianism Without Reserve." In *Writing and Difference*, translated by Alan Bass. Chicago: University of Chicago Press.

———. 2002. *Acts of Religion*. Edited by Gill Anidjar. London: Routledge.

Detienne, Marcel. 1967/1996. *Masters of Truth in Archaic Greece*. Translated by Janet Lloyd. New York: Zone.

Dews, Peter. 2008. Review of Alain Badiou's *Being and Event*. *Notre Dame Philosophical Reviews*. Online: http://ndpr.nd.edu/review.cfm?id=12406.

Dexter, Miriam Robbins, and Karlene Jones-Biley, editors. 1997. *The Kurgan Culture and the Indo-Europeanization of Europe: Selected Articles from 1952–1993*. Washington, DC: The Institute for the Study of Man.

Diner, Hasia R. 2004. *The Jews of the United States, 1654–2000*. Jewish Communities in the Modern World 4. Berkeley: University of California Press.

Dobbs Weinstein, Idit. Forthcoming a. "Gersonides: The Supercommenator on Aristotle: The Decisive Forgotten Link Between Averroes and Spinoza." In *Problems in Arabic Philosophy*, edited by Maroth Miklos.

———. Forthcoming b. "Necessity Revisited: Spinoza as a Radical Aristotelian." *Spinoza by 2000*. Vol. 5, edited by Yirmiyahu Yovel.

Dolan, Jay P. 2002. *In Search of an American Catholicism: A History of Religion and Culture in Tension*. Oxford: Oxford University Press

———. 1985. *The American Catholic Experience: A History from Colonial Times to the Present*. Garden City, NY: Doubleday.

———. 1983. *The Immigrant Church: New York's Irish and German Catholics, 1815–1865*. Notre Dame: University of Notre Dame Press.

Duhem, Pierre. 1906–1913. *Etudes sur Léonard de Vinci*. 3 vols. Paris: Hermann.

Duns Scotus, John. 1301/1965. *A Treatise on God as First Principle (De Primo Principio)*. Translated by Allan Wolter. Chicago: Franciscan Herald.

Dumézil, Georges. 1952. *Les Dieux des Indo-Europeans*. Paris: Presses Universitaires de France.

Durkheim, Émile. 1897/1951. *Suicide, A Study in Sociology*. Translated by John A. Spaulding and George Simpson. New York: Free Press.

———. 1893/1964. *The Division of Labor in Society*. Translated by George Simpson. New York: Free Press.

———. 1911/1965. *Elementary Forms of the Religious Life*. Translated by Joseph Ward Swain. New York: Free Press.

Dussel, Enrique. 1998. *Etica de la liberación en la edad de globaización y exclusión*. México: Trotta.

Edwards, Jonathan. 1746/1957–. *A Treatise Concerning Religious Affections*. In *The Works of Jonathan Edwards*, edited by Perry Miller, vol. 2. New Haven: Yale University Press.

Eggan, Fred. 1973. *The Social Organization of the Western Pueblos*. Chicago: University of Chicago.
Eisen, Arnold. 1995. *The Chosen People in America: Studies in Jewish Religious Ideology*. Bloomington: Indiana University Press
Eisenberg, Ellen. 1995. *Jewish Agricultural Colonies in New Jersey, 1882–1920*. Syracuse, NY: Syracuse University Press.
Elbaum, Max. 2002. *Revolution in the Air: Sixties Radicals Turn to Lenin, Mao and Che*. The Haymarket Series. London: Verso.
Elkins, James. 1999. *What Painting Is: How to Think about Oil Painting, Using the Language of Alchemy*. London: Routledge
Ellul, Jacques. 1975. *The Meaning of the City*. Translated by Dennis Pardee. Grand Rapids: Eerdmans.
Engels, Frederick. 1880/1940. *The Dialectics of Nature*. Translated by Clemens Dutt. New York: International.
———. 1880/1976. *Socialism: Utopian and Scientific*. New York: International.
Epic of Gilgamesh. Online: http://www.ancienttexts.org/library/mesopotamian/gilgamesh/
Farin, Ingo. 2007. "The First Draft of *Being and Time*." Paper presented to the North Texas Heidegger Symposium, Frisco, Texas, April 2007.
Ferguson. Niall. 2006. "The Next War of the World." *Foreign Affairs* 85:5:61–74.
Fischer, James T. 2002. *A Communion of Immigrants: A History of Catholics in America* Religion in American Life. Oxford University Press.
Frank, Andre Gunder. 1967. *Capitalism and Underdevelopment in Latin America: Historical Studies of Chile and Brazil*. New York: Monthly Review.
———. 1975. *On Capitalist Underdevelopment*. Oxford: Oxford University Press
———. 1998. *ReOrient: Global Economy in the Asian Age*. Berkeley: University of California Press.
Frank, A. G., and B. K. Gills. 1992. "The Five Thousand Year World System: An Introduction." *Humboldt Journal of Social Relations* 18:1.
———. 1993. *The World System: Five Hundred Years or Five Thousand?* London: Routledge.
Freud, Sigmund. 1927/1928. *The Future of An Illusion*. Translated by W. D. Robson-Scott. New York: Norton.
———. 1930. *Civilization and its Discontents*. Translation by John Riviere. New York: Norton.
Fromm, Erich. 1941. *Escape from Freedom*. New York: Holt Rinehart & Winston
———. 1947. *Man for Himself*. New York: Holt Rinehart & Winston
Fukuyama, Francis. 1989. "The End of History." *The National Interest* (Summer).
———. 2006. "After Neoconservatives." *New York Times*, 19 February 2006.
Fuller, R. Buckminster. 1975–1979. *Synergetics: Explorations into the Geometry of Thinking*. 2 vols. New York: Macmillan
———. 1981. *Critical Path*. New York: St. Martin's.
———. 1992. *Cosmography: A Posthumous Scenario for the Future of Humanity*. New York: Macmillan
Galbraith, James K. 1988. *Balancing Acts: Technology, Finance, and the American Future*. New York: Basic.
Gal-Or, Benjamin. 1987. *Cosmology: Physics and Philosophy*. New York: Springer.

Geissler, Suzanne. 1981. *Jonathan Edwards to Aaron Burr, Jr.: From the Great Awakening to Democratic Politics*. Lewiston: Mellen.

Genovese, Eugene D. 1974. *Roll, Jordan, Roll: The World the Slaves Made*. New York: Random House.

———. 1988. *The World the Slaveholders Made: Two Essays in Interpretation*. Middletown, CT: Wesleyan University Press.

Gernet, Jacques. 1985. *A History of Chinese Civilization*. Translated by J. R. Foster. Cambridge: Cambridge University Press.

Giambutas, Marija. 1991. *Civilization of the Goddess: The World of Old Europe*. Edited by Joan Marler. San Francisco: Harper.

Gilson, Etienne. 1936. *The Spirit of Medieval Philosophy*. Translated by A. H. C. Downes. Gifford Lectures, 1931–1932. New York: Scibners.

———. 1952. *Being and Some Philosophers*. 2nd ed. Toronto: Pontifical Institute of Medieval Studies.

———. 1968. *Dante and Philosophy*. Translated by David Moore. Gloucester, MA: Peter Smith.

Gleason, Sarell Everett. 1936. *An Ecclesiastical Barony of the Middle Ages: The Bishopric of Bayeux, 1066–1204*. Cambridge: Harvard University Press.

Glazer, Nathan. 1961. *Social Basis of American Communism*. Westport, CT: Greenwood.

———. 1988. *American Jewry or American Judaism*. Cambridge: Harvard University Press.

Goerner, E. A. 1965. *Peter and Caesar: The Catholic Church and Political Authority*. New York: Herder & Herder.

Gorbachev, Mihail. 1987. *Perestroika*. London: Collins.

Grant, Edward. 1978. "Cosmology." In *Science in the Middle Ages*, edited by David Lindberg. Chicago: University of Chicago Press.

Gramsci, Antonio. 1948. *Il materialismo storico e la filosofia di Benedetto Croce*. Torino: Einaudi.

———. 1949a. *Il Risorgimento*. Torino: Einaudi.

———. 1949b. *Note sul Macchiavelli, sulla politica, e sullo Stato Moderno*. Torino: Einaudi.

———. 1949c. *Gli intellectualli e l'organizzazione di cultura*. Torino: Einaudi.

———. 1950. *Letteratura e vita nazionale*. Torino: Einaudi.

———. 1951. *Passato e presente*. Torino: Einaudi.

———. 1954. *L'Ordine Nuovo*. Torino: Einaudi.

———. 1966. *La questione meridionale*. Roma: Riuniti.

Green, James. 1978. *Grassroots Socialism*. Baton Rouge: Louisiana State University.

Guttieriez, Ramon. 1990. *When Jesus Came the Corn Mothers Went Away*. Stanford: Stanford University Press.

Hardt, Michael, and Antonio Negri. 2001. *Empire*. Cambridge: Harvard University Press.

———. 2004. *Multitude: War and Democracy in the Age of Empire*. New York: Penguin.

Harris, Errol E. 1965. *The Foundations of Metaphysics in Science*. Muirhead Library of Philosophy. London: Allen & Unwin.

———. 1987. *Formal, Transcendental, and Dialectical Thinking: Logic and Reality*. Albany: State University of New York Press.

———. 1991. *Cosmos and Anthropos: A Philosophical Interpretation of the Anthropic Cosmological Principle*. Atlantic Highlands, NJ: Humanities.

———. 1992. *Cosmos and Theos: Ethical and Theological Implications of the Anthropic Cosmological Principle*. Atlantic Highlands, NJ: Humanities.

Hatch, Nathan O. 1977. *The Sacred Cause of Liberty: Republican Thought and the Millennium in Revolutionary New England*. New Haven: Yale University of Press.

Hayden, Brian. 1986. "Old Europe: Sacred matriarchy or complementary opposition?" In *Archaeology and Fertility Cult in the Ancient Mediterranean*, edited by A. Bonanno, 17–30. Amsterdam: Gruner.

———. 1998. "An Archaeological Evaluation of the Gimbutas Paradigm." *The Pomegranate* 6:35–46.

Hayek, F. A. 1973. *Law, Liberty, and Legislation, Volume One: Rules and Order*. Chicago: University of Chicago Press.

———. 1988. *The Fatal Conceit: The Errors of Socialism*. Chicago: University of Chicago Press.

He, Bingdi. 1959. *Studies on the Population of China, 1368–1953*. Harvard East Asian Studies 4. Cambridge: Harvard University Press.

Hegel, G. W. F. 1807/1967. *Phenomenology of Mind*. Translated by J. B. Baillie. New York: Harper & Row.

———. 1817/1990. *Encyclopaedia of the Philosophical Sciences (Outline)*. Translated by Steven Taubeneck. New York: Continuum.

———. 1830/1971. *Encyclopaedia of the Philosophical Sciences*. Translated by William Wallace. Oxford: Oxford University Press.

Heidegger, Martin. 1928/1968. *Being and Time*. Translated by John Macquarrie and Edward Robinson. New York: Harper & Row.

———. >1934/1989. *Beitrage sur Philosophie*. Frankfurt-Main: Klosterman.

———. >1941/1979–1987. *Nietzsche*. 4 vols. Translated by David Farrell Krell. San Francisco: Harper & Row.

Heimart, Alan. 1966. *Religion and the American Mind: From the Great Awakening to the Revolution*. Cambridge: Harvard University Press.

Heyd, Thomas, and John Clegg, editors. *Aesthetics and Rock Art*. Aldershot, UK: Ashgate.

Hill, Christopher. 1972. *The World Turned Upside Down: Radical Ideas During the English Revolution*. New York: Viking.

Hizb-ut-Tahrir. 2002. *The Inevitability of the Clash of Civilizations*. London: Al-Khilafah.

Hobsbawm, E. J. 1959. *Primitive Rebels: Studies in Archaic Forms of Social Movements in the 19th and 20th Centuries*. New York: Norton.

Hodges, Geoffrey. 1986. *The Intellectual Foundations of the Nicaraguan Revolution*. Austin: University of Texas Press.

Homer. ~750 BCE/1961. *The Iliad*. Translated by Richard Latimore. Chicago: University of Chicago Press.

———. ~750/1965. *The Odyssey*. Translated by Richard Latimore. New York: Harper

Houtart, Francois. 1957. *Aspects Sociologie de la Catholicism Americaine*. Paris : Ouvrière.

Hubbert, M. King. 1956. "Nuclear Energy and the Fossil Fuels." Paper presented before the Spring Meeting of the Southern District, American Petroleum Institute, Plaza Hotel, San Antonio, Texas, March 7–9.

———. 1974. "Oil: The Dwindling Treasure." *National Geographic* (June) 792–825.
Huntington, Samuel. 1993. "The Clash of Civilizations." *Foreign Affairs* (Summer).
Intergovernmental Panel on Climate Change. 2007. *Climate Change 2007: The Physical Science Basis: Summary for Policy Makers*. Paris: IPCC.
Jaspers, Karl. 1953. *The Origin and Goal of History*. Translated by Michael Bullock. New Haven: Yale University Press.
Johnson, Paul E. 1978. *A Shopkeeper's Millennium: Society and Revivals in Rochester, New York, 1815–1837*. New York: Hill & Wang.
Kalupahana, David J. 1992. *A History of Buddhist Philosophy: Continuities and Discontinuities*. Honolulu: University of Hawaii Press.
Kant, Immanuel. 1755/1968. *Universal Natural History and Theory of the Heavens*. Translated by W. Hastie. New York: Greenwood.
———. 1781/1969a. *Foundations of the Metaphysics of Morals*. Translated by Lewis White Beck. Indianapolis: Bobbs-Merrill.
———. 1781/1969b. *Critique of Pure Reason*. Translated by Lewis White Beck. Indianapolis: Bobbs-Merrill.
Kierkegaard, Søren. 1846/1941. *Kierkegaard's Concluding Unscientific Postscript*. Translated by David F. Swenson and Walter Lowrie. Princeton: Princeton University Press.
Kipp, Jacob, et al. 2006. "The Human Terrain System: ACORDS for the Twenty-First Century." *Military Review* (September and October). Online: http://www.army.mil/professionalwriting/volumes/volume4/december_2006/12_06_2.html
Kyrtatas, Dimitris. 1987. *The Social Structure of Early Christian Communities*. London: Verso.
Laclau, Ernesto. 1977. *Politics and Ideology in Marxist Theory: Capitalism, Fascism, Populism*. London: New Left.
Laclau, Ernesto, and Chantal Mouffe. 1985. *Hegemony and Socialist Strategy: Towards a Radical Democratic Politics*. London: Verso.
Lancaster, Roger N. 1988. *Thanks to God and the Revolution: Popular Religion and Class Consciousness in the New Nicaragua*. Berkeley: University of California Press.
Lasch, Christopher. 1977. *Haven in a Heartless World: The Family Besieged*. New York: Basic.
———. 1995. *The Revolt of the Elites: And the Betrayal of Democracy*. New York: Norton.
Lenin, V. I. 1894/1959. *The Development of Capitalism in Russia: The Process of the Formation of a Home Market for Large-Scale Industry*. Moscow: Progress
———. 1902/1929. *What is to Be Done?: Burning Questions of Our Movement*. New York: International.
———. 1905/1971. *Two Tactics of Social Democracy*. In *Selected Works of V. I. Lenin: One-volume Edition*. New York: International.
———. 1916/1971. *Imperialism*. In *Selected Works of V. I. Lenin: One-volume Edition*. New York: International.
———. 1908/1970. *Materialism and Empiriocriticism: Critical Comments on a Reactionary Philosophy*. Moscow: Progress.
———. 1920/1971. *Left-Wing Communism, an Infantile Disorder*. In *Selected Works of V. I. Lenin: One-volume Edition*. New York: International.
Lenski, Gerhard and Jean. 1982. *Human Societies: An Introduction to Macrosociology*. 4th ed. New York: McGraw Hill.

Lerner, Eric. 1991. *The Big Bang Never Happened*. New York: Vintage.
Lindberg, David C., editor. 1978. *Science in the Middle Ages*. Chicago History of Sciences and Medicine. Chicago: University of Chicago Press.
———. 1992. *The Beginnings of Western Science: The European Scientific Tradition in Philosophical, Religious, and Institutional Context, 600 B.C. to A.D. 1450*. Chicago: University of Chicago Press.
Lessing, Doris. 1979. *Shikasta: Re, Colonised Planet 5: Personal, Psychological, Historical Documents Relating to Visit by Johor (George Sherban) Emissary (Grade 9) 87th of the Period of the Last Days*. New York: Knopf.
———. 1980. *The Sirian Experiments: The Reports by Ambien II, of the Five*. New York: Knopf.
Lockridge, Kenneth. 1970. *A New England Town: The First Hundred Years*. New York: Norton.
Lovett, Clara. 1982. *The Democratic Movement in Italy, 1830–1876*. Cambridge: Harvard University Press.
Lukács, György. 1916/1974. *Theory of the Novel: A Historico-Philosophical Essay on the Forms of Great Epic Literature*. Translated by Anna Bostock. Cambridge: MIT Press.
———. 1922/1971. *History and Class Consciousness: Studies in Marxist Dialectics*. Translated by Rodney Livingstone. Cambridge: MIT Press.
———. 1953/1980. *The Destruction of Reason*. Translated by Peter Palmer. London: Merlin.
Lyotard, Jean Francois. 1979/1984. *The Postmodern Condition: A Report on Knowledge*. Translated by Geoff Bennington and Brian Massumi. Minneapolis: University of Minnesota Press.
Mallory, J. P. 1989. *In Search of the Indo-Europeans: Language, Archeology and Myth*. London: Thames & Huston.
Mallory, J. P., and D. Q. Adams, editors. 1997. *The Encyclopedia of Indo-European Culture*. London: Fitzroy-Dearborn.
Malthus, Thomas. 1798. *An Essay on the Principle of Population, As it Affects the Future Improvement of Society*. Online: http://www.ac.wwu.edu/~stephan/malthus/malthus.0.html
Mandel, Ernest. 1968. *Marxist Economic Theory*. Translated by Brian Pearce. New York: Monthly Review.
Mansueto, Anthony E. 1987 "Blessed Are the Meek: Religion and Socialism in Italian American History." In *The Melting Pot and Beyond: Italian Americans in the Year 2000: Proceedings of the XVIII Annual Conference of the American Italian Historical Association held at the Biltmore Plaza Hotel, Providence, Rhode Island, November 7–9, 1985*, edited by Jerome Krase and William Egelman. Staten Island, NY: Association.
———. 1988. "Religion, Solidarity, and Class Struggle." *Social Compass* 35:2.
———. 1995. *Towards Synergism: The Cosmic Significance of the Human Civilizational Project*. Lanham, MD: University Press of America.
———. 1998. "Against Philosophical Appeasement." *Dialectic, Cosmos, and Society* 11.
———. 2002a. *Religion and Dialectics*. Lanham, MD: University Press of America.
———. 2002b. *Knowing God: Restoring Reason in an Age of Doubt*. Aldershot, UK: Ashgate.

———. 2006. "A Question-Centered Approach to Liberal Education." *Journal of Liberal Education* 92:48–53.

———. 2010. *The Journey of the Dialectic: Knowing God, Volume 3*. Eugene, OR: Pickwick.

Mansueto, Anthony and Maggie. 2005. *Spirituality and Dialectics*. Lanham, MD: Lexington.

Mao Zedong. 1926/1971 "Analysis of the Classes in Chinese Society." In *Selected Works*. Peking: Foreign Languages.

———. 1927/1971. "Report on the Peasant Movement in Hunan." In *Selected Readings of the Works of Mao Tse-Tung*. Peking: Foreign Languages.

———. 1937a/1971. "On Contradiction." In *Selected Readings of the Works of Mao Tse-Tung*. Peking: Foreign Languages.

———. 1937b/1971. "On Practice." In *Selected Readings of the Works of Mao Tse-Tung*. Peking: Foreign Languages.

———. 1937c/1971. "Combat Liberalism." In *Selected Readings of the Works of Mao Tse-Tung*. Peking: Foreign Languages.

———. 1938/1971. "The Role of the Chinese Communist Party in the National War." In *Selected Readings of the Works of Mao Tse-Tung*. Peking: Foreign Languages.

———. 1940/1971. "Current Problems of Tactics in the Anti-Japanese United Front." In *Selected Readings of the Works of Mao Tse-Tung*. Peking: Foreign Languages.

———. 1945/1971. "The Foolish Old Man Who Removed the Mountains." In *Selected Readings of the Works of Mao Tse-Tung*. Peking: Foreign Languages.

———. 1949/1971. "On the People's Democratic Dictatorship." In *Selected Readings of the Works of Mao Tse-Tung*. Peking: Foreign Languages.

———. 1957a/1971. "On the Correct Handling of Contradictions Among the People." In *Selected Readings of the Works of Mao Tse-Tung*. Peking: Foreign Languages.

———. 1957b/1971. "Speech at the Chinese Communist Party's National Conference on Propaganda Work." In *Selected Readings of the Works of Mao Tse-Tung*. Peking: Foreign Languages.

———. 1963/1971. Where Do Correct Ideas Come From?" In *Selected Readings of the Works of Mao Tse-Tung*. Peking: Foreign Languages.

Marcuse, Herbert. 1962. *One Dimensional Man: Studies in the Ideology of Advanced Industrial Society*. Boston: Beacon.

Margulis, Lynn, and René Fester. 1991. *Symbiosis as a Source of Evolutionary Innovation: Speciation and Morphogenesis*. Cambridge: MIT Press.

Maritain, Jacques. 1932/1937. *The Degrees of Knowledge*. Translated by Bernard Wall and Margot R. Adamson. London: Bles.

———. 1936/1973. *Integral Humanism: Temporal and Spiritual Problems of a New Christendom*. Translated by Joseph W. Evans. Notre Dame, IN: University of Notre Dame Press.

———. 1951. *Man and the State*. Charles R. Walgreen Foundation Lectures. Chicago: University of Chicago Press

Marsden, George M. 1980. *Fundamentalism and American Culture: The Shaping of Twentieth Century Evangelicalism, 1870–1925*. New York: Oxford.

Marx, Karl. 1843/1978. "Contribution to the Critique of Hegel's Philosophy of Right: Introduction." In *The Marx-Engels Reader*, 2nd ed., edited by Robert C. Tucker. New York: Norton.

———. 1844/1978. *Economic and Philosophical Manuscripts*. New York: Norton.

———. 1846/1978. *The German Ideology*. In *The Marx-Engels Reader*. 2nd ed. Edited by Robert C. Tucker. New York: Norton.
———. 1848/1978. *The Communist Manifesto*. In *The Marx-Engels Reader*. 2nd ed. Edited by Robert C. Tucker. New York: Norton.
———. 1849/1978. *Wage Labor and Capital*. In *The Marx-Engels Reader*. 2nd ed. Edited by Robert C. Tucker. New York: Norton.
———. 1859/1961. *Contribution to the Critique of Political Economy: Preface*. Translated by T. B. Bottomore. In *Marx's Concept of Man*, by Erich Fromm. New York: F. Ungar.
———. 1867/1977. *Capital: A Critique of Political Economy*. Volume 1. Translated by Ben Fowkes. New York: Vintage.
———. 1881/1978. "Letter to Vera Zasulich." In *The Marx-Engels Reader*. 2nd ed. Edited by Robert C. Tucker. New York: Norton.
———. 1863/1963–1971. *Theories of Surplus Value*. 3 vols. Moscow: Progress.
McCool, Gerald A. 1977. *Catholic Theology in the Nineteenth Century*. New York: Seabury.
———. 1994. *The Neo-Thomists*. Marquette Studies in Philosophy 3. Milwaukee: Marquette University Press.
McGuire, Bill. 2003. "Will Global Warming Trigger a New Ice Age?" *The Guardian*, 13 November.
McLoughlin, William G. 1978. *Revivals, Awakening, and Reform: An Essay on Religion and Social Change in America, 1607–1977*. Chicago: University of Chicago Press.
Milbank, John. 1989. *Theology and Social Theory*. London: Blackwell.
———. 1997. *The Word Made Strange: Theology, Language, Culture*. Oxford: Blackwell.
———. 1999. "The Theological Critique of Philosophy in Hamman and Jacobi." In *Radical Orthodoxy*, edited by John Milbank, Catherine Pickstock and Graham Ward. London: Routledge.
———. 2006a "Geopolitical Theology." Unpublished Paper. Online: http://www.theologyphilosophycentre.co.uk/papers.php.
———. 2006b "Only Theology saves Metaphysics: On the Modalities of Terror." Unpublished Paper. Online: http://www.theologyphilosophycentre.co.uk/papers.php.
Miranda, José Porfirio. 1972. *Marx y la Biblia*. Salamanca: Sigueme.
———. 1973. *El se y el mesias*. Salamanca: Sigueme.
Moore, Barrington Jr. 1966. *Social Origins of Dictatorship and Democracy: Lord and Peasant in the Making of the Modern World*. Boston: Beacon
Murdoch, John, and Edith Sylla. 1978. "The Science of Motion." In *Science in the Middle Ages*, edited by David Lindberg. Chicago: University of Chicago Press.
Naess, Arne. 1989. *Ecology, Community, and Lifestyle: Outline of an Ecosophy*. Translated by David Rothenburg. Cambridge: Cambridge University Press.
Nash, Gary B. 1970. *Class and Society in Early America*. Interdisciplinary Approaches to History. Englewood Cliffs, NJ: Prentice-Hall.
Neusner, Jacob. 1998. *Invitation to the Talmud: A Teaching Book*. Scholars.
Nevin, John W. 2002. *The Mystical Presence: A Vindication of the Reformed or Calvinistic Doctrine of the Holy Eucharist*. 1867. Reprinted, Eugene, OR: Wipf & Stock.
Nichols, John Hastings. 1966. *The Mercersberg Theology*. A Library of Protestant Thought. New York: Oxford University Press.

Nietzsche, Friedreich. 1889/1968. *The Will to Power*. Translated by William Kaufmann and R. J. Hollingdale. New York: Random House.

Orsi, Robert A. 2002. *The Madonna of 115th Street: Faith and Community in Italian Harlem, 1880–1950*. New Haven: Yale University Press.

Paine, Thomas. 1776. *Common Sense*. Online: http://www.bartleby.com/133/

Parsons, Talcott. 1957. *The Social System*. New York: Free Press.

———. 1964. *The Structure of Social Action: A Study in Social Theory with Special Reference to a Group of Recent European Writers*. New York: Free Press.

Pew Forum on Religion and Public Life. 2008. *US Religious Landscape Survey*. Online: http://religions.pewforum.org/

Plato. c. 385 BCE/1968. *Republic*. Translated by Alan Bloom. New York: Basic.

———. c. 385 BCE/1960. *Timaeus*. New York: Penguin.

Prigogine, Ilya. 1977. *Self-Organization in Non-Equilibrium Systems: From Dissipative Structures to Order Through Fluctuations*. New York: Wiley.

———. 1979. *From Being to Becoming: Time and Complexity in the Physical Sciences*. New York: Freeman.

———. 1984. *Order Out of Chaos: Man's New Dialogue with Nature*. New York: Basic.

Prigogine, Ilya, with Tomio Petrosky. 1988. "An Alternative to Quantum Theory." *Physica* 147A:461–86.

Raschke, Carl. 2005 "Derrida and the Return of Religion: Religious Theory after Postmodernism." *Journal of Religious and Cultural Theory* 6:2.1–2

Reich, Robert. 1992. *The Work of Nations: Preparing Ourselves for 21st Century Capitalism*. New York: Vintage.

Romanell, Patrick. 1969. *Making of the Mexican Mind: A Study in Recent Mexican Thought*. Notre Dame, IN: University of Notre Dame.

Rowley, David G. 1987. *Millenarian Bolshevism, 1900 to 1920*. New York: Garland.

Rutman, Darret. 1965. *Winthrop's Boston: Portrait of a Puritan Town*. Chapel Hill: University of North Carolina Press.

Ste. Croix, C. E. M de. 1982. *The Class Struggle in the Ancient Greek World: From the Archaic Age to the Arab Conquests*. London: Duckworth.

Sarkisyanz, E. 1965. *Buddhist Backgrounds of the Burmese Revolution*. The Hague: Nijhoff.

Sarna, Jonathan D. 2004. *American Judaism: A History*. New Haven: Yale University Press.

Sartre, Jean Paul. 1943. *L'être et le néant, essai d'ontologie phénoménologique*. Paris: Gallimard.

Schaff, Phillip. 1964. *The Principle of Protestantism*. Translated by John W. Nevin. Philadelphia: United Church Press.

Sewell, William H. 1980. *Work and Revolution in France: The Language of Labor from the Old Regime to 1848*. New York: Cambridge University Press.

Service, Elman. 1966. *The Hunters*. Foundations of Modern Anthropology. Englewood Cliffs, NJ: Prentice Hall.

Shanbuch, R. 1981. *Chicago's Catholics: The Evolution of an American Identity*. Notre Dame, IN: Notre Dame University Press.

Shannon, Claude, and Warren Weaver. 1949. *The Mathematical Theory of Communication*. Urbana: University of Illinois Press.

Sheler, Jeffery. 1994. "The Christmas Covenant." *U.S. News & World Report*, December 19, 1994. 62.

Silberman, Neil Asher. 1998. *Heavenly Powers: Unraveling the Secret History of the Kabbalah.* New York: Grosset/Putnam.
Skocpol, Theda. 1979. *States and Social Revolutions: A Comparative Analysis of France, Russia, and China.* New York: Cambridge University Press.
Smith, Adam. 1776. *The Wealth of Nations.* Online: http://www.econlib.org/LIBRARY/Smith/smWN.html
Snodgrass, Anthony. 1980. *Archaic Greece: The Age of Experiment.* London: Dent.
Spencer, Herbert. 1857. *Progress: Its Laws and Causes.* Online: www.fordham.edu/halsall/mod/spencer-darwin.html
Spinoza, Baruch. 1677/1955. *Ethics.* In *The Chief Works of Benedict de Spinoza.* 2 vols. Translated by R. H. M. Elwes. New York: Dover.
Stern, Fritz. 1974. *The Politics of Cultural Despair: A Study in the Rise of Germanic Ideology.* California Library Reprint. Berkeley: University of California Press.
Stone, Merlin. 1976. *When God Was A Woman.* London: Dorset.
Stuart, David E. 2000. *Anasazi America: Seventeen Centuries on the Road from Center Place.* Albuquerque: University of New Mexico Press.
Subotnik, Rose Rosengard. 1976. "Adorno's Diagnosis of Beethoven's Late Style: Early Symptom of a Fatal Condition." *Journal of the American Musicological Society* 29 (Summer) 242–75.
Tabbert, Mark. 2005. *American Freemasonry: Three Centuries of Building Communities.* New York: New York University Press.
Taylor, Charles. 2007. *A Secular Age.* Cambridge, MA: Belknap.
Thapar, Romila. 2002. *Early India: From the Origins to 1300.* Berkeley: University of California Press.
Theissen, Gerd. 1982. *The Social Setting of Pauline Christianity: Essays on Corinth.* Translated by John H. Schütz. Philadelphia: Fortress.
Tillich, Paul, 1951–1963. *Systematic Theology.* 3 vols. Chicago: University of Chicago Press.
Tipler, Frank. 1994. *The Physics of Immortality: Modern Cosmology, God, and the Resurrection of the Dead.* New York: Doubleday.
Tocqueville, Alexis de. 1835/2003. *Democracy in America.* Translated by Arthur Goldhammer. New York: Penguin.
Turnbull, Herbert Westren. 1956. *The Great Mathematicians.* In *The World of Mathematics, Volume One,* edited by James R. Newman. New York: Simon & Schuster.
Tyler, Hamilton. 1964. *Pueblo Gods and Myths.* Norman: University of Oklahoma.
Vecoli, R. 1963. "Chicago Italians Prior to World War I." PhD diss., University of Wisconsin.
———. 1969. "Prelates and Peasants: Italian Immigrants and the Catholic Church." *Journal of Social History* 2:3.
Vernant, Jean-Pierre. 1962/1982. *The Origins of Greek Thought.* Ithaca, NY: Cornell University Press.
von Steenberghen, Fernand. 1980. *Thomas Aquinas and Radical Aristotelianism.* Washington, DC: Catholic University of America Press.
Wagar, W. Warren. 1999. *A Short History of the Future.* 3rd ed. Chicago: University of Chicago Press.

Wallerstein, Immanuel. 1974. *The Modern World System Volume I: Capitalist Agriculture and the Origins of the European World Economy in the Sixteenth Century.* New York: Academic.

———. 1980. *The Modern World System Volume II, 1600–1750: Mercantilism and the Consolidation of the European World Economy.* New York: Academic.

———. 1989 *The Modern World System Volume III: The Second Era of Great Expansion of the Capitalist World Economy, 1730–1840s.* New York: Academic.

Walzer, Michael. 1965. *The Revolution of the Saints: A Study in the Origins of Radical Politics.* Cambridge: Harvard University Press

Waters, Frank. 1963. *The Book of the Hopi.* New York: Viking.

Weber, Max. 1918/2004. "Science as a Vocation." In *The Vocation Lectures*, translated by Rodney Livingstone. New York: Hackett.

———. 1920/1958. *The Protestant Ethic and the Spirit of Capitalism.* Translated by Talcott Parsons. New York: Scribners.

———. 1921/1968. *Economy and Society: An Outline of Interpretive Sociology.* Translated by Ebrahim Fischoff et al. New York: Bedminster.

Winthrop, John 1630. *The Model of Christian Charity.* Online: http://www.animatedatlas.com/ecolonies/ecoloniessourceframe.html

Wolf, Eric R. 1969. *Peasant Wars of the Twentieth Century.* New York: Harper.

Wood, Ellen Meiksins, and Neal. 1978. *Class Ideology and Ancient Political Theory: Socrates, Plato, and Aristotle in Social Context.* Oxford: Blackwell.

Wood, Richard L. 2002. *Faith in Action: Religion, Race, and Democratic Organizing in America.* Morality and Society. Chicago: University of Chicago Press.

Wright, Eric Olin. *Class, Crisis, and the State.* London: Verso.

Wright, Robin. 1995. *The Moral Animal: Evolutionary Psychology and Everyday Life.* New York: Abacus.

Yovel, Yirmiyahu. 2001. *Spinoza and Other Heretics.* Princeton: Princeton University Press.

Zhao Ziyang, 1987. "Advance Along the Road to Socialism with Chinese Characteristics." *Beijing Review* 30:45.

Zupanic, Alenka. 2004. "The Fifth Condition." In *Think Again: Alain Badiou and the Future of Phlosophy.* Edited by Peter Hallward. London: Continuum.

www.ingramcontent.com/pod-product-compliance
Lightning Source LLC
Chambersburg PA
CBHW021648230426
43668CB00008B/557